Ultimate Recipes

Vegetarian

Ultimate Recipes

Vegetarian

p

This is a Parragon Publishing Book
This edition published in 2003

Parragon Publishing
Queen Street House
4 Queen Street
Bath BA1 1HE, UK

ISBN: 1-40540-180-X

Printed in China

Produced by Haldane Mason, London

Cover design by The Bridgewater Book Company

Notes

Use all metric or all imperial quantities, as the two are not interchangeable.
Cup measurements in this book are for American cups. Tablespoons are assumed to
be 15 ml. Unless otherwise stated, milk is assumed to be full fat, eggs are medium
and pepper is freshly ground black pepper.

The nutritional information provided for each recipe is per serving or per portion.
Optional ingredients, variations or serving suggestions have not been included in the
calculations. The times given for each recipe are an approximate guide only as the
preparation times may differ according to the techniques used by different people and
the cooking times may vary as a result of the type of oven used.

Contents

Introduction 10

Soups

Appetizers

Snacks & Light Meals

Pasta & Noodles

Grains & Legumes

Grains & Legumes
(continued)

Stir-fries & Sautés

Casseroles & Bakes

Casseroles & Bakes (continued)

Barbecues

Salads

Side Dishes

Side Dishes (continued)

Desserts

Introduction

Vegetarian food does not need to be boring, as this inspirational cookbook will demonstrate! Packed full of delicious recipes that are nutritious and substantial, even the most discerning palate is sure to be satisfied.

Healthy Eating

Variety, of course, is the key to healthy eating, whatever the diet. As long as the day's meals contain a good mixture of different food types—carbohydrates, proteins, and fats—a balanced diet and adequate supplies of essential vitamins and proteins are almost guaranteed. Typical dishes that are based on fresh vegetables, legumes, pasta or rice, for example, also have the advantage of being low in fats, particularly saturated fats, and high in complex carbohydrates and fiber, resulting in a diet that is in tune with modern nutritional thinking.

Vegetables are an important source of vitamins, especially vitamin C. Green vegetables and legumes contain many B-group vitamins. Both carrots and dark green vegetables contain high levels of carotene, which is used by the body to manufacture vitamin A. Carrots also contain useful quantities of vitamins B3, C, and E. Vegetable oils contain vitamin E and most are also high in polyunsaturated fats. Vegetables are also a particularly good source of many essential minerals, especially calcium, iron, magnesium, and potassium.

There is a long and honorable tradition of the specific, health-giving properties of different vegetables, which dates back at least as far as the Middle Ages. These qualities, once dismissed as old wives' tales, are now being recognized and valued again. Onions

and garlic, for example, contain cycloallin, an anticoagulant that helps protect against heart disease. Garlic also contains a strong antibiotic, is thought to protect the body against some major diseases, and increases the absorption of many vitamins.

There is no question that a sensible vegetarian diet is at least as healthy as a sensible meat-eating diet and some nutritionists maintain that it is better. However, there are

Healthy Eating

one or two particular points that are worth noting. Proteins are made up of "building blocks" called amino acids and, while all those essential to the human body are easily obtained from most animal products, they are not always present in many vegetarian foods. A good mixed diet will prevent this from being a problem. For example, legumes are an excellent source of protein, but they do lack one essential amino acid called methionine. Grains, on the other hand, contain this amino acid, although they lack two others, tryptophan and lysine. A dish that contains both rice and peas, a plate of hummus and pita bread or bowl of bean soup and a slice of whole wheat toast, for example, will ensure that all the necessary first-class proteins are available to the body.

Dairy products are also a valuable source of protein, but they are high in fat. It is very easy for busy people to fall into the habit of basing quite a lot of meals around cheese, for example, resulting in a high intake of cholesterol. Eaten in moderation, however, cheese is a very useful and versatile ingredient in the vegetarian diet. If you do use dairy products a lot, it may be worth considering buying low-fat types, such as skim or low-fat milk, low-fat yogurt, and soft cheeses.

It is important to be aware that the body cannot absorb iron from vegetable sources unless vitamin C is ingested at the same meal. Although many vegetables also contain vitamin C, this is easily destroyed through cooking. Some raw fruit, a glass of

fruit juice, or a side salad are simple and tasty solutions.

Vegans, who do not eat any dairy products, must be a little more scrupulous than straightforward vegetarians about making sure that they obtain all the necessary nutrients. A lack of calcium, in particular, can be a problem, but this can be countered with a mineral supplement or by using calcium-enriched soy milk. A vegan diet may be just as healthy as a vegetarian or meat-eating one.

No foods can really be said to be bad for you, although some are best eaten in moderation. It is sensible to keep an eye on the quantities of butter, cream, high-fat cheeses, dried fruits, oils, and unsalted nuts that you eat each day. Other popular vegetarian ingredients, such as grains, vegetables, legumes, fruit, bread, pasta, and noodles can be eaten more freely. All diets should include raw vegetables and fruit, and these should comprise as much as 40 percent of a vegetarian diet.

Finally, a hidden advantage to changing to a vegetarian diet is that, usually, it initially means thinking in a more detailed way about all the things you eat. This may extend across the whole spectrum of nutrition, including such things as your intake of salt, sugar, and refined foods. As a result, many long-term vegetarians have developed eating patterns that are among the healthiest in the world.

Vegetables

Vegetables are, of course, at the heart of a vegetarian diet, offering an almost endless choice of flavors and textures. Preparing and cooking them with care ensures that they may be enjoyed at their best and that they retain their full nutritional value.

Buying

The fresher vegetables are, the better. Nevertheless, some, such as root vegetables, can be stored for relatively long periods in a cool, dark place and most will keep for two or three days in a refrigerator. While supermarkets are very convenient and carry a wide range of good-quality vegetables, time spent finding a really high-quality supplier—possibly of organically-grown vegetables—will be repaid many times over in terms of flavor and nutritional value.

Whatever type you are buying, always look for unblemished and undamaged vegetables with no discoloration. Greens should have a good color, with no wilting leaves, root vegetables should be firm and crisp, vegetable fruits, such as tomatoes and bell peppers, should not have soggy patches or wrinkled skin. No vegetables should ever look or smell stale.

Preparing

Use vegetables as soon after buying them as possible, but try not to prepare them much in advance of cooking. If they are left exposed to air or soaking in water, many vitamins and other valuable nutrients are leached out or destroyed. The highest concentration of nutrients is in the layer directly under the skin, so if possible, avoid peeling them. If they must be peeled, try to do it very thinly. A swivel vegetable peeler is a worthwhile investment. Also, consider cooking potatoes, for example, in their skins—first scrubbing off any soil or dirt—and peeling them afterwards. The skin comes off in a much thinner layer than when they are peeled raw.

How thickly or thinly vegetables are sliced, or how large or small they are chopped, will depend, to some extent, on the method of cooking and the individual recipe instructions. However, remember that the smaller and finer the pieces, the greater the surface area from which nutrients can leach.

Green & Leafy Vegetables

Broccoli

Trim the stalk. Leave whole or break into flowerets—small "flowers" with a little stalk attached—according to the recipe. Wash thoroughly.

Brussels Sprouts

Trim the end of the stalk and remove the outer leaves. Leave whole.

Cabbage

Remove the outer leaves, if necessary, cut in quarters and cut out the stem. Slice or shred according to the recipe.

Cauliflower

Cut off the thick stalk level with the base of the head and cut out the core. Remove larger, coarse leaves, but smaller ones can be left. Leave the head whole or break into flowerets.

Chinese Cabbage

Remove the outer leaves and slice the quantity required.

Fava Beans

Trim and roughly slice very young beans less than 3 inches long. Shell older beans.

Green Beans

Trim young beans with kitchen shears or a knife and leave whole. Snap off the ends of older beans and pull off any strings. Slice diagonally or shred before cooking.

Kale & Curly Kale

Break the leaves from the stalk, cut out thick stalks, and cook whole or shredded.

Peas

Pop the fat end of the pod, split open, and remove the peas.

Runner Beans

Trim ends, remove string, then slice lengthwise, not diagonally.

Spinach

Rinse gently but thoroughly in two changes of cold water. Pull or cut off tough stalks.

Snowpeas & Sugar Snap Peas

Trim ends, then leave whole.

Shoots & Stems

Asparagus

Trim the woody end of the stalk. White asparagus stems usually require peeling.

Vegetables

Celery

Trim the base and separate the stalks. Wash thoroughly and slice thickly or thinly. If using raw in a salad, pull off any coarse strings.

Fennel

Remove the outer layer of skin, except from very young bulbs. Slice downwards or horizontally according to the recipe. Use the fronds for a garnish.

Globe Artichokes

Twist off the stem and cut the base flat, removing any small, spiky leaves. Cut off the top ½ inch and trim the points of the remaining leaves.

Root Vegetables

Carrots

Trim the ends and scrub young carrots—they do not need peeling. They may be left whole, sliced, or diced. Thinly peel older carrots and, if necessary, cut out the woody core.

Celery Root

Peel off the skin immediately before cooking, since the flesh quickly discolors. Slice or chop according to the recipe. If necessary, put the pieces into a bowl of water with a little lemon juice.

Green Onions

Trim the root and cut off any wilted green leaves. Slice or chop according to the recipe.

Jerusalem Artichokes

Scrub in cold water and cook in their skins before peeling. Otherwise peel immediately before use, placing them in water with a little lemon juice to prevent discoloration.

Leeks

Trim the root and the dark leaves. Cut in half lengthwise or prepare according to the recipe and wash well in plenty of cold water. Drain thoroughly.

Onions & Shallots

Peel off the papery skin, trim and slice or chop according to the recipe.

Parsnips

Trim and thinly peel. Small parsnips may be left whole, but older parsnips may be halved, sliced, or diced according to the recipe.

Potatoes

Wash new potatoes in cold running water and cook in their skins. Scrub

Vegetables

old potatoes and either cook in their skins, depending on the method, and peel afterwards, or thinly peel before cooking.

Rutabaga

Trim and peel off the thick skin. Chop or dice according to the recipe.

Sweet Potatoes

Scrub and cook in their skins and peel afterwards or peel thinly and put in water with lemon juice.

Turnips

Trim and thinly peel.

Salad Vegetables

Arugula

Discard any discolored leaves and wash the remainder.

Belgian Endive

Using a sharp, pointed knife, remove the core from the base. Discard any wilted leaves, then wash and dry thoroughly.

Cucumbers

Wash and peel, if you like. Always peel glossy, waxed cucumbers. Slice thinly or dice for salads. If cooking cucumber, first cut into wedges and remove the seeds.

Daikon

Trim, peel and wash. Slice, dice, or grate according to the recipe.

Escarole

Separate the leaves and discard any that are discolored. Wash thoroughly and pat dry.

Lettuce

Separate the leaves and wash in several changes of water. Adding vinegar to the first rinse will kill any insects in lettuce grown outdoors. Spin or wrap in a clean tea towel and shake dry. Tear loose-leafed lettuce into smaller pieces and slice or shred firm lettuce.

Radicchio

Separate the leaves and discard any that are discolored. Wash thoroughly and pat dry.

Radishes

Wash and leave whole or slice.

Watercress

Discard any wilted leaves and remove any thick stalks. Wash thoroughly.

Squashes

Pumpkins

Peel and chop.

Summer Squashes

Wash, then peel if the skin is tough or if the vegetable is to be braised or sautéed.

Zucchini

Leave tiny, baby zucchini whole— with their flowers. Trim ends, then slice, dice, or stuff, according to the recipe.

Vegetable Fruits

Avocados

Halve and remove the pit, then sprinkle the flesh with lemon juice to prevent discoloration. Leave in halves for serving with a vinaigrette. For other dishes, slice and then peel, or dice in the shells and then scoop out the diced flesh. (Peeled avocados are slippery and difficult to handle.)

Bell Peppers

For stuffing, cut a slice from the top, cut out the inner core and shake out any remaining seeds. For other dishes, halve and remove the core and seeds, then quarter, slice, or dice. To peel bell peppers, halve or quarter and broil, skin side up, until charred and beginning to blister. Transfer the pieces of bell pepper to a plastic bag, seal, and set

aside for 5–10 minutes. The skin will peel easily.

Eggplant

Newer varieties no longer require salting to remove the bitter taste; they are not so bitter as older varieties. However, salting still helps to draw out some of the moisture. Wash the eggplant, cut into slices or sections, according to the recipe, place in a colander, and sprinkle generously with salt. Leave for 30 minutes, rinse well and pat dry with paper towels.

Tomatoes

Wash well. To peel, cut a cross in the skin at the base, briefly blanch in boiling water and rinse in cold water. The skin should then peel off easily. Cut salad tomatoes and those for pizza toppings horizontally. Slice others according to the recipe.

Cooking Techniques

Vegetables can be cooked in a variety of ways and different cooking techniques are appropriate for different types of vegetable. See below for the best cooking methods for the vegetables you plan to use from the recipes in this book.

Different types of vegetables require particular cooking techniques in order to achieve their best potential. Robust root vegetables, such as rutabaga for example, require different treatment from delicate stems, such as asparagus.

However, all vegetables benefit from the minimum cooking required to make them tender, as vitamins and other valuable nutrients may be destroyed by heat or water. Minimum cooking also helps to preserve the texture, flavor, and color of vegetables.

Boiling

This is the traditional way to cook many vegetables—from potatoes to cabbage. It is one of the best methods for vegetables, such as globe artichokes, that require a long cooking time.

Use the minimum amount of water and cook until the vegetables are just tender, then drain immediately. Use a saucepan large enough to make sure that the water circulates. Cut vegetables, such as potatoes, into pieces of the same size, so that they are all ready at the same time. Use the cooking liquid to make gravy or a sauce.

Steaming

This is an increasingly popular method of cooking, often replacing traditional boiling. Less water comes into contact with the vegetables and they remain crisper. It is particularly suitable for vegetables that become limp when overcooked, such as snow peas, green beans, leeks, and zucchini. New potatoes are especially delicious when steamed. Use the cooking liquid to make a sauce or stock.

Stir-frying

This fast method of frying over a very high heat has long been established in China and South-east Asia. It is particularly healthy, because it requires less oil than shallow frying. Western vegetables also benefit from this technique in terms of flavor, texture, color, and nutritional content. Try thinly sliced cauliflower, Brussels sprouts, cucumber, carrots, or cabbage.

Cooking Techniques

Sautéing & Sweating

These are longer cooking processes at a lower temperature than stir-frying, but they are also ideal ways of preparing many vegetables, such as zucchini and onions.

Stewing & Braising

These methods involve much longer cooking times and are excellent with winter vegetables, such as turnips, rutabaga, celery, red cabbage, and carrots. Because the cooking juices are an integral part of the dish, fewer nutrients are lost. Braised vegetables, such as fennel or carrots, also make excellent side dishes.

Roasting

This involves cooking at a fairly high heat, so an outer layer quickly forms to seal the vegetables. Roast potatoes and sweet potatoes are traditional and popular dishes in North America. It is becoming fashionable to serve other roast vegetables. Try asparagus roasted briefly in a little olive oil, for example. Roast bell peppers and zucchini may be served hot or cold.

Frying

Frying is not an ideal technique for most vegetables, although it works well with some, such as sliced eggplant. Deep-frying, during which vegetables absorb less oil than when they are shallow-fried, is traditional for potatoes—french fries are known and enjoyed the world over. Coating vegetables in batter and then deep-frying is especially delicious and the coating forms a protective seal. Try Jerusalem artichokes, cauliflower, zucchini, fennel, and eggplant. Always make sure that the oil for deep-frying is hot before adding the vegetables, or they will absorb a lot of it and be soggy. Heat the oil to 350–375°F or until a cube of day-old bread browns in 30 seconds.

Grilling & Broiling

While not suitable for delicate vegetables, because the heat is too intense, or for dense vegetables, because the process is too rapid to tenderize them, these are excellent ways of cooking bell peppers, corn cobs, onions, eggplant, and tomatoes.

Baking

Baking is a traditional way of cooking stuffed vegetables, and foil-wrapped packages of mixed vegetables are quick, delicious, and nutritious. Baked potatoes lend themselves to a variety of toppings and fillings—from simple grated cheese to chili beans—to make a complete meal.

Microwaving

Finally remember that vegetables cooked in the microwave require less liquid or oil and a shorter cooking time than those cooked by conventional methods.

Vegetarian Ingredients

Although vegetables are extremely versatile, they are only a part of the story and many other ingredients are necessary to provide vegetarians with a balanced diet and interesting meals.

Legumes

These include an immense variety of peas, beans, and lentils. Some of the most common are adzuki beans, black kidney beans, black-eyed peas, borlotti beans, brown beans, brown lentils, lima beans, cannellini beans, garbanzo beans, green lentils, green split peas, gunga beans, navy beans, mung beans, pinto beans, Puy lentils, red kidney beans, soybeans, split red lentils, and yellow split peas. They are rich in proteins, carbohydrates, vitamins, especially B-group, and minerals, especially iron. They have a high fiber content and are inexpensive and versatile, so it is hardly surprising that they feature in so many dishes from across the world—dal curries in India, bean soups in the Mediterranean, Mexican refried beans, and the famous Boston baked beans. They do not have a strong flavor, so they combine well with other ingredients, including herbs and spices, and since they are quite substantial, they satisfy the appetite.

Most dried legumes require soaking before they are cooked in order to re-hydrate them and "plump" them up. The longer they have been stored, the greater the soaking time required. Wash them thoroughly under cold running water, then place in a bowl and cover with cold water and set aside to soak for as long as 8 hours, depending on the type. Alternatively, cover them with boiling water and soak for half the time. Lentils do not require soaking before cooking.

Some beans, including kidney beans and soybeans, contain a toxic substance. This can be destroyed after soaking by vigorously boiling kidney beans in fresh water over a high heat for 15 minutes before simmering. Boil soybeans for 1 hour before simmering.

Soy Products

A vast range of substitutes for dairy products are produced from soybeans, including "milk," "cream," spreads, and "ice cream," as well as other useful ingredients, such as flour, oil, and soy sauce. Tofu is one of the most versatile. It is widely available in a variety of forms and because it has little natural flavor, it combines well with other strong-tasting ingredients. It is high in protein and is a good source of B-group vitamins and iron. It is also high in fatty acids, essential for good nutrition, but contains no cholesterol.

Firm Tofu

This is sold in cakes and is the type best suited to such cooking techniques as stir-frying. It is easily cut into cubes with a sharp knife; do not use a blunt knife, as this will cause crumbling. Firm tofu can be roasted, broiled, stir-fried, or braised. Store, covered with water, in a sealed container in the refrigerator for up to 1 week. Change the water daily. Silken tofu may be used in place of cream or milk for sauces, soups, and sweet dishes.

Nuts & Seeds

Ideal for adding texture and flavor, as well as being an attractive garnish, nuts and seeds are small nutrition bombs. They are high in protein, carbohydrate, and fats, so they should be used in moderation. Most nuts and many seeds are best dry-roasted or dry-fried to release their full flavor and aroma before use. Almonds, cashews, hazelnuts, peanuts, pine nuts, pistachios, and walnuts are among the most useful and they can be used separately or in combination. Crushed nuts make a wonderful, crunchy coating. Useful seeds include fenugreek, melon, poppy, pumpkin, sesame, and sunflower. Both nuts and seeds will go rancid if stored for longer than six months, so buy in the quantities you use regularly and keep in an airtight container.

Sprouting Beans, Peas, & Seeds

Well known from many popular Chinese dishes, these are usually grown from mung beans, but many other fresh sprouts can add flavor, texture, and color to salads and stir-fries. They are rich in protein, vitamins, minerals, complex carbohydrates, and fiber, inexpensive and easy to grow yourself. Special layered sprouters are available, but most types will grow well in a jar covered with a piece of cheesecloth held in place with a rubber band. Place the seeds to be sprouted in the jar, cover with water, and set aside for 15

Vegetarian Ingredients

minutes. Pour out the excess water and leave in a moderate, even temperature (50–70°F) for 24 hours. Pour out any water and repeat the rinsing process. Within a few days, depending on the variety, sprouts will appear. They can be used when they are about 1 inch long. Always grow shoots from edible beans or seeds, rather than horticultural ones which may have been treated with preservatives. The following are suitable for sprouting: adzuki beans, alfalfa, garbanzo beans, fenugreek seeds, lentils, mung beans, poppy seeds, pumpkin seeds, sesame seeds, soybeans, and sunflower seeds. You can also sprout wheat grains.

Mushrooms & Other Fungi

Intensely flavored, mushrooms are an important and versatile addition to the vegetarian diet. They contain protein, B-group vitamins, and potassium, but have no cholesterol or fat. A huge variety of cultivated and wild mushrooms is available, each with its own individual qualities. Cultivated mushrooms are less strong-tasting than wild, although cultivated shiitake are very flavorful. Popular wild mushrooms, some of which are cultivated nowadays, include cepes, also called porcini, chanterelles, chestnut, also called champignons de Paris, field mushrooms, morels, and oyster mushrooms. Chinese straw mushrooms, which are valued for their slippery texture rather than their flavor, are usually only available in cans in the West.

Dried mushrooms are a useful stand-by, as they will keep virtually indefinitely in an airtight container. Although expensive, a little goes a long way, as the flavor intensifies when they are dried. They must be soaked in hot water before use.

Fresh mushrooms cannot be stored for longer than three days and wild mushrooms should be used on the day of purchase or when they are gathered. Gathering wild mushrooms is a popular and practical pastime in many European countries, where pharmacies are willing to check the identification of edible species. This activity is less popular in North America and it is vital that you never pick and eat any fungus that you cannot positively identify as edible.

Vegetarian Ingredients

Grains & Cereals

Once considered the ultimate evil in any diet, starchy ingredients have now been recognized as valuable foods which play an important role in ensuring good health and protection against disease. They release energy at a controlled rate over a period of time, which is much healthier than the sudden and short-lived "buzz" of sugar. Starchy foods also contain protein, B-group and other vitamins, iron, phosphorus, potassium, and zinc and they are high in fiber. Bread and many breakfast cereals have added vitamins and minerals, such as calcium.

Rice

This is one of the world's staples and a "must" for the vegetarian pantry. High in fiber, it satisfies the appetite and goes well with both sweet and savory ingredients. It contains proteins, B-group and other vitamins, and minerals. Basmati, the "prince of rices," is a fragrant Indian variety that goes well with many savory dishes and makes excellent salads. Use it whenever light, fluffy, separate grains are required. Long-grain rice, also excellent in savory dishes, is less expensive and very easy to cook. Risotto rice (arborio rice) is rounder than long-grain and absorbs a lot of liquid, which is what gives this

Italian dish its unique, creamy texture. Round grain and glutinous or sticky rice are usually used for desserts.

Brown rice is the whole grain with only the outer husk removed, whereas white rice has been polished and lost the layers of bran. Brown rice has a chewy texture and a nutty flavor and is available in both long- and round-grain varieties. It contains more proteins, vitamins, and minerals than white rice and is a good source of vitamin B1, riboflavin, niacin, calcium, and iron. It requires a longer cooking time than white rice, but this can be reduced by pre-soaking. Wild rice is an aquatic grass and not a true rice. It contains plenty of protein and has a delicious flavor. It is often served mixed with long-grain rice, but requires a longer cooking time.

Flour

A selection of different types of flour is a useful mainstay. Whole wheat flour has nothing added or removed, so it retains all its nutrients. It may be used on its own or mixed with other flours, such as all-purpose white or buckwheat.

Other cereals that are useful include cornmeal, bulgur or cracked wheat, couscous, which is made from semolina grains, and oats.

Pasta

This is another essential for the pantry. Arguably the most versatile ingredient in the world, it goes well with almost all vegetables, cheeses, cream, herbs, and spices. It is available in hundreds of shapes and many colors, and is both easy and quick to cook.

Fats & Oils

A valuable source of vitamins A, D, and E, a moderate amount of fats and oils is essential for a healthy diet. For general cooking, choose bland-flavored oils, such as sunflower, that are high in polyunsaturates. Extra virgin olive oil is best for salad dressings and virgin olive oil is a special treat when cooking Mediterranean dishes. Besides being high in monosaturates, which are thought to help reduce blood cholesterol levels, it has a delicious flavor. Use it to replace butter, margarine, or other spreads.

Basic Recipes

These recipes form the basis of several of the dishes contained throughout this book. Many of these basic recipes can be made ahead of time and stored in the refrigerator until required.

Fresh Vegetable Stock

8 oz shallots or onions

1 large carrot, diced

1 celery stalk, chopped

½ fennel bulb

1 garlic clove

1 bay leaf

a few fresh parsley and tarragon sprigs

8¾ cups water

pepper

1 Put all of the ingredients in a large saucepan and bring to a boil. Skim off the surface froth with a flat spoon and reduce to a gentle simmer. Partially cover and cook for 45 minutes. Leave to cool.

2 Line a strainer with clean cheesecloth and put over a large jug or bowl. Pour the stock through the strainer. Discard the herbs and vegetables. Cover and store in small quantities in the refrigerator for up to 3 days.

Tahini Cream

3 tbsp tahini

6 tbsp water

2 tsp lemon juice

1 garlic clove, crushed

salt and pepper

1 Blend together the tahini and water.

2 Stir in the lemon juice and garlic. Season with salt and pepper to taste. The tahini cream is now ready to serve.

Sesame Dressing

2 tbsp tahini

2 tbsp cider vinegar

2 tbsp medium sherry

2 tbsp sesame oil

1 tbsp soy sauce

1 garlic clove, crushed

1 Put the tahini in a bowl and gradually mix in the vinegar and sherry until smooth. Add the sesame oil, soy sauce, and garlic and mix together thoroughly.

Béchamel Sauce

2½ cups milk

4 cloves

1 bay leaf

pinch of freshly grated nutmeg

2 tbsp butter or margarine

2 tbsp all-purpose flour

salt and pepper

1 Put the milk in a saucepan and add the cloves, bay leaf, and nutmeg. Gradually bring to a boil. Remove from the heat and leave for 15 minutes.

2 Melt the butter or margarine in another saucepan and stir in the flour to make a roux. Cook, stirring, for 1 minute. Remove the pan from the heat.

3 Strain the milk and gradually blend into the roux. Return the pan to the heat and bring to a boil, stirring, until the sauce thickens. Season with salt and pepper to taste and add any flavorings.

Basic Recipes

Green Herb Dressing

¼ cup parsley

¼ cup mint

¼ cup chives

1 garlic clove, crushed

⅔ cup plain yogurt

salt and pepper

1 Remove the stalks from the parsley and mint and put the leaves in a blender or food processor.

2 Add the chives, garlic, and yogurt and salt and pepper to taste. Blend until smooth, then store in the refrigerator until needed.

Sesame Dressing

2 tbsp tahini

2 tbsp cider vinegar

2 tbsp medium sherry

2 tbsp sesame oil

1 tbsp soy sauce

1 garlic clove, crushed

1 Put the tahini in a bowl and gradually mix in the vinegar and sherry until smooth. Add the sesame oil, soy sauce, and garlic and mix together thoroughly.

Cucumber Dressing

1 cup plain yogurt

2-inch piece of cucumber, peeled

1 tbsp chopped fresh mint leaves

½ tsp grated lemon zest

pinch of sugar

salt and pepper

1 Put the yogurt, cucumber, mint, lemon zest, sugar, and salt and pepper to taste in a blender or food processor and work until smooth. Alternatively, finely chop the cucumber and combine with the other ingredients. Serve chilled.

Apple & Cider Vinegar Dressing

2 tbsp sunflower oil

2 tbsp concentrated apple juice

2 tbsp cider vinegar

1 tbsp mustard

1 garlic clove, crushed

salt and pepper

1 Put the oil, apple juice, cider vinegar, mustard, garlic, and salt and pepper to taste in a screw-top jar and shake vigorously until well-mixed.

Warm Walnut Dressing

6 tbsp walnut oil

3 tbsp white wine vinegar

1 tbsp honey

1 tsp wholegrain mustard

1 garlic clove, sliced

salt and pepper

1 Put the oil, vinegar, honey, mustard, and salt and pepper to taste in a saucepan and whisk together.

2 Add the garlic and heat very gently for 3 minutes. Remove the garlic slices with a perforated spoon and discard. Pour the dressing over the salad and serve immediately.

Tomato Dressing

½ cup tomato juice

1 garlic clove, crushed

2 tbsp lemon juice

1 tbsp soy sauce

1 tsp honey

2 tbsp chopped chives

salt and pepper

1 Put the tomato juice, garlic, lemon juice, soy sauce, honey, chives, and salt and pepper to taste in a screw-top jar and shake vigorously until well-mixed.

How to Use this Book

Each recipe contains a wealth of useful information, including a breakdown of nutritional quantities, preparation and cooking times, and level of difficulty. All of this information is explained in detail below.

This amount of time represents the actual cooking time.

The nutritional information provided for each recipe is per serving or per portion. Optional ingredients, variations, or serving suggestions have not been included in the calculations.

The number of chef's hats represents the difficulty of each recipe, ranging from easy (1 chef's hat) to difficult (5 chef's hats).

This amount of time represents the preparation of ingredients, including cooling, chilling, and soaking times.

The ingredients for each recipe are listed in the order that they are used.

The method is illustrated with step-by-step photographs, making the recipe easy to follow.

A full-color photograph of the finished dish.

Variations and cook's tips provide useful information regarding ingredients or cooking techniques.

The method is clearly explained with step-by-step instructions that are easy to follow.

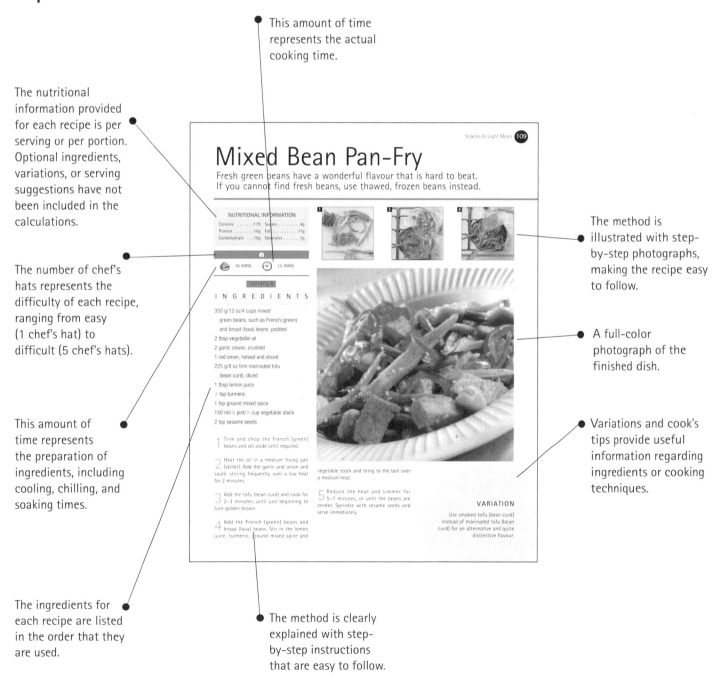

Snacks & Light Meals **109**

Mixed Bean Pan-Fry

Fresh green beans have a wonderful flavour that is hard to beat. If you cannot find fresh beans, use thawed, frozen beans instead.

NUTRITIONAL INFORMATION

Calories . . . . . . .179 Sugars 4g
Protein . . . . .10g Fat 11g
Carbohydrate . . .10g Saturates 1g

10 MINS   15 MINS

SERVES 4

INGREDIENTS

350 g/12 oz/4 cups mixed
    green beans, such as French (green)
    and broad (fava) beans, podded
2 tbsp vegetable oil
2 garlic cloves, crushed
1 red onion, halved and sliced
225 g/8 oz firm marinated tofu
    (bean curd), diced
1 tbsp lemon juice
½ tsp turmeric
1 tsp ground mixed spice
150 ml/¼ pint/⅔ cup vegetable stock
2 tsp sesame seeds

1 Trim and chop the French (green) beans and set aside until required.

2 Heat the oil in a medium frying pan (skillet). Add the garlic and onion and saute, stirring frequently, over a low heat for 2 minutes.

3 Add the tofu (bean curd) and cook for 2–3 minutes, until just beginning to turn golden brown.

4 Add the French (green) beans and broad (fava) beans. Stir in the lemon juice, turmeric, ground mixed spice and vegetable stock and bring to the boil over a medium heat.

5 Reduce the heat and simmer for 5–7 minutes, or until the beans are tender. Sprinkle with sesame seeds and serve immediately.

VARIATION

Use smoked tofu (bean curd) instead of marinated tofu (bean curd) for an alternative and quite distinctive flavour.

Soups

Soup is easy to make but always produces delicious results. There is an enormous variety of soups that you can make with vegetables. They can be rich and creamy, thick and chunky, light and delicate, and hot or chilled. The vegetables are often puréed to give a smooth consistency and thicken the soup, but you can also purée just some of

the mixture to give the soup more texture and interest. A wide range of ingredients can be used in addition to vegetables—legumes, grains, noodles, cheese, and yogurt all work well. You can also experiment with different substitutions if you don't have certain ingredients on hand. Whatever your preference, you are sure to enjoy the variety of tasty soups contained in this chapter. Serve with fresh, homemade bread for a truly delicious meal.

Bell Pepper & Chili Soup

This soup has a real Mediterranean flavor, using sweet red bell peppers, tomato, and basil. It is great served with an olive bread.

NUTRITIONAL INFORMATION

Calories	55	Sugars	........10g
Protein	.........2g	Fat	..........0.5g
Carbohydrate	....11g	Saturates	.....0.1g

 10 MINS   25 MINS

SERVES 4

INGREDIENTS

8 oz red bell peppers,
   seeded and sliced

1 onion, sliced

2 garlic cloves, crushed

1 green chili, chopped

1½ cups strained tomatoes

2½ cups vegetable stock

2 tbsp chopped basil

basil sprigs, to garnish

1 Put the bell peppers in a large saucepan with the onion, garlic, and chili. Add the strained tomatoes and vegetable stock and bring to a boil, stirring well.

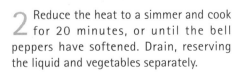

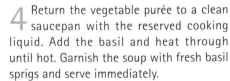

VARIATION

This soup is also delicious served cold with ⅔ cup of plain yogurt swirled into it.

2 Reduce the heat to a simmer and cook for 20 minutes, or until the bell peppers have softened. Drain, reserving the liquid and vegetables separately.

3 Press the vegetables through a strainer with the back of a spoon. Alternatively, process in a food processor until smooth.

4 Return the vegetable purée to a clean saucepan with the reserved cooking liquid. Add the basil and heat through until hot. Garnish the soup with fresh basil sprigs and serve immediately.

Avocado & Mint Soup

A rich and creamy pale green soup made with avocados and enhanced by a touch of chopped mint. Serve chilled in summer or hot in winter.

NUTRITIONAL INFORMATION

Calories 199	Sugars 3g
Protein 3g	Fat 18g
Carbohydrate 7g	Saturates 6g

 15 MINS 🕐 35 MINS

SERVES 6

I N G R E D I E N T S

3 tbsp butter or margarine

6 green onions, sliced

1 garlic clove, crushed

¼ cup all-purpose flour

2½ cups vegetable stock

2 ripe avocados

2–3 tsp lemon juice

pinch of grated lemon zest

⅔ cup milk

⅔ cup light cream

1–1½ tbsp chopped mint

salt and pepper

mint sprigs, to garnish

MINTED GARLIC BREAD

½ cup butter

1–2 tbsp chopped mint

1–2 garlic cloves, crushed

1 whole wheat or white baguette

1 Melt the butter or margarine in a large, heavy-bottomed saucepan. Add the green onions and garlic and fry over a low heat, stirring occasionally, for about 3 minutes, until soft and translucent.

2 Stir in the flour and cook, stirring, for 1–2 minutes. Gradually stir in the stock, then bring to a boil. Simmer gently while preparing the avocados.

3 Peel the avocados, discard the pits and chop coarsely. Add to the soup with the lemon juice and zest and seasoning. Cover and simmer for about 10 minutes, until tender.

4 Cool the soup slightly, then press through a strainer with the back of a spoon or process in a food processor or blender until a smooth purée forms. Pour into a bowl.

5 Stir in the milk and cream, adjust the seasoning, then stir in the mint. Cover and chill thoroughly.

6 To make the minted garlic bread, soften the butter and beat in the mint and garlic. Cut the loaf into slanting slices but leave a hinge on the bottom crust. Spread each slice with the butter and reassemble the loaf. Wrap in foil and place in a preheated oven at 350°F for about 15 minutes.

7 Serve the soup garnished with a sprig of mint and accompanied by the minted garlic bread.

Stilton & Walnut Soup

Full of flavor, this rich and creamy soup is very simple to make and utterly delicious to eat.

NUTRITIONAL INFORMATION

Calories 392	Sugars 8g	
Protein 15g	Fat 30g	
Carbohydrate ...15g	Saturates 16g	

  10 MINS   30 MINS

SERVES 4

I N G R E D I E N T S

4 tbsp butter

2 shallots, chopped

3 celery stalks, chopped

1 garlic clove, crushed

2 tbsp all-purpose flour

2½ cups vegetable stock

1¼ cups milk

1½ cups blue Stilton cheese, crumbled, plus extra to garnish

2 tbsp walnut halves, roughly chopped

⅔ cup plain yogurt

salt and pepper

chopped celery leaves, to garnish

1 Melt the butter in a large, heavy-bottomed saucepan and sauté the shallots, celery, and garlic, stirring occasionally, for 2–3 minutes, until softened.

2 Lower the heat, add the flour, and cook, stirring constantly, for 30 seconds.

3 Gradually stir in the vegetable stock and milk and bring to a boil.

4 Reduce the heat to a gentle simmer and add the crumbled blue Stilton cheese and walnut halves. Cover and simmer for 20 minutes.

5 Stir in the yogurt and heat through for 2 minutes more without boiling.

6 Season the soup to taste with salt and pepper, then transfer to a warm soup tureen or individual serving bowls, garnish with chopped celery leaves and extra crumbled blue Stilton cheese, and serve immediately.

COOK'S TIP

As well as adding protein, vitamins, and useful fats to the diet, nuts add important flavor and texture to vegetarian meals.

Leek, Potato, & Carrot Soup

A quick chunky soup, ideal for a snack or a quick lunch. The leftovers can be puréed to make one portion of creamed soup for the next day.

NUTRITIONAL INFORMATION

Calories	156	Sugars	.........7g
Protein	.........4g	Fat	...........6g
Carbohydrate	...22g	Saturates	.....0.7g

 10 MINS   25 MINS

SERVES 2

I N G R E D I E N T S

1 leek, about 6 oz

1 tbsp sunflower oil

1 garlic clove, crushed

3 cups vegetable stock

1 bay leaf

¼ tsp ground cumin

1 cup potatoes, diced

1 cup coarsely grated carrot

salt and pepper

chopped parsley, to garnish

P U R E E D   S O U P

5–6 tbsp milk

1–2 tbsp heavy cream, crème
    fraîche, or sour cream

1 Trim off and discard some of the coarse green part of the leek, then slice thinly and rinse thoroughly in cold water. Drain well.

2 Heat the sunflower oil in a heavy-bottomed saucepan. Add the leek and garlic, and fry over a low heat for about 2–3 minutes, until soft, but barely colored. Add the vegetable stock, bay leaf, and cumin and season to taste with salt and pepper. Bring the mixture to a boil, stirring constantly.

3 Add the diced potato to the saucepan, cover, and simmer over a low heat for 10–15 minutes until the potato is just tender, but not broken up.

4 Add the grated carrot and simmer for another 2–3 minutes. Adjust the seasoning, discard the bay leaf, and serve sprinkled liberally with chopped parsley.

5 To make a puréed soup, first process the leftovers (about half the original soup) in a blender or food processor or press through a strainer until smooth and then return to a clean saucepan with the milk. Bring to a boil and simmer for 2–3 minutes. Adjust the seasoning and stir in the cream or crème fraîche before serving sprinkled with chopped parsley.

Indian Bean Soup

A thick and hearty soup, nourishing and substantial enough to serve as a main meal with whole wheat bread.

NUTRITIONAL INFORMATION

Calories 237   Sugars 9g
Protein ....9g   Fat 9g
Carbohydrate ...33g   Saturates 1g

 20 MINS   50 MINS

SERVES 6

I N G R E D I E N T S

4 tbsp vegetable ghee or vegetable oil

2 onions, peeled and chopped

1½ cups potato, cut
    into chunks

1½ cups parsnip, cut
    into chunks

1½ cups turnip or rutabaga,
    cut into chunks

2 celery stalks, sliced

2 zucchini, sliced

1 green bell pepper, seeded and cut into
    ½-inch pieces

2 garlic cloves, crushed

2 tsp ground coriander

1 tbsp paprika

1 tbsp mild curry paste

5 cups vegetable stock

salt

14 oz can black-eyed peas,
    drained and rinsed

chopped cilantro,
    to garnish (optional)

1 Heat the ghee or oil in a saucepan, add all the prepared vegetables, except the zucchini and green bell pepper, and cook over a moderate heat, stirring frequently, for 5 minutes. Add the garlic, ground coriander, paprika, and curry paste and cook, stirring constantly, for 1 minute.

2 Stir in the stock and season with salt to taste. Bring to a boil, cover, and simmer over a low heat, stirring occasionally, for 25 minutes.

3 Stir in the black-eye peas, sliced zucchini, and green bell pepper, cover and continue cooking for 15 minutes more, or until all the vegetables are tender.

4 Process 1¼ cups of the soup mixture (about 2 ladlefuls) in a food processor or blender. Return the puréed mixture to the soup in the saucepan and reheat until piping hot. Sprinkle with chopped cilantro, if using, and serve hot.

Dal Soup

Dal is the name given to a delicious Indian lentil dish. This soup is a variation of the theme—it is made with red lentils and curry powder.

NUTRITIONAL INFORMATION

Calories	284	Sugars	........13g
Protein	........16g	Fat	..........9g
Carbohydrate	...38g	Saturates	.......5g

 5 MINS 40 MINS

SERVES 4

I N G R E D I E N T S

2 tbsp butter

2 garlic cloves, crushed

1 onion, chopped

½ tsp turmeric

1 tsp garam masala

¼ tsp chili powder

1 tsp ground cumin

2 lb 4 oz canned, diced
   tomatoes, drained

1 cup red lentils

2 tsp lemon juice

2½ cups vegetable stock

1¼ cups coconut milk

salt and pepper

chopped cilantro and lemon
   slices, to garnish

naan bread, to serve

1 Melt the butter in a large saucepan. Add the garlic and onion and sauté, stirring, for 2–3 minutes. Add the turmeric, garam masala, chili powder, and cumin and cook for another 30 seconds.

2 Stir in the tomatoes, red lentils, lemon juice, vegetable stock, and coconut milk and bring to a boil.

3 Reduce the heat to low and simmer the soup, uncovered, for about 25–30 minutes, until the lentils are tender and cooked.

4 Season to taste with salt and pepper and ladle the soup into a warm tureen. Garnish with chopped cilantro and lemon slices and serve immediately with warm naan bread.

COOK'S TIP

You can buy cans of coconut milk from supermarkets and delicatessens. It can also be made by grating creamed coconut, which comes in the form of a solid bar, and then mixing it with water.

Winter Soup

A thick vegetable soup which is a delicious meal in itself. Serve the soup with thin shavings of Parmesan and warm ciabatta or other Italian bread.

NUTRITIONAL INFORMATION

Calories	285	Sugars	........11g
Protein	........16g	Fat	..........12g
Carbohydrate	...29g	Saturates	.......3g

 10 MINS 20 MINS

SERVES 4

I N G R E D I E N T S

2 tbsp olive oil

2 leeks, thinly sliced

2 zucchini, chopped

2 garlic cloves, crushed

2 x 14 oz cans chopped tomatoes

1 tbsp tomato paste

1 bay leaf

3¾ cups vegetable stock

14 oz can garbanzo beans, drained

8 oz spinach

1 oz Parmesan cheese,
  thinly shaved

salt and pepper

crusty bread, to serve

1 Heat the oil in a heavy-bottomed saucepan. Add the sliced leeks and zucchini and cook over a medium heat, stirring constantly, for 5 minutes.

2 Add the garlic, chopped tomatoes, tomato paste, bay leaf, vegetable stock, and garbanzo beans. Bring to a boil, lower the heat, and simmer, stirring occasionally, for 5 minutes.

3 Shred the spinach finely, add to the soup and boil for 2 minutes. Season to taste with salt and pepper.

4 Remove the bay leaf. Pour into a soup tureen and sprinkle with the Parmesan. Serve with crusty bread.

Plum Tomato Soup

Homemade tomato soup is easy to make and always tastes better than bought varieties. Try this version with its Mediterranean influences.

NUTRITIONAL INFORMATION

Calories	402	Sugars	........14g
Protein	.........7g	Fat	..........32g
Carbohydrate	...16g	Saturates	.......3g

 20 MINS   30–35 MINS

SERVES 4

I N G R E D I E N T S

2 tbsp olive oil

2 red onions, chopped

2 celery stalks, chopped

1 carrot, chopped

1 lb 2 oz plum tomatoes, halved

3 cups vegetable stock

1 tbsp chopped oregano

1 tbsp chopped basil

⅔ cup dry white wine

2 tsp sugar

1 cup hazelnuts, toasted

1 cup black or green olives

handful of basil leaves

1 tbsp olive oil

1 loaf ciabatta bread (Italian-style loaf)

salt and pepper

basil sprigs to garnish

1 Heat the oil in a large saucepan. Add the onions, celery, and carrot and fry over a low heat, stirring frequently, until softened, but not colored.

2 Add the tomatoes, stock, chopped herbs, wine, and sugar. Bring to a boil, cover, and simmer for 20 minutes.

3 Place the toasted hazelnuts in a blender or food processor, together with the olives and basil leaves, and process until thoroughly combined, but not too smooth. Alternatively, finely chop the nuts, olives, and basil leaves and pound them together in a mortar with a pestle, then turn into a small bowl. Add the olive oil and process or beat thoroughly for a few seconds. Turn the mixture into a serving bowl.

4 Warm the ciabatta bread in a preheated oven at 375°F for 3–4 minutes.

5 Process the soup in a blender or a food processor, or press through a strainer, until smooth, Check the seasoning. Ladle into warmed soup bowls and garnish with sprigs of basil. Slice the warm bread and spread with the olive and hazelnut paste. Serve with the soup.

Mixed Bean Soup

This is a really hearty soup, filled with color, flavor, and goodness, which may be adapted to any vegetables that you have on hand.

NUTRITIONAL INFORMATION

Calories	190	Sugars	........9g
Protein	........10g	Fat	..........4g
Carbohydrate	...30g	Saturates	.....0.5g

 10 MINS   40 MINS

SERVES 4

INGREDIENTS

1 tbsp vegetable oil

1 red onion, halved and sliced

⅔ cup potato, diced

1 carrot, diced

1 leek, sliced

1 green chili, sliced

3 garlic cloves, crushed

1 tsp ground coriander

1 tsp chili powder

4 cups vegetable stock

1 lb mixed canned beans,
   such as red kidney or black-eyed
   peas, drained

salt and pepper

2 tbsp chopped cilantro,
   to garnish

COOK'S TIP

Serve this soup with slices of warm cornbread or a cheese loaf.

1 Heat the vegetable oil in a large saucepan. Add the onion, potato, carrot, and leek and sauté, stirring constantly, for about 2 minutes, until the vegetables are slightly softened.

2 Add the sliced chili and crushed garlic and cook for 1 minute more.

3 Stir in the ground coriander, chili powder, and the vegetable stock.

4 Bring the soup to a boil, reduce the heat, and cook for 20 minutes, or until the vegetables are tender.

5 Stir in the beans, season well with salt and pepper, and cook, stirring occasionally, for another 10 minutes.

6 Transfer the soup to a warm tureen or individual bowls, garnish with chopped cilantro, and serve.

Pumpkin Soup

This is a classic soup that has become popular worldwide. When pumpkin is out of season, use butternut squash in its place.

NUTRITIONAL INFORMATION

Calories 112	Sugars 7g
Protein 4g	Fat 7g
Carbohydrate 8g	Saturates 2g

 10 MINS   30 MINS

SERVES 6

I N G R E D I E N T S

2 lb 4 oz pumpkin

3 tbsp butter or margarine

1 onion, sliced thinly

1 garlic clove, crushed

3½ cups vegetable stock

½ tsp ground ginger

1 tbsp lemon juice

3–4 thinly pared strips of orange
    zest (optional)

1–2 bay leaves or 1 bouquet garni

1¼ cups milk

salt and pepper

TO GARNISH

4–6 tablespoons light or heavy cream, or
    plain yogurt

snipped chives

1 Peel the pumpkin, remove the seeds, and then cut the flesh into 1 inch cubes.

2 Melt the butter or margarine in a large, heavy-bottomed saucepan. Add the onion and garlic and fry over a low heat until soft but not colored.

3 Add the pumpkin and toss with the onion for 2–3 minutes.

4 Add the stock and bring to a boil over a medium heat. Season to taste with salt and pepper and add the ginger, lemon juice, strips of orange zest, if using, and bay leaves or bouquet garni. Cover and simmer over a low heat for about 20 minutes, until the pumpkin is tender.

5 Discard the orange zest, if using, and the bay leaves or bouquet garni. Cool the soup slightly, then press through a strainer or process in a food processor until smooth. Pour into a clean saucepan.

6 Add the milk and reheat gently. Adjust the seasoning. Garnish with a swirl of cream or plain yogurt and snipped chives, and serve.

Minted Pea & Yogurt Soup

A deliciously refreshing, summery soup that is full of goodness. It is also extremely tasty served chilled.

NUTRITIONAL INFORMATION

Calories 208	Sugars 9g	
Protein 10g	Fat 7g	
Carbohydrate ...26g	Saturates 2g	

 15 MINS 25 MINS

SERVES 6

INGREDIENTS

2 tbsp vegetable ghee or sunflower oil

2 onions, coarsely chopped

8 oz potato, coarsely chopped

2 garlic cloves, crushed

1 inch fresh ginger, chopped

1 tsp ground coriander

1 tsp ground cumin

1 tbsp all-purpose flour

3½ cups vegetable stock

1 lb frozen peas

2–3 tbsp chopped mint

salt and pepper

⅔ cup strained plain yogurt, plus extra
   to serve

½ tsp cornstarch

1¼ cups milk

mint sprigs, to garnish

1 Heat the vegetable ghee or sunflower oil in a saucepan, add the onions and potato, and cook over a low heat, stirring occasionally, for about 3 minutes, until the onion is soft and translucent.

2 Stir in the garlic, ginger, coriander, cumin, and flour and cook, stirring constantly, for 1 minute.

3 Add the vegetable stock, peas, and the chopped mint and bring to a boil, stirring. Reduce the heat, cover, and simmer gently for 15 minutes, or until the vegetables are tender.

4 Process the soup, in batches, in a blender or food processor. Return the mixture to the pan and season with salt and pepper to taste. Blend the yogurt with the cornstarch to a smooth paste and stir into the soup.

5 Add the milk and bring almost to a boil, stirring constantly. Cook very gently for 2 minutes. Serve the soup hot, garnished with the mint sprigs and a swirl of extra yogurt.

Thick Onion Soup

A delicious creamy soup with grated carrot and parsley for texture and color. Serve with crusty cheese biscuits for a hearty lunch.

NUTRITIONAL INFORMATION

Calories	277	Sugars 12g
Protein	.........6g	Fat 20g
Carbohydrate	...19g	Saturates 8g

 20 MINS   1HR 10 MINS

SERVES 6

INGREDIENTS

5 tbsp butter

1 lb 2 oz onions, finely chopped

1 garlic clove, crushed

6 tbsp all-purpose flour

2½ cups vegetable stock

2½ cups milk

2–3 tsp lemon or lime juice

good pinch of ground allspice

1 bay leaf

1 carrot, coarsely grated

4–6 tbsp heavy cream

2 tbsp chopped parsley

salt and pepper

CHEESE BISCUITS

2 cups whole wheat flour

2 tsp baking powder

¼ cup butter

4 tbsp grated Parmesan cheese

1 egg, beaten

about ⅓ cup milk

1 Melt the butter in a saucepan and fry the onions and garlic over a low heat, stirring frequently, for 10–15 minutes, until soft, but not colored. Stir in the flour and cook, stirring, for 1 minute, then gradually stir in the stock and bring to a boil, stirring frequently. Add the milk, then bring back to a boil.

2 Season to taste with salt and pepper and add 2 teaspoons of the lemon or lime juice, the allspice, and bay leaf. Cover and simmer for about 25 minutes until the vegetables are tender. Discard the bay leaf.

3 Meanwhile, make the biscuits. Combine the flour, baking powder, and seasoning and cut in the butter until the mixture resembles fine breadcrumbs. Stir in 3 tablespoons of the cheese, the egg, and enough milk to mix to a soft dough.

4 Shape into a bar about ¾-inch thick. Place on a floured cookie sheet and mark into slices. Sprinkle with the remaining cheese and bake in a preheated oven at 425°F for about 20 minutes, until risen and golden brown.

5 Stir the carrot into the soup and simmer for 2–3 minutes. Add more lemon or lime juice, if necessary. Stir in the cream and reheat. Garnish and serve with the warm biscuits.

Vegetable & Corn Chowder

This is a really filling soup, which should be served before a light main course. It is easy to prepare and filled with flavor.

NUTRITIONAL INFORMATION

Calories . . . . . . .378 Sugars 20g
Protein . . . . .16g Fat 13g
Carbohydrate . . .52g Saturates 6g

 15 MINS   30 MINS

SERVES 4

I N G R E D I E N T S

1 tbsp vegetable oil

1 red onion, diced

1 red bell pepper, seeded and diced

3 garlic cloves, crushed

1 large potato, diced

2 tbsp all-purpose flour

2½ cups milk

1¼ cups vegetable stock

1¾ oz broccoli flowerets

3 cups canned corn, drained

¾ cup cheddar cheese, grated

salt and pepper

1 tbsp chopped cilantro,
    to garnish

COOK'S TIP

Vegetarian cheeses are made with rennets of non-animal origin, using microbial or fungal enzymes.

1 Heat the oil in a large saucepan. Add the onion, bell pepper, garlic, and potato and sauté over a low heat, stirring frequently, for 2–3 minutes.

2 Stir in the flour and cook, stirring for 30 seconds. Gradually stir in the milk and stock.

3 Add the broccoli and corn. Bring the mixture to a boil, stirring constantly, then reduce the heat and simmer for about 20 minutes, or until all the vegetables are tender.

4 Stir in ½ cup of the cheese until it melts.

5 Season and spoon the chowder into a warm soup tureen. Garnish with the remaining cheese and the cilantro and serve.

Gazpacho

This Spanish soup is full of chopped and grated vegetables with a puréed tomato base. It requires chilling, so prepare well ahead of time.

NUTRITIONAL INFORMATION

Calories	140	Sugars	........12g
Protein	.........3g	Fat	...........9g
Carbohydrate	...13g	Saturates	.......1g

6¹/₂ HOURS   0 MINS

SERVES 4

INGREDIENTS

½ small cucumber

½ small green bell pepper, seeded and
   very finely chopped

1 lb 2 oz ripe tomatoes, peeled or
   14 oz can diced tomatoes

½ onion, coarsely chopped

2–3 garlic cloves, crushed

3 tbsp olive oil

2 tbsp white wine vinegar

1–2 tbsp lemon or lime juice

2 tbsp tomato paste

2 cups tomato juice

salt and pepper

TO SERVE

chopped green bell pepper

thinly sliced onion

garlic croutons

1 Coarsely grate the cucumber into a large bowl and add the chopped green bell pepper.

2 Process the tomatoes, onion, and garlic in a food processor or blender, then add the oil, vinegar, lemon or lime juice, and tomato paste and process until smooth. Alternatively, finely chop the tomatoes and finely grate the onion, then mix both with the garlic, oil, vinegar, lemon or lime juice, and tomato paste.

3 Add the tomato mixture to the bowl and mix well, then add the tomato juice and mix again.

4 Season, cover the bowl with plastic wrap, and chill thoroughly—for at least 6 hours and preferably longer so that the flavors have time to meld together.

5 Prepare the side dishes of green bell pepper, onion slices, and garlic croutons, and arrange them in individual serving bowls.

6 Ladle the soup into bowls, preferably from a soup tureen set on the table with the side dishes placed around it. Hand the dishes around to allow the guests to help themselves.

Gardener's Broth

This hearty soup uses a variety of green vegetables with a flavoring of ground coriander. A finishing touch of thinly sliced leeks adds texture.

NUTRITIONAL INFORMATION

Calories	169	Sugars	.........5g
Protein	.........4g	Fat	.........13g
Carbohydrate	....8g	Saturates	.......5g

  10 MINS 45 MINS

SERVES 6

I N G R E D I E N T S

3 tbsp butter

1 onion, chopped

1–2 garlic cloves, crushed

1 large leek

8 oz Brussels sprouts

4½ oz green or string beans

5 cups vegetable stock

1 cup frozen peas

1 tbsp lemon juice

½ tsp ground coriander

4 tbsp heavy cream

salt and pepper

M E L B A   T O A S T

4–6 slices white bread

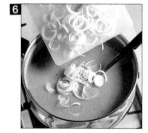  

1 Melt the butter in a saucepan. Add the onion and garlic and fry over a low heat, stirring occasionally, until they begin to soften, but not color.

2 Slice the white part of the leek very thinly and reserve; slice the remaining leek. Slice the Brussels sprouts and thinly slice the beans.

3 Add the green part of the leeks, the Brussels sprouts and beans to the saucepan. Add the stock and bring to a boil. Simmer for 10 minutes.

4 Add the frozen peas, seasoning, lemon juice, and coriander and continue to simmer for 10–15 minutes, until the vegetables are tender.

5 Cool the soup a little, then press through a strainer or process in a food processor or blender until smooth. Pour into a clean pan.

6 Add the reserved slices of leek to the soup, bring back to a boil and simmer for about 5 minutes, until the leek is tender. Adjust the seasoning, stir in the cream, and reheat gently.

7 To make the melba toast, toast the bread on both sides under a preheated broiler. Cut horizontally through the slices, then toast the uncooked sides until they curl up. Serve immediately with the soup.

Speedy Beet Soup

Quick and easy to prepare in a microwave oven, this deep red soup of puréed beets and potatoes makes a stunning first course.

NUTRITIONAL INFORMATION

Calories 120	Sugars 11g
Protein 4g	Fat 2g
Carbohydrate ...22g	Saturates 1g

 20 MINS   30 MINS

SERVES 6

INGREDIENTS

1 onion, chopped

12 oz potatoes, diced

1 small apple, peeled,
    cored, and grated

3 tbsp water

1 tsp cumin seeds

1 lb 2 oz cooked beets,
    peeled and diced

1 bay leaf

pinch of dried thyme

1 tsp lemon juice

2½ cups hot vegetable stock

4 tbsp sour cream

salt and pepper

few dill sprigs, to garnish

1 Place the onion, potatoes, apple, and water in a large bowl. Cover and cook on HIGH power for 10 minutes.

2 Stir in the cumin seeds and cook on HIGH power for 1 minute.

3 Stir in the beets, bay leaf, thyme, lemon juice, and hot vegetable stock. Cover and cook on HIGH power for 12 minutes, stirring halfway through the cooking time.

4 Leave to stand, uncovered, for 5 minutes. Remove and discard the bay leaf. Strain the vegetables and reserve the liquid. Process the vegetables with a little of the reserved liquid in a food processor or blender until they are smooth and creamy. Alternatively, either mash the vegetables with a potato masher or press them through a strainer with the back of a wooden spoon.

5 Pour the vegetable purée into a clean bowl with the reserved liquid and mix well. Season to taste. Cover and cook on HIGH power for 4–5 minutes, until the soup is piping hot.

6 Serve the soup in warmed bowls. Swirl 1 tablespoon of sour cream into each serving and garnish with a few sprigs of fresh dill.

Vichyssoise

This is a classic creamy soup made from potatoes and leeks. To achieve the delicate pale color, be sure to use only the white parts of the leeks.

NUTRITIONAL INFORMATION

Calories 208	Sugars 5g	
Protein 5g	Fat 12g	
Carbohydrate ...20g	Saturates 6g	

 10 MINS   40 MINS

SERVES 6

INGREDIENTS

3 large leeks

3 tbsp butter or margarine

1 onion, thinly sliced

1 lb 2 oz potatoes, chopped

3½ cups vegetable stock

2 tsp lemon juice

pinch of ground nutmeg

¼ tsp ground coriander

1 bay leaf

1 egg yolk

⅔ cup light cream

salt and white pepper

TO GARNISH

freshly snipped chives

1 Trim the leeks and remove most of the green part. Slice the white part of the leeks very finely.

2 Melt the butter or margarine in a saucepan. Add the leeks and onion and fry, stirring occasionally, for about 5 minutes without browning.

3 Add the potatoes, vegetable stock, lemon juice, nutmeg, coriander, and bay leaf to the pan, season to taste with salt and pepper, and bring to a boil. Cover and simmer for about 30 minutes, until all the vegetables are very soft.

4 Cool the soup a little, remove and discard the bay leaf, and then press through a strainer or process in a food processor or blender until smooth. Pour into a clean pan.

5 Blend the egg yolk into the cream, add a little of the soup to the mixture, and then whisk it all back into the soup and reheat gently, without boiling. Adjust the seasoning to taste. Cool and then chill thoroughly in the refrigerator.

6 Serve the soup sprinkled with freshly snipped chives.

Curried Parsnip Soup

Parsnips make a delicious soup as they have a slightly sweet flavor. In this recipe, spices are added to complement this sweetness.

NUTRITIONAL INFORMATION

Calories 152	Sugars 7g
Protein 3g	Fat 8g
Carbohydrate . . .18g	Saturates 3g

 10 MINS 35 MINS

SERVES 4

I N G R E D I E N T S

1 tbsp vegetable oil

1 tbsp butter

1 red onion, chopped

3 parsnips, chopped

2 garlic cloves, crushed

2 tsp garam masala

½ tsp chili powder

1 tbsp all-purpose flour

3¾ cups vegetable stock

grated zest and juice of 1 lemon

salt and pepper

lemon zest, to garnish

1 Heat the oil and butter in a large saucepan until the butter has melted. Add the onion, parsnips, and garlic and sauté, stirring frequently, for about 5–7 minutes, until the vegetables have softened, but not colored.

2 Add the garam masala and chili powder and cook, stirring constantly, for 30 seconds. Sprinkle in the flour, mixing well and cook, stirring constantly, for another 30 seconds.

3 Stir in the stock, lemon zest and juice and bring to a boil. Reduce the heat and simmer for 20 minutes.

4 Remove some of the vegetable pieces with a perforated spoon and reserve until required. Process the remaining soup and vegetables in a food processor or blender for about 1 minute, or until a smooth purée. Alternatively, press the vegetables through a strainer with the back of a wooden spoon.

5 Return the soup to a clean saucepan and stir in the reserved vegetables. Heat the soup through for 2 minutes until piping hot.

6 Season to taste with salt and pepper, then transfer to soup bowls, garnish with grated lemon zest, and serve.

Asparagus Soup

Fresh asparagus is now available for most of the year, so this soup can be made at any time. It can also be made using canned asparagus.

NUTRITIONAL INFORMATION

Calories	196	Sugars	.........7g
Protein	.........7g	Fat	..........12g
Carbohydrate	...15g	Saturates	.......4g

   5-10 MINS   55 MINS

SERVES 6

I N G R E D I E N T S

1 bunch asparagus, about 12 oz,

   or 2 packs mini asparagus,

   about 5½ oz each

3 cups vegetable stock

¼ cup butter or margarine

1 onion, chopped

3 tbsp all-purpose flour

¼ tsp ground coriander

1 tbsp lemon juice

2 cups milk

4–6 tbsp heavy or light cream

salt and pepper

1 Wash and trim the asparagus, discarding the woody part of the stem. Cut the rest into short lengths, keeping a few tips for garnish. Mini asparagus does not need to be trimmed.

2 Cook the tips in the minimum of boiling salted water for 5–10 minutes. Drain and set aside.

3 Put the asparagus in a saucepan with the stock, bring to a boil, cover, and simmer for about 20 minutes, until soft. Drain and reserve the stock.

4 Melt the butter or margarine in a saucepan. Add the onion and fry over a low heat until soft, but only barely colored. Stir in the flour and cook for 1 minute, then gradually whisk in the reserved stock and bring to a boil.

5 Simmer for 2–3 minutes, until thickened, then stir in the cooked asparagus, seasoning, coriander, and lemon juice. Simmer for 10 minutes, then cool a little and either press through a strainer or process in a blender or food processor until smooth.

6 Pour into a clean pan, add the milk and reserved asparagus tips, and bring to a boil. Simmer for 2 minutes. Stir in the cream, reheat gently, and serve.

COOK'S TIP

If using canned asparagus, drain the liquid and use as part of the measured stock. Remove a few small asparagus tips for garnish and chop the rest. Continue as above.

Jerusalem Artichoke Soup

Jerusalem artichokes are native to North America and have a nutty flavor which combines well with orange.

NUTRITIONAL INFORMATION

Calories 211	Sugars 17g	
Protein 7g	Fat 8g	
Carbohydrate ...29g	Saturates 4g	

 10 MINS   30 MINS

SERVES 4

I N G R E D I E N T S

1½ lb Jerusalem artichokes

5 tbsp orange juice

2 tbsp butter

1 leek, chopped

1 garlic clove, crushed

1¼ cups vegetable stock

⅔ cup milk

2 tbsp chopped cilantro

⅔ cup plain yogurt

grated orange zest, to garnish

1 Rinse the Jerusalem artichokes and place in a large saucepan with 2 tablespoons of the orange juice and enough water to cover. Bring to a boil, reduce the heat, and cook for 20 minutes, or until the artichokes are tender.

2 Drain the artichokes, reserving 2 cups of the cooking liquid. Leave the artichokes to cool, then peel and place in a large bowl. Mash the flesh with a potato masher.

3 Melt the butter in a large saucepan. Add the leek and garlic and fry over a low heat, stirring frequently, for 2–3 minutes, until the leek is soft.

4 Stir in the mashed artichoke, stock, milk, remaining orange juice, and reserved cooking water. Bring to a boil, then simmer for 2–3 minutes.

5 Remove a few pieces of leek with a perforated spoon and reserve. Process the remainder in a food processor for 1 minute until smooth. Alternatively, press through a strainer with the back of a spoon.

6 Return the soup to a clean saucepan and stir in the reserved leeks, cilantro, and yogurt and heat through. Transfer to individual soup bowls, garnish with orange zest, and serve.

Bean Soup

Beans feature widely in Mexican cooking, and here pinto beans are used to give an interesting texture. Pinto beans require soaking overnight.

NUTRITIONAL INFORMATION

Calories	188	Sugars	.........9g
Protein	........13g	Fat	...........1g
Carbohydrate	...33g	Saturates	.....0.3g

20 MINS   3 HOURS

SERVES 4

I N G R E D I E N T S

6 oz pinto beans

2¼ pints water

6–8 oz carrots, finely chopped

1 large onion, finely chopped

2–3 garlic cloves, crushed

½–1 chili, seeded and finely chopped

5 cups vegetable stock

2 tomatoes, peeled and finely chopped

2 celery stalks, very thinly sliced

salt and pepper

1 tbsp chopped cilantro (optional)

C R O U T O N S

3 slices white bread, crusts removed

oil, for deep-frying

1–2 garlic cloves, crushed

VARIATION

Pinto beans are widely available, but if you cannot find them or you wish to vary the recipe, you can use cannellini beans or black-eyed peas as an alternative.

1 Soak the beans overnight in cold water; drain and place in a pan with the water. Bring to a boil and boil vigorously for 10 minutes. Lower the heat, cover, and simmer for 2 hours, or until the beans are tender.

2 Add the carrots, onion, garlic, chili, and stock and bring back to a boil. Cover and simmer for 30 minutes, until very tender.

3 Remove half the beans and vegetables with the cooking juices and press through a strainer or process in a food processor or blender until smooth.

4 Return the bean purée to the saucepan and add the tomatoes and celery. Simmer for 10–15 minutes, or until the celery is just tender, adding a little more stock or water if necessary.

5 Meanwhile, make the croutons. Dice the bread. Heat the oil with the garlic in a small skillet and fry the croutons until golden brown. Drain on paper towels.

6 Season the soup and stir in the chopped cilantro, if using. Transfer to a warm tureen and serve immediately with the croutons.

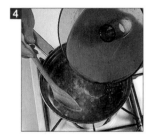

Beet Soup

Here are two variations using the same vegetable: a creamy soup made with puréed cooked borscht beets and a traditional clear soup.

NUTRITIONAL INFORMATION

Calories 106	Sugars 11g	
Protein 3g	Fat 5g	
Carbohydrate . . .13g	Saturates 3g	

25 MINS   35–55 MINS

SERVES 6

I N G R E D I E N T S

B O R S C H T

1 lb 2 oz raw beets, peeled
  and grated

2 carrots, finely chopped

1 large onion, finely chopped

1 garlic clove, crushed

1 bouquet garni

5 cups vegetable stock

2–3 tsp lemon juice

salt and pepper

⅔ cup sour cream, to serve

C R E A M E D   B E E T   S O U P

¼ cup butter or margarine

2 large onions, finely chopped

1–2 carrots, chopped

2 celery stalks, chopped

1 lb 2 oz cooked beets, diced

1–2 tbsp lemon juice

3½ cups vegetable stock

1¼ cups milk

salt and pepper

T O   S E R V E

grated cooked beets or 6 tbsp
  heavy cream, lightly whipped

1 To make borscht, place the beets, carrots, onion, garlic, bouquet garni, stock, and lemon juice in a saucepan and season to taste with salt and pepper. Bring to a boil, cover, and simmer for 45 minutes.

2 Press the soup through a fine strainer or a strainer lined with cheesecloth, then pour into a clean pan. Taste and adjust the seasoning and add extra lemon juice, if necessary.

3 Bring to a boil and simmer for 1–2 minutes. Serve with a spoonful of sour cream swirled through.

4 To make creamed beet soup, melt the butter or margarine in a saucepan. Add the onions, carrots, and celery and fry until just beginning to color.

5 Add the beet, 1 tablespoon of the lemon juice, the stock and seasoning, and bring to a boil. Cover and simmer for 30 minutes, until tender.

6 Cool slightly, then press through a strainer or process in a food processor or blender. Pour into a clean pan. Add the milk and bring to a boil. Adjust the seasoning and add extra lemon juice, if necessary. Top with grated beet or heavy cream.

Cauliflower & Broccoli Soup

Full of flavor, this creamy cauliflower and broccoli soup is simple to make and absolutely delicious to eat.

NUTRITIONAL INFORMATION

Calories	378	Sugars	........14g
Protein	........18g	Fat	..........26g
Carbohydrate	...20g	Saturates	.......7g

 10 MINS   35 MINS

SERVES 4

INGREDIENTS

3 tbsp vegetable oil

1 red onion, chopped

2 garlic cloves, crushed

10½ oz cauliflower flowerets

10½ oz broccoli flowerets

1 tbsp all-purpose flour

2½ cups milk

1¼ cups vegetable stock

¾ cup Gruyère cheese, grated

pinch of paprika

⅔ cup light cream

paprika and Gruyère cheese shavings,
    to garnish

1 Heat the oil in a large, heavy-bottomed saucepan. Add the onion, garlic, cauliflower flowerets, and broccoli flowerets, and sauté over a low heat, stirring constantly, for 3–4 minutes. Add the flour and cook, stirring constantly for another 1 minute.

2 Gradually stir in the milk and stock and bring to a boil, stirring constantly. Reduce the heat and simmer for 20 minutes.

3 Remove about a quarter of the vegetables with a perforated spoon and set aside. Put the remaining soup in a food processor or blender and process for about 30 seconds, until smooth. Alternatively, press the vegetables through a strainer with the back of a wooden spoon. Transfer the soup to a clean saucepan.

4 Return the reserved vegetable pieces to the soup. Stir in the grated cheese, paprika, and light cream and heat through over a low heat, without boiling, for 2–3 minutes, or until the cheese starts to melt.

5 Transfer to warmed individual serving bowls, garnish with shavings of Gruyère and dust with paprika, and serve immediately.

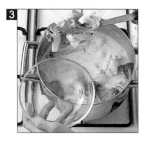

COOK'S TIP

The soup must not start to boil after the cream has been added, otherwise it will curdle. Use plain yogurt instead of the cream if preferred, but again do not allow it to boil.

Spanish Tomato Soup

This Mediterranean tomato soup is thickened with bread, as is traditional in some parts of Spain, and served with garlic bread.

NUTRITIONAL INFORMATION

Calories 297	Sugars 7g	
Protein 8g	Fat 13g	
Carbohydrate ...39g	Saturates 2g	

   10 MINS   20 MINS

SERVES 4

I N G R E D I E N T S

4 tbsp olive oil

1 onion, chopped

3 garlic cloves, crushed

1 green bell pepper, seeded and chopped

½ tsp chili powder

1 lb 2 oz tomatoes, chopped

8 oz French or Italian bread, cubed

4 cups vegetable stock

G A R L I C   B R E A D

4 slices ciabatta or French baguette

4 tbsp olive oil

2 garlic cloves, crushed

¼ cup grated cheddar cheese

chili powder, to garnish

1 Heat the olive oil in a large skillet. Add the onion, garlic, and bell pepper and sauté over a low heat, stirring frequently, for 2–3 minutes, or until the onion has softened.

2 Add the chili powder and tomatoes and cook over a medium heat until the mixture has thickened.

3 Stir in the bread cubes and stock and cook for 10–15 minutes, until the soup is thick and fairly smooth.

4 Meanwhile, make the garlic bread. Toast the bread slices under a medium broiler. Drizzle the oil over the top of the bread, rub with the garlic, sprinkle with the cheese, and return to the broiler for 2–3 minutes, until the cheese has melted. Sprinkle with chili powder and serve with the soup.

VARIATION

Replace the green bell pepper with red or orange bell pepper, if you prefer.

Broccoli & Potato Soup

This creamy soup has a delightful pale green coloring and rich flavor from the blend of tender broccoli and blue cheese.

NUTRITIONAL INFORMATION

Calories	452	Sugars	.........4g
Protein	........14g	Fat	.........35g
Carbohydrate	...20g	Saturates	......19g

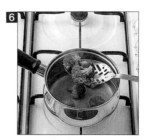

    5–10 MINS   40 MINS

SERVES 4

INGREDIENTS

2 tbsp olive oil

2 potatoes, diced

1 onion, diced

8 oz broccoli flowerets

4½ oz blue cheese, crumbled

4½ cups vegetable stock

⅔ cup heavy cream

pinch of paprika

salt and pepper

1 Heat the oil in a large saucepan. Add the potatoes and onion. Sauté, stirring constantly, for 5 minutes.

2 Reserve a few broccoli flowerets for the garnish and add the remaining broccoli to the pan. Add the cheese and vegetable stock.

COOK'S TIP

This soup freezes very successfully. Follow the method described here up to step 4, and freeze the soup after it has been puréed. Add the cream and paprika just before serving. Garnish and serve.

3 Bring to a boil, then reduce the heat, cover the pan, and simmer for 25 minutes, until the potatoes are tender.

4 Transfer the soup to a food processor or blender in batches and process until the mixture is smooth. Alternatively, press the vegetables through a strainer with the back of a wooden spoon.

5 Return the purée to a clean saucepan and stir in the heavy cream and a pinch of paprika. Season to taste with salt and pepper.

6 Blanch the reserved broccoli flowerets in a little boiling water for about 2 minutes, then lift them out of the pan with a perforated spoon.

7 Pour the soup into warmed individual bowls and garnish with the broccoli flowerets and a sprinkling of paprika. Serve immediately.

Spicy Dal & Carrot Soup

This nutritious soup uses split red lentils and carrots as the two main ingredients and includes a selection of spices to give it a kick.

NUTRITIONAL INFORMATION

Calories 173   Sugars 11g
Protein . . . . .9g   Fat 5g
Carbohydrate . . .24g   Saturates 1g

   15 MINS   45 MINS

SERVES 6

I N G R E D I E N T S

4½ oz split red lentils

5 cups vegetable stock

12 oz carrots, sliced

2 onions, chopped

8 oz can diced tomatoes

2 garlic cloves, chopped

2 tbsp vegetable ghee or oil

1 tsp ground cumin

1 tsp ground coriander

1 fresh green chili, seeded and chopped,
   or 1 tsp minced chili

½ tsp ground turmeric

1 tbsp lemon juice

salt

1¼ cups milk

2 tbsp chopped cilantro

plain yogurt, to serve

1 Place the lentils in a strainer and rinse well under cold running water. Drain and place in a large saucepan, together with 3½ cups of the stock, the carrots, onions, tomatoes, and garlic. Bring the mixture to a boil, reduce the heat, cover, and simmer for 30 minutes or until the vegetables and lentils are tender.

2 Meanwhile, heat the ghee or oil in a small pan. Add the cumin, ground coriander, chili, and turmeric and fry over a low heat for 1 minute. Remove from the heat and stir in the lemon juice. Season with salt to taste.

3 Process the soup in batches in a blender or food processor. Return the soup to the saucepan, add the spice mixture and the remaining 1¼ cups stock and simmer over a low heat for 10 minutes.

4 Add the milk, taste and adjust the seasoning, if necessary. Stir in the chopped cilantro and reheat gently. Serve hot with a swirl of yogurt.

Potato & Split Pea Soup

Split green peas are sweeter than other varieties of split pea and reduce down to a purée when cooked, which acts as a thickener in soups.

NUTRITIONAL INFORMATION

Calories 260	Sugars 5g
Protein 11g	Fat 10g
Carbohydrate ...32g	Saturates 3g

  5–10 MINS · 45 MINS

SERVES 4

INGREDIENTS

2 tbsp vegetable oil

2 unpeeled russet potatoes, diced

2 onions, diced

2¾ oz split green peas

4½ cups vegetable stock

5 tbsp grated Gruyère cheese

salt and pepper

CROUTONS

3 tbsp butter

1 garlic clove, crushed

1 tbsp chopped parsley

1 thick slice white bread, cubed

1 Heat the vegetable oil in a large saucepan. Add the potatoes and onions and sauté over a low heat, stirring constantly, for about 5 minutes.

VARIATION

For a richly colored soup, red lentils could be used instead of split green peas. Add a large pinch of brown sugar to the recipe for extra sweetness if red lentils are used.

2 Add the split green peas to the pan and stir to mix together well.

3 Pour the vegetable stock into the pan and bring to a boil. Reduce the heat to low and simmer for 35 minutes, until the potatoes are tender and the split peas cooked.

4 Meanwhile, make the croutons. Melt the butter in a skillet. Add the garlic, parsley and bread cubes, and cook, turning frequently, for about 2 minutes, until the bread cubes are golden brown on all sides.

5 Stir the grated cheese into the soup and season to taste with salt and pepper. Heat gently until the cheese is starting to melt.

6 Pour the soup into warmed individual bowls and sprinkle the croutons on top. Serve immediately.

Avocado & Vegetable Soup

Avocado has a rich flavor and color which makes a creamy flavored soup. It is best served chilled, but may be eaten warm as well.

NUTRITIONAL INFORMATION

Calories 167	Sugars 5g
Protein 4g	Fat 13g
Carbohydrate 8g	Saturates 3g

 15 MINS 10 MINS

SERVES 4

I N G R E D I E N T S

1 large, ripe avocado

2 tbsp lemon juice

1 tbsp vegetable oil

½ cup canned corn, drained

2 tomatoes, peeled and seeded

1 garlic clove, crushed

1 leek, chopped

1 red chili, chopped

2 cups vegetable stock

⅔ cup milk

shredded leek, to garnish

1 Peel the avocado and mash the flesh with a fork, stir in the lemon juice, and reserve until required.

2 Heat the oil in a large saucepan. Add the corn, tomatoes, garlic, leek, and chili and sauté over a low heat for 2–3 minutes, or until the vegetables have softened.

3 Put half the vegetable mixture in a food processor or blender, together with the mashed avocado and process until smooth. Transfer the mixture to a clean saucepan.

4 Add the vegetable stock, milk and reserved vegetables and cook over a low heat for 3–4 minutes, until hot. Transfer to a warmed individual serving bowls, garnish with shredded leek, and serve immediately.

COOK'S TIP

If serving chilled, transfer from the food processor to a bowl, stir in the vegetable stock and milk, cover, and chill in the refrigerator for at least 4 hours.

Indian Potato & Pea Soup

A slightly hot and spicy Indian flavor is given to this soup with the use of garam masala, chili, cumin, and coriander.

NUTRITIONAL INFORMATION

Calories 153	Sugars 6g	
Protein 6g	Fat 6g	
Carbohydrate ...18g	Saturates 1g	

 10 MINS   35 MINS

SERVES 4

I N G R E D I E N T S

2 tbsp vegetable oil

8 oz russet potatoes, diced

1 large onion, chopped

2 garlic cloves, crushed

1 tsp garam masala

1 tsp ground coriander

1 tsp ground cumin

3¾ cups vegetable stock

1 red chili, chopped

scant 1 cup frozen peas

4 tbsp plain yogurt

salt and pepper

chopped cilantro,
   to garnish

warm bread, to serve

VARIATION

For slightly less heat, seed the chili before adding it to the soup. Always wash your hands after handling chilies as they contain volatile oils that can irritate the skin and make your eyes burn if you touch your face.

1 Heat the vegetable oil in a large saucepan. Add the potatoes, onion, and garlic and sauté over a low heat, stirring constantly, for about 5 minutes.

2 Add the garam masala, ground coriander, and cumin and cook, stirring constantly, for 1 minute.

3 Stir in the vegetable stock and chopped red chili and bring the mixture to a boil. Reduce the heat, cover the pan, and simmer for 20 minutes, until the potatoes begin to break down.

4 Add the peas and cook for another 5 minutes. Stir in the yogurt and season to taste with salt and pepper.

5 Pour into warmed soup bowls, garnish with chopped fresh cilantro, and serve hot with warm bread.

Cream Cheese & Herb Soup

Make the most of home-grown herbs to create this wonderfully creamy soup with its marvelous garden-fresh fragrance.

NUTRITIONAL INFORMATION

Calories 275	Sugars 5g	
Protein 7g	Fat 22g	
Carbohydrate ...14g	Saturates 11g	

15 MINS   35 MINS

SERVES 4

INGREDIENTS

2 tbsp butter or margarine

2 onions, chopped

3½ cups vegetable stock

1 oz coarsely chopped mixed
    herbs, such as parsley, chives, thyme,
    basil, and oregano

1 cup full-fat cream cheese

1 tbsp cornstarch

1 tbsp milk

chopped chives, to garnish

1 Melt the butter or margarine in a large, heavy-bottomed saucepan. Add the onions and fry over a medium heat for 2 minutes, then cover and turn the heat to low. Continue to cook the onions for 5 minutes, then remove the lid.

2 Add the vegetable stock and herbs to the saucepan. Bring to a boil over a moderate heat. Lower the heat, cover, and simmer gently for 20 minutes.

3 Remove the saucepan from the heat. Transfer the soup to a food processor or blender and process for about 15 seconds, until smooth. Alternatively, press it through a strainer with the back of a wooden spoon. Return the soup to the saucepan.

4 Reserve a little of the cheese for garnish. Spoon the remaining cheese into the soup and whisk until it has melted and is incorporated.

5 Mix the cornstarch with the milk to a paste, then stir the mixture into the soup. Heat, stirring constantly, until thickened and smooth.

6 Pour the soup into warmed individual bowls. Spoon some of the reserved cheese into each bowl and garnish with chives. Serve immediately.

Fava Bean Soup

Fresh fava beans are best for this scrumptious soup, but if they are unavailable, use frozen beans instead.

NUTRITIONAL INFORMATION

Calories	224	Sugars	........4g
Protein	........12g	Fat	..........6g
Carbohydrate	...31g	Saturates	.......1g

 15 MINS   40 MINS

SERVES 4

INGREDIENTS

2 tbsp olive oil

1 red onion, chopped

2 garlic cloves, crushed

2 potatoes, diced

3 cups fava beans,
   thawed if frozen

3¾ cups vegetable stock

2 tbsp freshly chopped mint

mint sprigs and plain yogurt, to garnish

1 Heat the olive oil in a large saucepan. Add the onion and garlic and sauté for 2–3 minutes, until softened.

2 Add the potatoes and cook, stirring constantly, for 5 minutes.

3 Stir in the beans and the stock, cover, and simmer for 30 minutes, or until the beans and potatoes are tender.

4 Remove a few vegetables with a perforated spoon and set aside until required. Place the remainder of the soup in a food processor or blender and process until smooth.

5 Return the soup to a clean saucepan and add the reserved vegetables and chopped mint. Stir thoroughly and heat through gently.

6 Transfer the soup to a warm tureen or individual serving bowls. Garnish with swirls of yogurt and sprigs of fresh mint and serve immediately.

VARIATION

Use fresh cilantro and ½ tsp ground cumin as flavorings in the soup, if you prefer.

Spinach & Mascarpone Soup

Spinach is the basis for this delicious soup, which has creamy mascarpone cheese stirred through it to give it a wonderful texture.

NUTRITIONAL INFORMATION

Calories 402	Sugars 2g
Protein 11g	Fat 36g
Carbohydrate ...10g	Saturates 21g

 15 MINS 30 MINS

SERVES 4

I N G R E D I E N T S

¼ cup butter

1 bunch green onions,
   trimmed and chopped

2 celery stalks, chopped

3 cups spinach or sorrel, or
   3 bunches watercress

3½ cups vegetable stock

1 cup mascarpone cheese

1 tbsp olive oil

2 slices thick-cut bread, cut into cubes

½ tsp caraway seeds

salt and pepper

sesame bread sticks, to serve

1 Melt half the butter in a very large saucepan. Add the green onions and celery, and cook over a medium heat, stirring frequently, for about 5 minutes, until softened.

2 Pack the spinach, sorrel, or watercress into the saucepan. Add the stock and bring to a boil, then reduce the heat, cover, and simmer for 15–20 minutes.

3 Transfer the soup to a blender or food processor and process until smooth. Alternatively, rub it through a strainer. Return to the saucepan.

4 Add the mascarpone to the soup and heat gently, stirring constantly, until smooth and blended. Season to taste with salt and pepper.

5 Heat the remaining butter with the oil in a skillet. Add the bread cubes and fry, turning frequently, until golden brown, adding the caraway seeds toward the end of cooking, so that they do not burn.

6 Ladle the soup into warmed bowls. Sprinkle with the croutons and serve with the sesame bread sticks.

VARIATION

Any leafy vegetable can be used to make this soup to give variations to the flavor. For anyone who grows their own vegetables, it is the perfect recipe for experimenting with a glut of produce. Try young beet leaves or surplus lettuces for a change.

Appetizers

With so many fresh ingredients easily available, it is very easy to create some deliciously different appetizers and first courses to introduce a vegetarian meal. The ideas in this chapter are an inspiration to cook and a treat to eat, and they give an edge to the appetite that makes the main course even more enjoyable. When choosing an appetizer,

make sure that you provide a good balance of flavors, colors, and textures that offer variety and contrast. Balance the nature of the recipes too—a rich main course is best preceded by a light appetizer, which is just enough to interest the palate and stimulate the tastebuds.

Mushroom & Garlic Soufflés

These individual soufflés are very impressive first courses, but must be cooked just before serving to prevent them from sinking.

NUTRITIONAL INFORMATION

Calories	179	Sugars	.........3g
Protein	.........6g	Fat	..........14g
Carbohydrate	....8g	Saturates	.......8g

10 MINS 20 MINS

SERVES 4

I N G R E D I E N T S

4 tbsp butter

1 cup chopped mushrooms

2 tsp lime juice

2 garlic cloves, crushed

2 tbsp chopped marjoram

$1/_4$ cup all-purpose flour

1 cup milk

salt and pepper

2 eggs, separated

1 Lightly grease the inside of four $2/_3$ cup individual soufflé dishes with a little butter.

2 Melt 2 tbsp of the butter in a skillet. Add the mushrooms, lime juice, and garlic and sauté for 2–3 minutes. Remove the mushroom mixture with a slotted spoon and transfer to a bowl. Stir in the marjoram.

COOK'S TIP

Insert a skewer into the center of the soufflés to test if they are cooked through—it should come out clean. If not, cook for a few minutes longer, but do not overcook otherwise they will become rubbery.

3 Melt the remaining butter in a pan. Add the flour and cook for 1 minute, then remove from the heat. Stir in the milk and return to the heat. Bring to a boil, stirring until thickened.

4 Mix the sauce into the mushroom mixture and beat in the egg yolks.

5 Whisk the egg whites until they form peaks and then fold into

the mushroom mixture until fully incorporated.

6 Divide the mixture between the soufflé dishes. Place the dishes on a cookie sheet and cook in a preheated oven, 400°F, for about 8–10 minutes, or until the soufflés have risen and are cooked through. Serve immediately.

Feta Cheese Tartlets

These crisp-baked bread cases, filled with sliced tomatoes, feta cheese, black olives, and quail's eggs, are quick to make and taste delicious.

NUTRITIONAL INFORMATION

Calories 570   Sugars 3g
Protein . . . . .14g   Fat 42g
Carbohydrate . . .36g   Saturates 23g

30 MINS   10 MINS

SERVES 4

INGREDIENTS

8 slices bread from a medium-cut large loaf

½ cup butter, melted

4½ oz feta cheese,
    cut into small cubes

4 cherry tomatoes, cut into wedges

8 pitted black or green olives, halved

8 quail's eggs, hard-boiled

2 tbsp olive oil

1 tbsp wine vinegar

1 tsp wholegrain mustard

pinch of sugar

salt and pepper

parsley sprigs, to garnish

1 Remove the crusts from the bread. Trim the bread into squares and flatten each piece with a rolling pin.

2 Brush the bread with melted butter, and then arrange them in bun or muffin tins. Press a piece of crumpled foil into each bread case to secure in place. Bake in a preheated oven, 375°F, for about 10 minutes, or until crisp and browned.

3 Meanwhile, mix together the feta cheese, tomatoes, and olives. Shell the eggs and quarter them. Mix together the olive oil, wine vinegar, mustard and sugar. Season according to taste with salt and pepper.

4 Remove the bread cases from the oven and discard the foil. Leave to cool.

5 Just before serving, fill the bread cases with the cheese and tomato mixture. Arrange the eggs on top and spoon over the dressing. Garnish with parsley sprigs.

Mixed Bhajis

These small bhajis are often served as accompaniments to a main meal, but they are delicious as a first course with a salad and yogurt sauce.

NUTRITIONAL INFORMATION

Calories 414   Sugars 7g
Protein . . . . .9g   Fat 26g
Carbohydrate . . .38g   Saturates 3g

 25 MINS   30 MINS

SERVES 4

I N G R E D I E N T S

B H A J I S

1¼ cups gram or besan flour

1 tsp baking soda

2 tsp ground coriander

1 tsp garam masala

1½ tsp turmeric

1½ tsp chili powder

2 tbsp chopped cilantro

1 small onion, halved and sliced

1 small leek, sliced

3½ oz cooked cauliflower

9–12 tbsp cold water

salt and pepper

vegetable oil, for deep-frying

S A U C E

⅔ cup plain yogurt

2 tbsp chopped mint

½ tsp turmeric

1 garlic clove, crushed

mint sprigs, to garnish

1 Sift the flour, baking soda, and salt to taste into a mixing bowl and add the spices and fresh cilantro. Mix thoroughly.

2 Divide the mixture into 3 and place in separate bowls. Stir the onion into one bowl, the leek into another and the cauliflower into the third bowl. Add 3–4 tbsp of water to each bowl and mix each to form a smooth paste.

3 Heat the oil for deep-frying in a deep fryer to 350°F or until a cube of bread browns in 30 seconds. Using 2 dessert spoons, form the mixture into rounds and cook each in the oil for 3–4 minutes, until browned. Remove with a slotted spoon and drain well on absorbent paper towels. Keep the bhajis warm in the oven while cooking the remainder.

4 Mix all of the sauce ingredients together and pour into a small serving bowl. Garnish with mint sprigs and serve with the warm bhajis.

Dumplings in Yogurt Sauce

Adding a baghaar (seasoned oil dressing) just before serving makes this a mouth-watering accompaniment to any meal.

NUTRITIONAL INFORMATION

Calories	719	Sugars	........9g
Protein	.........9g	Fat	.........60g
Carbohydrate	...38g	Saturates	.......7g

 35 MINS   35 MINS

SERVES 4

INGREDIENTS

DUMPLINGS

¾ cup gram or besan flour

1 tsp chili powder

½ tsp baking soda

1 medium onion, finely chopped

2 green chilies

cilantro leaves

⅔ cup water

1¼ cups vegetable oil

salt

YOGURT SAUCE

1¼ cups plain yogurt

3 tbsp gram flour

⅔ cup water

1 tsp chopped ginger

1 tsp crushed garlic

1½ tsp chili powder

½ tsp turmeric

1 tsp ground coriander

1 tsp ground cumin

SEASONED DRESSING

⅔ cup vegetable oil

1 tsp white cumin seeds

6 dried red chilies

1 To make the dumplings, sift the gram flour into a large bowl. Add the chili powder, ½ teaspoon salt, baking soda, onion, green chilies, and cilantro and mix. Add the water and mix to form a thick paste. Heat the oil in a skillet. Place teaspoonfuls of the paste in the oil and fry over a medium heat, turning once, until a crisp golden brown. Set aside.

2 To make the sauce, place the yogurt in a bowl and whisk with the gram flour and the water. Add all of the spices and 1½ teaspoons salt and mix well.

3 Press this mixture through a large strainer into a saucepan. Bring to a boil over a low heat, stirring constantly. If the yogurt sauce becomes too thick, add a little extra water.

4 Pour the sauce into a deep serving dish and arrange all the dumplings on top. Set aside and keep warm.

5 To make the dressing, heat the oil in a skillet. Add the white cumin seeds and the dried red chilies and fry until darker in color and giving off their aroma. Pour the dressing over the dumplings and serve hot.

Vegetable Timbales

This is a great way to serve pasta as a first course, wrapped in an eggplant mold. It looks really impressive, yet it is very easy.

NUTRITIONAL INFORMATION

Calories 291	Sugars 11g
Protein 8g	Fat 18g
Carbohydrate . . .25g	Saturates 4g

30 MINS   45 MINS

SERVES 4

INGREDIENTS

1 large eggplant

½ cup macaroni

1 tbsp vegetable oil

1 onion, chopped

2 garlic cloves, crushed

2 tbsp drained canned corn

2 tbsp frozen peas, thawed

3½ oz spinach

¼ cup grated cheddar cheese

1 egg, beaten

3 cups canned,
    diced tomatoes

1 tbsp chopped basil

salt and pepper

SAUCE

4 tbsp olive oil

2 tbsp white wine vinegar

2 garlic cloves, crushed

3 tbsp chopped basil

1 tbsp sugar

1 Cut the eggplant lengthwise into thin strips, using a potato peeler. Place in a bowl of salted boiling water and leave to stand for 3–4 minutes. Drain well.

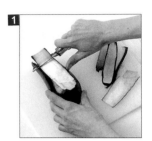

2 Lightly grease four ⅔-cup individual ramekin dishes and use the eggplant slices to line the dishes, leaving 1 inch of eggplant overlapping.

3 Cook the pasta in a pan of boiling water for 8–10 minutes until al dente. Drain. Heat the oil in a pan and sauté the onion and garlic for 2–3 minutes. Stir in the corn and peas and remove from the heat.

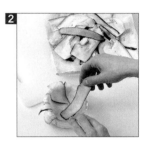

4 Blanch the spinach, drain well, chop and reserve. Add the pasta to the onion mixture with the cheese, egg, tomatoes and basil. Season and mix.

5 Half-fill each ramekin with some of the pasta. Place the spinach on top and then the remaining pasta mixture. Fold the eggplant over the pasta filling to cover. Put the ramekins in a roasting pan half-filled with boiling water, cover and cook in a preheated oven, 350°F, for 20–25 minutes, or until set. Meanwhile, heat the sauce ingredients in a pan. Turn out the ramekins and serve immediately with the sauce.

Mint & Cannellini Bean Dip

This dip is ideal for pre-dinner drinks or for passing around at a party.
The cannellini beans require soaking overnight, so prepare in advance.

NUTRITIONAL INFORMATION

Calories ....208 Sugars 1g
Protein ....10g Fat 12g
Carbohydrate ...16g Saturates 2g

  40 MINS   30 MINS

SERVES 6

I N G R E D I E N T S

1 cup dried cannellini beans

1 small garlic clove, crushed

1 bunch green onions,
    roughly chopped

handful of mint leaves

2 tbsp tahini

2 tbsp olive oil

1 tsp ground cumin

1 tsp ground coriander

lemon juice

salt and pepper

sprigs of mint, to garnish

T O   S E R V E

fresh vegetable crudités, such as
    cauliflower flowerets, carrots, cucumber,
    radishes, and bell peppers

1 Soak the cannellini beans overnight in plenty of cold water.

2 Rinse and drain the beans, put them into a large saucepan and cover them with cold water. Bring to a boil and boil rapidly for 10 minutes. Reduce the heat, cover and simmer until tender.

3 Drain the beans and transfer them to a bowl or food processor. Add the garlic, green onions, mint, tahini, and olive oil.

4 Process the mixture for about 15 seconds or mash well by hand, until smooth.

5 Transfer the mixture to a bowl, stir in the cumin, coriander and lemon juice and season to taste with salt and pepper. Mix thoroughly, cover and leave in a cool place for 30 minutes to allow the flavors to develop fully.

6 Spoon the dip into serving bowls, garnish with sprigs of fresh mint and surround with vegetable crudités. Serve at room temperature.

Spinach Phyllo Baskets

If you use frozen spinach, it only needs to be thawed and drained before being mixed with the cheeses and seasonings.

NUTRITIONAL INFORMATION

Calories . . . . . . .533 Sugars 3g
Protein . . . . .24g Fat 38g
Carbohydrate . . .26g Saturates 22g

 55 MINS   30 MINS

MAKES 2

I N G R E D I E N T S

3 cups fresh leaf spinach,
   washed and chopped roughly, or
   ½ cup thawed frozen spinach

2–4 green onions, trimmed and
   chopped, or 1 tbsp finely chopped onion

1 garlic clove, crushed

2 tbsp grated Parmesan cheese

¾ cup grated mature (sharp)
   cheddar cheese

pinch of ground allspice

1 egg yolk

4 sheets phyllo pastry

2 tbsp butter, melted

salt and pepper

2 green onions, to garnish

1 If using fresh spinach, cook it in the minimum of boiling salted water for 3–4 minutes, until tender. Drain very thoroughly, using a potato masher to remove excess liquid, then chop and put into a bowl. If using frozen spinach, simply drain and chop.

2 Add the green onions or onion, garlic, cheeses, allspice, egg yolk, and seasoning, and mix well.

3 Grease 2 individual ovenproof dishes about 5 inches in diameter, and 1½ inches deep. Cut the phyllo pastry sheets in half to make 8 pieces and brush each lightly with melted butter.

4 Place one piece of phyllo pastry in a pan or dish and then cover with a second piece at right angles to the first. Add two more pieces at right angles, so that all the corners are in different places. Line the other dish in the same way.

5 Spoon the spinach mixture into the 'baskets' and cook in a preheated oven, 350°F, for about 20 minutes, or until the pastry is golden brown. Garnish with a green onion tassel and serve hot or cold.

6 Make green onion tassels about 30 minutes before required. Trim off the root end and cut to a length of 2–3 inches. Make a series of cuts from the green end to within ¾ inch of the other end. Place in a bowl of iced water to open out. Drain well before use.

Vegetable Fritters

These mixed vegetable fritters are coated in a light batter and deep-fried until golden. They are ideal with the sweet and sour dipping sauce.

NUTRITIONAL INFORMATION

Calories	.479	Sugars	.18g
Protein	.8g	Fat	.32g
Carbohydrate	.42g	Saturates	.5g

20 MINS · 20 MINS

SERVES 4

INGREDIENTS

¾ cup whole wheat flour

pinch of cayenne pepper

4 tsp olive oil

12 tbsp cold water

3½ oz broccoli flowerets

3½ oz cauliflower flowerets

1¾ oz snow peas

1 large carrot, cut into sticks

1 red bell pepper, seeded and sliced

2 egg whites, beaten

oil, for deep-frying

salt

SAUCE

⅔ cup pineapple juice

⅔ cup vegetable stock

2 tbsp white wine vinegar

2 tbsp light brown sugar

2 tsp cornstarch

2 green onions, chopped

1 Sift the flour and a pinch of salt into a mixing bowl and add the cayenne pepper. Make a well in the center and gradually beat in the oil and cold water to make a smooth batter.

2 Cook the vegetables in boiling water for 5 minutes and drain well.

3 Whisk the egg whites until they form peaks and gently fold them into the flour batter.

4 Dip the vegetables into the batter, turning to coat well. Drain off any excess batter. Heat the oil for deep-frying in a deep-fryer to 350°F or until a cube of bread browns in 30 seconds. Fry the coated vegetables, in batches, for 1–2 minutes, until golden. Remove from the oil with a slotted spoon and drain on paper towels.

5 Place all of the sauce ingredients in a pan and bring to a boil, stirring, until thickened and clear. Serve with the fritters.

Walnut, Egg, & Cheese Pâté

This unusual pâté, flavored with parsley and dill, can be served with crackers, crusty bread, or toast. The pâté requires chilling until set.

NUTRITIONAL INFORMATION

Calories 438	Sugars 2g	
Protein 21g	Fat 38g	
Carbohydrate 2g	Saturates 18g	

20 MINS · 2 MINS

SERVES 2

INGREDIENTS

1 celery stalk

1–2 green onions, trimmed

¼ cup shelled walnuts

1 tbsp chopped fresh parsley

1 tsp chopped fresh dill or ½ tsp dried dill

1 garlic clove, crushed

dash of vegetarian Worcestershire sauce

½ cup cottage cheese

½ cup blue cheese, such as
    Stilton or Danish Blue

1 hard-boiled egg

2 tbsp butter

salt and pepper

herbs, to garnish

crackers, toast or crusty bread, and
    crudités, to serve

COOK'S TIP

You can also use this as a stuffing for vegetables. Cut the tops off extra-large tomatoes, scoop out the seeds and fill with the pâté, piling it well up, or spoon into the hollows of celery stalks cut into 2-inch pieces.

1 Finely chop the celery, slice the green onions very finely, and chop the walnuts evenly. Place in a bowl.

2 Add the chopped herbs and garlic and Worcestershire sauce to taste and mix well, then stir the cottage cheese evenly through the mixture.

3 Grate the blue cheese and hard-boiled egg finely into the pâté mixture, and season with salt and pepper.

4 Melt the butter and stir through the pâté, then spoon into one serving dish or two individual dishes, but do not press down firmly. Chill until set.

5 Garnish with fresh herbs and serve with crackers, toast or fresh, crusty bread and a few crudités, if you like.

Samosas

Samosas, which are an Indian vegetable pastry, make excellent snacks. In India, they are popular snacks at roadside stalls.

NUTRITIONAL INFORMATION

Calories 261	Sugars 0.4g
Protein 2g	Fat 23g
Carbohydrate . . .13g	Saturates 4g

  40 MINS 40 MINS

MAKES 12

INGREDIENTS

PASTRY

¾ cup self-rising flour

½ tsp salt

3 tbsp butter, cut into
   small pieces

4 tbsp water

FILLING

3 medium potatoes, boiled

1 tsp finely chopped ginger

1 tsp crushed garlic

½ tsp white cumin seeds

½ tsp mixed onion and mustard seeds

1 tsp salt

½ tsp crushed red chilies

2 tbsp lemon juice

2 small green chilies, finely chopped

ghee or oil, for deep-frying

1 Sift the flour and salt into a bowl. Add the butter and rub into the flour until the mixture resembles fine breadcrumbs.

2 Pour in the water and mix with a fork to form a dough. Pat it into a ball and knead for 5 minutes, or until smooth. Cover and leave to rise.

3 To make the filling, mash the boiled potatoes gently and mix with the ginger, garlic, white cumin seeds, onion and mustard seeds, salt, crushed red chilies, lemon juice, and green chilies.

4 Break small balls off the dough and roll each out very thinly to form a round. Cut in half, dampen the edges and shape into cones. Fill the cones with a little of the filling, dampen the top and bottom edges of the cones and pinch together to seal. Set aside.

5 Fill a deep pan one-third full with oil and heat to 350°F or until a small cube of bread browns in 30 seconds. Carefully lower the samosas into the oil, a few at a time, and fry for 2–3 minutes, or until golden brown. Remove from the oil and drain thoroughly on paper towels. Serve hot or cold.

Heavenly Garlic Dip

Anyone who loves garlic will adore this dip—it is very potent! Serve it at a barbecue and dip raw vegetables or chunks of French bread into it.

NUTRITIONAL INFORMATION

Calories 344   Sugars 2g
Protein ....6g   Fat 34g
Carbohydrate ....3g   Saturates 5g

 15 MINS   20 MINS

SERVES 4

I N G R E D I E N T S

2 bulbs garlic

6 tbsp olive oil

1 small onion, finely chopped

2 tbsp lemon juice

3 tbsp tahini

2 tbsp chopped parsley

salt and pepper

TO SERVE

fresh vegetable crudités

French bread or warmed pita breads

1 Separate the bulbs of garlic into individual cloves. Place them on a cookie sheet and roast in a preheated oven, 400°F, for 8–10 minutes. Set aside to cool for a few minutes.

2 When they are cool enough to handle, peel the garlic cloves and then chop them finely.

3 Heat the olive oil in a saucepan or skillet and add the garlic and onion. Fry over a low heat, stirring occasionally, for 8–10 minutes, until softened. Remove the pan from the heat.

4 Mix in the lemon juice, tahini, and parsley. Season to taste with salt and pepper. Transfer to a small heatproof bowl and keep warm at one side of the barbecue.

5 Serve with fresh vegetable crudités, chunks of French bread or warm pita breads.

VARIATION

If you come across smoked garlic, use it in this recipe—it tastes wonderful. There is no need to roast the smoked garlic, so omit the first step. This dip can also be used to baste kabobs and vegetarian burgers.

Mixed Bean Pâté

This is a really quick appetizer to prepare if canned beans are used. Choose a wide variety of beans for color and flavor.

NUTRITIONAL INFORMATION

Calories	126	Sugars	.........3g
Protein	.........5g	Fat	...........6g
Carbohydrate	...13g	Saturates	.......1g

 45 MINS 0 MINS

SERVES 4

INGREDIENTS

14 oz can mixed beans, drained

2 tbsp olive oil

juice of 1 lemon

2 garlic cloves, crushed

1 tbsp chopped cilantro

2 green onions, chopped

salt and pepper

shredded green onions,
    to garnish

1 Rinse the beans thoroughly under cold running water and drain well.

2 Transfer the beans to a food processor or blender and process until smooth. Alternatively, place the beans in a bowl and mash thoroughly with a fork or potato masher.

3 Add the olive oil, lemon juice, garlic, cilantro, and green onions and blend until fairly smooth. Season with salt and pepper to taste.

4 Transfer the pâté to a serving bowl and chill in the refrigerator for at least 30 minutes.

5 Garnish with shredded green onions and serve.

Avocado Cream Terrine

The smooth, rich taste of ripe avocados combines well with thick, creamy yogurt and light cream to make this impressive terrine.

NUTRITIONAL INFORMATION

Calories	327	Sugars	.........3g
Protein	.........6g	Fat	.........32g
Carbohydrate	....4g	Saturates	.......8g

 2¼ HOURS   0 MINS

SERVES 6

I N G R E D I E N T S

2 ripe avocados

4 tbsp cold water

2 tsp vegetarian gelatin

1 tbsp lemon juice

4 tbsp mayonnaise

⅔ cup thick plain yogurt

⅔ cup light cream

salt and pepper

mixed salad greens, to serve

TO GARNISH

cucumber slices

nasturtium flowers

1 Peel the avocados and remove and discard the stones. Put the flesh in a blender or food processor or a large bowl, together with the water, vegetarian gelatin, lemon juice, mayonnaise, yogurt, and cream. Season to taste with salt and pepper.

2 Process for about 10–15 seconds, or beat by hand, using a fork or whisk, until smooth.

3 Transfer the mixture to a small saucepan and heat gently, stirring constantly, until just boiling.

4 Pour the mixture into a 3½-cup plastic container or terrine and smooth the top. Allow the mixture to cool and set, and then leave to chill in the refrigerator for about 1½–2 hours.

5 Turn the mixture out of its container and cut into neat slices. Arrange a bed of salad greens on 6 serving plates. Place a slice of avocado terrine on top and garnish with cucumber slices and nasturtium flowers.

Vegetable Medley

This is a colorful dish of shredded vegetables in a fresh garlic and honey dressing. It is delicious served with crusty bread.

NUTRITIONAL INFORMATION

Calories . . . . . . .209 Sugars 10g
Protein . . . . .2g Fat 14g
Carbohydrate . . .20g Saturates 2g

  15 MINS   5 MINS

SERVES 4

I N G R E D I E N T S

2 tbsp olive oil

1 potato, cut into thin strips

1 fennel bulb, cut into thin strips

2 carrots, grated

1 red onion, cut into thin strips

chopped chives and fennel fronds,
    to garnish

D R E S S I N G

3 tbsp olive oil

1 tbsp garlic wine vinegar

1 garlic clove, crushed

1 tsp Dijon mustard

2 tsp honey

salt and pepper

1 Heat the olive oil in a skillet, add the potato and fennel slices and cook over a medium heat for about 2–3 minutes, until beginning to brown. Remove from the skillet with a slotted spoon and drain on paper towels.

2 Arrange the carrot, red onion, potato and fennel in separate piles on a serving platter.

3 Mix the dressing ingredients together and pour over the vegetables. Toss

well and sprinkle with chopped chives and fennel fronds. Serve immediately or leave in the refrigerator until required.

VARIATION

Use mixed, grilled bell peppers or shredded leeks in this dish for variety, or add bean sprouts and a segmented orange, if you prefer.

Spanish Tortilla

This classic Spanish dish is often served as part of a tapas selection. A variety of cooked vegetables can be added to this recipe.

NUTRITIONAL INFORMATION

Calories	430	Sugars	.........6g
Protein	........16g	Fat	..........20g
Carbohydrate	...50g	Saturates	.......4g

10 MINS   35 MINS

SERVES 4

I N G R E D I E N T S

2 lb 4 oz potatoes, thinly sliced

4 tbsp vegetable oil

1 onion, sliced

2 garlic cloves, crushed

1 green bell pepper, seeded and diced

2 tomatoes, seeded and chopped

1 oz canned corn, drained

6 large eggs, beaten

2 tbsp chopped parsley

salt and pepper

1 Parboil the potatoes in a saucepan of lightly salted boiling water for 5 minutes. Drain well.

2 Heat the oil in a large skillet, add the potato and onions and sauté over a low heat, stirring constantly, for 5 minutes, until the potatoes have browned.

COOK'S TIP

Ensure that the handle of your pan is heatproof before placing it under the broiler and be sure to use an oven mitt when removing it as it will be very hot.

3 Add the garlic, diced bell pepper, chopped tomatoes, and corn, mixing well.

4 Pour in the eggs and add the chopped parsley. Season well with salt and pepper. Cook for 10–12 minutes, until the underside is cooked through.

5 Remove the skillet from the heat and continue to cook the tortilla under a preheated medium broiler for 5–7 minutes, or until the tortilla is set and the top is golden brown.

6 Cut the tortilla into wedges or cubes, depending on your preference, and transfer to serving dishes. Serve with salad. In Spain tortillas are served hot, cold, or warm.

Hyderabad Pickles

This is a very versatile dish that will go with almost anything and can be served warm or cold. It is perfect to start off a dinner party.

NUTRITIONAL INFORMATION

Calories	732	Sugars	.........6g
Protein	.........6g	Fat	..........75g
Carbohydrate	....8g	Saturates	......10g

🥘 30 MINS 🕐 30 MINS

SERVES 6

INGREDIENTS

2 tsp ground coriander

2 tsp ground cumin

2 tsp shredded coconut

2 tsp sesame seeds

1 tsp mixed mustard and onion seeds

1¼ cups vegetable oil

3 medium onions, sliced

1 tsp finely chopped ginger

1 tsp crushed garlic

½ tsp turmeric

1½ tsp chili powder

1½ tsp salt

3 medium eggplant,
   halved lengthwise

1 tbsp tamarind paste

1¼ cups water

3 hard-boiled eggs, halved,
   to garnish

BAGHAAR

1 tsp mixed onion and mustard seeds

1 tsp cumin seeds

4 dried red chilies

⅔ cup vegetable oil

cilantro leaves

1 green chili, finely chopped

1 Dry-fry the ground coriander, cumin, coconut, sesame seeds, and mustard and onion seeds in a pan. Grind in a pestle and mortar or food processor and set aside.

2 Heat the oil in a skillet and fry the onions until golden. Reduce the heat and add the ginger, garlic, turmeric, chili powder, and salt, stirring. Leave to cool, then grind this mixture to form a paste.

3 Make 4 cuts across each eggplant half. Blend the spices with the onion paste. Spoon this mixture into the slits in the eggplants.

4 In a bowl, mix the tamarind paste and 3 tbsp water to make a fine paste and set aside.

5 For the baghaar, fry the onion and mustard seeds, cumin seeds, and chilies in the oil. Reduce the heat, place the eggplants in the baghaar and stir gently. Stir in the tamarind paste and remaining water and cook over a medium heat for 15–20 minutes. Add the cilantro and chilies.

6 When cool, transfer to a serving dish and serve garnished with the hard-boiled eggs.

Hummus & Garlic Toasts

Hummus is a real favorite spread on these flavorful garlic toasts for a delicious appetizer or snack.

NUTRITIONAL INFORMATION

Calories 731	Sugars 2g
Protein 22g	Fat 55g
Carbohydrate . . .39g	Saturates 8g

 20 MINS   3 MINS

SERVES 4

I N G R E D I E N T S

H U M M U S

14 oz can garbanzo beans

juice of 1 large lemon

6 tbsp tahini

2 tbsp olive oil

2 garlic cloves, crushed

salt and pepper

chopped cilantro and
    black olives, to garnish

T O A S T S

1 ciabatta loaf (Italian bread), sliced

2 garlic cloves, crushed

1 tbsp chopped cilantro

4 tbsp olive oil

COOK'S TIP

Make the hummus 1 day in advance, and chill, covered, in the refrigerator until required. Garnish and serve.

  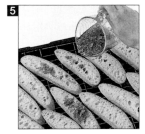

1 To make the hummus, firstly drain the garbanzo beans, reserving a little of the liquid. Put the garbanzo beans in a food processor and process, gradually adding the reserved liquid and lemon juice. Blend well after each addition until smooth.

2 Stir in the tahini and all but 1 teaspoon of the olive oil. Add the garlic, season to taste, and blend again until smooth.

3 Spoon the hummus into a serving dish and smooth the top. Drizzle the

remaining olive oil over the top, garnish with chopped cilantro and olives. Set aside in the refrigerator to chill while you are preparing the toasts.

4 Place the slices of ciabatta (Italian bread) on a broiler rack in a single layer.

5 Mix the garlic, cilantro and olive oil together and drizzle over the bread slices. Cook under a hot broiler, turning once, for about 2–3 minutes, until golden brown. Serve the toasts immediately with the hummus.

Fiery Salsa

Make this Mexican-style salsa to perk up jaded palates. Its lively flavors really get the tastebuds going. Serve with hot tortilla chips.

NUTRITIONAL INFORMATION

Calories	328	Sugars	.........2g
Protein	.........4g	Fat	..........26g
Carbohydrate	...21g	Saturates	.......5g

 30 MINS   🕐 0 MINS

SERVES 4

INGREDIENTS

2 small fresh red chilies

1 tbsp lime or lemon juice

2 large ripe avocados

2-inch piece of cucumber

2 tomatoes, peeled

1 small garlic clove, crushed

few drops of Tabasco sauce

salt and pepper

lime or lemon slices, to garnish

tortilla chips, to serve

1 Remove and discard the stem and seeds from 1 fresh red chili. Chop the flesh very finely and place in a large mixing bowl.

2 To make a chili 'flower' for garnish, using a small, sharp knife, slice the remaining chili from the stem to the tip several times without removing the stem. Place in a bowl of iced water, so that the 'petals' open out.

3 Add the lime or lemon juice to the mixing bowl. Halve, pit and peel the avocados. Add the flesh to the mixing bowl and mash thoroughly with a fork. The salsa should be slightly chunky. (The lime or lemon juice prevents the avocado from turning brown.)

4 Chop the cucumber and tomatoes finely and add to the avocado mixture with the crushed garlic.

5 Stir in the Tabasco sauce and season with salt and pepper. Transfer the dip to a serving bowl. Garnish with slices of lime or lemon and the chili flower.

6 Put the bowl on a large plate, surround with tortilla chips and serve. Do not keep this dip standing for long or it will discolor.

Egg Rolls

Thin slices of vegetables are wrapped in pastry and deep-fried until crisp. Eggroll wrappers are available fresh or frozen.

NUTRITIONAL INFORMATION

Calories 186	Sugars 2g	
Protein 4g	Fat 11g	
Carbohydrate ...18g	Saturates 1g	

45 MINS   25–30 MINS

MAKES 12

INGREDIENTS

5 Chinese dried mushrooms (if unavailable,

   use button mushrooms)

1 large carrot

1 cup canned bamboo shoots

2 green onions

2 oz Chinese cabbage

2 tbsp vegetable oil

4 cups bean sprouts

1 tbsp soy sauce

12 spring roll wrappers

1 egg, beaten

vegetable oil, for deep-frying

salt

1 Place the dried mushrooms in a small bowl and cover with warm water. Leave to soak for 20–25 minutes.

2 Drain the mushrooms and squeeze out the excess water. Remove the tough centers and slice the mushroom caps thinly. Cut the carrot and bamboo shoots into very thin julienne strips. Chop the green onions and shred the Chinese cabbage.

3 Heat the 2 tablespoons of oil in a wok. Add the mushrooms, carrot and bamboo shoots and stir-fry for 2 minutes. Add the green onions, Chinese cabbage, bean sprouts, and soy sauce. Season with salt and stir-fry for 2 minutes. Leave to cool.

4 Divide the mixture into 12 equal portions and place one portion on the edge of each spring roll wrapper. Fold in the sides and roll each one up, brushing the join with a little beaten egg to seal.

5 Deep-fry the spring rolls in batches in hot oil in a wok or large saucepan for 4–5 minutes, or until golden and crispy. Take care that the oil is not too hot or the spring rolls will brown on the outside before cooking on the inside. Remove and drain on paper towels. Keep each batch warm while the others are being cooked. Serve immediately.

COOK'S TIP

If eggroll wrappers are unavailable, use sheets of phyllo pastry instead.

Toasted Nibbles

These tiny cheese balls are rolled in fresh herbs, toasted nuts, or paprika to make tasty nibbles for parties, buffets, or pre-dinner drinks.

NUTRITIONAL INFORMATION

Calories 310   Sugars 1g
Protein . . . . .15g   Fat 27g
Carbohydrate . . . .1g   Saturates 12g

🥪 40 MINS   🕑 5 MINS

SERVES 4

INGREDIENTS

½ cup ricotta cheese

1 cup finely grated brick cheese

2 tsp chopped parsley

½ cup chopped mixed nuts

3 tbsp chopped herbs, such as parsley, chives, marjoram, lovage, and chervil

2 tbsp mild paprika

pepper

herb sprigs, to garnish

1 Mix together the ricotta and brick cheeses. Add the parsley and pepper and work together until thoroughly combined.

2 Form the mixture into small balls and place on a plate. Cover and chill in the refrigerator for about 20 minutes, until they are firm.

3 Scatter the chopped nuts onto a cookie sheet and place them under a preheated broiler until lightly browned. Take care as they can easily burn. Leave them to cool.

4 Sprinkle the nuts, herbs and paprika into 3 separate small bowls. Remove the cheese balls from the refrigerator and

divide into 3 equal piles. Roll 1 quantity of the cheese balls in the nuts, 1 quantity in the herbs, and 1 quantity in the paprika until they are all well coated.

5 Arrange the coated cheese balls alternately on a large serving platter. Chill in the refrigerator until ready to serve and then garnish with sprigs of fresh herbs.

Bite-sized Bhajis

Don't be surprised at the shape these form—they are odd but look lovely when arranged on a tray with the yogurt dipping sauce.

NUTRITIONAL INFORMATION

Calories 122	Sugars 2g
Protein 2g	Fat 10g
Carbohydrate 6g	Saturates 1g

 15 MINS 15 MINS

MAKES 20

INGREDIENTS

2 heaping tbsp gram or besan flour

½ tsp turmeric

½ tsp cumin seeds, ground

1 tsp garam masala

pinch of cayenne pepper

1 egg

1 large onion, quartered and sliced

1 tbsp chopped cilantro

3 tbsp breadcrumbs (optional)

vegetable oil, for deep-frying

salt

SAUCE

1 tsp coriander seeds, ground

1½ tsp cumin seeds, ground

1 cup plain yogurt

salt and pepper

COOK'S TIP

Make sure that the pan and all the utensils are properly dried before use. Do not let any water come into contact with the hot oil or the oil will spit and splutter, which could be dangerous.

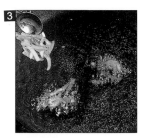

1 Put the gram flour into a large bowl and mix in the turmeric, cumin, garam masala and cayenne. Make a well in the center and add the egg. Stir to form a gluey mixture. Add the onion and sprinkle in a little salt. Add the cilantro and stir. If the mixture is not stiff enough, add the breadcrumbs.

2 Heat the oil for deep-frying over a medium heat until fairly hot—it should just be starting to smoke.

3 Push a teaspoonful of the mixture into the oil with a second teaspoon to form fairly round balls. The bhajis should firm up quite quickly. Cook in batches of 8–10. Keep stirring them so that they brown evenly. Drain on plenty of paper towels and keep them warm in the oven until ready to serve.

4 To make the sauce, roast the spices in a skillet. Remove from the heat and stir in the yogurt. Season well.

Lentil Pâté

Red lentils are used in this spicy recipe for speed since they do not need pre-soaking. You can substitute other types of lentils, if preferred.

NUTRITIONAL INFORMATION

Calories	267	Sugars	........12g
Protein	........14g	Fat	...........8g
Carbohydrate	...37g	Saturates	.......1g

 30 MINS   1¼ HOURS

SERVES 4

I N G R E D I E N T S

1 tbsp vegetable oil, plus extra for greasing

1 onion, chopped

2 garlic cloves, crushed

1 tsp garam masala

½ tsp ground coriander

3¾ cups vegetable stock

¾ cup red lentils

1 small egg

2 tbsp milk

2 tbsp mango chutney

2 tbsp chopped parsley

parsley sprigs, to garnish

salad greens and toast, to serve

1 Heat the oil in a large saucepan and sauté the onion and garlic, stirring constantly, for 2–3 minutes. Add the spices and cook for a further 30 seconds.

2 Stir in the stock and lentils and bring the mixture to a boil. Reduce the heat and simmer for 20 minutes, until the lentils are cooked and softened. Remove the pan from the heat and drain off any excess moisture.

3 Put the mixture in a food processor and add the egg, milk, mango chutney and parsley. Process until smooth.

4 Grease and line the base of a 1 lb loaf pan and spoon in the mixture, levelling the surface. Cover and cook in a preheated oven, 400°F, for 40–45 minutes, or until firm to the touch.

5 Cool in the pan for 20 minutes, then transfer to the refrigerator.

6 Turn out the pâté on to a serving plate, slice and garnish with fresh parsley. Serve with salad greens and toast.

COOK'S TIP

It is always better to make your own stock, if you have time, rather than use stock cubes, as the flavor is far superior.

Cauliflower Roulade

A light-as-air mixture of eggs and vegetables produces a stylish vegetarian dish that can be enjoyed hot or cold.

NUTRITIONAL INFORMATION

Calories	.271	Sugars	.4g
Protein	.15g	Fat	.20g
Carbohydrate	.7g	Saturates	.11g

 30 MINS 🕐 40 MINS

SERVES 6

INGREDIENTS

1 small cauliflower, divided into flowerets

4 eggs, separated

¾ cup grated cheddar cheese

¼ cup cottage cheese

pinch of grated nutmeg

½ tsp mustard powder

salt and pepper

FILLING

1 bunch watercress, trimmed

¼ cup butter

¼ cup flour

¾ cup plain yogurt

¼ cup grated cheddar cheese

¼ cup cottage cheese

1 Line a jelly roll pan with baking parchment.

2 Steam the cauliflower until just tender, then drain under cold water. Process the cauliflower in a food processor or chop and press through a strainer.

3 Beat the egg yolks, then stir in the cauliflower, ½ cup of the Cheddar, and the cottage cheese. Season with nutmeg, mustard, and salt and pepper. Whisk the egg whites until stiff but not dry, then fold them in.

4 Spread the mixture evenly in the pan. Bake in a preheated oven, 375°F, for about 20–25 minutes, until risen and a golden color.

5 Chop the watercress, reserving a few sprigs for garnish. Melt the butter in a small pan. Cook the watercress, stirring, for 3 minutes, until wilted. Blend in the flour, then stir in the yogurt and simmer for 2 minutes. Stir in the cheeses.

6 Turn out the roulade onto a damp tea towel covered with baking parchment. Peel off the paper and leave for a minute to allow the steam to escape. Roll up the roulade, including a new sheet of paper, starting from one narrow end.

7 Unroll the roulade, spread the filling to within 1 inch of the edges, and roll up. Transfer to a cookie sheet, sprinkle with the remaining cheddar, and return to the oven for 5 minutes. Serve immediately if serving hot, or allow to cool completely.

Mini Vegetable Puffs

These are ideal with a more formal meal, as they take a little time to prepare and look really impressive.

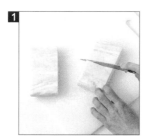

NUTRITIONAL INFORMATION

Calories	649	Sugars	.........3g
Protein	.........9g	Fat	..........45g
Carbohydrate	...57g	Saturates	......18g

15 MINS   35 MINS

SERVES 4

INGREDIENTS

1 lb puff pastry, thawed if frozen

1 egg, beaten

FILLING

8 oz sweet potato, cubed

3½ oz baby asparagus spears

2 tbsp butter or margarine

1 leek, sliced

2 small mushrooms, sliced

1 tsp lime juice

1 tsp chopped thyme

pinch of dried mustard

salt and pepper

1 Cut the pastry into 4 equal pieces. Roll each piece out on a lightly floured surface to form a 5-inch square. Place on a dampened cookie sheet and score a smaller 2.5-inch square inside each one.

2 Brush with beaten egg and cook in a preheated oven, 400°F, for 20 minutes, or until risen and golden brown.

3 Meanwhile, make the filling. Cook the sweet potato in a saucepan of boiling water for 15 minutes, until tender. Drain well and set aside. Blanch the asparagus in a saucepan of boiling water for about 10 minutes, or until tender. Drain and reserve.

4 Remove the pastry squares from the oven, then carefully cut out the central square of pastry with a sharp knife, lift out and reserve.

5 Melt the butter or margarine in a saucepan and sauté the leek and mushrooms for 2–3 minutes. Add the lime juice, thyme, and mustard, season well and stir in the sweet potatoes and asparagus. Spoon the mixture into the pastry shells, top with the reserved pastry squares, and serve immediately.

Vegetable & Nut Samosas

These delicious little fried pastries are really quite simple to make. Serve them hot or cold as an appetizer to an Indian meal.

NUTRITIONAL INFORMATION

Calories . . . . . . .343 Sugars 2g
Protein . . . . .5g Fat 26g
Carbohydrate . . .24g Saturates 5g

30 MINS   40 MINS

MAKES 12

I N G R E D I E N T S

12 oz potatoes, diced

salt

1 cup frozen peas

3 tbsp vegetable oil

1 onion, chopped

1-inch piece of ginger, chopped

1 garlic clove, crushed

1 tsp garam masala

2 tsp mild curry paste

½ tsp cumin seeds

2 tsp lemon juice

½ cup unsalted cashews,
    coarsely chopped

vegetable oil, for shallow frying

cilantro sprigs, to garnish

mango chutney, to serve

P A S T R Y

2 cups all-purpose flour

¼ cup butter

6 tbsp warm milk

1 Cook the potatoes in a saucepan of boiling, salted water for 5 minutes. Add the peas and cook for a further 4 minutes, or until the potatoes are tender. Drain well. Heat the oil in a skillet and fry the onion, potato and pea mixture, ginger, garlic and spices for 2 minutes. Stir in the lemon juice and cook gently, uncovered, for 2 minutes. Remove from the heat, slightly mash the potato and peas, then add the cashews, mix well and season with salt.

2 To make the pastry, put the flour in a bowl and cut in the butter. Mix in the milk to form a dough. Knead lightly and divide into 6 portions. Form each into a ball and roll out to a 7-inch round. Cut each one in half.

3 Divide the filling equally between the semi-circles of pastry, spreading it out to within ¼ inch of the edges. Brush the edges of pastry all the way round with water and fold over to form triangular shapes, sealing the edges well together to enclose the filling completely.

4 Heat the vegetable oil in a skillet to 350°F or until a cube of bread browns in 30 seconds. Fry the samosas, a few at a time, turning frequently until golden brown and heated through. Drain on paper towels and keep warm while cooking the remainder. Garnish with cilantro sprigs and serve hot.

Onions à la Grecque

This is a well-known method of cooking vegetables
and is perfect with shallots or onions, served with a crisp salad.

NUTRITIONAL INFORMATION

Calories	200	Sugars	........26g
Protein	.........2g	Fat	..........9g
Carbohydrate	...28g	Saturates	.......1g

 10 MINS 15 MINS

SERVES 4

INGREDIENTS

1 lb shallots

3 tbsp olive oil

3 tbsp honey

2 tbsp garlic wine vinegar

3 tbsp dry white wine

1 tbsp tomato paste

2 celery stalks, sliced

2 tomatoes, seeded and chopped

salt and pepper

chopped celery leaves, to garnish

1 Peel the shallots. Heat the oil in a large saucepan, add the shallots and cook, stirring, for 3–5 minutes, or until they begin to brown.

2 Add the honey and cook over a high heat for a further 30 seconds, then add the garlic wine vinegar and dry white wine, stirring well.

3 Stir in the tomato paste, celery, and tomatoes and bring the mixture to a boil. Cook over a high heat for 5–6 minutes. Season to taste and leave to cool slightly.

4 Garnish with chopped celery leaves and serve warm. Alternatively chill in the refrigerator before serving.

Garlicky Mushroom Pakoras

Whole mushrooms are dunked in a spiced garlicky batter and deep-fried until golden. They are at their most delicious served piping hot.

NUTRITIONAL INFORMATION

Calories	297	Sugars	.........3g
Protein	.........5g	Fat	..........21g
Carbohydrate	...24g	Saturates	.......2g

    20 MINS   10–15 MINS

SERVES 6

I N G R E D I E N T S

1½ cups gram or besan flour

½ tsp salt

¼ tsp baking powder

1 tsp cumin seeds

½–1 tsp chili powder

1 cup water

2 garlic cloves, crushed

1 small onion, finely chopped

vegetable oil, for deep-frying

1 lb 2 oz mushrooms, trimmed
    and wiped

lemon wedges and cilantro
    sprigs, to garnish

COOK'S TIP

Gram flour, also known as
besan flour, is a pale yellow
flour made from garbanzo beans.
It is now readily available from
larger supermarkets, as well as
Indian food shops and some ethnic
delicatessens. Gram flour is also
used to make onion bhajis.

1 Put the gram flour, salt, baking powder, cumin and chili powder into a bowl and mix well together. Make a well in the center of the mixture and gradually stir in the water, mixing thoroughly to form a batter.

2 Stir the crushed garlic and the chopped onion into the batter and leave the mixture to infuse for 10 minutes. One-third fill a deep-fat fryer or pan with vegetable oil and heat to 350°F or until a cube of bread browns in 30 seconds. Lower the basket into the hot oil.

3 Meanwhile, mix the mushrooms into the batter, stirring to coat. Remove a few at a time and place them into the hot oil. Fry for about 2 minutes, or until golden brown.

4 Remove the mushrooms from the pan with a slotted spoon and drain on paper towels while you are cooking the remainder in the same way.

5 Serve hot, sprinkled with coarse salt and garnished with lemon wedges and cilantro sprigs.

Cheese, Garlic, & Herb Pâté

This wonderful cream cheese pâté is fragrant with the aroma of fresh herbs and garlic. Serve with triangles of Melba toast.

NUTRITIONAL INFORMATION

Calories 392	Sugars 1g
Protein 17g	Fat 28g
Carbohydrate . . .18g	Saturates 18g

 20 MINS   10 MINS

SERVES 4

I N G R E D I E N T S

1 tbsp butter

1 garlic clove, crushed

3 green onions, finely chopped

½ cup full-fat cream cheese

2 tbsp chopped mixed herbs,
    such as parsley, chives, marjoram,
    oregano, and basil

1½ cups finely grated mature (sharp)
    cheddar cheese

pepper

4–6 slices of white bread from a
    medium-cut sliced loaf

mixed salad greens and cherry
tomatoes, to serve

TO GARNISH

ground paprika

herb sprigs

1 Melt the butter in a small skillet and gently fry the garlic and green onions together for 3–4 minutes, until softened. Allow to cool.

2 Beat the cream cheese in a large mixing bowl until smooth, then add the garlic and green onions. Stir in the herbs, mixing well.

3 Add the cheddar and work the mixture together to form a stiff paste. Cover and chill until ready to serve.

4 To make the Melba toast, toast the slices of bread on both sides, and then cut off the crusts. Using a sharp bread knife, cut through the slices horizontally to make very thin slices. Cut into triangles and then lightly broil the untoasted sides until golden.

5 Arrange the mixed salad greens on 4 serving plates with the cherry tomatoes. Pile the cheese pâté on top and sprinkle with a little paprika. Garnish with sprigs of fresh herbs and serve with the Melba toast.

Tzatziki & Black Olive Dip

Tzatziki is a Greek dish made with yogurt, mint, and cucumber.
It tastes superb with warm pita bread.

NUTRITIONAL INFORMATION

Calories 381	Sugars 8g
Protein 11g	Fat 15g
Carbohydrate . . .52g	Saturates 2g

1 HOUR 3 MINS

SERVES 4

I N G R E D I E N T S

½ cucumber

1 cup thick plain yogurt

1 tbsp chopped mint

salt and pepper

4 pita breads

D I P

2 garlic cloves, crushed

1 cup pitted black olives

4 tbsp olive oil

2 tbsp lemon juice

1 tbsp chopped parsley

T O   G A R N I S H

mint sprigs

parsley sprigs

COOK'S TIP

Sprinkling the cucumber
with salt draws out some of its
moisture, making it crisper. If
you are in a hurry, you can omit
this procedure. Use green olives
instead of black ones if you prefer.

1 To make the tzatziki, peel the cucumber and chop roughly. Sprinkle it with salt and leave to stand for 15–20 minutes. Rinse with cold water and drain well.

2 Mix the cucumber, yogurt and mint together. Season to taste with salt and pepper and transfer to a serving bowl. Cover and chill for 20–30 minutes.

3 To make the black olive dip, put the crushed garlic and olives into a blender or food processor and process for 15–20 seconds. Alternatively, chop them very finely.

4 Add the olive oil, lemon juice, and parsley to the blender or food processor and process for a few more seconds. Alternatively, mix with the chopped garlic and olives and mash together. Season with salt and pepper.

5 Wrap the pita breads in foil and place over a barbecue for 2–3 minutes, turning once to warm through. Alternatively, heat in the oven or under the broiler. Cut into pieces and serve with the tzatziki and black olive dip, garnished with sprigs of fresh mint and parsley.

Soft Dumplings in Yogurt

These are very light and make a good summer afternoon snack, as well as a good appetizer to any vegetarian meal.

NUTRITIONAL INFORMATION

Calories ....476 Sugars 29g
Protein ....11g Fat 21g
Carbohydrate ...64g Saturates 3g

 15 MINS   20 MINS

SERVES 4

I N G R E D I E N T S

1½ cups urid dal powder (lentil powder)

1 tsp baking powder

½ tsp ground ginger

1¼ cups water

oil, for deep-frying

1½ cups plain yogurt

5 tbsp sugar

M A S A L A

6 tbsp ground coriander

6 tbsp ground white cumin

1 oz crushed red chilies

½ cup citric acid

chopped fresh red chilies, to garnish

1 Place the powdered urid dal in a large mixing bowl. Add the baking powder and ginger and stir to combine. Add the water and mix to form a paste.

2 Heat the oil in a deep saucepan. Pour in the batter, 1 tsp at a time, and deep-fry the dumplings until golden brown, lowering the heat when the oil gets too hot. Set the dumplings aside.

3 Place the yogurt in a separate bowl. Add 1⅔ cups water and the sugar and

mix together with a whisk or fork. Set aside.

4 To make the masala, roast the ground coriander and the white cumin in a saucepan until a little darker in color and giving off their aroma. Grind coarsely in a food processor or in a mortar with a

pestle. Add the crushed red chilies and citric acid and blend well together.

5 Sprinkle about 1 tbsp of the masala over the dumplings and store the remainder in an airtight jar for future use. Garnish with chopped red chilies. Serve with the reserved yogurt mixture.

Avocado Margherita

This classic Italian combination of tomatoes, basil, and mozzarella cheese is easy to prepare in this microwave recipe.

NUTRITIONAL INFORMATION

Calories 284   Sugars 3g
Protein . . . . .6g   Fat 27g
Carbohydrate . . . .6g   Saturates 7g

10 MINS   7 MINS

SERVES 4

INGREDIENTS

1 small red onion, sliced

1 garlic clove, crushed

1 tbsp olive oil

2 small tomatoes

2 avocados, halved and pitted

4 fresh basil leaves, torn into shreds

2 oz mozzarella cheese, thinly sliced

salt and pepper

TO GARNISH

mixed salad

fresh basil leaves

1 Place the onion, garlic and the olive oil in a bowl. Cover and cook on HIGH power for 2 minutes.

COOK'S TIP

This recipe is for combination microwave ovens with a broiler. Arrange the avocados on the low rack of the broiler or on the turntable. Cook on combination broiler 1 and LOW power for 8 minutes until browned and bubbling.

 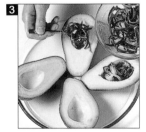 

2 Meanwhile, peel the tomatoes by cutting a cross in the base of the tomatoes and placing them in a small bowl. Pour on boiling water and leave for about 45 seconds. Drain and then plunge into cold water. The skins will slide off without too much difficulty.

3 Arrange the avocado halves on a plate, narrow ends towards the center. Spoon the onions into the hollows.

4 Cut the tomatoes into slices. Divide the tomatoes, basil and thin slices of mozzarella between the avocado halves. Season to taste with salt and pepper.

5 Cook on MEDIUM power for 5 minutes until the avocados are heated through and the cheese has melted. Serve immediately with a mixed salad and garnished with basil leaves.

Tofu Tempura

Crispy coated vegetables and tofu accompanied by a sweet, spicy dip give a real taste of Asia to this Japanese-style dish.

NUTRITIONAL INFORMATION

Calories	582	Sugars	........10g
Protein	........16g	Fat	.........27g
Carbohydrate	...65g	Saturates	.......4g

 15 MINS   20 MINS

SERVES 4

INGREDIENTS

4½ oz baby zucchini

4½ oz baby carrots

4½ oz baby corn cobs

4½ oz baby leeks

2 baby eggplants

8 oz tofu

vegetable oil, for deep-frying

julienne strips of carrot, ginger, and
  baby leek to garnish

noodles, to serve

BATTER

2 egg yolks

1¼ cups water

2 cups all-purpose flour

DIPPING SAUCE

5 tbsp mirin or dry sherry

5 tbsp tamari

2 tsp honey

1 garlic clove, crushed

1 tsp grated ginger

1 Slice the zucchini and carrots in half lengthwise. Trim the corn. Trim the leeks at both ends. Quarter the eggplants. Cut the tofu into 1-inch cubes.

2 To make the batter, mix the egg yolks with the water. Sift in 1½ cups of the flour and beat with a whisk to form a thick batter. Don't worry if there are any lumps. Heat the oil for deep-frying to 350°F or until a cube of bread browns in 30 seconds.

3 Place the remaining flour on a large plate and toss the vegetables and tofu until lightly coated.

4 Dip the tofu in the batter and deep-fry for 2–3 minutes, until lightly golden. Drain on paper towels and keep warm.

5 Dip the vegetables in the batter and deep-fry, a few at a time, for 3–4 minutes, until golden. Drain and place on a warmed serving plate.

6 To make the dipping sauce, mix all the ingredients together. Serve with the vegetables and tofu, accompanied with noodles and garnished with julienne strips of vegetables.

Buttered Nut & Lentil Dip

This tasty dip is very easy to make. It is perfect to have at barbecues, as it gives your guests something to nibble while they are waiting.

NUTRITIONAL INFORMATION

Calories	395	Sugars	.........4g
Protein	........12g	Fat	..........31g
Carbohydrate	...18g	Saturates	......10g

 5-10 MINS   40 MINS

SERVES 4

INGREDIENTS

¼ cup butter

1 small onion, chopped

⅓ cup red lentils

1¼ cups vegetable stock

½ cup blanched almonds

½ cup pine nuts

½ tsp ground coriander

½ tsp ground cumin

½ tsp grated ginger

1 tsp chopped fresh cilantro

salt and pepper

sprigs of cilantro to garnish

TO SERVE

fresh vegetable crudités

bread sticks

VARIATION

Green or brown lentils can be used, but they will take longer to cook than red lentils. If you wish, substitute peanuts for the almonds. Ground ginger can be used instead of fresh—substitute ½ teaspoon and add it with the other spices.

1 Melt half the butter in a saucepan and fry the onion over a medium heat, stirring frequently, until golden brown.

2 Add the lentils and vegetable stock. Bring to a boil, then reduce the heat and simmer gently, uncovered, for about 25–30 minutes, until the lentils are tender. Drain well.

3 Melt the remaining butter in a small skillet. Add the almonds and pine nuts and fry them over a low heat, stirring frequently, until golden brown. Remove from the heat.

4 Put the lentils, almonds and pine nuts, with any remaining butter, into a food processor blender. Add the ground coriander, cumin, ginger, and cilantro. Process for about 15–20 seconds, until the mixture is smooth. Alternatively, press the lentils through a strainer to purée them and then mix with the finely chopped nuts, spices, and herbs.

5 Season the dip with salt and pepper and garnish with sprigs of cilantro. Serve with fresh vegetable crudités and bread sticks.

Pakoras

Pakoras are eaten all over India. They are made in many different ways and with a variety of fillings. Sometimes they are served in yogurt.

NUTRITIONAL INFORMATION

Calories . . . . .331 Sugars 5g
Protein . . . . .9g Fat 22g
Carbohydrate . . .27g Saturates 3g

 15 MINS   15–20 MINS

SERVES 4

I N G R E D I E N T S

6 tbsp gram or besan flour

½ tsp salt

1 tsp chili powder

1 tsp baking powder

1½ tsp white cumin seeds

1 tsp pomegranate seeds

1¼ cups water

cilantro leaves, finely chopped

vegetables of your choice: cauliflower, cut
    into small flowerets; onions, cut into
    rings; potatoes, sliced; eggplant,
    sliced; or fresh spinach leaves

oil, for deep-frying

1 Sift the gram flour into a large mixing bowl. Add the salt, chili powder, baking powder, cumin and pomegranate seeds and blend together well. Pour in the water and beat thoroughly to form a smooth batter.

2 Add the cilantro and mix. Set the batter aside.

3 Dip the prepared vegetables of your choice into the batter, carefully shaking off any of the excess batter.

4 Heat the oil in a large heavy-bottomed pan. Place the battered vegetables of your choice in the oil and deep-fry, in batches, turning once.

5 Repeat this process until all of the batter has been used up.

6 Transfer the battered vegetables to kitchen paper and drain thoroughly. Serve immediately.

COOK'S TIP

When deep-frying, it is important to use oil at the correct temperature. If the oil is too hot, the outside of the food will burn as will the spices, before the inside is cooked. If the oil is too cool, the food will be sodden with oil before a crisp batter forms.

Snacks & Light Meals

The ability to rustle up a simple snack or a quickly-prepared light meal can be very important in our busy lives. Sometimes we may not feel like eating a full-scale

meal, but nevertheless want something appetizing and satisfying. Or if lunch or dinner is going to be served very late, then we may want something to tide us over and hold off those hunger pangs! Whether it is for a sustaining snack to break the day, or hearty bites to serve with pre-dinner drinks, or an informal lunch or supper party, you will find a mouthwatering collection of recipes in this chapter.

Roasted Vegetables

Roasted vegetables are delicious and attractive. Served on warm English muffins with a herb sauce, they are unbeatable.

NUTRITIONAL INFORMATION

Calories 509   Sugars 12g
Protein . . . . .15g   Fat 28g
Carbohydrate . . .50g   Saturates 12g

🍞 1¼ HOURS   🕐 30 MINS

SERVES 4

I N G R E D I E N T S

1 red onion, cut into 8 pieces

1 eggplant, halved and sliced

1 yellow bell pepper, seeded and sliced

1 zucchini, sliced

4 tbsp olive oil

1 tbsp garlic vinegar

2 tbsp vermouth

2 garlic cloves, crushed

1 tbsp chopped thyme

2 tsp light brown sugar

4 English muffins, halved

salt and pepper

S A U C E

2 tbsp butter

1 tbsp flour

⅔ cup milk

⅓ cup vegetable stock

¾ cup grated cheddar cheese

1 tsp wholegrain mustard

3 tbsp chopped mixed herbs

1 Arrange the vegetables in a shallow ovenproof dish. Mix together the oil, vinegar, vermouth, garlic, thyme, and sugar and pour over the vegetables. Set aside to marinate for 1 hour.

2 Transfer the vegetables to a cookie sheet. Cook in a preheated oven at 400°F for 20–25 minutes, or until the vegetables have softened and become tender.

3 Meanwhile, make the sauce. Melt the butter in a small pan and add the flour. Cook for 1 minute, stirring constantly, and then remove from the heat. Gradually, stir in the milk and stock and return the pan to the heat. Bring to a boil, stirring constantly, until thickened. Stir in the cheese, mustard, and mixed herbs and season to taste with salt and pepper.

4 Preheat the broiler to high. Cut the English muffins in half and broil for 2–3 minutes, until golden brown, then remove and arrange on a serving plate.

5 Spoon the roasted vegetables onto the English muffins and pour the sauce over the top. Serve immediately.

Falafel

These are a very tasty, well-known Middle Eastern dish of small garbanzo bean-based balls, spiced and deep-fried.

NUTRITIONAL INFORMATION

Calories 491   Sugars 3g
Protein . . . . .15g   Fat 30g
Carbohydrate . . .43g   Saturates 3g

🍲 25 MINS   🕐 10-15 MINS

SERVES 4

I N G R E D I E N T S

6 cups canned garbanzo beans, drained

1 red onion, chopped

3 garlic cloves, crushed

3½ oz whole wheat bread

2 small fresh red chilies

1 tsp ground cumin

1 tsp ground coriander

½ tsp turmeric

1 tbsp chopped cilantro, plus
    extra to garnish

1 egg, beaten

1 cup whole wheat breadcrumbs

vegetable oil, for
    deep-frying

salt and pepper

tomato and cucumber salad
    and lemon wedges, to serve

1 Put the garbanzo beans, onion, garlic, bread, chilies, spices, and cilantro in a food processor and process for 30 seconds. Stir and season to taste with salt and pepper.

2 Remove the mixture from the food processor and shape into walnut-sized balls.

3 Place the beaten egg in a shallow bowl and place the whole wheat breadcrumbs on a plate. Dip the balls first into the egg to coat and then roll them in the breadcrumbs, shaking off any excess.

4 Heat the oil for deep-frying to 350°F or until a cube of bread browns in 30 seconds. Fry the falafel, in batches if necessary, for 2–3 minutes, until crisp and browned. Remove from the oil with a perforated spoon and dry on absorbent paper towels. Garnish with cilantro and serve with a tomato and cucumber salad and lemon wedges.

Potato Fritters with Relish

These are incredibly simple to make and sure to be popular served as a tempting snack or as an accompaniment to almost any Indian meal.

NUTRITIONAL INFORMATION

Calories	294	Sugars	........4g
Protein	.........4g	Fat	.........24g
Carbohydrate	...18g	Saturates	.......3g

 40 MINS   15 MINS

SERVES 8

I N G R E D I E N T S

½ cup whole wheat flour

½ tsp ground coriander

½ tsp cumin seeds

¼ tsp chili powder

½ tsp ground turmeric

¼ tsp salt

1 egg

3 tbsp milk

12 oz potatoes, peeled

1–2 garlic cloves, crushed

4 green onions, chopped

2 oz corn kernels

vegetable oil, for shallow frying

O N I O N & T O M A T O
R E L I S H

1 onion, peeled

8 oz tomatoes

2 tbsp chopped cilantro

2 tbsp chopped mint

2 tbsp lemon juice

½ tsp roasted cumin seeds

¼ tsp salt

pinch of cayenne pepper

1 First make the relish. Cut the onion and tomatoes into small dice and place in a bowl with the remaining ingredients. Mix together well and leave to stand for at least 15 minutes before serving to allow time for the flavors to blend.

2 Place the flour in a bowl, stir in the spices and salt, and make a well in the center. Add the egg and milk and mix to form a fairly thick batter.

3 Coarsely grate the potatoes, place in a strainer, and rinse well under cold running water. Drain and squeeze dry, then stir into the batter with the garlic, scallions, and corn.

4 Heat about ¼ inch vegetable oil in a large skillet and add a few tablespoonfuls of the mixture at a time, flattening each one to form a thin cake. Fry over a low heat, turning frequently, for 2–3 minutes, or until golden brown and cooked through.

5 Drain on paper towels and keep hot while frying the remaining mixture in the same way. Serve hot with onion and tomato relish.

Mixed Bean Pan-Fry

Fresh green beans have a wonderful flavor that is hard to beat.
If you cannot find fresh beans, use thawed frozen beans instead.

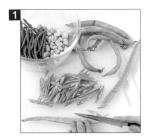

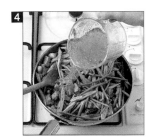

NUTRITIONAL INFORMATION

Calories 179	Sugars 4g	
Protein 10g	Fat 11g	
Carbohydrate . . .10g	Saturates 1g	

10 MINS   15 MINS

SERVES 4

INGREDIENTS

4 cups mixed green beans, such as green
and fava beans, podded

2 tbsp vegetable oil

2 garlic cloves, crushed

1 red onion, halved and sliced

8 oz firm tofu, diced

1 tbsp lemon juice

½ tsp turmeric

1 tsp ground allspice

⅔ cup vegetable stock

2 tsp sesame seeds

1 Trim and chop the green beans and
set aside until required.

2 Heat the oil in a medium skillet. Add
the garlic and onion and sauté,
stirring frequently, over a low heat for
2 minutes.

3 Add the tofu and cook for 2–3
minutes, until just beginning to turn
golden brown.

4 Add the green beans and fava beans.
Stir in the lemon juice, turmeric,
ground mixed spice, and vegetable stock
and bring to a boil over a medium heat.

5 Reduce the heat and simmer for
5–7 minutes, or until the beans are
tender. Sprinkle with sesame seeds and
serve immediately.

VARIATION

Use smoked bean curd
instead of marinated
bean curd for an alternative
and quite distinctive flavor.

Spinach Crêpes

Serve these crêpes as a light lunch or supper dish, with a tomato and basil salad for a dramatic color contrast.

NUTRITIONAL INFORMATION

Calories 663	Sugars 9g
Protein 32g	Fat 48g
Carbohydrate . . .28g	Saturates 18g

 25 MINS   1¼ HOURS

SERVES 4

I N G R E D I E N T S

¾ cup whole wheat flour

1 egg

⅔ cup plain yogurt

3 tbsp water

1 tbsp vegetable oil, plus extra for brushing

7 oz frozen leaf spinach, thawed
    and puréed

pinch of grated nutmeg

salt and pepper

T O   G A R N I S H

lemon wedges

fresh cilantro sprigs

F I L L I N G

1 tbsp vegetable oil

3 green onions,
    thinly sliced

1 cup ricotta cheese

4 tbsp plain yogurt

1¾ cup grated Gruyère cheese

1 egg, lightly beaten

1 cup unsalted cashews

2 tbsp chopped parsley

pinch of cayenne pepper

1 Sift the flour and salt into a bowl and tip in any bran in the strainer. Beat together the egg, yogurt, water, and oil. Gradually pour it onto the flour, beating constantly. Stir in the spinach and season with pepper and nutmeg.

2 To make the filling, heat the oil in a pan and fry the green onions until translucent. Remove with a perforated spoon and drain on paper towels. Beat together the ricotta, yogurt, and half the Gruyère. Beat in the egg and stir in the cashews and parsley. Season with salt and cayenne.

3 Lightly brush a small, heavy skillet with oil and heat. Pour in 3–4 tablespoons of the crêpe batter and tilt the pan so that it covers the base.

Cook for about 3 minutes, until bubbles appear in the center. Turn and cook the other side for about 2 minutes, until lightly browned. Slide the crêpe onto a warmed plate, cover with foil, and keep warm while you cook the remainder. The batter should make 8–12 crêpes.

4 Spread a little filling over each crêpe and fold in half and then half again, envelope style. Spoon the remaining filling into the opening.

5 Grease a shallow, ovenproof dish and arrange the crêpes in a single layer. Sprinkle on the remaining cheese and cook in a preheated oven at 350°F for about 15 minutes. Serve hot, garnished with lemon wedges and cilantro sprigs.

Broiled Potatoes

This dish is ideal with broiled or grilled foods, since the potatoes themselves may be cooked by either method.

NUTRITIONAL INFORMATION

Calories 417	Sugars 1g	
Protein 3g	Fat 37g	
Carbohydrate . . .20g	Saturates 10g	

 15 MINS   20 MINS

SERVES 4

INGREDIENTS

1 lb potatoes, unpeeled and scrubbed

3 tbsp butter, melted

2 tbsp chopped thyme

paprika, for dusting

LIME MAYONNAISE

⅔ cup mayonnaise

2 tsp lime juice

finely grated zest of 1 lime

1 garlic clove, crushed

pinch of paprika

salt and pepper

1 Cut the potatoes into ½-inch thick slices.

2 Cook the potatoes in a saucepan of boiling water for 5–7 minutes—they should still be quite firm. Remove the potatoes with a perforated spoon and drain thoroughly.

3 Line a broiler pan with aluminum foil. Place the potato slices on top of the foil.

4 Brush the potatoes with the melted butter and sprinkle the chopped thyme on top. Season to taste with salt and pepper.

5 Cook the potatoes under a preheated broiler at medium heat for 10 minutes, turning once.

6 Meanwhile, make the lime mayonnaise. Thoroughly combine the mayonnaise, lime juice, lime zest, garlic, paprika, and salt and pepper to taste in a small bowl.

7 Dust the hot potato slices with a little paprika and serve immediately with the lime mayonnaise.

COOK'S TIP

The lime mayonnaise may be spooned over the broiled potatoes to coat them just before serving, if you prefer.

Paprika Chips

These wafer-thin potato chips are great cooked over a grill and served with spicy vegetable kabobs. They also work well broiled.

NUTRITIONAL INFORMATION

Calories	149	Sugars	.......0.6g
Protein	.........2g	Fat	...........8g
Carbohydrate	...17g	Saturates	.......1g

 5 MINS   7 MINS

SERVES 4

I N G R E D I E N T S

2 large potatoes

3 tbsp olive oil

½ tsp paprika

salt

1 Using a sharp knife, slice the potatoes very thinly so that they are almost transparent. Drain the potato slices thoroughly and pat dry with paper towels.

2 Heat the oil in a large skillet and add the paprika, stirring constantly to ensure that the paprika doesn't stick and burn.

3 Add the potato slices to the skillet and cook them in a single layer for about 5 minutes or until the potato slices just begin to curl slightly at the edges.

VARIATION

You could use curry powder or any other spice to flavor the chips instead of the paprika, if you prefer.

4 Remove the potato slices from the pan using a slotted spoon and transfer them to paper towels to drain thoroughly.

5 Thread the potato slices onto several wooden kabob skewers.

6 Sprinkle the potato slices with a little salt and cook over a medium hot grill or under a medium broiler, turning frequently, for 10 minutes, until the potato slices begin to crispen. Sprinkle with a little more salt, if preferred, and serve immediately.

Marinated Fennel

Fennel has a wonderful aniseed flavor which is ideal for grilling or broiling. This marinated recipe is really delicious.

NUTRITIONAL INFORMATION

Calories 117   Sugars 3g
Protein ....1g   Fat 11g
Carbohydrate ....3g   Saturates 2g

 1¼ HOURS   10 MINS

SERVES 4

INGREDIENTS

2 fennel bulbs

1 red bell pepper, seeded and cut into
   large cubes

1 lime, cut into 8 wedges

MARINADE

2 tbsp lime juice

4 tbsp olive oil

2 garlic cloves, crushed

1 tsp wholegrain mustard

1 tbsp chopped thyme

fennel fronds, to garnish

crisp salad, to serve

1 Cut each of the fennel bulbs into 8 pieces and place in a shallow dish. Mix in the bell peppers.

2 To make the marinade, combine the lime juice, oil, garlic, mustard, and thyme. Pour the marinade over the fennel and bell peppers, toss to coat thoroughly, and set aside to marinate for 1 hour.

3 Thread the fennel and bell peppers onto wooden skewers with the lime wedges. Preheat a broiler to medium and broil the kabobs, turning and basting frequently with the marinade, for about 10 minutes.

4 Transfer to serving plates, garnish with fennel fronds, and serve immediately with a crisp salad.

COOK'S TIP

Soak the skewers in cold water for 20 minutes before using to prevent them from burning during broiling. You could substitute 2 tablespoons orange juice for the lime juice and add 1 tbsp honey, if you prefer.

Garlic Mushrooms on Toast

This is so simple to prepare and looks great if you use a variety of mushrooms for shape and texture.

NUTRITIONAL INFORMATION

Calories	366	Sugars	.........2g
Protein	.........9g	Fat	..........18g
Carbohydrate	...45g	Saturates	.......4g

 10 MINS   10 MINS

SERVES 4

INGREDIENTS

6 tbsp margarine

2 garlic cloves, crushed

4 cups mixed mushrooms,
   such as button, oyster, and
   shiitake, sliced

8 slices French baguette

1 tbsp chopped parsley

salt and pepper

1 Melt the margarine in a skillet. Add the crushed garlic and cook, stirring constantly, for 30 seconds.

2 Add the mushrooms and cook, turning occasionally, for 5 minutes.

3 Toast the French baguette slices under a preheated medium broiler for 2–3 minutes, turning once. Transfer the toasts to a serving plate.

COOK'S TIP

Always store mushrooms for a maximum of 24–36 hours in the refrigerator, in paper bags, as they sweat in plastic. Wild mushrooms should be washed but other varieties can simply be wiped with paper towels.

4 Toss the parsley into the mushrooms, mixing well, and season well with salt and pepper to taste.

5 Spoon the mushroom mixture over the bread and serve immediately.

Corn & Potato Fritters

An ideal supper dish for two, or for one if you halve the quantities.
You can use the remaining corn in another recipe.

 20 MINS   20 MINS

SERVES 2

INGREDIENTS

2 tbsp oil

1 small onion, thinly sliced

1 garlic clove, crushed

12 oz potatoes

7 oz can of corn, drained

½ tsp dried oregano

1 egg, beaten

½ cup grated Edam or
  Gouda cheese

salt and pepper

2–4 eggs

2–4 tomatoes, sliced

parsley sprigs, to garnish

1 Heat 1 tablespoon of the oil in a non-stick skillet. Add the onion and garlic and fry very gently, stirring frequently, until soft, but only lightly colored. Remove from the heat.

2 Grate the potatoes coarsely into a bowl and mix in the corn, oregano, beaten egg, and salt and pepper to taste. Add the fried onion.

3 Heat the remaining oil in the skillet. Divide the potato mixture in half and add to the skillet to make 2 oval-shaped cakes, leveling and shaping the cakes with a metal spatula.

4 Cook the fritters over a low heat for about 10 minutes, until golden brown underneath and almost cooked through, keeping them tidily in shape with the metal spatula and loosening so they don't stick.

5 Sprinkle each potato fritter with the grated cheese and place under a preheated moderately hot broiler until golden brown.

6 Meanwhile, poach 1 or 2 eggs for each person until just cooked. Transfer the fritters to warmed plates and top with the eggs and sliced tomatoes. Garnish with parsley and serve immediately.

Lentils & Mixed Vegetables

The green lentils used in this recipe require soaking but are worth it for the flavor. If time is short, you could use red split peas instead.

NUTRITIONAL INFORMATION

Calories	386	Sugars	........16g
Protein	........12g	Fat	..........23g
Carbohydrate	...35g	Saturates	......12g

45 MINS   40–45 MINS

SERVES 4

INGREDIENTS

¾ cups green lentils

4 tbsp butter or margarine

2 garlic cloves, crushed

2 tbsp olive oil

1 tbsp cider vinegar

1 red onion, cut into 8 chunks

1¾ oz baby corn cobs,
    halved lengthwise

1 yellow bell pepper, seeded and
    cut into strips

1 red bell pepper, seeded and
    cut into strips

1¾ oz green beans, halved

6 tbsp vegetable stock

2 tbsp honey

salt and pepper

crusty bread, to serve

VARIATION

This pan-fry is very versatile:
you can use a mixture of your
favorite vegetables, if you prefer.
Try zucchini, carrots, or snow peas.

1 Soak the lentils in a large saucepan of cold water for 25 minutes. Bring to a boil, reduce the heat, and simmer for 20 minutes. Drain thoroughly.

2 Add 1 tablespoon of the butter or margarine, 1 garlic clove, 1 tablespoon of oil, and the vinegar to the lentils and mix well.

3 Melt the remaining butter, garlic, and oil in a skillet and stir-fry the onion,

corn cobs, bell peppers, and beans for 3–4 minutes.

4 Add the vegetable stock and bring to a boil. Boil for about 10 minutes, or until the liquid has evaporated.

5 Add the honey and season with salt and pepper to taste. Stir in the lentil mixture and cook for 1 minute to heat through. Spoon onto warmed serving plates and serve with crusty bread.

Creamy Mushroom & Potato

These oven-baked mushrooms are covered with a creamy potato and mushroom filling topped with melted cheese.

NUTRITIONAL INFORMATION

Calories 214	Sugars 1g
Protein 5g	Fat 17g
Carbohydrate . . : . .11g	Saturates 11g

 40 MINS   40 MINS

SERVES 4

I N G R E D I E N T S

25 g/1 oz dried ceps

225 g/8 oz floury (mealy) potatoes, diced

25 g/1 oz/2 tbsp butter, melted

4 tbsp double (heavy) cream

2 tbsp chopped fresh chives

25 g/1 oz/¼ cup grated Emmenthal cheese

8 large open-capped mushrooms

150 ml/¼ pint/⅔cup vegetable stock

salt and pepper

fresh chives, to garnish

1 Place the dried ceps in a small bowl. Add sufficient boiling water to cover and set aside to soak for 20 minutes.

2 Meanwhile, cook the potatoes in a medium saucepan of lightly salted boiling water for 10 minutes, until cooked through and tender. Drain well and mash until smooth.

3 Drain the soaked ceps and then chop them finely. Mix them into the mashed potato.

4 Thoroughly blend the butter, cream and chives together and pour the mixture into the ceps and potato mixture, mixing well. Season to taste with salt and pepper.

5 Remove the stalks from the open-capped mushrooms. Chop the stalks and stir them into the potato mixture. Spoon the mixture into the open-capped mushrooms and sprinkle the cheese over the top.

6 Arrange the filled mushrooms in a shallow ovenproof dish and pour in the vegetable stock.

7 Cover the dish and cook in a preheated oven, 220°C/ 425°F/Gas Mark 7, for 20 minutes. Remove the lid and cook for 5 minutes until golden.

8 Garnish the mushrooms with fresh chives and serve at once.

VARIATION

Use fresh mushrooms instead of the dried ceps, if preferred, and stir a mixture of chopped nuts into the mushroom stuffing mixture for extra crunch.

Indian-Style Omelet

Omelets are very versatile: they go with almost anything and you can also serve them at any time of the day.

NUTRITIONAL INFORMATION

Calories	132	Sugars	.........1g
Protein	.........7g	Fat	...........11g
Carbohydrate	....2g	Saturates	.......2g

 10 MINS   20 MINS

SERVES 4

I N G R E D I E N T S

1 small onion, very finely chopped

2 green chilies, finely chopped

cilantro leaves, finely chopped

4 medium eggs

1 tsp salt

2 tbsp oil

toasted bread or crisp
green salad, to serve

1 Place the onion, chilies, and cilantro in a large mixing bowl. Mix together until well combined.

2 Place the eggs in a separate bowl and whisk together.

3 Add the onion mixture to the eggs and mix together.

4 Add the salt to the egg and onion mixture and whisk together well.

5 Heat 1 tbsp of the oil in a large skillet. Place a ladleful of the omelet batter into the pan.

6 Fry the omelet, turning once and pressing down with a flat spoon to make sure that the egg is cooked right through, until the omelet is a golden brown color.

7 Repeat the same process for the remaining batter. Set the omelets aside and keep warm while you make the remaining batches of omelets.

8 Serve the omelets immediately with toasted bread. Alternatively, simply serve the omelets with a crisp green salad for a light lunch.

COOK'S TIP

Indian cooks use a variety of vegetable oils, and peanut or sunflower oils make good alternatives for most dishes, although sometimes more specialist ones, such as coconut oil, mustard oil, and sesame oil, are called for.

Cabbage & Walnut Stir-Fry

This is a really quick, one-pan dish using green and red cabbage for both color and flavor.

NUTRITIONAL INFORMATION

Calories . . . . . . .422 Sugars 9g
Protein . . . . .13g Fat 37g
Carbohydrate . . .10g Saturates 5g

 10 MINS   10 MINS

SERVES 4

I N G R E D I E N T S

12 oz green cabbage

12 oz red cabbage

4 tbsp peanut oil

1 tbsp walnut oil

2 garlic cloves, crushed

8 green onions

8 oz firm tofu, cubed

2 tbsp lemon juice

3½ oz walnut halves

2 tsp Dijon mustard

2 tsp poppy seeds

salt and pepper

1 Using a sharp knife, shred the green and red cabbages thinly and set aside until required.

2 Heat the peanut and walnut oils in a preheated wok or heavy-bottomed skillet. Add the garlic, cabbage, green onions, and tofu and cook, stirring constantly, for 5 minutes.

3 Add the lemon juice, walnuts, and Dijon mustard, season to taste with salt and pepper, and cook for another 5 minutes, or until the cabbage is tender.

4 Transfer the stir-fry to a warm serving bowl, sprinkle with poppy seeds, and serve immediately.

COOK'S TIP

As well as adding protein, vitamins, and useful fats to the diet, nuts and seeds add flavor and texture to vegetarian meals. Keep a good supply of them in your pantry as they can be used in a great variety of dishes—salads, bakes, stir-fries, to name but a few.

Crispy Potato Skins

Potato skins are always a favorite. Prepare the skins in advance and warm through before serving with the salad fillings.

NUTRITIONAL INFORMATION

Calories	332	Sugars	. . . . .18g
Protein	. . . . .8g	Fat	. . . . .14g
Carbohydrate	. . .47g	Saturates	. . . . . . .5g

 30 MINS   1HR 10 MINS

SERVES 4

I N G R E D I E N T S

4 large baking potatoes

2 tbsp vegetable oil

4 tsp salt

snipped chives, to garnish

⅔ cup sour cream

  and 2 tbsp chopped chives, to serve

B E A N   S P R O U T   S A L A D

½ cup bean sprouts

1 celery stalk, sliced

1 orange, peeled and segmented

1 red eating apple, chopped

½ red bell pepper, seeded and chopped

1 tbsp chopped parsley

1 tbsp light soy sauce

1 tbsp honey

1 small garlic clove, crushed

B E A N   F I L L I N G

1½ cups canned mixed
  beans, drained

1 onion, halved and sliced

1 tomato, chopped

2 green onions, chopped

2 tsp lemon juice

salt and pepper

1 Scrub the potatoes and put on a cookie sheet. Prick the potatoes all over with a fork and rub the oil and salt into the skins.

2 Cook in a preheated oven at 400°F for 1 hour or until soft and cooked through.

3 Cut the potatoes in half lengthwise and scoop out the flesh, leaving a ½-inch thick shell. Put the shells, skin side up, in the oven for 10 minutes, until crisp.

4 Mix the ingredients for the bean sprout salad in a bowl, tossing in the soy sauce, honey, and garlic to coat.

5 Mix the ingredients for the bean filling in a separate bowl.

6 Mix the sour cream and chives in another bowl.

7 Serve the potato skins hot, with the two salad fillings, garnished with snipped chives, and the sour cream and chive sauce.

Cress & Cheese Tartlets

These individual tartlets are great for lunchtime or for picnic food.
Watercress is a good source of folic acid, important in early pregnancy.

NUTRITIONAL INFORMATION

Calories 410	Sugars 4g
Protein 15g	Fat 29g
Carbohydrate . . .24g	Saturates 19g

20 MINS   25 MINS

SERVES 4

INGREDIENTS

¾ cup all-purpose flour

pinch of salt

½ cup butter or margarine

2–3 tbsp cold water

2 bunches watercress

2 garlic cloves, crushed

1 shallot, chopped

1½ cups grated
    cheddar cheese

4 tbsp plain yogurt

½ tsp paprika

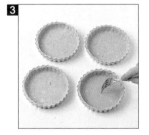

1 Sift the flour into a mixing bowl and add the salt. Cut in ⅓ cup of the butter or margarine into the flour until the mixture resembles breadcrumbs.

2 Stir in enough of the cold water to make a smooth dough.

3 Roll the dough out on a lightly floured surface and use to line four 4-inch tartlet pans. Prick the bases with a fork and leave to chill.

4 Heat the remaining butter or margarine in a skillet. Discard the stems from the watercress and add to the pan with the garlic and shallot, cooking for 1–2 minutes, until the watercress has wilted.

5 Remove the pan from the heat and stir in the grated cheese, yogurt, and paprika.

6 Spoon the mixture into the pastry shells and cook in a preheated oven, at 350°F for 20 minutes, or until the filling is firm. Turn out the tartlets and serve immediately.

VARIATION

Use spinach instead of the watercress, making sure it is well drained before mixing with the remaining filling ingredients.

Hash Browns

Hash browns are a popular recipe made of fried potato squares, often served at brunch. This recipe includes extra vegetables.

NUTRITIONAL INFORMATION

Calories 339	Sugars 9g
Protein 10g	Fat 21g
Carbohydrate ...29g	Saturates 7g

 20 MINS 45 MINS

SERVES 4

I N G R E D I E N T S

1 lb 2 oz potatoes

1 carrot, diced

1 celery stalk, diced

2 oz mushrooms, diced

1 onion, diced

2 garlic cloves, crushed

¼ cup frozen peas, thawed

⅔ cup grated Parmesan cheese

4 tbsp vegetable oil

2 tbsp butter

salt and pepper

S A U C E

1¼ cups strained tomatoes

2 tbsp chopped fresh cilantro

1 tbsp vegetarian Worcestershire sauce

½ tsp chili powder

2 tsp brown sugar

2 tsp mustard

⅓ cup vegetable stock

1 Cook the potatoes in a saucepan of lightly salted boiling water for 10 minutes. Drain and leave to cool. Meanwhile, cook the carrot in lightly salted boiling water for 5 minutes.

2 Set the potato aside to cool. When cool enough to handle, grate it with a coarse grater.

3 Drain the carrot and add it to the grated potato, together with the celery, mushrooms, onion, garlic, peas, and cheese. Season to taste with salt and pepper.

4 Put all of the sauce ingredients in a small saucepan and bring to a boil. Reduce the heat to low and simmer for 15 minutes.

5 Divide the potato mixture into 8 portions of equal size and shape into flattened rectangles with your hands.

6 Heat the oil and butter in a skillet and cook the hash browns over a low heat for 4–5 minutes on each side, until crisp and golden brown.

7 Transfer the hash browns to a serving plate and serve immediately with the tomato sauce.

Corn Patties

These are a delicious addition to any party buffet, and very simple to prepare. Serve with a sweet chili sauce.

NUTRITIONAL INFORMATION

Calories	90	Sugars	........3g
Protein	.........2g	Fat	..........5g
Carbohydrate	....11g	Saturates	.....0.6g

 10 MINS 10 MINS

SERVES 6

INGREDIENTS

11½ oz canned corn, drained

1 onion, finely chopped

1 tsp curry powder

1 garlic clove, crushed

1 tsp ground coriander

2 green onions, chopped

3 tbsp all-purpose flour

½ tsp baking powder

1 large egg

4 tbsp sunflower oil

salt

1 Mash the drained corn lightly in a medium-sized bowl. Add the onion, curry powder, garlic, ground coriander, green onions, flour, baking powder, and egg, one at a time, stirring after each addition. Season to taste with salt.

2 Heat the sunflower oil in a skillet. Drop tablespoonfuls of the mixture carefully onto the hot oil, far enough apart for them not to run into each other as they cook.

3 Cook for about 4–5 minutes, turning each patty once, until they are golden brown and firm to the touch. Take care not to turn them too soon, or they will break up in the pan.

4 Remove the patties from the pan with a slice and drain on paper towels. Serve immediately while still warm.

COOK'S TIP

To make this dish more attractive, you can serve the patties on large leaves, like those shown in the photograph. Be sure to cut the green onions on the diagonal, as shown, for a more elegant appearance.

Buck Rarebit

This substantial version of cheese on toast—a creamy cheese sauce topped with a poached egg—makes a tasty, filling snack.

NUTRITIONAL INFORMATION

Calories	478	Sugars	.........2g
Protein	........29g	Fat	.........34g
Carbohydrate	...14g	Saturates	......20g

10 MINS   15-20 MINS

SERVES 4

I N G R E D I E N T S

12 oz sharp cheddar cheese

4½ oz Dutch, Gruyère, or Swiss cheese

1 tsp mustard powder

1 tsp wholegrain mustard

2–4 tbsp brown ale or milk

½ tsp vegetarian Worcestershire sauce

4 thick slices white or brown bread

4 eggs

salt and pepper

TO GARNISH

tomato wedges

watercress sprigs

1 Grate the cheeses and place in a non-stick saucepan.

2 Add the mustards, seasoning, brown ale or milk, and the Worcestershire sauce and mix well.

VARIATION

For a change, you can use part or all Stilton or other blue cheese; the appearance is not so attractive but the flavor is very good.

3 Heat the cheese mixture gently, stirring until it has melted and is completely thick and creamy. Remove from the heat and leave to cool a little.

4 Toast the slices of bread on each side under a preheated broiler, then spread the rarebit mixture evenly over each piece. Put under a moderate broiler until golden brown and bubbling.

5 Meanwhile, poach the eggs. If using a poacher, grease the cups, heat the

water in the pan and, when just boiling, break the eggs into the cups. Cover and simmer for 4–5 minutes until just set. Alternatively, bring about 1½ inches of water to a boil in a skillet or large saucepan and for each egg quickly swirl the water with a knife and drop the egg into the "hole" created. Cook for about 4 minutes until just set.

6 Top the rarebits with a poached egg and serve garnished with tomato wedges and sprigs of watercress.

Carrot & Potato Soufflé

Hot soufflés have a reputation for being difficult to make, but this one is both simple and impressive. Make sure you serve it as soon as it is ready.

NUTRITIONAL INFORMATION

Calories 294	Sugars 6g
Protein 10g	Fat 9g
Carbohydrate ...46g	Saturates 4g

 1¼ HOURS 40 MINS

SERVES 4

INGREDIENTS

2 tbsp butter, melted

4 tbsp fresh whole wheat
   breadcrumbs

1½ lb russet potatoes, baked
   in their skins

2 carrots, grated

2 eggs, separated

2 tbsp orange juice

¼ tsp grated nutmeg

salt and pepper

carrot curls, to garnish

1 Brush the inside of a 3¾-cup soufflé dish with butter. Sprinkle three-quarters of the breadcrumbs over the base and sides.

2 Cut the baked potatoes in half and scoop the flesh into a mixing bowl.

3 Add the carrot, egg yolks, orange juice, and nutmeg to the potato flesh. Season to taste with salt and pepper.

4 In a separate bowl, whisk the egg whites until soft peaks form, then gently fold into the potato mixture with a metal spoon until well incorporated.

5 Gently spoon the potato and carrot mixture into the prepared soufflé dish. Sprinkle the remaining breadcrumbs over the top of the mixture.

6 Cook in a preheated oven at 400°F for 40 minutes, until risen and golden. Do not open the oven door during the cooking time, otherwise the soufflé will sink. Serve immediately, garnished with carrot curls.

COOK'S TIP

To bake the potatoes, prick the skins and cook in a pre-heated oven at 375°F for about 1 hour.

Vegetable Kabobs

These kabobs, made from a spicy vegetable mixture, are delightfully easy to make and taste delicious.

NUTRITIONAL INFORMATION

Calories	268	Sugars	.........1g
Protein	.........2g	Fat	..........25g
Carbohydrate	....9g	Saturates	.......3g

 20 MINS   25–30 MINS

MAKES 12

I N G R E D I E N T S

2 large potatoes, sliced

1 medium onion, sliced

½ medium cauliflower, cut into
   small flowerets

½ cup peas

1 tbsp spinach paste

2–3 green chilies

fresh cilantro leaves

1 tsp finely chopped fresh ginger

1 tsp crushed garlic

1 tsp ground coriander

1 pinch turmeric

1 tsp salt

1 cup breadcrumbs

1¼ cups vegetable oil

fresh chili strips, to garnish

1 Place the potatoes, onion, and cauliflower flowerets in a pan of water and bring to a boil. Reduce the heat and simmer until the potatoes are cooked through. Remove the vegetables from the pan with a perforated spoon and drain thoroughly. Set aside.

2 Add the peas and spinach to the vegetables and mix, mashing down thoroughly with a fork.

3 Using a sharp knife, finely chop the green chilies and fresh cilantro leaves.

4 Mix the chilies and cilantro with the ginger, garlic, ground coriander, turmeric, and salt.

5 Blend the spice mixture into the vegetables, mixing with a fork to make a paste.

6 Scatter the breadcrumbs onto a large plate.

7 Break off 10-12 small balls from the spice paste. Flatten them with the palm of your hand to make flat, round shapes.

8 Dip each kabob in the breadcrumbs, coating well.

9 Heat the oil in a heavy-bottomed skillet and shallow-fry the kabobs, in batches, until golden brown, turning occasionally. Transfer to serving plates and garnish with fresh chili strips. Serve hot.

Lentil Croquettes

These croquettes are an ideal light lunch served with a crisp salad and a tahini dip.

NUTRITIONAL INFORMATION

Calories	409	Sugars	.........5g
Protein	........19g	Fat	..........17g
Carbohydrate	...48g	Saturates	.......2g

🥔 10 MINS 🕐 55 MINS

SERVES 4

I N G R E D I E N T S

1¼ cups split red lentils

1 green bell pepper, seeded and
   finely chopped

1 red onion, finely chopped

2 garlic cloves, crushed

1 tsp garam masala

½ tsp chili powder

1 tsp ground cumin

2 tsp lemon juice

2 tbsp chopped unsalted peanuts

2½ cups water

1 egg, beaten

3 tbsp all-purpose flour

1 tsp turmeric

1 tsp chili powder

4 tbsp vegetable oil

salt and pepper

salad greens and herbs, to serve

1 Put the lentils in a large saucepan with the bell pepper, onion, garlic, garam masala, chili powder, ground cumin, lemon juice, and peanuts. Add the water and bring to a boil. Reduce the heat and simmer, stirring occasionally, for about 30 minutes, or until the liquid has been absorbed.

2 Remove the mixture from the heat and leave to cool slightly. Beat in the egg and season to taste with salt and pepper. Leave to cool completely.

3 With floured hands, form the mixture into 8 rectangles

4 Mix the flour, turmeric, and chili powder together on a small plate. Roll the croquettes in the spiced flour mixture to coat thoroughly.

5 Heat the oil in a large skillet. Add the croquettes, in batches, and fry, turning once, for about 10 minutes, until crisp on both sides. Transfer to warm serving plates and serve the croquettes with crisp salad greens and fresh herbs.

Scrambled Tofu

This is a delicious dish which would serve equally well as a light lunch or supper and makes an excellent after-school snack.

NUTRITIONAL INFORMATION

Calories	392	Sugars	.........6g
Protein	........16g	Fat	..........22g
Carbohydrate	...35g	Saturates	.......4g

 5–10 MINS   5 MINS

SERVES 4

I N G R E D I E N T S

6 tbsp margarine

1 lb firm tofu

1 red onion, chopped

1 red bell pepper, seeded and chopped

4 ciabatta (Italian bread) rolls

2 tbsp chopped mixed herbs

salt and pepper

fresh herbs, to garnish

1 Melt the margarine in a skillet and crumble the tofu into it.

2 Add the onion and bell pepper and cook, stirring occasionally, for 3–4 minutes.

COOK'S TIP

Rub the cut surface of a garlic clove over the toasted ciabatta rolls for extra flavor.

3 Meanwhile, slice the ciabatta rolls in half and toast them under a hot broiler for about 2–3 minutes, turning once.

4 Remove the toasts and transfer to a serving plate.

5 Add the mixed herbs to the tofu mixture, combine, and season to taste with salt and pepper.

6 Spoon the tofu mixture onto the toast and garnish with fresh herbs. Serve immediately.

Stuffed Vegetable Snacks

In this recipe, eggplant are filled with a spicy bulgur wheat and vegetable stuffing for a delicious light meal.

NUTRITIONAL INFORMATION

Calories 360   Sugars 17g
Protein . . . . .9g   Fat 16g
Carbohydrate . . .50g   Saturates 2g

 40 MINS   30 MINS

SERVES 4

INGREDIENTS

4 medium eggplant

salt

¾ cup bulgur wheat

1¼ cups boiling water

3 tbsp olive oil

2 garlic cloves, crushed

2 tbsp pine nuts

½ tsp turmeric

1 tsp chili powder

2 celery stalks, chopped

4 green onions, chopped

1 carrot, grated

¾ cup mushrooms, chopped

2 tbsp raisins

2 tbsp chopped cilantro

green salad, to serve

water over the top. Leave to stand for 20 minutes, or until the water has been completely absorbed.

3 Heat the oil in a skillet. Add the garlic, pine nuts, turmeric, chili powder, celery, green onions, carrot, mushrooms, and raisins and cook for 2–3 minutes.

4 Stir in the reserved eggplant flesh and cook for 2–3 minutes more. Add the chopped cilantro, mixing well.

5 Remove the pan from the heat and stir in the bulgur wheat. Rinse the eggplant shells under cold water and pat dry with paper towels.

6 Spoon the bulgur filling into the eggplant and place in a roasting pan. Pour in a little boiling water and cook in a preheated oven at 350°F for about 15–20 minutes, until piping hot. Remove from the oven and serve hot with a green salad.

1 Cut the eggplant in half lengthwise and scoop out the flesh with a teaspoon. Chop the flesh and set aside. Rub the insides of the eggplant with a little salt and leave to stand for 20 minutes.

2 Meanwhile, put the bulgur wheat in a mixing bowl and pour the boiling

Potato Mushroom Cakes

These cakes will be loved by vegetarians and meat-eaters alike. Packed with creamy potato and as wide a variety of mushrooms as possible.

NUTRITIONAL INFORMATION

Calories 298	Sugars 0.8g
Protein 5g	Fat 22g
Carbohydrate . . .22g	Saturates 5g

 20 MINS 25 MINS

SERVES 4

I N G R E D I E N T S

1 lb mealy potatoes, diced

2 tbsp butter

6 oz mixed mushrooms, chopped

2 garlic cloves, minced

1 small egg, beaten

1 tbsp chopped fresh chives, plus extra
   to garnish

flour, for dusting

oil, for frying

salt and pepper

1 Cook the potatoes in a pan of lightly salted boiling water for 10 minutes, or until cooked through

2 Drain the potatoes well, mash with a potato masher or fork, and set aside.

3 Meanwhile, melt the butter in a skillet. Add the mushrooms and garlic and cook, stirring constantly, for 5 minutes. Drain well.

4 Stir the mushrooms and garlic into the potato, together with the beaten egg and chives.

5 Divide the mixture equally into 4 portions and shape them into round cakes. Toss them in the flour until the outsides of the cakes are completely coated.

6 Heat the oil in a skillet. Add the potato cakes and fry over a medium heat for 10 minutes until they are golden brown, turning them over halfway through. Serve the cakes at once, with a simple crisp salad.

COOK'S TIP

Prepare the cakes in advance, cover, and leave to chill in the refrigerator for up to 24 hours, if you wish.

Refried Beans with Tortillas

Refried beans are a classic Mexican dish and are usually served as an accompaniment. They are, however, delicious served with warm tortillas.

NUTRITIONAL INFORMATION

Calories 519	Sugars 14g
Protein 25g	Fat 28g
Carbohydrate . . .44g	Saturates 9g

🐻 🐻

🍳 15 MINS   🕐 15 MINS

SERVES 4

I N G R E D I E N T S

B E A N S

2 tbsp olive oil

1 onion, finely chopped

3 garlic cloves, crushed

1 green chili, chopped

14 oz can red kidney beans, drained

14 oz can pinto beans, drained

2 tbsp chopped cilantro

⅔ cup vegetable stock

8 flour tortillas

¼ cup grated cheddar cheese

salt and pepper

R E L I S H

4 green onions, chopped

1 red onion, chopped

1 green chili, chopped

1 tbsp garlic wine vinegar

1 tsp sugar

1 tomato, chopped

1 Heat the oil for the beans in a large skillet over a medium heat. Add the onion and sauté, stirring frequently, for 3–5 minutes. Add the garlic and chili and cook for 1 minute.

2 Mash the beans with a potato masher and stir into the pan, together with the cilantro.

3 Stir in the vegetable stock and cook the beans, stirring constantly, for 5 minutes until soft and pulpy.

4 Meanwhile, place the tortillas on a cookie sheet and heat through in a preheated oven at 350°F for about 1–2 minutes.

5 Mix the relish ingredients together. Spoon the beans into a serving dish and top with the cheese. Season to taste with salt and pepper. Roll the warm tortillas and serve with the onion relish and refried beans.

Spicy Potato Fries

These homemade fries with a difference are flavored with spices and cooked in the oven. Serve with Lime Mayonnaise (see page 111).

NUTRITIONAL INFORMATION

Calories	328	Sugars	.........2g
Protein	.........5g	Fat	...........11g
Carbohydrate	...56g	Saturates	.......7g

 35 MINS   40 MINS

SERVES 4

I N G R E D I E N T S

4 large potatoes

2 sweet potatoes

4 tbsp butter, melted

½ tsp chili powder

1 tsp garam masala

salt

1 Cut the potatoes and sweet potatoes into slices about ½-inch thick, then cut them into fries shapes.

2 Place the potatoes in a large bowl of cold salted water. Set aside to soak for 20 minutes.

3 Remove the potato slices with a perforated spoon and drain thoroughly. Pat with paper towels until completely dry.

COOK'S TIP

Rinsing the potatoes in cold water before cooking removes the starch, thus preventing them from sticking together. Soaking the potatoes in a bowl of cold salted water actually makes the cooked fries crisper.

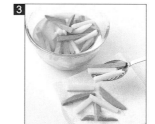

4 Pour the melted butter onto a cookie sheet. Transfer the potato slices to the cookie sheet.

5 Sprinkle with the chili powder and garam masala, turning the potato slices to coat them with the mixture.

6 Cook the fries in a preheated oven, 400°F, turning frequently, for 40 minutes, until browned and cooked through.

7 Drain the fries on paper towels to remove the excess oil and serve immediately.

Vegetable Samosas

These Indian snacks are perfect for a quick or light meal. Served with a salad they can be made in advance and frozen for ease.

NUTRITIONAL INFORMATION

Calories 291	Sugars 2g
Protein 4g	Fat 23g
Carbohydrate . . .18g	Saturates 3g

  20 MINS   30 MINS

MAKES 12

INGREDIENTS

FILLING

2 tbsp vegetable oil

1 onion, chopped

½ tsp ground coriander

½ tsp ground cumin

pinch of turmeric

½ tsp ground ginger

½ tsp garam masala

1 garlic clove, crushed

1½ cups potatoes, diced

1 cup frozen peas, thawed

2 cups spinach, chopped

PASTRY

12 sheets phyllo pastry

oil, for deep-frying

1 To make the filling, heat the oil in a skillet. Add the onion and sauté, stirring frequently, for 1–2 minutes, until softened. Stir in all of the spices and garlic and cook for 1 minute.

2 Add the potatoes and cook over a low heat, stirring frequently, for 5 minutes, until they begin to soften.

3 Stir in the peas and spinach and cook for another 3–4 minutes.

4 Lay the phyllo pastry sheets out on a clean work counter and fold each sheet in half lengthwise.

5 Place 2 tablespoons of the vegetable filling at one end of each folded pastry sheet. Fold over one corner to make a triangle. Continue folding in this way to make a triangular package and seal the edges with water.

6 Repeat with the remaining pastry and the remaining filling.

7 Heat the oil for deep-frying to 350°F or until a cube of bread browns in 30 seconds. Fry the samosas, in batches, for 1–2 minutes until golden. Drain on absorbent paper towels and keep warm while cooking the remainder. Serve immediately.

Stuffed Globe Artichokes

This imaginative and attractive recipe for artichokes stuffed with nuts, tomatoes, olives and mushrooms, has been adapted for the microwave.

NUTRITIONAL INFORMATION

Calories 248	Sugars 8g	
Protein 5g	Fat 19g	
Carbohydrate ...16g	Saturates 2g	

🍲 30 MINS   🕐 25 MINS

SERVES 4

INGREDIENTS

4 globe artichokes

8 tbsp water

4 tbsp lemon juice

1 onion, chopped

1 garlic clove, crushed

2 tbsp olive oil

225 g/8 oz/2 cups button
    mushrooms, chopped

40 g/1½ oz/½ cup pitted black
    olives, sliced

60 g/2 oz/¼ cup sun-dried tomatoes in oil,
    drained and chopped

1 tbsp chopped fresh basil

60 g/2 oz/1 cup fresh
    white breadcrumbs

25 g/1 oz/¼ cup pine nuts, toasted

oil from the jar of sun-dried tomatoes
    for drizzling

salt and pepper

1 Cut the stalks and lower leaves off the artichokes. Snip off the leaf tips with scissors. Place 2 artichokes in a large bowl with half the water and half the lemon juice. Cover and cook on HIGH power for 10 minutes, turning the artichokes over halfway through, until a leaf pulls away easily from the base. Leave to stand, covered, for 3 minutes before draining. Turn the artichokes upside down and leave to cool. Repeat to cook the remaining artichokes.

2 Place the onion, garlic and oil in a bowl. Cover and cook on HIGH power for 2 minutes, stirring once. Add the mushrooms, olives and sun-dried tomatoes. Cover and cook on HIGH power for 2 minutes.

3 Stir in the basil, breadcrumbs and pine nuts. Season to taste with salt and pepper.

4 Turn the artichokes the right way up and carefully pull the leaves apart. Remove the purple-tipped central leaves. Using a teaspoon, scrape out the hairy choke and discard.

5 Divide the stuffing into 4 equal portions and spoon into the centre of each artichoke. Push the leaves back around the stuffing.

6 Arrange in a shallow dish and drizzle over a little oil from the jar of sun-dried tomatoes. Cook on HIGH power for 7–8 minutes to reheat, turning the artichokes around halfway through.

Ciabatta Rolls

Sandwiches are always a welcome snack, but can be mundane. These crisp rolls filled with roast bell peppers and cheese are irresistible.

NUTRITIONAL INFORMATION

Calories 328	Sugars 6g
Protein 8g	Fat 19g
Carbohydrate ...34g	Saturates 9g

15 MINS   10 MINS

SERVES 4

INGREDIENTS

4 ciabatta (Italian bread) rolls

2 tbsp olive oil

1 garlic clove, crushed

FILLING

1 red bell pepper

1 green bell pepper

1 yellow bell pepper

4 radishes, sliced

1 bunch watercress

8 tbsp cream cheese

1 Slice the ciabatta rolls in half. Heat the olive oil and crushed garlic in a saucepan. Pour the garlic and oil mixture over the cut surfaces of the rolls and leave to stand.

2 Halve the bell peppers and place, skin side uppermost, on a broiler rack. Cook under a hot broiler for 8–10 minutes, until just beginning to char. Remove the bell peppers from the broiler, peel, and slice thinly.

3 Arrange the radish slices on one half of each roll with a few watercress leaves. Spoon the cream cheese on top. Pile the bell peppers on top of the cream cheese and top with the other half of the roll. Serve immediately.

Brown Rice Gratin

This dish is extremely versatile and could be made with any vegetables that you have to hand.

NUTRITIONAL INFORMATION

Calories 321   Sugars 6g
Protein . . . . .10g   Fat 18g
Carbohydrate . . .32g   Saturates 9g

15 MINS   1 HOUR

SERVES 4

I N G R E D I E N T S

⅓ cup brown rice

2 tbsp butter or margarine, plus extra
   for greasing

1 red onion, chopped

2 garlic cloves, crushed

1 carrot, cut into thin sticks

1 zucchini, sliced

2¾ oz baby corn cobs,
   halved lengthwise

2 tbsp sunflower seeds

3 tbsp chopped mixed herbs

1 cup grated mozzarella cheese

2 tbsp whole wheat breadcrumbs

salt and pepper

VARIATION

Use an alternative rice, such
as basmati, and flavor the dish
with curry spices, if
you prefer.

1 Cook the rice in a saucepan of boiling lightly salted water for 20 minutes. Drain well.

2 Lightly grease a 3¾-cup ovenproof dish with butter.

3 Heat the butter in a skillet. Add the onion and cook, stirring constantly, for 2 minutes, or until soft and translucent.

4 Add the garlic, carrot, zucchini, and corn and cook, stirring constantly, for 5 minutes more.

5 Mix the rice with the sunflower seeds and mixed herbs and stir into the pan.

6 Stir in half of the mozzarella cheese and season with salt and pepper to taste.

7 Spoon the mixture into the prepared dish and top with the breadcrumbs and remaining cheese. Cook in a preheated oven at 350°F for about 25–30 minutes, or until the cheese has begun to turn golden. Serve immediately.

Stuffed Parathas

This bread can be quite rich and is usually made for special occasions. It can be eaten on its own or with a vegetable curry.

NUTRITIONAL INFORMATION

Calories 391   Sugars 2g
Protein . . . . .6g   Fat 24g
Carbohydrate . . .40g   Saturates 2.5g

 25 MINS   30–35 MINS

SERVES 6

INGREDIENTS

DOUGH

1¾ cups whole wheat flour (ata
or chapati flour)

½ tsp salt

1 cup water

8 tbsp vegetable ghee

2 tbsp ghee, for frying

FILLING

3 medium potatoes

½ tsp turmeric

1 tsp garam masala

1 tsp finely chopped fresh ginger

fresh cilantro leaves

3 green chilies, finely chopped

1 tsp salt

1 To make the parathas, mix the flour, salt, water, and ghee in a bowl to form a dough.

2 Divide the dough into 6–8 equal portions. Roll each portion out onto a floured work counter. Brush the middle of the dough portions with ½ tsp ghee. Fold the dough portions in half, roll into a pipe-like shape, flatten with the palms of your hand, then roll around your finger to form a coil. Roll out again, using flour to dust as and when necessary, to form a round about 7 inches in diameter.

3 Place the potatoes in a saucepan of boiling water and cook until soft enough to be mashed.

4 Blend the turmeric, garam masala, ginger, cilantro, chilies, and salt together in a bowl.

5 Add the spice mixture to the mashed potato and mix well. Spread about 1 tablespoon of the spicy potato mixture on each dough portion and cover with another rolled-out piece of dough. Seal the edges well.

6 Heat 2 teaspoons ghee in a heavy-bottomed skillet. Place the paratas gently in the pan, in batches, and fry, turning and moving them about gently with a flat spoon, until golden.

7 Remove the parathas from the skillet and serve immediately.

Cheese & Onion Rosti

These grated potato cakes are also known as straw cakes, as they resemble a straw mat! Serve them with a tomato sauce or salad.

NUTRITIONAL INFORMATION

Calories	307	Sugars	.........4g
Protein	.........8g	Fat	.........13g
Carbohydrate	...42g	Saturates	.......6g

 10 MINS   40 MINS

SERVES 4

INGREDIENTS

2 lb potatoes

1 onion, grated

½ cup grated Gruyère cheese

2 tbsp chopped parsley

1 tbsp olive oil

2 tbsp butter

salt and pepper

TO GARNISH

shredded green onion

1 small tomato, quartered

1 Parboil the potatoes in a pan of lightly salted boiling water for 10 minutes and leave to cool. Peel the potatoes and grate with a coarse grater. Place the grated potatoes in a large mixing bowl.

COOK'S TIP

The potato cakes should be flattened as much as possible during cooking, otherwise the outside will be cooked before the center.

2 Stir in the onion, cheese, and parsley. Season well with salt and pepper. Divide the potato mixture into 4 portions of equal size and form them into cakes.

3 Heat half of the olive oil and butter in a skillet and cook 2 of the potato cakes over a high heat for 1 minute, then reduce the heat and cook

for 5 minutes, until they are golden underneath. Turn them over and cook for a another 5 minutes.

4 Repeat with the other half of the oil and the remaining butter to cook the remaining 2 cakes. Transfer to warm individual serving plates, garnish, and serve immediately.

Mini Kabobs

Cubes of tofu are speared on bamboo satay sticks with crisp vegetables and marinated with lemon juice and olive oil.

NUTRITIONAL INFORMATION

Calories ....322 Sugars 9g
Protein ....13g Fat 24g
Carbohydrate ...13g Saturates 7g

25 MINS   15–20 MINS

SERVES 6

I N G R E D I E N T S

10½ oz tofu, cut into cubes

1 large red bell pepper, seeded and
    cut into small squares

1 large yellow bell pepper, seeded and
    cut into small squares

6 oz mushrooms

1 small zucchini, sliced

finely grated zest and juice of 1 lemon

3 tbsp olive oil

1 tbsp chopped parsley

1 tsp sugar

salt and pepper

parsley sprigs, to garnish

S A U C E

1 cup cashews

1 tbsp butter

1 garlic clove, crushed

1 shallot, finely chopped

1 tsp ground coriander

1 tsp ground cumin

1 tbsp sugar

1 tbsp shredded coconut

⅔ cup plain yogurt

1 Thread the tofu cubes, bell peppers, mushrooms, and zucchini on to bamboo satay sticks. Arrange them in a shallow dish.

2 Mix together the lemon zest and juice, olive oil, parsley and sugar. Season to taste with salt and pepper. Pour over the kabobs, and brush them with the mixture. Leave for 10 minutes.

3 To make the sauce, scatter the cashews onto a cookie sheet and toast them under a hot broiler until lightly browned.

4 Melt the butter in a saucepan and sauté the garlic and shallot gently until softened. Transfer to a blender or food processor and add the nuts, coriander, cumin, sugar, coconut, and yogurt. Process for about 15 seconds, or until combined. Alternatively, chop the nuts very finely and mix with the remaining ingredients.

5 Place the kabobs under a preheated broiler and cook, turning and basting with the lemon juice mixture, until lightly browned. Garnish with sprigs of parsley, and serve with the cashew sauce.

Stuffed Mushrooms

Use large mushrooms for this recipe for their flavor and suitability for filling.

NUTRITIONAL INFORMATION

Calories 273   Sugars 5g
Protein . . . . .13g   Fat 18g
Carbohydrate . . .15g   Saturates 5g

15 MINS   25 MINS

SERVES 4

I N G R E D I E N T S

8 large mushrooms

1 tbsp olive oil

1 small leek, chopped

1 celery stalk, chopped

3½ oz firm tofu, diced

1 zucchini, chopped

1 carrot, chopped

1 cup whole wheat breadcrumbs

2 tbsp chopped basil

1 tbsp tomato paste

2 tbsp pine nuts

¾ cup grated cheddar cheese

⅔ cup vegetable stock

salt and pepper

salad, to serve

1 Remove the stalks from the mushrooms and chop finely. Reserve the caps.

2 Heat the olive oil in a large, heavy-bottomed skillet over a medium heat. Add the chopped mushroom stalks, leek, celery, tofu, zucchini, and carrot and cook, stirring constantly, for 3–4 minutes.

3 Stir in the breadcrumbs, chopped basil, tomato paste, and pine nuts. Season with salt and pepper to taste and mix thoroughly.

4 Spoon the mixture into the mushroom caps and top with the grated cheese.

5 Place the mushrooms in a shallow ovenproof dish and pour the vegetable stock around them.

6 Cook in a preheated oven at 425°F for 20 minutes, or until cooked through and the cheese has melted. Remove the mushrooms from the dish and serve immediately with a salad.

Potato Fritters

Chunks of cooked potato are coated first in Parmesan cheese, then in a light batter before being fried until golden for a delicious hot snack.

NUTRITIONAL INFORMATION

Calories ....599 Sugars 9g
Protein ....22g Fat 39g
Carbohydrate ...42g Saturates 13g

 20 MINS   20-25 MINS

SERVES 4

INGREDIENTS

1 lb 2 oz potatoes, cut into
　large cubes

1¼ cups grated Parmesan cheese

oil, for deep-frying

SAUCE

2 tbsp butter

1 onion, halved and sliced

2 garlic cloves, crushed

¼ cup all-purpose flour

1¼ cups milk

1 tbsp chopped parsley

BATTER

½ cup all-purpose flour

1 small egg

⅔ cup milk

1 To make the sauce, melt the butter in a saucepan and cook the sliced onion and garlic over a low heat, stirring frequently, for 2–3 minutes. Add the flour and cook, stirring constantly, for 1 minute.

2 Remove from the heat and stir in the milk and parsley. Return to the heat and bring to a boil. Keep warm.

3 Meanwhile, cook the cubed potatoes in a saucepan of boiling water for 5–10 minutes, until just firm. Do not overcook or they will fall apart.

4 Drain the potatoes and toss them in the Parmesan cheese. If the potatoes are still slightly wet, the cheese sticks to them and coats them well.

5 To make the batter, place the flour in a mixing bowl and gradually beat in the egg and milk until smooth. Dip the potato cubes into the batter to coat them.

6 In a large saucepan or deep-fryer, heat the oil to 350°F or until a cube of bread browns in 30 seconds. Add the fritters and cook for 3–4 minutes, or until golden.

7 Remove the fritters with a perforated spoon and drain well. Transfer them to a warm serving bowl and serve immediately with the garlic sauce.

Bombay Bowl

You can use dried garbanzo beans for this popular snack, but the canned sort are quick and easy without sacrificing much flavor.

NUTRITIONAL INFORMATION

Calories 183	Sugars 6g
Protein 9g	Fat 3g
Carbohydrate ...33g	Saturates 0.3g

 15 MINS   15 MINS

SERVES 4

INGREDIENTS

14 oz can garbanzo beans, drained

2 medium potatoes

1 medium onion

2 tbsp tamarind paste

6 tbsp water

1 tsp chili powder

2 tsp sugar

1 tsp salt

TO GARNISH

1 tomato, sliced

2 fresh green chilies, chopped

fresh cilantro leaves

COOK'S TIP

Cream-colored and resembling a hazelnut in appearance, garbanzo beans have a nutty flavor and slightly crunchy texture. Indian cooks grind these to make a flour called gram or besan, which is used to make breads and thicken sauces.

1 Place the drained garbanzo beans in a bowl.

2 Using a sharp knife, cut the potatoes into even-size dice.

3 Place the diced potatoes in a saucepan of water and boil until cooked through. Test by inserting the tip of a knife into the potatoes—they should feel soft and tender. Drain and set the potatoes aside until required.

4 Using a sharp knife, finely chop the onion. Set aside until required.

5 Mix together the tamarind paste and water in a small mixing bowl.

6 Add the chili powder, sugar, and salt to the tamarind paste mixture and mix together. Pour the mixture over the garbanzo beans.

7 Add the onion and the diced potatoes, and stir to mix. Season to taste with a little salt.

8 Transfer to a serving bowl and garnish with tomatoes, chilies, and cilantro leaves.

Spiced Corn & Nut Mix

A tasty mixture of buttery-spiced nuts, raisins, and popcorn to enjoy as a snack or with pre-dinner drinks.

NUTRITIONAL INFORMATION

Calories 372	Sugars 9g
Protein 8g	Fat 31g
Carbohydrate ...16g	Saturates 9g

5 MINS   10 MINS

SERVES 6

INGREDIENTS

2 tbsp vegetable oil

¼ cup popping corn

¼ cup butter

1 garlic clove, crushed

⅓ cup unblanched almonds

½ cup unsalted cashews

½ cup unsalted peanuts

1 tsp vegetarian Worcestershire sauce

1 tsp curry powder or paste

¼ tsp chili powder

⅓ cup seedless raisins

salt

1 Heat the oil in a saucepan. Add the popping corn, stir well, then cover and cook over a fairly high heat for 3-5 minutes, holding the saucepan lid firmly and shaking the pan frequently until the popping stops.

2 Turn the popped corn into a dish, discarding any unpopped corn kernels.

3 Melt the butter in a skillet, add the garlic, almonds, cashews, and peanuts, then stir in the Worcestershire sauce, curry powder or paste and chili powder and cook over a medium heat, stirring frequently, for 2–3 minutes.

4 Remove the pan from the heat and stir in the raisins and popped corn. Season with salt to taste and mix thoroughly. Transfer to a serving bowl and serve warm or cold.

VARIATION

Use a mixture of any unsalted nuts of your choice—walnuts, pecans, hazelnuts, Brazils, macadamia, and pine nuts. For a less fiery flavor, omit the curry and chili powder and add 1 tsp cumin seeds, 1 tsp ground coriander, and tsp paprika.

Potato & Mushroom Bake

Use any mixture of mushrooms on hand for this creamy layered bake. It can be served straight from the dish in which it is cooked.

NUTRITIONAL INFORMATION

Calories	304	Sugars	.........2g
Protein	.........4g	Fat	..........24g
Carbohydrate	...20g	Saturates	......15g

🥔 15 MINS 🕐 1 HOUR

SERVES 4

I N G R E D I E N T S

2 tbsp butter

1 lb 2 oz potatoes, thinly sliced

2 cups sliced mixed mushrooms

1 tbsp chopped rosemary

4 tbsp chopped chives

2 garlic cloves, crushed

⅔ cup heavy cream

salt and pepper

snipped chives, to garnish

1 Grease a shallow, round ovenproof dish with butter.

2 Parboil the sliced potatoes in a saucepan of boiling water for 10 minutes. Drain well. Layer a quarter of the potatoes in the base of the dish.

COOK'S TIP

For a special occasion, bake in a lined cake pan and then turn out to serve.

3 Arrange one-quarter of the mushrooms on top of the potatoes and sprinkle with one-quarter of the rosemary, chives, and garlic. Continue making layers in the same order, finishing with a layer of potatoes on top.

4 Pour the cream over the top of the potatoes. Season to taste with salt and pepper.

5 Cook in a preheated oven at 375°F for about 45 minutes, or until the bake is golden brown and piping hot.

6 Garnish with snipped chives and serve immediately straight from the dish.

Vegetable Enchiladas

This Mexican dish uses prepared tortillas, readily available in supermarkets, which are then filled with a spicy vegetable mixture.

NUTRITIONAL INFORMATION

Calories 309	Sugars 14g
Protein 12g	Fat 19g
Carbohydrate . . .23g	Saturates 8g

🍽 20 MINS   🕐 55 MINS

SERVES 4

I N G R E D I E N T S

4 flour tortillas

¾ cup grated cheddar cheese

F I L L I N G

2¾ oz spinach

2 tbsp olive oil

8 baby corn cobs, sliced

1 tbsp frozen peas, thawed

1 red bell pepper, seeded and diced

1 carrot, diced

1 leek, sliced

2 garlic cloves, crushed

1 red chili, chopped

salt and pepper

S A U C E

1¼ cups strained tomatoes

2 shallots, chopped

1 garlic clove, crushed

1¼ cups vegetable stock

1 tsp sugar

1 tsp chili powder

1 To make the filling, blanch the spinach in a pan of boiling water for 2 minutes. Drain well, pressing out as much excess moisture as possible, and chop.

2 Heat the oil in a skillet over a medium heat. Add the baby corn cobs, peas, bell pepper, carrot, leek, garlic, and chili and sauté, stirring briskly, for 3–4 minutes. Stir in the spinach and season well with salt and pepper to taste.

3 Put all the sauce ingredients in a heavy-bottomed saucepan and bring to a boil, stirring constantly. Cook over a high heat, stirring constantly, for 20 minutes, until thickened and reduced by a third.

4 Spoon a quarter of the filling along the center of each tortilla. Roll the tortillas around the filling and place, seam side down, in a single layer in an ovenproof dish.

5 Pour the sauce over the tortillas and sprinkle the cheese on top. Cook in a preheated oven at 350°F for 20 minutes, or until the cheese has melted and browned. Serve immediately.

Vegetable Burgers & Fries

These spicy vegetable burgers are delicious, especially when served with the light oven-baked fries and in a warm bun or roll.

NUTRITIONAL INFORMATION

Calories	.461	Sugars	.4g
Protein	.18g	Fat	.17g
Carbohydrate	.64g	Saturates	.2g

 45 MINS 1 HOUR

SERVES 4

I N G R E D I E N T S

VEGETABLE BURGERS

3½ oz spinach

1 tbsp olive oil

1 leek, chopped

2 garlic cloves, crushed

1½ cups chopped mushrooms

10½ oz firm tofu, chopped

1 tsp chili powder

1 tsp curry powder

1 tbsp chopped cilantro

1½ cups fresh whole wheat breadcrumbs

1 tbsp olive oil

burger roll and salad, to serve

FRIES

2 large potatoes

2 tbsp flour

1 tsp chili powder

2 tbsp olive oil

1 To make the burgers, cook the spinach in a little boiling water for 2 minutes. Drain thoroughly and pat dry with paper towels.

2 Heat the oil in a skillet and sauté the leek and garlic for 2–3 minutes. Add the remaining ingredients, except the breadcrumbs, and cook for 5–7 minutes, until the vegetables have softened. Toss in the spinach and cook for 1 minute.

3 Transfer the mixture to a food processor and process for 30 seconds, until almost smooth. Transfer to a bowl, stir in the breadcrumbs, mixing well, and leave until cool enough to handle. Using floured hands, form the mixture into four equal-size burgers. Leave to chill for 30 minutes.

4 To make the fries, cut the potatoes into thin wedges and cook in a pan of boiling water for 10 minutes. Drain and toss in the flour and chili powder. Lay the fries on a cookie sheet and sprinkle with the oil. Cook in a preheated oven at 400°F for 30 minutes, or until golden.

5 Meanwhile, heat 1 tbsp oil in a skillet and cook the burgers for 8–10 minutes, turning once. Serve with salad in a roll with the fries.

Potato Omelet

This quick chunky omelet has pieces of potato cooked into
the egg mixture and is then filled with feta cheese and spinach.

NUTRITIONAL INFORMATION

Calories	564	Sugars 6g
Protein	. . . . .30g	Fat 39g
Carbohydrate	. . .25g	Saturates 19g

 20 MINS   25-30 MINS

SERVES 4

INGREDIENTS

⅓ cup butter

6 potatoes, diced

3 garlic cloves, crushed

1 tsp paprika

2 tomatoes, peeled, seeded, and diced

12 eggs

pepper

FILLING

8 oz baby spinach

1 tsp fennel seeds

4½ oz feta cheese, diced

4 tbsp plain yogurt

1 Heat 2 tbsp of the butter in a skillet and cook the potatoes over a low heat, stirring constantly, for 7–10 minutes until golden. Transfer to a bowl.

2 Add the garlic, paprika, and tomatoes to the pan and cook for 2 minutes more.

3 Whisk the eggs together and season with pepper. Pour the eggs into the potatoes and mix well.

4 Cook the spinach in boiling water for 1 minute, until just wilted. Drain and refresh under cold running water. Pat dry

with paper towels. Stir in the fennel seeds, feta cheese, and yogurt.

5 Heat a quarter of the remaining butter in a 6 inch omelet pan. Ladle a quarter of the egg and potato mixture into the pan. Cook, turning once, for 2 minutes, until set.

6 Transfer the omelet to a serving plate. Spoon a quarter of the spinach mixture onto one half of the omelet, then fold the omelet in half over the filling. Repeat to make 4 omelets.

VARIATION

Use any other cheese, such as blue cheese, instead of the feta and blanched broccoli in place of the baby spinach, if you prefer.

Three-Cheese Fondue

A hot cheese dip made from three different cheeses can be prepared easily and with guaranteed success in the microwave.

NUTRITIONAL INFORMATION

Calories 565	Sugars 1g
Protein 29g	Fat 38g
Carbohydrate . . .15g	Saturates 24g

 15 MINS   10 MINS

SERVES 4

I N G R E D I E N T S

1 garlic clove

1¼ cups dry white wine

2 cups grated mild cheddar cheese

1 cup grated Gruyère cheese

1 cup grated mozzarella cheese

2 tbsp cornstarch

pepper

TO SERVE

French bread

vegetables, such as zucchini, mushrooms, baby corn cobs, and cauliflower

COOK'S TIP

Make sure you add the cheese to the wine gradually, mixing well in between each addition, otherwise the mixture might curdle.

1 Bruise the garlic by placing the flat side of a knife on top and pressing down with the heel of your hand.

2 Rub the garlic around the inside of a large bowl. Discard the garlic.

3 Pour the wine into the bowl and heat, uncovered, on HIGH power for 3–4 minutes, until hot but not boiling.

4 Gradually add the cheddar and Gruyère cheeses, stirring well after each addition, then add the mozzarella. Stir until completely melted.

5 Mix the cornstarch with a little water to a smooth paste and stir into the cheese mixture. Season to taste with pepper.

6 Cover and cook on MEDIUM power for 6 minutes, stirring twice during cooking, until the sauce is smooth.

7 Cut the French bread into cubes and the vegetables into sticks, slices, or flowerets. To serve, keep the fondue warm over a fondue burner or reheat as necessary in the microwave. Dip in cubes of French bread and sticks, slices, or flowerets of vegetables.

Casseroled Potatoes

This potato dish is cooked in the oven with leeks and white wine. It is very quick and simple to make and is delicious for lunch.

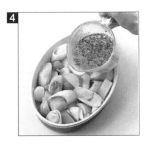

NUTRITIONAL INFORMATION

Calories	200	Sugars	.........3g
Protein	.........6g	Fat	...........4g
Carbohydrate	...32g	Saturates	.......2g

15 MINS   45 MINS

SERVES 4

I N G R E D I E N T S

1½ lb potatoes, cut into chunks

1 tbsp butter

2 leeks, sliced

⅔ cup dry white wine

⅔ cup vegetable stock

1 tbsp lemon juice

2 tbsp chopped mixed herbs

salt and pepper

salad, to serve

T O   G A R N I S H

grated lemon zest

mixed herbs (optional)

1 Cook the potato chunks in a saucepan of lightly salted boiling water for 5 minutes. Drain thoroughly.

2 Meanwhile, melt the butter in a skillet and sauté the leeks for 5 minutes, or until they have softened.

3 Spoon the partly cooked potatoes and leeks into an ovenproof dish and spread out over the base.

4 Mix together the white wine, vegetable stock, lemon juice, and chopped mixed herbs. Season to taste with salt and pepper, then pour the mixture over the potatoes.

5 Cook in a preheated oven at 375°F for 35 minutes, or until the potatoes are tender.

6 Garnish the potato casserole with lemon zest and fresh herbs, if using, and serve immediately with salad.

COOK'S TIP

Cover the ovenproof dish halfway through cooking if the leeks start to brown on the top.

Vegetable Crêpes

Crêpes are ideal for filling with your favorite ingredients. In this recipe they are packed with a spicy vegetable filling.

NUTRITIONAL INFORMATION

Calories	509	Sugars	........10g
Protein	........17g	Fat	..........34g
Carbohydrate	...36g	Saturates	.......9g

 15 MINS   45 MINS

SERVES 4

I N G R E D I E N T S

CREPES

¾ cup all-purpose flour

pinch of salt

1 egg, beaten

1¼ cups milk

vegetable oil, for frying

FILLING

2 tbsp vegetable oil

1 leek, shredded

½ tsp chili powder

½ tsp ground cumin

1¾ oz snow peas

3½ oz button mushrooms,

1 red bell pepper, sliced

¼ cup cashews, chopped

SAUCE

2 tbsp margarine

3 tbsp all-purpose flour

⅔ cup vegetable stock

⅔ cup milk

1 tsp Dijon mustard

¾ cup grated cheddar cheese

2 tbsp chopped cilantro

1 For the crêpes, sift the flour and salt into a bowl. Beat in the egg and milk to make a batter.

2 For the filling, heat the oil and sauté the leek for 2–3 minutes. Add the remaining ingredients and cook, stirring, for 5 minutes.

3 For the sauce, melt the margarine in a pan and add the flour. Cook, stirring, for 1 minute. Remove from the heat, stir in the stock and milk, and return to the heat. Bring to a boil, stirring until thick.

Add the mustard, half the cheese and the cilantro; cook for 1 minute.

4 Heat 1 tbsp of oil in a small skillet. Pour off the oil and add an eighth of the batter. Tilt to cover the base. Cook for 2 minutes, turn, and cook the other side for 1 minute. Repeat with the remaining batter. Spoon a little of the filling along the center of each crêpe and roll up. Place in a flameproof dish and pour the sauce on top. Top with cheese and heat under a hot broiler for 3–5 minutes or until the cheese melts.

Cheese & Potato Slices

This recipe takes a while to prepare but it is well worth the effort. The golden potato slices coated in breadcrumbs and cheese are delicious.

NUTRITIONAL INFORMATION

Calories 560	Sugars 3g	
Protein 19g	Fat 31g	
Carbohydrate ...55g	Saturates 7g	

🥪 10 MINS   🕐 40 MINS

SERVES 4

INGREDIENTS

3 large potatoes, unpeeled and
thickly sliced

1 cup fresh white breadcrumbs

½ cup grated Parmesan cheese

1½ tsp chili powder

2 eggs, beaten

oil, for deep frying

chili powder, for dusting (optional)

1 Cook the sliced potatoes in a saucepan of boiling water for about 10–15 minutes, or until the potatoes are just tender. Drain thoroughly.

2 Mix the breadcrumbs, cheese, and chili powder together in a bowl, then transfer to a shallow dish. Pour the beaten eggs into a separate shallow dish.

3 Dip the potato slices first in egg and then roll them in the breadcrumbs to coat completely.

4 Heat the oil in a large saucepan or deep-fryer to 350°F or until a cube of bread browns in 30 seconds. Cook the cheese and potato slices, in several batches, for 4–5 minutes or until a golden brown color.

5 Remove the cheese and potato slices from the oil with a perforated spoon and drain thoroughly on paper towels. Keep the cheese and potato slices warm while you cook the remaining batches.

6 Transfer the cheese and potato slices to warm individual serving plates. Dust lightly with chili powder, if using, and serve immediately.

COOK'S TIP

The cheese and potato slices may be coated in the breadcrumb mixture ahead of time and then stored in the refrigerator until ready to use.

Spiced Semolina

A south Indian savory snack which is very quick and easy to prepare, this should be served warm. It has a really lovely aroma.

NUTRITIONAL INFORMATION

Calories	556	Sugars	.........2g
Protein	.........9g	Fat	..........41g
Carbohydrate	...40g	Saturates	.......5g

5 MINS   15 MINS

SERVES 4

I N G R E D I E N T S

⅔ cup vegetable oil

1 tsp mixed onion and mustard seeds

4 dried red chilies

4 curry leaves (fresh or dried)

8 tbsp coarse semolina

½ cup cashews

1 tsp salt

⅔ cup water

1 Heat the vegetable oil in a large, heavy-bottomed skillet over a fairly low heat.

2 Add the mixed onion and mustard seeds, dried red chilies, and curry leaves and fry, stirring constantly, for about 1 minute.

3 Reduce the heat to low and add the coarse semolina and the cashews. Stir-fry for about 5 minutes, moving the mixture around the pan all the time to prevent it from catching and burning on the base.

4 Add the salt to the pan, mixing well, and continue to stir-fry over a low heat, keeping the mixture moving all the time.

5 Add the water and cook, stirring constantly, until the mixture is beginning to thicken.

6 Serve the spiced semolina warm as a delicious snack with Indian tea.

COOK'S TIP

Curry leaves are very similar in appearance to bay leaves but are very different in flavor. They can be bought both fresh and dried. They are mainly used to flavor lentil dishes and vegetable curries.

Vegetable Hash

This is a quick one-pan dish which is ideal for a snack. Packed with color and flavor, it is very versatile because you can add other vegetables.

NUTRITIONAL INFORMATION

Calories ....182 Sugars 6g
Protein ....5g Fat 4g
Carbohydrate ...34g Saturates 0.5g

🥔 15 MINS   🕐 30 MINS

SERVES 4

INGREDIENTS

1½ lb potatoes, cubed

1 tbsp olive oil

2 garlic cloves, crushed

1 green bell pepper, seeded
   and cubed

1 yellow bell pepper, seeded
   and cubed

3 tomatoes, diced

1 cup mushrooms, halved

1 tbsp vegetarian Worcestershire sauce

2 tbsp chopped basil

salt and pepper

basil sprigs, to garnish

warm, crusty bread, to serve

1 Cook the potatoes in a saucepan of boiling salted water for 7–8 minutes. Drain well and reserve.

2 Heat the olive oil in a large, heavy-bottomed skillet. Add the potatoes and cook, stirring constantly, for 8–10 minutes, until browned.

3 Add the garlic and bell peppers and cook, stirring frequently, for 2–3 minutes.

4 Stir in the tomatoes and mushrooms and cook, stirring frequently, for 5–6 minutes.

5 Stir in the Worcestershire sauce and basil and season to taste with salt and pepper. Transfer to a warm serving dish, garnish with basil sprigs, and serve with warm bread.

COOK'S TIP

Most brands of Worcestershire sauce contain anchovies, so check the label to make sure you choose a vegetarian variety.

Vegetable Jambalaya

This dish traditionally contains spicy sausage, but it is equally delicious filled with vegetables in this spicy vegetarian version.

NUTRITIONAL INFORMATION

Calories 181   Sugars 8g
Protein . . . . .6g   Fat 7g
Carbohydrate . . .25g   Saturates 1g

10 MINS   55 MINS

SERVES 4

I N G R E D I E N T S

½ cup brown rice

2 tbsp olive oil

2 garlic cloves, crushed

1 red onion, cut into eight

1 eggplant, diced

1 green bell pepper, diced

1¾ oz baby corn cobs,
   halved lengthwise

½ cup frozen peas

3½ oz small broccoli flowerets

⅔ cup vegetable stock

8 oz can chopped tomatoes

1 tbsp tomato paste

1 tsp creole seasoning

½ tsp chili flakes

salt and pepper

COOK'S TIP

Use a mixture of different kinds of rice, such as wild or red rice, for color and texture. Cook the rice ahead of time for a speedier recipe.

1 Cook the rice in a large saucepan of salted boiling water for 20 minutes, or until cooked through. Drain, rinse with boiling water, drain again, and set aside.

2 Heat the oil in a heavy-bottomed skillet and cook the garlic and onion, stirring constantly, for 2–3 minutes.

3 Add the eggplant, bell pepper, corn, peas, and broccoli to the pan and cook, stirring occasionally, for 2–3 minutes.

4 Stir in the vegetable stock and canned tomatoes, tomato paste, creole seasoning, and chili flakes.

5 Season to taste and cook over a low heat for 15–20 minutes, or until the vegetables are tender.

6 Stir the brown rice into the vegetable mixture and cook, mixing well, for 3–4 minutes, or until hot. Transfer the vegetable jambalaya to a warm serving dish and serve immediately.

Potato & Spinach Triangles

These small pastries are made with crisp phyllo and filled with a tasty spinach and potato mixture flavored with chili and tomato.

NUTRITIONAL INFORMATION

Calories 514	Sugars 4g	
Protein 9g	Fat 37g	
Carbohydrate . . .37g	Saturates 8g	

🥔 25 MINS   🕐 35 MINS

SERVES 4

I N G R E D I E N T S

2 tbsp butter, melted, plus extra
   for greasing

8 oz potatoes, finely diced

1 lb 2 oz baby spinach

1 tomato, seeded and chopped

¼ tsp chili powder

½ tsp lemon juice

8 oz phyllo pastry, thawed if frozen

salt and pepper

crisp salad, to serve

L E M O N   M A Y O N N A I S E

⅔ cup mayonnaise

2 tsp lemon juice

zest of 1 lemon

1 Lightly grease a cookie sheet with a little butter.

2 Cook the potatoes in a saucepan of lightly salted boiling water for 10 minutes, or until cooked through. Drain thoroughly and place in a mixing bowl.

3 Meanwhile, put the spinach in a saucepan with 2 tbsp of water, cover, and cook over a low heat for 2 minutes, until wilted. Drain the spinach thoroughly, squeezing out excess moisture, and add to the potato.

4 Stir in the chopped tomato, chili powder, and lemon juice. Season to taste with salt and pepper.

5 Lightly brush 8 sheets of phyllo pastry with melted butter. Spread out 4 of the sheets and lay the other 4 on top of each. Cut them into rectangles about 8 x 4 inches.

6 Spoon the potato and spinach mixture on to one end of each rectangle. Fold a corner of the pastry over the filling, fold the pointed end back over the pastry strip, then fold over the remaining pastry to form a triangle.

7 Place the triangles on the cookie sheet and bake in a preheated oven at 375°F for 20 minutes, or until golden brown.

8 To make the mayonnaise, mix the mayonnaise, lemon juice, and lemon zest together in a small bowl. Serve the potato and spinach phyllo triangles warm or cold with the lemon mayonnaise and a crisp salad.

Mixed Rice, Nuts, & Raisins

This is one of the most popular nut mixtures in India and is very tasty.
Make a large quantity and store it in an airtight container.

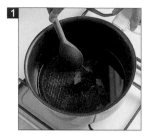

NUTRITIONAL INFORMATION

Calories 568	Sugars 28g	
Protein 6g	Fat 39g	
Carbohydrate . . .51g	Saturates 4g	

  3¼ HOURS   15–20 MINS

SERVES 4

INGREDIENTS

1¼ cups vegetable oil

2 tsp onion seeds

6 curry leaves

3 cups parva (flaked rice)

2 tbsp peanuts

2 tbsp raisins

5 tbsp sugar

2 tsp salt

2 tsp chili powder

1¾ oz sev (optional)

⅓ cup chana dal, soaked in
   cold water for 3 hours

1 Heat the oil in a saucepan. Add the onion seeds and the curry leaves and fry, stirring constantly, until the onion seeds are crisp and golden.

2 Add the parva (flaked rice) to the mixture in the pan and fry until crisp and golden (do not allow to burn).

3 Remove the mixture from the pan and drain on paper towels so that any excess oil is soaked up.

4 Fry the peanuts in the remaining oil, stirring constantly.

5 Add the peanuts to the flaked rice mixture, stirring to mix well.

6 Add the raisins, sugar, salt, and chili powder and mix together. Mix in the sev (if using). Transfer to a serving dish.

7 Re-heat the oil remaining in the pan. Drain the soaked chana dal, add to the pan, and fry until golden. Add to the other ingredients in the serving dish and mix together.

8 This dish can be eaten immediately or stored in an airtight container until you need it.

COOK'S TIP

Sev are very thin sticks made of gram flour which can be bought in Indian and Pakistani grocers.

Cumin Seed Pastries

A simple-to-make snack which will retain its crispness if stored in an airtight container. Serve with drinks or at a coffee break.

NUTRITIONAL INFORMATION

Calories 465	Sugars 0.6g
Protein 4g	Fat 38g
Carbohydrate ...29g	Saturates 4g

 15 MINS   15-20 MINS

SERVES 4

I N G R E D I E N T S

1⅓ cups all-purpose flour

1 tsp baking powder

½ tsp salt

1 tbsp black cumin seeds

½ cup water

1¼ cups oil

1 Place the flour in a large mixing bowl. Add the baking powder, salt, and the black cumin seeds and stir to mix.

2 Add the water to the dry ingredients and mix together until combined to form a soft, elastic dough.

3 Roll out the dough on to a clean work counter to about ¼ inch thick.

4 Using a sharp knife, score the dough to form diamond shapes. Re-roll the trimmings and cut out more diamond shapes until all of the dough has been used up.

5 Heat the oil in a large pan to 350°F or until a cube of bread browns in 30 seconds.

6 Carefully place the pastry diamonds in the oil, in batches if necessary, and deep-fry until golden brown.

7 Remove the diamond pastries with a perforated spoon and drain on paper towels. Serve with a dal for dipping or store and serve when required.

COOK'S TIP

Black cumin seeds are used here for their strong aromatic flavor. White cumin seeds may not be used as a substitute.

Pasta & Noodles

Pasta is one of the most popular and versatile ingredients available, and it is both nourishing and satisfying. Fresh or dried pasta is made in a variety of flavors and colors,

shapes and sizes, all of which work well with a number of vegetarian sauces. Pasta combines well with vegetables, herbs, nuts, and cheeses to provide scores of interesting and tasty meals. Noodles are also quick to cook and provide good basic food that can be dressed up in all kinds of different ways. Often flavored with Asian ingredients, the noodle recipes in this chapter are sure to liven up a vegetarian diet.

Baked Pasta

This pasta dish is baked in a bowl and served cut into slices. It looks and tastes terrific and is great when you want to impress.

NUTRITIONAL INFORMATION

Calories	179	Sugars	.........6g
Protein	.........8g	Fat	..........10g
Carbohydrate	...16g	Saturates	.......3g

10 MINS   1 HR 5 MINS

SERVES 8

INGREDIENTS

1 cup dried pasta shapes,
   such as penne

1 tbsp olive oil

1 leek, chopped

3 garlic cloves, crushed

1 green bell pepper, seeded and chopped

14 oz can diced tomatoes

2 tbsp chopped, pitted black olives

2 eggs, beaten

1 tbsp chopped basil

TOMATO SAUCE

1 tbsp olive oil

1 onion, chopped

8 oz can diced tomatoes

1 tsp sugar

2 tbsp tomato paste

¾ cup vegetable stock

salt and pepper

1 Cook the pasta in a saucepan of boiling lightly salted water for 8 minutes. Drain thoroughly.

2 Meanwhile, heat the oil in a saucepan. Add the leek and garlic and sauté, stirring constantly, for 2 minutes. Add the bell pepper, tomatoes, and olives and cook for a further 5 minutes.

3 Remove the pan from the heat and stir in the pasta, beaten eggs, and basil. Season well, and spoon into a lightly greased 4 cup ovenproof bowl.

4 Place the bowl in a roasting pan and half-fill the pan with boiling water. Cover and cook in a preheated oven at 350°F for 40 minutes, until set.

5 To make the sauce, heat the oil in a pan and sauté the onion for 2 minutes. Add the remaining ingredients and cook for 10 minutes. Put the sauce in a food processor or blender and process until smooth. Return to a clean saucepan and heat through.

6 Turn the pasta out of the bowl onto a warm plate. Slice and serve with the tomato sauce.

Pasta Provençale

A Mediterranean mixture of red bell peppers, garlic, and zucchini cooked in olive oil and tossed with pasta.

NUTRITIONAL INFORMATION

Calories	487	Sugars	........14g
Protein	........17g	Fat	..........24g
Carbohydrate	...53g	Saturates	.......8g

5 MINS   (clock) 20 MINS

SERVES 4

I N G R E D I E N T S

3 tbsp olive oil

1 onion, sliced

2 garlic cloves, chopped

3 red bell peppers, seeded
and cut into strips

3 zucchini, sliced

14 oz can diced tomatoes

3 tbsp sun-dried tomato paste

2 tbsp chopped fresh basil

8 oz fresh pasta spirals

1 cup grated Gruyère cheese

salt and pepper

fresh basil sprigs, to garnish

1 Heat the oil in a heavy-bottomed saucepan or flameproof casserole dish. Add the onion and garlic and cook, stirring occasionally, until softened. Add the bell peppers and zucchini and fry , stirring occasionally, for 5 minutes.

2 Add the tomatoes, sun-dried tomato paste, and basil and season to taste with salt and pepper. Cover and cook for 5 minutes more.

3 Meanwhile, bring a large saucepan of salted water to a boil and add the pasta. Stir and bring back to a boil.

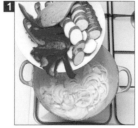

Reduce the heat slightly and cook, uncovered, for 3 minutes, until just tender. Drain thoroughly and add to the vegetables. Toss gently to mix well.

4 Transfer to a shallow ovenproof dish and sprinkle with the cheese.

5 Cook under a preheated broiler for 5 minutes, until the cheese is golden brown and bubbling. Garnish with basil sprigs and serve immediately.

Vegetable Cannelloni

This dish is made with prepared cannelloni tubes, but may also be made by rolling ready-bought lasagne sheets.

NUTRITIONAL INFORMATION

Calories 594	Sugars 12g
Protein 13g	Fat 38g
Carbohydrate ...52g	Saturates 7g

10 MINS   45 MINS

SERVES 4

I N G R E D I E N T S

1 eggplant

½ cup olive oil

8 oz spinach

2 garlic cloves, crushed

1 tsp ground cumin

1 cup mushrooms, chopped

12 cannelloni tubes

salt and pepper

TOMATO SAUCE

1 tbsp olive oil

1 onion, chopped

2 garlic cloves, crushed

2 x 14 oz cans diced tomatoes

1 tsp sugar

2 tbsp chopped basil

½ cup sliced mozzarella

COOK'S TIP

You can prepare the tomato sauce in advance and store it in the refrigerator for up to 24 hours.

1 Cut the eggplant into small dice.

2 Heat the oil in a skillet. Add the eggplant and cook over a moderate heat, stirring frequently, for 2–3 minutes.

3 Add the spinach, garlic, cumin, and mushrooms. Season and cook, stirring, for 2–3 minutes. Spoon the mixture into the cannelloni tubes and place in an ovenproof dish in a single layer.

4 To make the sauce, heat the olive oil in a saucepan and sauté the onion and garlic for 1 minute. Add the tomatoes, sugar, and chopped basil and bring to a boil. Reduce the heat and simmer for about 5 minutes. Pour the sauce over the cannelloni tubes.

5 Arrange the sliced mozzarella on top of the sauce and cook in a preheated oven at 375°F for 30 minutes, or until the cheese is bubbling and golden brown. Serve immediately.

Pear & Walnut Pasta

This is quite an unusual combination of ingredients in a savory dish, but is absolutely wonderful tossed into a thin pasta, such as spaghetti.

NUTRITIONAL INFORMATION

Calories	508	Sugars 9g
Protein	........15g	Fat 27g
Carbohydrate	...50g	Saturates 11g

 10 MINS　　 20 MINS

SERVES 4

INGREDIENTS

8 oz dried spaghetti

2 small ripe pears, peeled and sliced

1¾ cup vegetable stock

6 tbsp dry white wine

2 tbsp butter

1 tbsp olive oil

1 red onion, quartered and sliced

1 garlic clove, crushed

½ cup walnut halves

2 tbsp chopped oregano

1 tbsp lemon juice

2¾ oz dolcelatte or ricotta cheese

salt and pepper

oregano sprigs, to garnish

1 Cook the pasta in a saucepan of boiling lightly salted water for about 8–10 minutes, or until al dente. Drain thoroughly and keep warm until required.

2 Meanwhile, place the pears in a pan and pour over the stock and wine. Poach the pears over a low heat for 10 minutes. Drain and reserve the cooking liquid and set the pears aside.

3 Heat the butter and oil in a saucepan until the butter melts. Add the onion and garlic and sauté over a low heat, stirring frequently for 2–3 minutes.

4 Stir in the walnut halves, oregano, and lemon juice.

5 Stir in the reserved pears with 4 tablespoons of the poaching liquid.

6 Crumble the dolcelatte or ricotta cheese into the pan and cook over a low heat, stirring occasionally, for 1–2 minutes, or until the cheese is just beginning to melt. Season with salt and pepper to taste.

7 Add the pasta and toss in the sauce, using two forks. Garnish and serve.

Penne & Vegetables

The sweet cherry tomatoes in this recipe add color and flavor and are complemented by the black olives and bell peppers.

NUTRITIONAL INFORMATION

Calories 380	Sugars 6g
Protein 8g	Fat 16g
Carbohydrate ...48g	Saturates 7g

 10 MINS   25 MINS

SERVES 4

I N G R E D I E N T S

2 cups dried penne

2 tbsp olive oil

2 tbsp butter

2 garlic cloves, crushed

1 green bell pepper, seeded and
   thinly sliced

1 yellow bell pepper, seeded and
   thinly sliced

16 cherry tomatoes, halved

1 tbsp chopped oregano

½ cup dry white wine

2 tbsp quartered, pitted black olives

1 bunch arugula

salt and pepper

oregano sprigs, to garnish

VARIATION

If arugula is unavailable, spinach makes a good substitute. Follow the same cooking instructions as for arugula.

1 Cook the pasta in a saucepan of boiling salted water for 8–10 minutes or until al dente. Drain thoroughly.

2 Heat the oil and butter in a pan until the butter melts. Sauté the garlic for 30 seconds. Add the bell peppers and cook, stirring, for 3–4 minutes.

3 Stir in the cherry tomatoes, oregano, wine, and olives and cook for 3–4 minutes. Season well with salt and pepper and stir in the arugula until just wilted.

4 Transfer the pasta to a serving dish, spoon over the sauce, and garnish.

Vegetable Lasagna

This colorful and tasty lasagna has layers of vegetables in tomato sauce and eggplant, all topped with a rich cheese sauce.

NUTRITIONAL INFORMATION

Calories 544   Sugars 18g
Protein ....20g   Fat 26g
Carbohydrate ...61g   Saturates 12g

35 MINS   55 MINS

SERVES 4

INGREDIENTS

1 eggplant, sliced

3 tbsp olive oil

2 garlic cloves, crushed

1 red onion, halved and sliced

3 mixed bell peppers, seeded and diced

8 oz mixed mushrooms, sliced

2 celery stalks, sliced

1 zucchini, diced

½ tsp chili powder

½ tsp ground cumin

2 tomatoes, chopped

1¼ cups strained tomatoes

2 tbsp chopped basil

8 oven-ready green lasagna sheets

salt and pepper

CHEESE SAUCE

2 tbsp butter or margarine

1 tbsp flour

⅔ cup vegetable stock

1¼ cups milk

¾ cup grated cheddar cheese

1 tsp Dijon mustard

1 tbsp chopped basil

1 egg, beaten

1 Place the eggplant slices in a colander, sprinkle with salt, and leave for 20 minutes. Rinse under cold water, drain and reserve.

2 Heat the oil in a pan and sauté the garlic and onion for 1–2 minutes. Add the bell peppers, mushrooms, celery, and zucchini and cook, stirring constantly, for 3–4 minutes.

3 Stir in the spices and cook for 1 minute. Mix in the tomatoes, strained tomatoes, and basil and season to taste with salt and pepper.

4 For the sauce, melt the butter in a pan, stir in the flour, and cook for 1 minute. Remove from the heat, stir in the stock and milk, return to the heat and add half the cheese and the mustard. Boil, stirring, until thickened. Stir in the basil. Remove from the heat and stir in the egg.

5 Place half the lasagna in an ovenproof dish. Top with half the vegetable mixture then half the eggplant. Repeat and spoon the cheese sauce on top. Sprinkle with cheese and cook in a preheated oven at 350°F for 40 minutes.

Spinach & Nut Pasta

Use any pasta shapes that you have for this recipe. Multicolored pasta is visually the most attractive to use.

NUTRITIONAL INFORMATION

Calories	603	Sugars	.........5g
Protein	........12g	Fat	.........41g
Carbohydrate	...46g	Saturates	.......6g

 5 MINS　　 15 MINS

SERVES 4

INGREDIENTS

2 cups dried pasta shapes

½ cup olive oil

2 garlic cloves, crushed

1 onion, quartered and sliced

3 large flat mushrooms, sliced

8 oz spinach

2 tbsp pine nuts

6 tbsp dry white wine

salt and pepper

Parmesan shavings, to garnish

1 Cook the pasta in a saucepan of boiling salted water for 8–10 minutes, or until al dente. Drain well.

2 Meanwhile, heat the oil in a large saucepan and sauté the garlic and onion for 1 minute.

COOK'S TIP

Grate a little nutmeg over the dish for extra flavor, as this spice has a particular affinity with spinach.

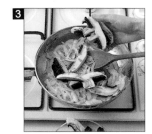

3 Add the sliced mushrooms to the pan and cook over a medium heat, stirring occasionally, for 2 minutes.

4 Lower the heat, add the spinach to the pan, and cook, stirring occasionally, for 4–5 minutes, or until the spinach has wilted.

5 Stir in the pine nuts and wine, season to taste with salt and pepper, and cook for 1 minute.

6 Transfer the pasta to a warm serving bowl and toss the sauce into it, mixing well. Garnish with shavings of Parmesan cheese and serve.

Macaroni Cheese & Tomato

This is a really simple, family dish which is inexpensive and easy to prepare and cook. Serve with a salad or fresh green vegetables.

NUTRITIONAL INFORMATION

Calories 592   Sugars 6g
Protein ....28g   Fat 29g
Carbohydrate ...57g   Saturates 17g

 15 MINS   35–40 MINS

SERVES 4

INGREDIENTS

2 cups dried elbow macaroni

1½ cups grated cheddar cheese

1 cup grated Parmesan cheese

4 tbsp fresh white breadcrumbs

1 tbsp chopped basil

1 tbsp butter or margarine, plus extra
   for greasing

TOMATO SAUCE

1 tbsp olive oil

1 shallot, finely chopped

2 garlic cloves, crushed

1 lb 2 oz canned diced tomatoes

1 tbsp chopped basil

salt and pepper

1 To make the tomato sauce, heat the oil in a heavy-bottomed saucepan. Add the shallots and garlic and sauté for 1 minute. Add the tomatoes and basil and season with salt and pepper to taste. Cook over a medium heat, stirring constantly, for 10 minutes.

2 Meanwhile, cook the macaroni in a large pan of boiling lightly salted water for 8 minutes, or until al dente. Drain thoroughly and set aside.

3 Mix the cheddar and Parmesan together in a bowl. Grease a deep, ovenproof dish. Spoon one-third of the tomato sauce into the base of the dish, top with one-third of the macaroni and then one-third of the cheeses. Season to taste with salt and pepper. Repeat these layers twice, ending with a layer of grated cheese.

4 Combine the breadcrumbs and basil and sprinkle evenly over the top. Dot the topping with the butter or margarine and cook in a preheated oven at 375°F for 25 minutes, or until the the topping is golden brown and bubbling. Serve immediately.

Summertime Tagliatelle

This is a really fresh-tasting dish, made with zucchini and cream, which is ideal with a crisp white wine and some bread.

NUTRITIONAL INFORMATION

Calories 502	Sugars 5g	
Protein 16g	Fat 30g	
Carbohydrate ...44g	Saturates 9g	

10 MINS   20 MINS

SERVES 4

INGREDIENTS

1½ lb zucchini

6 tbsp olive oil

3 garlic cloves, crushed

3 tbsp chopped basil

2 red chilies, sliced

juice of 1 large lemon

5 tbsp light cream

4 tbsp grated Parmesan cheese

8 oz dried tagliatelle (ribbon pasta)

salt and pepper

crusty bread, to serve

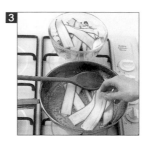

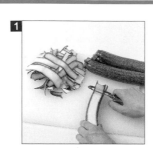

1 Using a swivel vegetable peeler, slice the zucchini into thin ribbons.

2 Heat the oil in a skillet and sauté the garlic for 30 seconds.

COOK'S TIP

Lime juice could be used instead of the lemon. As limes are usually smaller, squeeze the juice from two.

3 Add the zucchini ribbons and cook over a low heat, stirring constantly, for 5–7 minutes.

4 Stir in the basil, chilies, lemon juice, light cream, and grated Parmesan cheese and season with salt and pepper to taste. Keep warm over a very low heat.

5 Meanwhile, cook the tagliatelle in a large pan of lightly salted boiling water for 10 minutes until al dente. Drain the pasta thoroughly and put in a warm serving bowl.

6 Pile the zucchini mixture on top of the pasta. Serve immediately with crusty bread.

Thai-Style Stir-fried Noodles

This dish is considered the Thai national dish, as it is made and eaten everywhere—a one-dish, fast food for eating on the move.

NUTRITIONAL INFORMATION

Calories	407	Sugars	11g
Protein	14g	Fat	16g
Carbohydrate	56g	Saturates	3g

 15 MINS   5 MINS

SERVES 4

INGREDIENTS

8 oz dried rice noodles

2 red chilies, seeded and
   finely chopped

2 shallots, finely chopped

2 tbsp sugar

2 tbsp tamarind water

1 tbsp lime juice

2 tbsp light soy sauce

1 tbsp sunflower oil

1 tsp sesame oil

¾ cup diced tofu

pepper

2 tbsp chopped roasted peanuts,
   to garnish

1 Cook the rice noodles as directed on the pack, or soak them in boiling water for 5 minutes.

2 Grind together the chilies, shallots, sugar, tamarind water, lime juice, light soy sauce, and pepper to taste.

3 Heat both the oils together in a preheated wok or large, heavy skillet over a high heat. Add the tofu and stir for 1 minute.

4 Add the chili mixture, bring to a boil, and cook, stirring constantly, for about 2 minutes, until thickened.

5 Drain the rice noodles and add them to the chili mixture. Use 2 spoons to lift and stir them until they are no longer steaming. Serve immediately, garnished with the peanuts.

COOK'S TIP

This is a quick one-dish meal that is very useful if you are catering for a single vegetarian in the family.

Stir-fried Japanese Noodles

This quick dish is an ideal lunchtime meal, packed with whatever mixture of mushrooms you like in a sweet sauce.

NUTRITIONAL INFORMATION

Calories	379	Sugars	.........8g
Protein	........12g	Fat	.........13g
Carbohydrate	...53g	Saturates	.......3g

 15 MINS   15 MINS

SERVES 4

I N G R E D I E N T S

8 oz Japanese egg noodles

2 tbsp sunflower oil

1 red onion, sliced

1 garlic clove, crushed

1 lb 2 oz mixed mushrooms, such as
  shiitake, oyster, and brown

12 oz bok choy

2 tbsp sweet sherry

6 tbsp soy sauce

4 green onions, sliced

1 tbsp toasted sesame seeds

1 Place the egg noodles in a large bowl. Pour over enough boiling water to cover and leave to soak for 10 minutes.

2 Heat the sunflower oil in a large preheated wok.

COOK'S TIP

The variety of mushrooms in supermarkets has greatly improved and a good mixture should be easily obtainable. If not, use the more common mushrooms.

3 Add the red onion and garlic to the wok and stir-fry for 2–3 minutes, or until softened.

4 Add the mushrooms to the wok and stir-fry for about 5 minutes, or until the mushrooms have softened.

5 Drain the Japanese egg noodles thoroughly and set aside.

6 Add the the bok choy, noodles, sweet sherry, and soy sauce to the wok. Toss all of the ingredients together to mix well and stir-fry for 2–3 minutes, or until the liquid is just bubbling.

7 Transfer the mushroom noodles to warm serving bowls and scatter with sliced green onions and toasted sesame seeds. Serve immediately.

Spicy Fried Noodles

This is a simple idea to add an extra kick to noodles, which accompany many main course dishes in Thailand.

NUTRITIONAL INFORMATION

Calories	568	Sugars	.........3g
Protein	........16g	Fat	..........19g
Carbohydrate	...90g	Saturates	.......4g

 15 MINS   3–5 MINS

SERVES 4

I N G R E D I E N T S

1 lb 2 oz medium egg noodles

1 cup bean sprouts

½ oz chives

3 tbsp sunflower oil

1 garlic clove, crushed

4 fresh green chilies, seeded, sliced, and
    soaked in 2 tbsp rice vinegar

salt

1 Place the noodles in a bowl, cover with boiling water, and soak for 10 minutes. Drain and set aside.

2 Pick over the bean sprouts and soak in cold water while you cut the chives into 1-inch pieces. Set a few chives aside for the garnish. Drain the bean sprouts thoroughly.

3 Heat the oil in a preheated wok or large, heavy-bottomed skillet. Add the crushed garlic and stir; then add the chilies and stir-fry for about 1 minute, until fragrant.

4 Add the bean sprouts, stir, and then add the noodles. Stir in salt to taste and add the chives. Using 2 spoons or a wok scoop, lift and toss the noodles for 1 minute.

5 Transfer the noodles to a warm serving dish, garnish the with the reserved chives, and serve immediately.

COOK'S TIP

Soaking a chili in rice vinegar has the effect of distributing the hot chili flavor throughout the dish. To reduce the heat, you can slice the chili more thickly before soaking.

Chow Mein

Egg noodles are cooked and then fried with a colorful variety of vegetables to make this well-known and ever-popular dish.

NUTRITIONAL INFORMATION

Calories 669   Sugars 9g
Protein . . . . .19g   Fat 23g
Carbohydrate . .100g   Saturates 4g

 15 MINS   🕑 10 MINS

SERVES 4

I N G R E D I E N T S

1 lb 2 oz egg noodles
4 tbsp vegetable oil
1 onion, thinly sliced
2 carrots, cut into thin sticks
1⅓ cups mushrooms, quartered
4½ oz snow peas
½ cucumber, cut into sticks
2 cups spinach, shredded
2 cups bean sprouts
2 tbsp dark soy sauce
1 tbsp sherry
1 tsp salt
1 tsp sugar
1 tsp cornstarch
1 tsp sesame oil

COOK'S TIP

For a spicy hot chow mein, add 1 tablespoon chili sauce or substitute chili oil for the sesame oil.

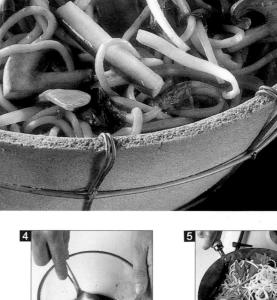

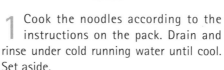

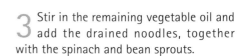

1 Cook the noodles according to the instructions on the pack. Drain and rinse under cold running water until cool. Set aside.

2 Heat 3 tablespoons of the vegetable oil in a preheated wok or skillet. Add the onion and carrots, and stir-fry for 1 minute. Add the mushrooms, snow peas, and cucumber and stir-fry for 1 minute.

3 Stir in the remaining vegetable oil and add the drained noodles, together with the spinach and bean sprouts.

4 Blend together all the remaining ingredients and pour over the noodles and vegetables.

5 Stir-fry until the noodle mixture is thoroughly heated, transfer to a warm serving dish, and serve.

Spicy Japanese Noodles

These noodles are highly spiced with chili and flavored with sesame seeds for a nutty taste that is a true delight.

NUTRITIONAL INFORMATION

Calories 381	Sugars 12g	
Protein 11g	Fat 13g	
Carbohydrate . . .59g	Saturates 2g	

5 MINS   15 MINS

SERVES 4

INGREDIENTS

1 lb 2 oz fresh Japanese noodles

1 tbsp sesame oil

1 tbsp sesame seeds

1 tbsp sunflower oil

1 red onion, sliced

3½ oz snow peas

6 oz carrots, thinly sliced

12 oz white cabbage, shredded

3 tbsp sweet chili sauce

2 green onions, sliced, to garnish

1 Bring a large saucepan of water to a boil. Add the Japanese noodles to the pan and cook for 2–3 minutes. Drain the noodles thoroughly.

2 Toss the noodles with the sesame oil and sesame seeds.

3 Heat the sunflower oil in a large preheated wok.

4 Add the onion slices, snow peas, carrot slices, and shredded cabbage to the wok and stir-fry for about 5 minutes.

5 Add the sweet chili sauce to the wok and cook, stirring occasionally, for 2 minutes more.

6 Add the sesame noodles to the wok, toss thoroughly to combine, and heat through for another 2–3 minutes. (You may wish to serve the noodles separately, so transfer them to the serving bowls.)

7 Transfer the Japanese noodles and spicy vegetables to warm individual serving bowls, scatter over the sliced green onions to garnish, and serve immediately.

COOK'S TIP

If fresh Japanese noodles are difficult to get hold of, use dried rice noodles or thin egg noodles instead.

Grains & Legumes

Grains and legumes are universally important staple foods. They are highly nutritious as they are an excellent source of protein, iron, calcium, and B vitamins, and are virtually

fat-free. Grains include wheat, corn, barley, rye, oats, buckwheat, and many different varieties of rice, as well as associated flours. Legumes include garbanzo beans, yellow and green split peas, a fascinating variety of beans, together with many types of lentil. Grains and legumes form a substantial base to which other ingredients can be added. Each has its own flavor and texture, so it is worth experimenting.

Risotto Verde

Risotto is an Italian dish which is easy to make and uses arborio rice, onion, and garlic as a base for a range of savory recipes.

NUTRITIONAL INFORMATION

Calories . . . . .374 Sugars 5g
Protein . . . . .10g Fat 9g
Carbohydrate . . .55g Saturates 2g

 5 MINS   35 MINS

SERVES 4

I N G R E D I E N T S

7½ cups vegetable stock

2 tbsp olive oil

2 garlic cloves, crushed

2 leeks, shredded

1¼ cups arborio rice

1¼ cups dry white wine

4 tbsp chopped mixed herbs

8 oz baby spinach

3 tbsp plain yogurt

salt and pepper

shredded leek, to garnish

COOK'S TIP

Do not try to hurry the process of cooking the risotto as the rice must absorb the liquid slowly in order for it to reach the correct consistency.

1 Pour the stock into a large saucepan and bring to a boil. Reduce the heat to a simmer.

2 Meanwhile, heat the oil in a separate pan. Add the garlic and leeks and sauté over a low heat, stirring occasionally, for 2–3 minutes, until softened.

3 Stir in the rice and cook for 2 minutes, stirring until each grain is coated with oil.

4 Pour in half of the wine and a little of the hot stock. Cook over a low heat until all of the liquid has been absorbed. Add the remaining stock and the wine, a little at a time, and cook over a low heat for 25 minutes, or until the rice is creamy.

5 Stir in the chopped mixed herbs and baby spinach, season to taste with salt and pepper, and cook for 2 minutes.

6 Stir in the plain yogurt. Transfer to a warm serving dish, garnish with the shredded leek, and serve immediately.

Rice with Fruit & Nuts

Here is a tasty and filling rice dish that is nice and spicy and includes fruits for a refreshing flavor and toasted nuts for a crunchy texture.

NUTRITIONAL INFORMATION

Calories 423	Sugars 19g
Protein 10g	Fat 17g
Carbohydrate ...62g	Saturates 2g

20 MINS   1 HOUR

SERVES 6

INGREDIENTS

4 tbsp vegetable ghee or oil

1 large onion, chopped

2 garlic cloves, crushed

1-inch piece fresh ginger, chopped

1 tsp chili powder

1 tsp cumin seeds

1 tbsp mild or medium curry powder
    or paste

1½ cups brown rice

3½ cups boiling vegetable stock

14 oz can diced tomatoes

salt and pepper

6 oz dried apricots or
    peaches, cut into slivers

1 red bell pepper, seeded and diced

¾ cup frozen peas

1-2 small, slightly green bananas

⅓-½ cup toasted nuts,
    such as almonds, cashews, and
    hazelnuts, or pine nuts

cilantro sprigs, to garnish

1 Heat the ghee or oil in a large saucepan. Add the onion and fry over a low heat for 3 minutes. Stir in the garlic, ginger, spices and rice and cook gently, stirring constantly, for 2 minutes, until the rice is coated in the spiced oil.

2 Pour in the boiling stock, add the chopped tomatoes and season with salt and pepper to taste. Bring to the boil, then reduce the heat, cover and simmer gently for 40 minutes, or until the rice is almost cooked and most of the liquid has been absorbed.

3 Add the slivered apricots or peaches, diced red (bell) pepper and peas. Cover and continue cooking for 10 minutes. Remove from the heat and allow to stand for 5 minutes without uncovering.

4 Peel and slice the bananas. Uncover the rice mixture and fork through to mix the ingredients together. Add the toasted nuts and sliced banana and toss lightly. Transfer to a warm serving platter and garnish with coriander (cilantro) sprigs. Serve hot.

Thai Jasmine Rice

Every Thai meal has as its centerpiece a big bowl of steaming, fluffy Thai jasmine rice, to which salt should not be added.

NUTRITIONAL INFORMATION

Calories 239	Sugars 0g
Protein 5g	Fat 2g
Carbohydrate . . .54g	Saturates 0.6g

 5 MINS   10–15 MINS

SERVES 4

INGREDIENTS

OPEN-PAN METHOD

1 cup Thai jasmine rice

4 cups water

ABSORPTION METHOD

1 cup Thai jasmine rice

2 cups water

1 For the open-pan method, rinse the rice in a strainer under cold running water and leave to drain.

2 Bring the water to a boil. Add the rice, stir once, and return to a medium boil. Cook, uncovered, for 8–10 minutes, until tender.

3 Drain thoroughly and fork through lightly before serving.

4 For the absorption method, rinse the rice under cold running water.

5 Put the rice and water into a saucepan and bring to a boil. Stir once and then cover the pan tightly. Lower the heat as much as possible. Cook for 10 minutes. Leave to rest for 5 minutes.

6 Fork through lightly and serve the rice immediately.

COOK'S TIP

Thai jasmine rice can be frozen. Freeze in a plastic sealed container. Frozen rice is ideal for stir-fry dishes, as the process seems to separate the grains.

Couscous Royale

Serve this stunning dish as a centerpiece for a North African-style feast; it will prove to be a truly memorable meal.

NUTRITIONAL INFORMATION

Calories 329	Sugars 31g	
Protein 6g	Fat 13g	
Carbohydrate ...50g	Saturates 6g	

 25 MINS   45 MINS

SERVES 6

INGREDIENTS

3 carrots

3 zucchini

12 oz pumpkin or squash

5 cups vegetable stock

2 cinnamon sticks, broken in half

2 tsp ground cumin

1 tsp ground coriander

pinch of saffron strands

2 tbsp olive oil

pared zest and juice of 1 lemon

2 tbsp honey

2¾ cups pre-cooked couscous

¼ cup butter or margarine, softened

1 cup large seedless raisins

salt and pepper

cilantro, to garnish

1 Cut the carrots and zucchini into 3 inch pieces and cut in half lengthwise.

2 Trim the pumpkin or squash and discard the seeds. Peel and cut into pieces the same size as the carrots and zucchini.

3 Put the stock, spices, saffron, and carrots in a large saucepan. Bring to a boil, skim off any froth, and add the olive oil. Simmer for 15 minutes.

4 Add the lemon zest and juice to the pan, together with the honey, zucchini, and pumpkin or squash. Season well. Bring back to a boil and simmer for another 10 minutes.

5 Meanwhile, soak the couscous according to the pack instructions. Transfer to a steamer or large strainer lined with cheesecloth and place over the vegetable pan. Cover and steam as directed. Stir in the butter.

6 Pile the couscous on to a warmed serving plate. Drain the vegetables, reserving the stock, lemon zest, and cinnamon. Arrange the vegetables on top of the couscous. Put the raisins on top and spoon over 6 tablespoons of the reserved stock. Keep warm.

7 Return the remaining stock to the heat and boil for 5 minutes to reduce slightly. Discard the lemon zest and cinnamon. Garnish with sprigs of cilantro and serve immediately, handing the sauce separately.

Spiced Basmati Pilaf

The whole spices are not meant to be eaten and may be removed before serving. Omit the broccoli and mushrooms for a plain, spiced pilaf.

NUTRITIONAL INFORMATION

Calories 450	Sugars 3g
Protein 9g	Fat 15g
Carbohydrate . . .76g	Saturates 2g

 20 MINS   🕐 25 MINS

SERVES 6

I N G R E D I E N T S

2½ cups basmati rice

6 oz broccoli, trimmed

6 tbsp vegetable oil

2 large onions, chopped

3 cups sliced mushrooms

2 garlic cloves, crushed

6 cardamom pods, split

6 whole cloves

8 black peppercorns

1 cinnamon stick

1 tsp ground turmeric

5 cups boiling vegetable
   stock or water

salt and pepper

⅓ cup seedless raisins

½ cup unsalted pistachios,
   coarsely chopped

VARIATION

For added richness, you could stir a spoonful of vegetable ghee through the rice mixture just before serving. A little diced red bell pepper and a few cooked peas forked through at step 4 add a colorful touch.

1 Place the rice in a strainer and wash well under cold running water. Drain. Trim off most of the broccoli stalk and cut into small flowerets, then quarter the stalk lengthwise and cut diagonally into ½ inch pieces.

2 Heat the oil in a large saucepan. Add the onions and broccoli stalks and cook over a low heat, stirring frequently, for 3 minutes. Add the mushrooms, rice, garlic, and spices and cook for 1 minute, stirring, until the rice is coated in oil.

3 Add the boiling stock and season to taste with salt and pepper. Stir in the broccoli flowerets and return the mixture to a boil. Cover, reduce the heat and cook over a low heat for 15 minutes without uncovering the pan.

4 Remove from the heat and leave to stand for 5 minutes without uncovering. Add the raisins and pistachios and gently fork through to fluff up the grains. Serve hot.

Tabbouleh Salad

This kind of salad is eaten widely throughout the Middle East. The flavor improves as it is kept, so it tastes even better on the second day.

NUTRITIONAL INFORMATION

Calories . . . . . . .637 Sugars 8g
Protein . . . . .20g Fat 41g
Carbohydrate . . .50g Saturates 11g

1½ HOURS   5–10 MINS

SERVES 2

I N G R E D I E N T S

1 cup bulgur wheat

2½ cups boiling water

1 red bell pepper, seeded and halved

3 tbsp olive oil

1 garlic clove, crushed

grated zest of ½ lime

about 1 tbsp lime juice

1 tbsp chopped mint

1 tbsp chopped parsley

3–4 green onions, trimmed and
    thinly sliced

8 pitted black olives, halved

½ cup large salted peanuts or
    cashews

1–2 tsp lemon juice

2–3 oz Gruyère cheese

salt and pepper

mint sprigs, to garnish

warm pita bread or crusty rolls,
    to serve

1 Put the bulgur wheat into a bowl and cover with the boiling water to reach about 1 inch above the bulgur. Set aside to soak for up to 1 hour, until most of the water is absorbed and is cold.

2 Meanwhile, put the halved red bell pepper, skin side upwards, on a broiler rack and cook under a preheated moderate broiler until the skin is thoroughly charred and blistered. Leave to cool slightly.

3 When cool enough to handle, peel off the skin and discard the seeds. Cut the bell pepper flesh into narrow strips.

4 Whisk together the oil, garlic, and lime zest and juice. Season to taste and whisk until thoroughly blended. Add 4½ teaspoons of the dressing to the bell peppers and mix lightly.

5 Drain the soaked bulgur wheat thoroughly, squeezing it in a dry cloth to make it even drier, then place in a bowl.

6 Add the chopped herbs, green onions, olives, and peanuts or cashews to the bulgur and toss . Add the lemon juice to the remaining dressing, and stir through the salad. Spoon the salad on to 2 serving plates.

7 Cut the cheese into narrow strips and mix with the bell pepper strips. Spoon alongside the bulgur salad. Garnish with mint sprigs and serve with warm pita bread or crusty rolls.

Deep South Rice & Beans

Cajun spices add a flavor of the American South to this colorful rice and red kidney bean salad.

NUTRITIONAL INFORMATION

Calories ....336 Sugars 8g
Protein ....7g Fat 13g
Carbohydrate ...51g Saturates 2g

10 MINS   15 MINS

SERVES 4

INGREDIENTS

1 cup long grain rice

4 tbsp olive oil

1 small green bell pepper, seeded
   and chopped

1 small red bell pepper, seeded
   and chopped

1 onion, finely chopped

1 small red or green chili, seeded and
   finely chopped

2 tomatoes, chopped

½ cup canned red kidney
   beans, rinsed and drained

1 tbsp chopped fresh basil

2 tsp chopped fresh thyme

1 tsp Cajun spice

salt and pepper

fresh basil leaves, to garnish

1 Cook the rice in plenty of boiling, lightly salted water for about 12 minutes, until just tender. Rinse with cold water and drain well.

2 Meanwhile, heat the olive oil in a skillet and fry the green and red bell peppers and onion gently for about 5 minutes, until softened.

3 Add the chili and tomatoes, and cook for 2 minutes more.

4 Add the vegetable mixture and red kidney beans to the rice. Stir well to combine thoroughly.

5 Stir the chopped herbs and Cajun spice into the rice mixture. Season to taste with salt and pepper, and serve, garnished with basil leaves.

Vegetable Biryani

The biryani originated in the North of India, and was a dish reserved for festivals. The vegetables are marinated in a yogurt-based marinade.

NUTRITIONAL INFORMATION

Calories	449	Sugars	........18g
Protein	........12g	Fat	.........12g
Carbohydrate	...79g	Saturates	.......6g

2¼ HOURS   1 HR 5 MINS

SERVES 4

INGREDIENTS

1 large potato, cubed

3½ oz baby carrots

1¾ oz okra, thickly sliced

2 celery stalks, sliced

2¾ oz baby mushrooms, halved

1 eggplant, halved and sliced

1¼ cups plain yogurt

1 tbsp grated fresh ginger

2 large onions, grated

4 garlic cloves, crushed

1 tsp turmeric

1 tbsp curry powder

2 tbsp butter

2 onions, sliced

1¼ cups basmati rice

chopped cilantro, to garnish

1 Cook the potato cubes, carrots, and okra in a pan of boiling salted water for 7–8 minutes. Drain well and place in a large bowl. Mix with the celery, mushrooms, and eggplant.

2 Mix the plain yogurt, ginger, grated onions, garlic, turmeric, and curry powder and spoon over the vegetables. Set aside in a cool place to marinate for at least 2 hours.

3 Heat the butter in a heavy-bottomed skillet. Add the sliced onions and cook over a medium heat for 5–6 minutes, until golden brown. Remove a few onions from the pan and reserve for the garnish.

4 Cook the rice in a large pan of boiling water for 7 minutes. Drain thoroughly and set aside.

5 Add the marinated vegetables to the onions and cook for 10 minutes.

6 Put half of the rice in an 8¾ cup casserole dish. Spoon the vegetables on top and cover with the remaining rice. Cover and cook in a preheated oven at 375°F for 20–25 minutes, or until the rice is tender.

7 Spoon the biryani onto a serving plate, garnish with the reserved onions and cilantro, and serve.

White Radish Curry

This is rather an unusual recipe for a vegetarian curry. The dish is good served hot with chapatis.

NUTRITIONAL INFORMATION

Calories 384   Sugars 4g
Protein . . . . .3g   Fat 38g
Carbohydrate . . . .9g   Saturates 4g

 10 MINS   20 MINS

SERVES 4

INGREDIENTS

1 lb 2 oz white radish (daikon),
  preferably with leaves

1 tbsp moong dal

2½ cups water

⅔ cup vegetable oil

1 medium onion, thinly sliced

1 tsp crushed garlic

1 tsp crushed dried red chilies

1 tsp salt

1 Rinse, peel, and roughly slice the white radish, together with its leaves, if using.

2 Place the white radish, the leaves, if using, and the moong dal in a large saucepan and pour over the water. Bring to a boil and cook over a medium heat

until the white radish has softened enough to handle.

3 Drain the white radish thoroughly and squeeze out any excess water, using your hands.

4 Heat the vegetable oil in a heavy-bottomed saucepan. Add the onion, garlic, crushed red chilies, and salt and fry over a medium heat, stirring from time to time, for about 5–7 minutes, until the

onions have softened and turned light golden brown in color.

5 Stir the white radish mixture into the spiced onion mixture and combine well. Reduce the heat and continue cooking, stirring frequently, for about 3–5 minutes.

6 Transfer the white radish curry to individual serving plates and serve hot with chapatis.

COOK'S TIP

The vegetable used in this recipe, white radish (daikon), looks a bit like a parsnip without the tapering end and is sold in supermarkets, as well as in Indian grocers.

Kofta Kabobs

Traditionally, koftas are made from a spicy meat mixture, but this bean and wheat version makes a tasty vegetarian alternative.

NUTRITIONAL INFORMATION

Calories	598	Sugars	.........7g
Protein	........26g	Fat	.......17g
Carbohydrate	...90g	Saturates	.......3g

1 HR 20 MINS 1½ HOURS

SERVES 4

INGREDIENTS

1 cup adzuki beans

1 cup bulgur wheat

2 cups vegetable stock

3 tbsp olive oil, plus extra for brushing

1 onion, finely chopped

2 garlic cloves, crushed

1 tsp ground coriander

1 tsp ground cumin

2 tbsp chopped fresh cilantro

3 eggs, beaten

¾ cup dried breadcrumbs

salt and pepper

TABBOULEH

1 cup bulgur wheat

2 tbsp lemon juice

1 tbsp olive oil

6 tbsp chopped parsley

4 green onions, finely chopped

2 oz cucumber, finely chopped

3 tbsp chopped mint

1 extra-large tomato, finely chopped

TO SERVE

black olives

pita bread

1 Cook the adzuki beans in boiling water for 40 minutes, until tender. Drain, rinse, and leave to cool. Cook the bulgur wheat in the stock for 10 minutes, until the stock is absorbed. Set aside.

2 Heat 1 tablespoon of the oil in a skillet and fry the onion, garlic, and spices for 4–5 minutes.

3 Transfer to a bowl, together with the beans, cilantro, seasoning, and eggs and mash with a potato masher or fork. Add the breadcrumbs and bulgur wheat and stir well. Cover and chill for 1 hour, until firm.

4 To make the tabbouleh, soak the bulgur wheat in slightly less than 2 cups of boiling water for 15 minutes. Combine with the remaining ingredients. Cover and chill.

5 With wet hands, mold the kofta mixture into 32 oval shapes.

6 Press on to skewers, brush with oil, and broil for 5–6 minutes. until golden. Turn, brush with oil again and cook for 5–6 minutes. Drain on paper towels. Garnish and serve with the tabbouleh, black olives, and pita bread.

Vegetable Couscous

Couscous is a semolina grain which is very quick and easy to cook, and it makes a pleasant change from rice or pasta.

NUTRITIONAL INFORMATION

Calories 280   Sugars 13g
Protein . . . . .10g   Fat 7g
Carbohydrate . . .47g   Saturates 1g

🕒 20 MINS   🕐 40 MINS

SERVES 4

INGREDIENTS

2 tbsp vegetable oil

1 large onion, coarsely chopped

1 carrot, chopped

1 turnip, chopped

2½ cups vegetable stock

1 cup couscous

2 tomatoes, peeled and quartered

2 zucchini, chopped

1 red bell pepper, seeded and chopped

4½ oz green beans, chopped

grated zest of 1 lemon

pinch of ground turmeric (optional)

1 tbsp finely chopped fresh cilantro or
    parsley

salt and pepper

fresh flat-leaf parsley sprigs,
    to garnish

1 Heat the oil in a large saucepan and fry the onion, carrot, and turnip for 3–4 minutes. Add the stock, bring to a boil, cover, and simmer for 20 minutes.

2 Meanwhile, put the couscous in a bowl and moisten with a little boiling water, stirring, until the grains have swollen and separated.

3 Add the tomatoes, zucchini, bell pepper, and green beans to the saucepan.

4 Stir the lemon zest into the couscous and add the turmeric, if using, the and mix thoroughly. Put the couscous in a steamer and position it over the saucepan of vegetables. Simmer the vegetables so

that the couscous steams for about 8–10 minutes.

5 Pile the couscous onto warmed serving plates. Ladle the vegetables and some of the liquid over the top. Scatter with the cilantro or parsley and serve immediately, garnished with parsley sprigs.

Risotto in Shells

An eggplant is halved and filled with a risotto mixture, topped with cheese, and baked to make a snack or quick meal for two.

NUTRITIONAL INFORMATION

Calories 444	Sugars 20g	
Protein 13g	Fat 23g	
Carbohydrate ... 50g	Saturates 8g	

20 MINS   55 MINS

SERVES 2

INGREDIENTS

¼ cup mixed long grain and wild rice

1 eggplant, about 12 oz

1 tbsp olive oil

1 small onion, finely chopped

1 garlic clove, crushed

½ small red bell pepper, seeded
  and chopped

2 tbsp water

3 tbsp raisins

¼ cup cashews, roughly chopped

½ tsp dried oregano

⅓ cup grated sharp cheddar or
  Parmesan cheese

salt and pepper

oregano or parsley to garnish

1 Cook the rice in boiling salted water for about 15 minutes, until just tender. Drain, rinse, and drain again.

2 Bring a large saucepan of water to a boil. Cut the stem off the eggplant and cut in half lengthwise. Cut out the flesh from the center carefully, leaving about a ½ inch shell. Blanch the shells in the boiling water for 3–4 minutes. Drain thoroughly. Chop the eggplant flesh finely.

3 Heat the oil in a saucepan or skillet. Add the onion and garlic and fry over a low heat until beginning to soften, then add the bell pepper and eggplant flesh and continue cooking for a 2–3 minutes before adding the water and cooking for another 2–3 minutes.

4 Stir the raisins, cashews, dried oregano, and rice into the eggplant mixture and season to taste with salt and pepper.

5 Place the eggplant shells in an ovenproof dish and spoon in the rice mixture, piling it up well. Cover and cook in a preheated oven at 375°F for 20 minutes.

6 Remove the lid and sprinkle the cheese over the rice. Place under a preheated moderate broiler and cook for 3–4 minutes, until golden brown and bubbling. Serve hot garnished with oregano or parsley.

Special Fried Rice

In this simple recipe, cooked rice is fried with vegetables and cashews. It can either be eaten on its own or served as an accompaniment.

NUTRITIONAL INFORMATION

Calories	355	Sugars 6g
Protein	. . . . .9g	Fat 15g
Carbohydrate	. . .48g	Saturates 3g

 10 MINS   30 MINS

SERVES 4

I N G R E D I E N T S

¾ cup long grain rice

½ cup cashews

1 carrot

½ cucumber

1 yellow bell pepper

2 green onions

2 tbsp vegetable oil

1 garlic clove, crushed

¾ cup frozen peas, thawed

1 tbsp soy sauce

1 tsp salt

cilantro leaves, to garnish

1 Bring a large pan of water to a boil. Add the rice and simmer for 15 minutes. Tip the rice into a strainer and rinse; drain thoroughly.

COOK'S TIP

You can replace any of the vegetables in this recipe with others suitable for a stir-fry, and using leftover rice makes this a perfect last-minute dish.

2 Heat a wok or large, heavy-bottomed skillet, add the cashews, and dry-fry until lightly browned. Remove and set aside.

3 Cut the carrot in half along the length, then slice thinly into semi-circles. Halve the cucumber and remove the seeds, using a teaspoon, then dice the flesh. Seed and slice the bell pepper and chop the green onions.

4 Heat the oil in a wok or large skillet. Add the prepared vegetables and the garlic. Stir-fry for 3 minutes. Add the rice, peas, soy sauce, and salt. Continue to stir-fry until well mixed and thoroughly heated.

5 Stir in the reserved cashews. Transfer to a warmed serving dish, garnish with cilantro leaves, and serve immediately.

Spinach & Nut Pilaf

Fragrant basmati rice is cooked with porcini mushrooms, spinach, and pistachios in this easy microwave recipe.

NUTRITIONAL INFORMATION

Calories 403	Sugars 7g	
Protein 10g	Fat 15g	
Carbohydrate ...62g	Saturates 2g	

 55 MINS   15–20 MINS

SERVES 4

INGREDIENTS

⅓ oz dried porcini mushrooms

1¼ cups hot water

1 onion, chopped

1 garlic clove, crushed

1 tsp grated fresh ginger

½ fresh green chili, seeded and chopped

2 tbsp oil

generous 1 cup basmati rice

1 large carrot, grated

¾ cup vegetable stock

½ tsp ground cinnamon

4 cloves

½ tsp saffron strands

6 cups fresh spinach, long stalks removed

½ cup pistachios

1 tbsp chopped cilantro

salt and pepper

cilantro leaves, to garnish

1 Place the porcini mushrooms in a small bowl. Pour over the hot water and leave to soak for 30 minutes.

2 Place the onion, garlic, ginger, chili, and oil in a large bowl. Cover and cook on HIGH power for 2 minutes. Rinse the rice, then stir it into the bowl, together with the carrot. Cover and cook on HIGH power for 1 minute.

3 Strain and coarsely chop the mushrooms. Add the mushroom soaking liquid to the stock to make 2 cups. Pour onto the rice. Stir in the mushrooms, cinnamon, cloves, saffron, and ½ teaspoon salt. Cover and cook on HIGH power for 10 minutes, stirring once. Leave to stand, covered, for 10 minutes.

4 Place the spinach in a large bowl. Cover and cook on HIGH power for 3½ minutes, stirring once. Drain well and chop coarsely.

5 Stir the spinach, pistachios, and chopped cilantro into the rice. Season to taste with salt and pepper and garnish with cilantro leaves. Serve immediately.

Pulao Rice

Plain boiled rice is eaten by most people in India every day, but for entertaining, a more interesting rice dish, such as this, is served.

NUTRITIONAL INFORMATION

Calories . . . . . . .265 Sugars 0g
Protein . . . . .4g Fat 10g
Carbohydrate . . .43g Saturates 6g

 5 MINS   25 MINS

SERVES 4

INGREDIENTS

1 cup basmati rice

2 tbsp vegetable ghee

3 green cardamoms

2 cloves

3 peppercorns

½ tsp salt

½ tsp saffron

2 cups water

1 Rinse the rice twice under running water and set aside until required.

2 Heat the ghee in a saucepan. Add the cardamoms, cloves, and peppercorns to the pan and fry, stirring constantly, for about 1 minute.

3 Add the rice and stir-fry over a medium heat for another 2 minutes.

4 Add the salt, saffron, and water to the rice mixture and reduce the heat. Cover the pan and simmer over a low heat until the water has been absorbed.

5 Transfer the pulao rice to a serving dish and serve hot.

COOK'S TIP

The most expensive of all spices, saffron strands are the stamens of a type of crocus. They give dishes a rich, golden color, as well as adding a distinctive, slightly bitter taste. Saffron is sold as a powder or in the more expensive strands.

Tomato Rice

Rice cooked with tomatoes and onions will add color to your table, especially when garnished with green chilies and cilantro.

NUTRITIONAL INFORMATION

Calories	866	Sugars	.........7g
Protein	........15g	Fat	..........46g
Carbohydrate	..106g	Saturates	.......6g

10 MINS   35 MINS

SERVES 4

INGREDIENTS

⅔ cup vegetable oil

2 medium onions, sliced

1 tsp onion seeds

1 tsp, finely chopped fresh ginger

1 tsp crushed garlic

½ tsp turmeric

1 tsp chili powder

1½ tsp salt

14 oz can tomatoes

2¼ cups basmati rice

2½ cups water

TO GARNISH

3 fresh green chilies, finely chopped

fresh cilantro leaves, chopped

3 hard-cooked eggs

1 Heat the oil in a saucepan. Add the onions and fry over a moderate heat, stirring frequently, for 5 minutes, until golden brown.

2 Add the onion seeds, ginger, garlic, turmeric, chili powder, and salt, stirring to combine.

3 Reduce the heat, add the tomatoes, and stir-fry for 10 minutes, breaking them up.

4 Add the rice to the tomato mixture, stirring gently to coat the rice completely in the mixture. Stir in the water. Cover the pan and cook over a low heat until the water has been absorbed and the rice is cooked.

5 Transfer the tomato rice to a warmed serving dish. Garnish with the finely chopped green chilies, cilantro leaves, and hard-cooked eggs. Serve the tomato rice immediately.

COOK'S TIP

Onion seeds are always used whole in Indian cooking. They are used in pickles and often sprinkled over the top of naan breads. Onion seeds don't have anything to do with the vegetable, but they look similar to the plant's seed, hence the name.

Green Rice

Based on the Mexican dish *Arroz Verde*, this recipe is perfect for bell pepper and chili lovers. Serve with iced lemonade to quell the fire!

NUTRITIONAL INFORMATION

Calories	445	Sugars	.........6g
Protein	........13g	Fat	..........12g
Carbohydrate	...76g	Saturates	.......2g

 25 MINS   30 MINS

SERVES 4

INGREDIENTS

2 large green bell peppers

2 fresh green chilies

2 tbsp, plus 1 tsp vegetable oil

1 large onion, finely chopped

1 garlic clove, crushed

1 tbsp ground coriander

1½ cups long grain rice

3 cups vegetable stock

2 cups frozen peas

6 tbsp chopped cilantro

1 egg, beaten

salt and pepper

cilantro, to garnish

TO SERVE

tortilla chips

lime wedges

COOK'S TIP

There are hundreds of varieties of chilies, many of them very similar in appearance, so it is not always easy to tell how hot they are. As a general rule, small, pointed chilies are hotter than larger, more rounded ones, but this is not invariable.

1 Halve, core, and seed the bell peppers. Cut the flesh into small cubes. Seed and finely chop the chilies.

2 Heat 2 tablespoons of the oil in a saucepan and fry the onion, garlic, bell peppers, and chilies for 5–6 minutes, until softened, but not browned.

3 Stir in the ground coriander, rice, and stock. Bring to a boil, cover, and simmer for 10 minutes. Add the peas, bring back to a boil, cover, and simmer for 5 minutes more, until the rice is tender. Remove from the heat and leave to stand, covered, for 10 minutes.

4 Season to taste with salt and pepper and mix in the fresh cilantro. Pile into a warmed serving dish and keep warm.

5 Heat the remaining oil in a small omelet pan. Pour in the egg and cook over a medium heat for 1–2 minutes on each side, until set. Slide the omelet onto a plate, roll up loosely, and slice into thin rounds.

6 Arrange the omelet strips on top of the rice. Garnish with cilantro and serve immediately with tortilla chips and lime wedges.

Kitchouri

The traditional breakfast plate of kedgeree reputedly has its roots in this Indian flavored rice dish, which English colonists adopted.

NUTRITIONAL INFORMATION

Calories 318	Sugars 5g
Protein 12g	Fat 10g
Carbohydrate . . .48g	Saturates 6g

 10 MINS   30 MINS

SERVES 4

I N G R E D I E N T S

2 tbsp vegetable ghee or butter

1 red onion, finely chopped

1 garlic clove, crushed

½ celery stalk, finely chopped

1 tsp turmeric

½ tsp garam masala

1 green chili, seeded and finely chopped

½ tsp cumin seeds

1 tbsp chopped cilantro

½ cup basmati rice, rinsed under cold water

½ cup green lentils

1¼ cups vegetable juice

2½ cups vegetable stock

1 Heat the ghee or butter in a large heavy-bottomed saucepan. Add the onion, garlic, and celery and cook for about 5 minutes, until soft.

2 Add the turmeric, garam masala, green chili, cumin seeds, and cilantro. Cook over a moderate heat, stirring constantly, for about 1 minute, until fragrant.

3 Add the rice and lentils and cook for 1 minute, until the rice is translucent.

4 Pour the vegetable juice and stock into the saucepan and bring to a boil over a medium heat. Cover and simmer over a low heat, stirring occasionally, for about 20 minutes, or until the lentils are cooked. (They should be tender when pressed between two fingers.)

5 Transfer the kitchouri to a warmed serving dish and serve piping hot.

COOK'S TIP

This is a versatile dish, and can be served as a great-tasting and satisfying one-pot meal. It can also be served as a winter lunch dish with tomatoes and yogurt.

Bulgur Pilaf

Bulgur wheat is very easy to use and, as well as being full of nutrients, it is a delicious alternative to rice, having a distinctive nutty flavor.

NUTRITIONAL INFORMATION

Calories	637	Sugars	........25g
Protein	........16g	Fat	.........26g
Carbohydrate	...90g	Saturates	......11g

15 MINS   35–40 MINS

SERVES 4

I N G R E D I E N T S

6 tbsp butter or margarine

1 red onion, halved and sliced

2 garlic cloves, crushed

2 cups bulgur wheat

6 oz tomatoes, seeded and chopped

1¾ oz baby corn cobs,
   halved lengthwise

2¾ oz small broccoli flowerets

3¾ cups vegetable stock

2 tbsp honey

1¾ oz golden raisins

½ cup pine nuts

½ tsp ground cinnamon

½ tsp ground cumin

salt and pepper

sliced green onions, to garnish

COOK'S TIP

The dish is left to stand for
10 minutes so that the bulgur
can finish cooking and the flavors
will mingle.

1 Melt the butter or margarine in a large flameproof casserole.

2 Add the onion and garlic and sauté for 2–3 minutes, stirring occasionally.

3 Add the bulgur wheat, tomatoes, corn, broccoli, and stock and bring to a boil. Reduce the heat, cover, and cook, stirring occasionally, for 15–20 minutes.

4 Stir in the honey, golden raisins, pine nuts, ground cinnamon, and cumin and season with salt and pepper to taste, mixing well. Remove the casserole from the heat, cover, and set aside for 10 minutes.

5 Spoon the bulgur pilaf into a warmed serving dish.

6 Garnish the bulgur pilaf with thinly sliced green onions and serve immediately.

Fried Spicy Rice

Ginger and garlic give this beautifully aromatic rice dish its lovely flavor. If desired, you can add a few peas to it for extra color.

NUTRITIONAL INFORMATION

Calories 507	Sugars 2g	
Protein 9g	Fat 11g	
Carbohydrate . . .99g	Saturates 6g	

10 MINS   35 MINS

SERVES 4

INGREDIENTS

2¼ cups rice

1 medium onion

2 tbsp vegetable ghee

1 tsp finely chopped fresh ginger

1 tsp crushed garlic

1 tsp salt

1 tsp black cumin seeds

3 whole cloves

3 whole green cardamoms

2 cinnamon sticks

4 peppercorns

3¼ cups water

1 Rinse the rice thoroughly under cold running water.

2 Using a sharp knife, cut the onion into thin slices.

3 Heat the ghee in a large saucepan. Add the onion and fry over a medium heat, stirring occasionally, until crisp and golden brown.

4 Add the ginger, garlic, and salt to the onions in the pan, stirring to combine.

5 Remove half of the spicy onions from the saucepan and set aside.

6 Add the rice, black cumin seeds, cloves, cardamoms, cinnamon sticks, and peppercorns to the pan and stir-fry for 3–5 minutes.

7 Add the water to the pan and bring to a boil over a medium heat. Reduce the heat, cover, and simmer until steam comes out through the lid. Check to see whether the rice is cooked and the liquid has been absorbed.

8 Transfer the fried spicy rice to a warmed serving dish and serve immediately garnished with the reserved fried onions.

Creamy Vegetable Curry

Vegetables are cooked in a mildly spiced curry sauce with yogurt and fresh cilantro stirred in just before serving.

NUTRITIONAL INFORMATION

Calories	423	Sugars	.......24g
Protein	........16g	Fat	.........19g
Carbohydrate	...50g	Saturates	.......7g

  20 MINS   25 MINS

SERVES 4

INGREDIENTS

2 tbsp sunflower oil

1 onion, sliced

2 tsp cumin seeds

2 tbsp ground coriander

1 tsp ground turmeric

2 tsp ground ginger

1 tsp chopped fresh red chili

2 garlic cloves, chopped

14 oz can chopped tomatoes

3 tbsp powdered coconut mixed with
    1¼ cups boiling water

1 small cauliflower, broken into flowerets

2 zucchini, sliced

2 carrots, sliced

1 potato, diced

14 oz can garbanzo beans, drained
    and rinsed

¾ cup thick plain yogurt

2 tbsp mango chutney

3 tbsp chopped fresh cilantro

salt and pepper

fresh herbs, to garnish

1 Heat the oil in a saucepan and fry the onion until softened. Add the cumin, ground coriander, turmeric, ginger, chili, and garlic and fry for 1 minute.

2 Add the tomatoes and coconut mixture and mix well.

3 Add the cauliflower flowerets, zucchini, carrots, diced potato, and garbanzo beans and season to taste with salt and pepper. Cover and simmer for 20 minutes, until the vegetables are tender.

4 Stir in the yogurt, mango chutney, and fresh cilantro and heat through gently, but do not boil. Transfer to a warm serving dish, garnish with fresh herbs, and serve.

Rice & Nuts

Here is a tasty and filling rice dish that is nice and spicy and includes fruits for a refreshing flavor and toasted nuts for a crunchy texture.

NUTRITIONAL INFORMATION

Calories 612   Sugars 31g
Protein . . . . .15g   Fat 21g
Carbohydrate . . .96g   Saturates 3g

20 MINS   55 MINS

SERVES 4

INGREDIENTS

4 tbsp vegetable ghee or oil

1 large onion, chopped

2 garlic cloves, crushed

1 inch fresh ginger, chopped finely

1 tsp chili powder

1 tsp cumin seeds

1 tbsp mild or medium curry powder
    or paste

1½ cups brown rice

3½ cups boiling vegetable stock

14 oz can chopped tomatoes

6 oz soaked dried apricots or
    peaches, cut into slivers

1 red bell pepper, cored, seeded, and diced

3 oz frozen peas

1-2 small, slightly green bananas

⅓-½ cup toasted mixed nuts

salt and pepper

1 Heat the ghee or oil in a large saucepan, add the onion and fry gently for 3 minutes.

2 Stir in the garlic, ginger, chili powder, cumin seeds, curry powder or paste, and rice. Cook gently for 2 minutes, stirring all the time, until the rice is coated in the spiced oil.

3 Pour in the boiling stock, stirring to mix. Add the tomatoes and season with salt and pepper to taste. Bring the mixture to a boil, then reduce the heat, cover the pan, and leave to simmer gently for 40 minutes or until the rice is almost cooked and most of the liquid is absorbed.

4 Add the apricots or peaches, red bell pepper and peas to the rice mixture in the pan. Cover and cook for 10 minutes.

5 Remove the pan from the heat and leave to stand for 5 minutes without uncovering.

6 Peel and slice the bananas. Uncover the rice mixture and toss with a fork to mix. Add the toasted nuts and sliced banana and toss lightly.

7 Transfer the brown rice and fruit and nuts to a serving platter and serve piping hot.

Stuffed Rice Pancakes

Dosas (pancakes) are widely eaten in southern India. The rice and urid dal need to soak and ferment, so prepare well ahead of time.

NUTRITIONAL INFORMATION

Calories 748	Sugars 1g
Protein 10g	Fat 47g
Carbohydrate ...76g	Saturates 5g

6¼ HOURS 40-45 MINS

SERVES 4

INGREDIENTS

1 cup rice and ¼ cup urid dal (lentil flour), or
1¾ cups ground rice and 7 tbsp urid
dal flour (ata)

2–2½ cups water

1 tsp salt

4 tbsp vegetable oil

FILLING

4 medium potatoes, diced

3 fresh green chilies, chopped

½ tsp turmeric

1 tsp salt

⅔ cup oil

1 tsp mixed mustard and onion seeds

3 dried chilies

4 curry leaves

2 tbsp lemon juice

1 To make the dosas (pancakes), soak the rice and urid dal for 3 hours. Grind the rice and urid dal to a smooth consistency, adding water if necessary. Set aside for a further 3 hours to ferment. Alternatively, if you are using ground rice and urid dal flour (ata), mix together in a bowl. Add the water and salt and stir until a batter is formed.

2 Heat about 1 tbsp of oil in a large, non-stick skillet. Using a ladle, spoon the batter into the skillet. Tilt the skillet to spread the mixture over the base. Cover and cook over a medium heat for about 2 minutes. Remove the lid and turn the dosa over very carefully. Pour a little oil around the edge, cover, and cook for 2 minutes more. Repeat with the remaining batter.

3 To make the filling, cook the potatoes in a pan of boiling water. Add the chilies, turmeric, and salt and cook until the potatoes are just soft. Drain and mash lightly with a fork.

4 Heat the oil in a saucepan and fry the mustard and onion seeds, dried red chilies and curry leaves, stirring constantly, for about 1 minute. Pour the spice mixture over the mashed potatoes, then sprinkle over the lemon juice and mix well. Spoon the potato filling on one half of each of the dosas (pancakes) and fold the other half over it. Transfer to a warmed serving dish and serve hot.

Oriental-Style Millet Pilaf

Millet makes an interesting alternative to rice, which is the more traditional ingredient for a pilaf. Serve with a crisp oriental salad.

NUTRITIONAL INFORMATION

Calories 660	Sugars 28g
Protein 15g	Fat 27g
Carbohydrate ...94g	Saturates 5g

  20 MINS 30 MINS

SERVES 4

I N G R E D I E N T S

1½ cups millet

1 tbsp vegetable oil

1 bunch green onions,
   white and green parts, chopped

1 garlic clove, crushed

1 tsp grated fresh ginger

1 orange bell pepper, seeded and diced

2½ cups water

1 orange

¾ cup chopped pitted dates

2 tsp sesame oil

1 cup roasted cashews

2 tbsp pumpkin seeds

salt and pepper

oriental salad vegetables, to serve

1 Place the millet in a large saucepan and toast over a medium heat, shaking the pan occasionally, for 4–5 minutes, until the grains begin to crack and pop.

2 Heat the oil in another saucepan. Add the green onions, garlic, ginger, and bell pepper and fry, stirring frequently, for 2–3 minutes, until just softened, but not browned. Add the millet and pour in the water.

3 Using a vegetable peeler, pare the zest from the orange and add the zest to the pan. Squeeze the juice from the orange into the pan. Season to taste with salt and pepper.

4 Bring to a boil, reduce the heat, cover, and cook gently for 20 minutes, until all the liquid has been absorbed. Remove from the heat, stir in the dates and sesame oil, and leave to stand for 10 minutes.

5 Discard the orange zest and stir in the cashews. Pile into a warmed serving dish, sprinkle with pumpkin seeds, and serve with salad vegetables.

Green Herb Rice

This is a deliciously different way to serve plain rice for a special occasion or to liven up a simple meal.

NUTRITIONAL INFORMATION

Calories	652	Sugars	.........9g
Protein	........15g	Fat	..........17g
Carbohydrate	...116g	Saturates	.......6g

 1HR 10 MINS   35 MINS

SERVES 4

I N G R E D I E N T S

2 tbsp olive oil

2¼ cups basmati or Thai jasmine rice,
   soaked for 1 hour, washed and drained

3 cups coconut milk

1 tsp salt

1 bay leaf

2 tbsp chopped cilantro

2 tbsp chopped mint

2 green chilies, seeded and finely chopped

1 Heat the oil in a saucepan, add the rice, and stir over a medium heat until it becomes translucent.

2 Add the coconut milk, salt, and bay leaf. Bring to a boil and cook until all the liquid is absorbed.

COOK'S TIP

The contrasting colors of this dish make it particularly attractive, and it can be made to look even more interesting with a carefully chosen garnish. Two segments of fresh lime compliment the cilantro perfectly.

3 Reduce the heat to very low, cover the saucepan tightly, and cook for 10 minutes. Take great care that the rice does not catch and burn on the base of the saucepan.

4 Remove the bay leaf and stir in the cilantro, mint, and green chilies. Fork through the rice gently to fluff up the grains. Transfer to a warm serving dish and serve immediately.

Vegetable Pulao

This is a lovely way of cooking rice and vegetables together, and the saffron gives it a beautiful aroma. Serve this with any kabob.

NUTRITIONAL INFORMATION

Calories 557	Sugars 9g	
Protein 11g	Fat 14g	
Carbohydrate ..104g	Saturates 7g	

 20 MINS   55 MINS

SERVES 6

INGREDIENTS

2 medium potatoes, each cut into 6

1 medium eggplant, cut into 6

7 oz carrots, sliced

1¾ oz green beans, cut into pieces

4 tbsp vegetable ghee

2 medium onions, sliced

¾ cup plain yogurt

2 tsp finely chopped fresh ginger

2 tsp crushed garlic

2 tsp garam masala

2 tsp black cumin seeds

½ tsp turmeric

3 black cardamoms

3 cinnamon sticks

2 tsp salt

1 tsp chili powder

½ tsp saffron strands

1¼ cups milk

3 cups basmati rice

5 tbsp lemon juice

TO GARNISH

4 green chilies, chopped

cilantro leaves, chopped

1 Prepare the vegetables. Heat the ghee in a skillet. Add the potatoes, eggplant, carrots, and beans and fry, turning frequently, until softened. Remove from the pan and set aside.

2 Add the onions and fry, stirring frequently, until soft. Add the yogurt, ginger, garlic, garam masala, 1 teaspoon black cumin seeds, the turmeric, 1 cardamom, 1 cinnamon stick, 1 teaspoon salt, and the chili powder and stir-fry for 3–5 minutes. Return the vegetables to the pan and fry for 4–5 minutes.

3 Put the saffron and milk in a saucepan and bring to a boil, stirring. Remove from the heat and set aside.

4 In a pan of boiling water, half-cook the rice with 1 teaspoon salt, 2 cinnamon sticks, 2 black cardamoms, and 1 teaspoon black cumin seeds. Drain the rice, leaving half in the pan, while transferring the other half to a bowl. Pour the vegetable mixture on top of the rice in the pan. Pour half of the lemon juice and half of the saffron milk over the vegetables and rice, cover with the remaining rice and pour the remaining lemon juice and saffron milk over the top. Garnish with chilies and cilantro, return to the heat, and cover. Cook over a low heat for about 20 minutes. Serve hot.

Spiced Rice & Lentils

This is a lovely combination of rice and masoor dal and is simple to cook. You can add a dollop of unsalted butter before serving, if desired.

NUTRITIONAL INFORMATION

Calories	394	Sugars	.........3g
Protein	........14g	Fat	...........8g
Carbohydrate	...70g	Saturates	.......1g

 5 MINS   30 MINS

SERVES 4

INGREDIENTS

1 cup basmati rice

¾ cup masoor dal

2 tbsp vegetable ghee

1 small onion, sliced

1 tsp finely chopped fresh ginger

1 tsp crushed garlic

½ tsp turmeric

2½ cups water

1 tsp salt

1 Combine the rice and dal and rinse thoroughly in cold running water. Set aside until required.

2 Heat the ghee in a large saucepan. Add the onion and fry, stirring occasionally, for about 2 minutes.

COOK'S TIP

Many Indian recipes specify using ghee as the cooking fat. This is because it is similar to clarified butter in that it can be heated to a very high temperature without burning. Ghee adds a nutty flavor to dishes and a glossy shine to sauces.

3 Reduce the heat, add the ginger, garlic, and turmeric and stir-fry for 1 minute.

4 Add the rice and dal to the mixture in the pan and blend together, mixing gently, but thoroughly.

5 Add the water to the mixture in the pan and bring to a boil over a medium heat. Reduce the heat, cover, and cook for 20–25 minutes, until the rice is tender and the liquid is absorbed.

6 Just before serving, add the salt and mix to combine.

7 Transfer the spiced rice and lentils to a large warmed serving dish and serve immediately.

Channa Dal & Rice

Saffron is used to flavor this dish, which makes it rather special.
It is absolutely delicious served with any curry.

NUTRITIONAL INFORMATION

Calories 479	Sugars 7g	
Protein 12g	Fat 14g	
Carbohydrate ...80g	Saturates 8g	

3¼ HOURS   1 HOUR

SERVES 6

I N G R E D I E N T S

¾ cup channa dal

4 tbsp ghee

2 medium onions, sliced

1 tsp finely chopped fresh ginger

1 tsp crushed garlic

½ tsp turmeric

2 tsp salt

½ tsp chili powder

1 tsp garam masala

5 tbsp plain yogurt

5⅔ cups water

⅔ cup milk

1 tsp saffron

3 tbsp lemon juice

2 fresh green chilies

fresh cilantro leaves

3 black cardamoms

3 black cumin seeds

2¼ cups basmati rice

1 Rinse and soak the channa dal for 3 hours. Rinse the rice under running water and set aside.

2 Heat the ghee in a skillet. Add the onion and fry until golden brown. Using a perforated spoon, remove half of the onion with a little of the ghee and set aside in a bowl.

3 Add the ginger, garlic, turmeric, 1 tsp of the salt, the chili powder, and garam masala to the mixture remaining in the pan and stir-fry for 5 minutes. Stir in the yogurt and add the chana dal and ⅔ cup water. Cook, covered, for 15 minutes. Set aside.

4 Meanwhile, boil the milk with the saffron and set aside with the reserved fried onion, lemon juice, green chilies, and cilantro leaves.

5 Boil the rest of the water and add the salt, black cardamoms, black cumin seeds, and the rice, and cook, stirring, until the rice is half-cooked. Drain, and place half of the fried onion, saffron, lemon juice, green chilies, and cilantro on top of the channa dal mixture. Place the remaining rice on top of this and the rest of the fried onion, saffron, lemon juice, chilies, and cilantro on top of the rice. Cover tightly with a lid and cook for 20 minutes over a very low heat. Mix with a perforated spoon before transferring to a warmed serving dish. Serve immediately.

Vegballs with Chili Sauce

These tasty, nutty morsels are delicious served with a fiery, tangy sauce that counteracts the richness of the peanuts.

NUTRITIONAL INFORMATION

Calories	.615	Sugars	.13g
Protein	.23g	Fat	.43g
Carbohydrate	.37g	Saturates	.8g

25 MINS   30 MINS

SERVES 4

INGREDIENTS

3 tbsp peanut oil

1 onion, finely chopped

1 celery stalk, chopped

1 tsp dried mixed herbs

2 cups roasted unsalted
   peanuts, ground

1 cup canned garbanzo beans, drained
   and mashed

1 tsp yeast extract

1 cup fresh whole wheat breadcrumbs

1 egg yolk

¼ cup all-purpose flour

strips of fresh red chili, to garnish

HOT CHILI SAUCE

2 tsp peanut oil

1 large red chili, seeded and finely chopped

2 green onions, finely chopped

2 tbsp red wine vinegar

7 oz can diced tomatoes

2 tbsp tomato paste

2 tsp sugar

salt and pepper

rice and salad greens, to serve

1 Heat 1 tablespoon of the oil in a skillet and gently fry the onion and celery for 3–4 minutes, until softened, but not browned.

2 Place all the other ingredients, except the remaining oil and the flour, in a mixing bowl and add the onion and celery. Mix well.

3 Divide the mixture into 12 portions and roll into small balls. Coat all over with the flour.

4 Heat the remaining oil in a skillet. Add the garbanzo bean balls and cook over a medium heat, turning frequently, for 15 minutes, until cooked through and golden. Drain on paper towels.

5 Meanwhile, make the hot chili sauce. Heat the oil in a small skillet and gently fry the chili and green onions for 2–3 minutes. Stir in the remaining ingredients and season. Bring to a boil and simmer for 5 minutes.

6 Serve the garbanzo bean and peanut balls with the hot chili sauce, rice, and a salad.

Red Bean Stew & Dumplings

There's nothing better on a cold day than a hearty dish topped with dumplings. This recipe is very quick and easy to prepare.

NUTRITIONAL INFORMATION

Calories	508	Sugars	........15g
Protein	........22g	Fat	.........12g
Carbohydrate	...83g	Saturates	.......4g

20 MINS   40 MINS

SERVES 4

INGREDIENTS

1 tbsp vegetable oil

1 red onion, sliced

2 celery stalks, chopped

3½ cups vegetable stock

8 oz carrots, diced

8 oz potatoes, diced

8 oz zucchini, diced

4 tomatoes, peeled and chopped

½ cup split red lentils

14 oz can kidney beans,
   rinsed and drained

1 tsp paprika

salt and pepper

DUMPLINGS

1 cup all-purpose flour

½ tsp salt

2 tsp baking powder

1 tsp paprika

1 tsp dried mixed herbs

2 tbsp shortening

7 tbsp water

sprigs of flat-leaf parsley, to garnish

1 Heat the oil in a flameproof casserole or a large saucepan. Add the onion and celery and fry over a low heat, stirring frequently, for about 3–4 minutes until just softened.

2 Pour in the stock and stir in the carrots and potatoes. Bring to a boil, cover, and cook for 5 minutes.

3 Stir in the zucchini, tomatoes, lentils, kidney beans, paprika, and seasoning. Bring to a boil, cover, and cook for 5 minutes.

4 Meanwhile, make the dumplings. Sift the flour, salt, baking powder, and paprika into a bowl. Stir in the herbs and shortening. Bind together with the water to form a soft dough. Divide into 8 portions and roll gently to form balls.

5 Uncover the stew, stir, then add the dumplings, pushing them slightly into the stew. Cover, reduce the heat so the stew simmers, and cook for 15 minutes more, until the dumplings have risen and are cooked through. Garnish with flat-leaf parsley and serve immediately.

Savory Flan

This tasty flan combines lentils and red bell peppers in a crisp whole wheat pie shell.

NUTRITIONAL INFORMATION

Calories 287   Sugars 5g
Protein ....10g   Fat 5g
Carbohydrate ...35g   Saturates 3g

45 MINS   50 MINS

SERVES 8

I N G R E D I E N T S

PASTRY

1¾ cups all-purpose whole wheat flour

⅓ cup margarine,
    cut into small pieces

4 tbsp water

FILLING

¾ cup red lentils, rinsed

1¼ cups vegetable stock

11 tbsp margarine

1 onion, chopped

2 red bell peppers, seeded and diced

1 tsp yeast extract

1 tbsp tomato paste

3 tbsp chopped parsley

pepper

1 To make the pie dough, place the flour in a mixing bowl and cut in the margarine with your fingertips until the mixture resembles fine breadcrumbs. Stir in the water and bring together to form a dough. Wrap and chill for 30 minutes.

2 Meanwhile, make the filling. Put the lentils in a saucepan with the stock, bring to a boil, and then simmer for 10 minutes, until the lentils are tender and can be mashed to a purée.

3 Melt the margarine in a small pan, add the chopped onion and diced red bell peppers, and fry, stirring frequently, until just soft.

4 Add the lentil purée, yeast extract, tomato paste, and parsley. Season to taste with pepper. Mix until well combined.

5 On a lightly floured surface, roll out the dough and line a 9½ inch loose-based quiche pan. Prick the base of the dough with a fork and spoon the lentil mixture into the pie shell.

6 Bake in a preheated oven at 400°F for 30 minutes, until the filling is firm.

VARIATION

Add corn to the flan in step 4 for a colorful and tasty change, if you prefer.

Fragrant Curry

There are many different ways of cooking garbanzo beans, but this version is probably one of the most delicious and popular.

NUTRITIONAL INFORMATION

Calories 313   Sugars 5g
Protein . . . . .8g   Fat 19g
Carbohydrate . . .29g   Saturates 2g

🕙 10 MINS   🕐 20 MINS

SERVES 4

I N G R E D I E N T S

6 tbsp vegetable oil

2 medium onions, sliced

1 tsp finely chopped fresh ginger

1 tsp ground cumin

1 tsp ground coriander

1 tsp crushed garlic

1 tsp chili powder

2 fresh green chilies

cilantro leaves

⅔ cup water

1 large potato

14 oz can garbanzo beans, drained

1 tbsp lemon juice

1 Heat the oil in a large saucepan. Add the onions and fry over a medium heat, stirring occasionally, for 5–8 minutes, until golden brown.

2 Reduce the heat, add the ginger, ground cumin, ground coriander, garlic, chili powder, fresh green chilies, and cilantro leaves to the pan and stir-fry for 2 minutes.

3 Add the water to the mixture in the pan and stir well to mix.

4 Using a sharp knife, cut the potato into small diced pieces. Add the potato and the drained garbanzo beans to the mixture in the pan. Lower the heat, cover, and simmer, stirring occasionally, for 5–7 minutes.

5 Sprinkle the lemon juice over the curry and stir.

6 Transfer the garbanzo bean curry to warmed individual serving dishes and serve immediately.

COOK'S TIP

Using canned garbanzo beans saves time, but you can use dried garbanzo beans if you prefer. Soak them overnight, then boil them for 15–20 minutes, or until soft.

Semolina Fritters

Based on a gnocchi recipe, these delicious cheese-flavored fritters are accompanied by a fruity homemade apple relish.

NUTRITIONAL INFORMATION

Calories ....682 Sugars 40g
Protein ....19g Fat 32g
Carbohydrate ...85g Saturates 11g

 30 MINS   40-45 MINS

SERVES 4

INGREDIENTS

2½ cups milk

1 small onion

1 celery stalk

1 bay leaf

2 cloves

⅔ cup semolina

1 cup grated sharp cheddar cheese

½ tsp dried mustard powder

2 tbsp all-purpose flour

1 egg, beaten

¾ cup dried white breadcrumbs

6 tbsp vegetable oil

salt and pepper

celery leaves, to garnish

coleslaw, to serve

RELISH

2 celery stalks, chopped

2 small apples, cored and diced

½ cup golden raisins

½ cup dried apricots, chopped

6 tbsp cider vinegar

pinch of ground cloves

½ tsp ground cinnamon

1 Pour the milk into a saucepan and add the onion, celery, bay leaf, and cloves. Bring to a boil, remove from the heat, and allow to stand for 15 minutes.

2 Strain into another saucepan, bring to a boil and sprinkle in the semolina, stirring constantly. Reduce the heat and simmer for 5 minutes, until very thick, stirring occasionally to prevent it sticking.

3 Remove the pan from the heat. Beat in the cheese, mustard, and seasoning. Place in a greased bowl and allow to cool.

4 To make the relish, put all the ingredients in a saucepan, bring to a boil, cover, and simmer gently for 20 minutes, until tender. Allow to cool.

5 Put the flour, egg, and breadcrumbs on separate plates. Divide the cooled semolina mixture into 8 and press into 2½ inch rounds, flouring the hands if necessary.

6 Coat lightly in flour, then in egg and, finally, in breadcrumbs. Heat the oil in a large skillet and gently fry the fritters for 3–4 minutes on each side, until golden. Drain on paper towels. Garnish with celery leaves and serve immediately with the apple relish and coleslaw.

Lemon Dal

This dal is eaten almost every day in most households in Hyderabad in India. Traditionally, it is cooked with tamarind, but lemon juice is easier.

NUTRITIONAL INFORMATION

Calories 386   Sugars 0.7g
Protein ....5g   Fat 35g
Carbohydrate ...12g   Saturates 4g

 10 MINS   30 MINS

SERVES 4

INGREDIENTS

½ cup masoor dal

1 tsp finely chopped fresh ginger

1 tsp crushed garlic

1 tsp chili powder

½ tsp turmeric

2 cups water

1 tsp salt

3 tbsp lemon juice

2 fresh green chilies

cilantro leaves

BAGHAAR

¾ cup oil

4 garlic cloves

6 dried red chilies

1 tsp white cumin seeds

1 Rinse the masoor dal and place in a large saucepan. Add the ginger, garlic, chili powder, and turmeric. Stir in 1¼ cups of the water and bring to a boil over a medium heat. Half-cover the pan and simmer until the dal is soft enough to be mashed.

2 Mash the dal. Add the salt, lemon juice, and the remaining water, stir to mix thoroughly. It should be of a fairly smooth consistency.

3 Add the green chilies and cilantro leaves to the dal and set aside.

4 To make the baghaar, heat the oil in a heavy-bottomed pan. Add the garlic, red chilies, and white cumin seeds and fry for about 1 minute. Turn off the heat.

5 When the baghaar has cooled slightly, pour it over the dal. If the dal is too runny, set it, uncovered, over a medium heat for 3–5 minutes, until it has thickened slightly.

6 Transfer the dal to a warmed serving dish and serve hot.

Midweek Curry Special

This easy curry is always enjoyed. Double the quantities for a great dish if you're cooking for a crowd.

NUTRITIONAL INFORMATION

Calories 403	Sugars 19g
Protein 19g	Fat 15g
Carbohydrate ...51g	Saturates 3g

20 MINS   40–45 MINS

SERVES 4

I N G R E D I E N T S

2 tbsp vegetable oil

2 garlic cloves, crushed

1 large onion, chopped

1 large carrot, sliced

1 apple, cored and chopped

2 tbsp medium-hot curry powder

1 tsp finely grated fresh ginger

2 tsp paprika

3½ cups vegetable stock

2 tbsp tomato paste

½ small cauliflower, broken into flowerets

15 oz can garbanzo beans, rinsed and
    drained

2 tbsp golden raisins

2 tbsp cornstarch

2 tbsp water

4 hard-cooked eggs

salt and pepper

paprika, to garnish

C U C U M B E R   D I P

3-inch piece of cucumber, chopped

1 tbsp chopped mint

¾ cup plain yogurt

mint sprigs, to garnish

1 Heat the oil in a large saucepan. Add the garlic, onion, carrot, and apple and fry, stirring frequently, for 4–5 minutes, until softened.

2 Add the curry powder, ginger, and paprika and fry for 1 minute. Stir in the vegetable stock and tomato paste.

3 Add the cauliflower, garbanzo beans, and golden raisins. Bring to a boil, then reduce the heat, cover, and simmer, for 25–30 minutes, until the vegetables are tender.

4 Blend the cornstarch with the water to a smooth paste and add to the curry, stirring until thickened. Cook gently for 2 minutes. Season to taste with salt and pepper.

5 To make the dip, mix together the cucumber, mint, and yogurt in a small serving bowl.

6 Ladle the curry on to 4 warmed serving plates. Shell and quarter the eggs and arrange them on top of the curry. Sprinkle with a little paprika. Garnish the cucumber and mint dip with mint and serve with the curry.

Lentil & Vegetable Biryani

A delicious mix of vegetables, basmati rice, and lentils produces
a wholesome and nutritious dish.

NUTRITIONAL INFORMATION

Calories	.516	Sugars	.9g
Protein	.20g	Fat	.19g
Carbohydrate	.72g	Saturates	.3g

20 MINS   45 MINS

SERVES 6

INGREDIENTS

¾ cup lentils

4 tbsp vegetable ghee or oil

2 onions, quartered and sliced

2 garlic cloves, crushed

1 inch piece of fresh ginger, chopped

1 tsp ground turmeric

½ tsp chili powder

1 tsp ground coriander

2 tsp ground cumin

3 tomatoes, peeled and chopped

1 eggplant, trimmed and
    cut in ½ inch pieces

6¼ cups boiling vegetable stock

1 red or green bell pepper, seeded
    and diced

1¾ cups basmati rice

1 cup green beans, halved

1⅓ cups cauliflower flowerets

1½ cups mushrooms,
    sliced or quartered

½ cup unsalted cashews

3 hard-cooked eggs, shelled, and cilantro
sprigs, to garnish

1 Rinse the lentils under cold running water and drain. Heat the ghee or oil in a saucepan, add the onions, and fry gently for 2 minutes. Stir in the garlic, ginger, and spices and fry gently, stirring frequently, for 1 minute.

2 Add the lentils, tomatoes, eggplant, and 2½ cups of the stock, mix well, then cover and simmer gently for 20 minutes.

3 Add the red or green bell pepper and cook for another 10 minutes, or until the lentils are tender and all the liquid has been absorbed.

4 Meanwhile, rinse the rice under cold running water. Drain and place in another pan with the remaining stock. Bring to a boil, add the green beans, cauliflower, and mushrooms, then cover and cook gently for 15 minutes, or until rice and vegetables are tender. Remove from the heat and set aside, covered, for 10 minutes.

5 Add the lentil mixture and the cashews to the cooked rice and mix lightly together. Pile onto a warm serving platter and garnish with wedges of hard-cooked egg and cilantro sprigs. Serve hot.

Dry Moong Dal

This dal has a baghaar (seasoned oil dressing) of butter, dried red chilies, and white cumin seeds. It is simple to cook and tastes very good.

NUTRITIONAL INFORMATION

Calories 304	Sugars 1g
Protein 9g	Fat 21g
Carbohydrate ...21g	Saturates 14g

  5 MINS   30–35 MINS

SERVES 4

I N G R E D I E N T S

1 cup moong dal

1 tsp finely chopped fresh ginger

½ tsp ground cumin

½ tsp ground coriander

1 tsp fresh garlic, crushed

½ tsp chili powder

2½ cups water

1 tsp salt

B A G H A A R

8 tbsp unsalted butter

5 dried red chilies

1 tsp white cumin seeds

T O S E R V E

chapati

vegetable curry

COOK'S TIP

Moong dal are tear-drop-shaped yellow split lentils, more popular in northern India than in the south. Dried red chilies are the quickest way to add heat to a dish.

1 Rinse the lentils under cold running water and place them in a large saucepan. Add the ginger, ground cumin, ground coriander, garlic, and chili powder, and stir to mix well.

2 Pour in enough of the water to cover the lentil mixture. Cook over a medium heat, stirring frequently, until the lentils are soft but not mushy.

3 Stir in the salt, transfer to a serving dish, and keep warm.

4 Meanwhile, make the baghaar. Melt the butter in a heavy-bottomed saucepan over a fairly low heat. Add the dried red chilies and white cumin seeds and fry, stirring constantly, until they begin to pop.

5 Pour the baghaar over the lentils and serve immediately with chapati and a vegetable curry.

Vegetable & Lentil Koftas

A mixture of vegetables, nuts and lentils is shaped into small balls and baked in the oven with a sprinkling of aromatic garam masala.

NUTRITIONAL INFORMATION

Calories 679   Sugars 20g
Protein ....29g   Fat 33g
Carbohydrate ...73g   Saturates 5g

 30 MINS   50 MINS

SERVES 4

INGREDIENTS

6 tbsp vegetable ghee or oil

1 onion, finely chopped

2 carrots, finely chopped

2 celery stalks, finely chopped

2 garlic cloves, minced

1 fresh green chili, seeded and
   finely chopped

4½ tsp curry powder or paste

1¼ cups split red lentils

2½ cups vegetable stock

2 tbsp tomato paste

2 cups fresh whole wheat bread crumbs

¾ cup unsalted cashews, finely chopped

2 tbsp chopped cilantro

1 egg, beaten

salt and pepper

garam masala, for sprinkling

YOGURT DRESSING

1 cup unsweetened yogurt

1-2 tbsp chopped cilantro

1-2 tbsp mango chutney,
   chopped if necessary

1 Heat 4 tablespoons of ghee or oil in a large saucepan and gently fry the onion, carrots, celery, garlic, and chili, stirring frequently, for 5 minutes. Add the curry powder or paste and the lentils and cook, stirring constantly, for 1 minute.

2 Add the stock and tomato paste and bring to a boil. Reduce the heat, cover, and simmer for 20 minutes or until the lentils are tender and all the liquid is absorbed.

3 Remove from the heat and cool slightly. Add the bread crumbs, nuts, cilantro, egg, and seasoning to taste. Mix well and leave to cool. Shape into rounds about the size of golf balls (use 2 spoons to help shape the rounds).

4 Place the balls on an oiled baking sheet, drizzle with the remaining oil and sprinkle with a little garam masala, to taste. Cook in a preheated oven, at 350°F, for 15-20 minutes, or until very hot and lightly golden in color.

5 Meanwhile, make the yogurt dressing. Mix all the ingredients together in a bowl. Serve the koftas hot with the yogurt dressing.

Black-Eyed Peas

This is very good served with chapatis and a vegetable curry. The peas need to be soaked overnight so prepare well ahead of time.

NUTRITIONAL INFORMATION

Calories 757   Sugars 5g
Protein . . . . .10g   Fat 69g
Carbohydrate . . .26g   Saturates 7g

  5 MINS   1 HOUR

SERVES 4

I N G R E D I E N T S

1 cup black-eyed peas

1¼ cups vegetable oil

2 medium onions, sliced

1 tsp finely chopped fresh ginger

1 tsp crushed garlic

1 tsp chili powder

1½ tsp salt

1½ tsp ground coriander

1½ tsp ground cumin

⅔ cup water

2 green chilies

cilantro leaves

1 tbsp lemon juice

1 Rinse the black-eyed peas, place them in a bowl, cover with cold water, and set aside to soak overnight.

2 Drain the black-eyed peas, place in a pan of water and bring to a boil over a low heat. Simmer for about 30 minutes. Drain the peas thoroughly and set aside.

3 Heat the oil in a heavy-bottomed pan. Add the onions and fry, stirring frequently, for 5–8 minutes, until golden brown. Add the ginger, garlic, chili powder, salt, ground coriander, and ground cumin and stir-fry the mixture for 3–5 minutes.

4 Add the water to the pan, cover, and simmer until all of the water has completely evaporated.

5 Add the black-eyed peas, green chilies, and cilantro leaves to the onions and stir-fry for 3-5 minutes.

6 Transfer the black-eyed peas to a serving dish, sprinkle over the lemon juice, and serve immediately. Alternatively, allow the black-eyed peas to cool and serve cold.

COOK'S TIP

Black-eyed peas are oval-shaped, gray or beige peas with a dark dot in the center. They have a slightly smoky flavor. They are sold canned, as well as dried.

Midweek Medley

Canned garbanzo beans are used in this dish, but you could use black-eyed peas or red kidney beans, if preferred.

NUTRITIONAL INFORMATION

Calories	480	Sugars	.........8g
Protein	........11g	Fat	..........38g
Carbohydrate	...25g	Saturates	......13g

15 MINS   20-25 MINS

SERVES 4

INGREDIENTS

1 large eggplant

2 zucchini

6 tbsp vegetable ghee or oil

1 large onion, quartered and sliced

2 garlic cloves, crushed

1–2 fresh green chilies, seeded and
    chopped, or 1–2 tsp minced chili

2 tsp ground coriander

2 tsp cumin seeds

1 tsp ground turmeric

1 tsp garam masala

14 oz can diced tomatoes

1¼ cups vegetable stock
    or water

salt and pepper

14 oz can garbanzo beans, drained and
rinsed

2 tbsp chopped mint

⅔ cup heavy cream

1 Trim the leaf end off eggplant and cut into cubes. Trim and slice the zucchini.

2 Heat the ghee or oil in a saucepan and fry the eggplant, zucchini, onion, garlic, and chilies over a low heat, stirring frequently, for about 5 minutes, adding a little more oil to the pan, if necessary.

3 Stir in the spices and cook for 30 seconds. Add the tomatoes and stock and season with salt and pepper to taste. Cook for 10 minutes.

4 Add the garbanzo beans to the pan and cook for 5 minutes more.

5 Stir in the mint and cream and reheat gently. Taste and adjust the seasoning, if necessary. Transfer to a warm serving dish and serve hot with plain or pilaf rice, or with parathas, if preferred.

Aloo Chat

Aloo Chat is one of a variety of Indian foods served at any time of the day. The garbanzo beans need to be soaked overnight.

NUTRITIONAL INFORMATION

Calories 262   Sugars 6g
Protein ....13g   Fat 4g
Carbohydrate ...46g   Saturates 0.5g

 35 MINS   1 HR 5 MINS

SERVES 4

INGREDIENTS

½ cup garbanzo beans soaked
    overnight in cold water and drained

1 dried red chili

1 lb 2 oz potatoes, boiled in
    their skins and peeled

1 tsp cumin seeds

2 tsp salt

1 tsp black peppercorns

½ tsp dried mint

½ tsp chili powder

½ tsp ground ginger

2 tsp mango powder

½ cup plain yogurt

oil, for deep frying

4 pappadums

VARIATION

Instead of garbanzo beans, diced tropical fruits can be stirred into the potatoes and spice mix; add a little lemon juice to balance the sweetness.

1 Boil the garbanzo beans with the chili in plenty of water for about 1 hour, until tender. Drain.

2 Cut the potatoes into 1 inch dice and mix into the garbanzo beans while they are still warm. Set aside.

3 Grind together the cumin, salt, and peppercorns in a spice grinder or with a pestle and mortar. Stir in the mint, chili powder, ginger, and mango powder.

4 Put a small saucepan or skillet over a low heat and add the spice mix. Stir until the spices give off their aroma and then immediately remove the pan from the heat.

5 Stir half of the spice mix into the garbanzo bean and potato mixture and stir the other half into the yogurt.

6 Cook the pappadums according to the instructions on the pack. Drain on plenty of paper towels. Break into bite-size pieces and stir into the potatoes and garbanzo beans, spoon over the spiced yogurt, and serve immediately.

Egg & Lentil Curry

A nutritious meal that is easy and relatively quick to make. The curried lentil sauce would also be delicious served with cooked vegetables.

NUTRITIONAL INFORMATION

Calories	298	Sugars	.........6g
Protein	........17g	Fat	..........17g
Carbohydrate	...20g	Saturates	.......4g

🍲 10 MINS   🕐 35 MINS

SERVES 4

I N G R E D I E N T S

3 tbsp vegetable ghee or oil

1 large onion, chopped

2 garlic cloves, chopped

1-inch piece fresh
    ginger chopped

½ tsp minced chili or chili powder

1 tsp ground coriander

1 tsp ground cumin

1 tsp paprika

⅓ cup split red lentils

1¾ cups vegetable stock

8 oz can diced tomatoes

6 eggs

¼ cup coconut milk

salt

2 tomatoes, cut into wedges,
    and cilantro sprigs, to garnish

parathas, chapatis, or naan bread,
    to serve

1 Heat the ghee or oil in a saucepan, add the onion, and fry gently for 3 minutes. Stir in the garlic, ginger, chili, and spices and cook gently, stirring frequently, for 1 minute. Stir in the lentils, stock, and diced tomatoes and bring to a boil. Reduce the heat, cover, and simmer, stirring occasionally, for 30 minutes, until the lentils are tender.

2 Meanwhile, place the eggs in a saucepan of cold water and bring to a boil. Reduce the heat and simmer for 10 minutes. Drain and cover immediately with cold water.

3 Stir the coconut milk into the lentil mixture and season well with salt to taste. Process the mixture in a blender or food processor until smooth. Return to the pan and heat through.

4 Shell the hard-cooked eggs and cut in half lengthwise. Arrange 3 halves, in a petal design, on each serving plate. Spoon the hot lentil sauce over the eggs, adding enough to flood the plate. Arrange a tomato wedge and a cilantro sprig between each halved egg. Serve hot with parathas, chapatis, or naan bread.

Spinach & Chana Dal

An attractive-looking dish, this makes a good accompaniment to almost any dish. For a contrast in color and taste, serve with a tomato curry.

NUTRITIONAL INFORMATION

Calories ....175 Sugars 1g
Protein ....6g Fat 12g
Carbohydrate ...12g Saturates 1g

3 HRS 5 MINS 45 MINS

SERVES 6

INGREDIENTS

4 tbsp channa dal

6 tbsp oil

1 tsp mixed onion and mustard seeds

4 dried red chilies

14-15 oz can spinach, drained

1 tsp finely chopped fresh ginger

1 tsp ground coriander

1 tsp ground cumin

1 tsp salt

1 tsp chili powder

2 tbsp lemon juice

1 green chili, to garnish

1 Soak the chana dal in a bowl of warm water for at least 3 hours, preferably overnight.

COOK'S TIP

Very similar in appearance to moong dal—the yellow split peas—channa dal have slightly less shiny grains. It is used as a binding agent and may be bought from Indian and Pakistani grocers.

2 Place the lentils in a saucepan, cover with water, and bring to a boil. Simmer for 30 minutes.

3 Heat the oil in a saucepan. Add the mixed onion and mustard seeds and dried red chilies and fry, stirring constantly, until they turn a shade darker.

4 Add the drained spinach to the pan, mixing gently. Add the ginger, ground coriander, ground cumin, salt, and chili

powder to the mixture in the pan. Reduce the heat and gently stir-fry the mixture for 7-10 minutes.

5 Add the lentils to the pan and blend into the spinach mixture well, stirring gently so that it does not break up.

6 Transfer the mixture to a warm serving dish. Sprinkle over the lemon juice and garnish with the green chili. Serve immediately.

Kabli Channa Sag

Legumes such as garbanzo beans are widely used in India. They need to be soaked overnight so prepare well ahead of time.

NUTRITIONAL INFORMATION

Calories 217   Sugars 5g
Protein . . . . .12g   Fat 9g
Carbohydrate . . .25g   Saturates 1g

10 MINS   1 HOUR

SERVES 6

INGREDIENTS

1 cup garbanzo beans soaked overnight
    and drained

5 cloves

1 inch piece cinnamon stick

2 garlic cloves

3 tbsp sunflower oil

1 small onion, sliced

3 tbsp lemon juice

1 tsp coriander seeds

2 tomatoes, peeled, seeded, and chopped

1 lb 2 oz spinach, rinsed and any
    tough stems removed

1 tbsp chopped cilantro

TO GARNISH

cilantro sprigs

lemon slices

1 Put the garbanzo beans into a saucepan with enough water to cover. Add the cloves, cinnamon, and 1 whole unpeeled garlic clove that has been lightly crushed with the back of a knife to release the juices. Bring to a boil, reduce the heat, and simmer for 40–50 minutes, or until the garbanzo beans are tender when tested with a skewer. Skim off any foam that comes to the surface.

2 Meanwhile, heat 1 tablespoon of the oil in a saucepan. Crush the remaining garlic clove. Put this into the pan with the oil and the onion, and cook over a moderate heat for about 5 minutes.

3 Remove the cloves, cinnamon, and garlic from the pan of garbanzo beans. Drain the garbanzo beans. Using a food processor or a fork, blend ½ cup of the garbanzo beans with the onion and garlic, the lemon juice and 1 tablespoon of the oil until smooth. Stir this purée into the remaining garbanzo beans.

4 Heat the remaining oil in a large skillet, add the coriander seeds and stir for 1 minute. Add the tomatoes, stir, and add the spinach. Cover and cook for 1 minute over a moderate heat. The spinach should be wilted, but not soggy. Stir in the chopped cilantro and remove from the heat.

5 Transfer the garbanzo beans to a warm serving dish and spoon over the spinach. Garnish with the cilantro and slices of lemon and serve immediately.

Spiced Spinach & Lentils

This interesting combination of lentils and spiced vegetables is delicious served with parathas, chapatis, or naan bread and yogurt.

NUTRITIONAL INFORMATION

Calories	362	Sugars	........9g
Protein	........20g	Fat	..........13g
Carbohydrate	...44g	Saturates	.......2g

15 MINS   30 MINS

SERVES 4

INGREDIENTS

1 cup split red lentils

3 cups water

1 onion

1 eggplant

1 red bell pepper

2 zucchini

4½ oz mushrooms

8 oz leaf spinach

4 tbsp vegetable ghee or oil

1 fresh green chili, seeded and chopped

1 tsp ground cumin

1 tsp ground coriander

1 inch piece of fresh
    ginger, chopped

⅔ cup vegetable stock

salt

cilantro sprigs, to garnish

COOK'S TIP

Wash the spinach thoroughly in several changes of cold water as it can be gritty. Drain well and shake off excess water from the leaves before adding it to the pan.

1 Wash the lentils and place in a saucepan with the water. Cover and simmer for 15 minutes, until the lentils are soft but still whole.

2 Meanwhile, quarter and slice the onion. Trim the leaf end and cut the eggplant into ½ inch pieces. Remove the stalk end and seeds from the bell pepper and cut into ½ inch pieces. Trim and cut the zucchini into ½ inch thick slices. Thickly slice the mushrooms. Discard any coarse stalks from the spinach leaves and wash the spinach well.

3 Heat the ghee or oil in a large saucepan, add the onion and red bell pepper, and fry gently for 3 minutes, stirring frequently. Stir in the eggplant, mushrooms, chili, spices, and ginger and fry gently for 1 minute. Add the spinach and stock and season with salt to taste. Stir and turn until the spinach leaves wilt. Cover and simmer for about 10 minutes, or until the vegetables are just tender.

4 Make a border of the lentils on a warm serving plate and spoon the vegetable mixture into the center. (The lentils may be stirred into the vegetable mixture, instead of being used as a border, if wished.) Garnish with cilantro sprigs and serve immediately.

White Lentils

This dal is dry when cooked, so give it a baghaar (seasoned oil dressing). It makes an excellent accompaniment to any meal of kormas.

NUTRITIONAL INFORMATION

Calories 129	Sugars 1g	
Protein 6g	Fat 6g	
Carbohydrate ...14g	Saturates 1g	

 5 MINS   45 MINS

SERVES 4

I N G R E D I E N T S

½ cup urid dal

1 tsp finely chopped fresh ginger

2½ cups water

1 tsp salt

1 tsp pepper

2 tbsp vegetable ghee

2 garlic cloves

2 fresh red chilies, finely chopped

mint leaves, to garnish

chapatis, to serve

1 Rinse the lentils thoroughly and put them in a large saucepan, together with the ginger.

2 Add the water and bring to a boil. Cover and simmer over a medium heat for about 30 minutes. Check to see whether the lentils are cooked by rubbing them between your finger and thumb. If they are still a little hard in the middle, cook for another 5–7 minutes. If necessary, remove the lid and cook until any remaining water has evaporated.

3 Add the salt and pepper to the lentils, mix well, and set aside.

4 To make the baghaar, heat the ghee in a separate saucepan. Add the cloves of garlic and chopped red chilies and stir well to mix thoroughly.

5 Pour the garlic and chili mixture over the lentils and then garnish with the fresh mint leaves.

6 Transfer the white lentils to warm individual serving dishes and serve hot with chapatis.

COOK'S TIP

Ghee was traditionally made from clarified butter, which can withstand higher temperatures than ordinary butter. Vegetable ghee has largely replaced it now because it is lower in saturated fats.

Split Peas with Vegetables

Here is a simple, yet nourishing and flavorful way of cooking yellow split peas. Vary the choice of vegetables and spices according to taste.

NUTRITIONAL INFORMATION

Calories 490   Sugars 8g
Protein . . . . .21g   Fat 19g
Carbohydrate . . .63g   Saturates 3g

  🍲 🍲 🍲

🥘 4¼ HOURS   🕐 1 HOUR

SERVES 4

INGREDIENTS

1 cup dried yellow split peas

5 cups water

½ tsp ground turmeric (optional)

1 lb 2 oz new potatoes

⅓ cup vegetable oil

2 onions, coarsely chopped

6 oz button mushrooms

1 tsp ground coriander

1 tsp ground cumin

1 tsp chili powder

1 tsp garam masala

salt and pepper

1¾ cups vegetable stock

½ cauliflower, broken into flowerets

¾ cup frozen peas

6 oz cherry tomatoes, halved

mint sprigs, to garnish

VARIATION

Channa dal (popular with vegetarians because of its high protein content) may be used instead of yellow split peas, if preferred. Channa dal is similar to yellow split peas, although the grains are smaller and the flavor sweeter.

1 Place the split peas in a bowl, add the water and set aside to soak for at least 4 hours or overnight.

2 Place the peas and the soaking liquid in a fairly large saucepan, stir in the turmeric, if using, and bring to the boil. Skim off any surface scum, half-cover the pan with a lid and simmer gently for 20 minutes, or until the peas are tender and almost dry. Remove the pan from the heat and set aside.

3 Meanwhile, cut the potatoes into 5 mm/¼ inch thick slices. Heat the oil in a flameproof casserole, add the onions, potatoes and mushrooms and cook over a low heat, stirring frequently, for 5 minutes. Stir in the spices and fry, stirring frequently, for 1 minute, then add salt and pepper to taste, the stock and cauliflower florets.

4 Cover the pan and simmer, stirring occasionally, for 25 minutes, or until the potato is tender. Add the split peas (and any of the cooking liquid) and the frozen peas. Bring to the boil, cover and continue cooking for 5 minutes.

5 Stir in the halved cherry tomatoes and cook for 2 minutes. Taste and adjust the seasoning, if necessary. Serve hot, garnished with mint sprigs.

Channa Dal

Dried legumes and lentils can be cooked in similar ways, but the soaking and cooking times do vary, so check the pack for instructions.

NUTRITIONAL INFORMATION

Calories	195	Sugars	.........4g
Protein	........11g	Fat	...........5g
Carbohydrate	...28g	Saturates	.......3g

  1 HR 10 MINS   50 MINS

SERVES 6

I N G R E D I E N T S

2 tbsp vegetable ghee

1 large onion, finely chopped

1 garlic clove, crushed

1 tbsp grated fresh ginger

1 tbsp cumin seeds, ground

2 tsp coriander seeds, ground

1 dried red chili

1 inch piece of cinnamon stick

1 tsp salt

½ tsp ground turmeric

1 cup split yellow peas, soaked
  in cold water for 1 hour and drained

14 oz can plum tomatoes

1¼ cups water

2 tsp garam masala

1 Heat the ghee in a large saucepan, add the onion, garlic, and ginger and fry for 3–4 minutes, until the onion has softened slightly.

2 Add the cumin, coriander, chili, cinnamon, salt, and turmeric, then stir in the split peas until well mixed.

3 Add the tomatoes, together with their can juices, breaking the tomatoes up slightly with the back of a spoon.

4 Add the water and bring to a boil. Reduce the heat to very low and simmer, uncovered, stirring occasionally, for about 40 minutes, until most of the liquid has been absorbed and the split peas are tender. Skim the surface occasionally with a slotted spoon to remove any froth.

5 Gradually stir in the garam masala, tasting after each addition, until it is of the required flavor. Serve hot.

COOK'S TIP

Use a non-stick saucepan if you have one, because the mixture is quite dense and does stick to the base of the pan occasionally. If the dal is overstirred, the split peas will break up and the dish will not have much texture or bite.

Onion Dal

This dal is semi-dry when cooked, so it is best to serve it with a curry which has a sauce. Ordinary onions can be used as a substitute.

NUTRITIONAL INFORMATION

Calories	232	Sugars	.........1g
Protein	.........6g	Fat	........17g
Carbohydrate	...15g	Saturates	.......2g

 5 MINS 30 MINS

SERVES 4

INGREDIENTS

½ cup masoor dal

6 tbsp vegetable oil

1 small bunch green onions, chopped

1 tsp finely chopped fresh ginger

1 tsp crushed garlic

½ tsp chili powder

½ tsp turmeric

1¼ cups water

1 tsp salt

1 fresh green chili, finely chopped

fresh cilantro leaves

1 Rinse the lentils thoroughly and set aside until required.

2 Heat the oil in a heavy-bottomed saucepan. Add the green onions to the pan and fry over a medium heat, stirring frequently, until lightly browned.

3 Reduce the heat and add the ginger, garlic, chili powder, and turmeric. Briefly stir-fry the green onions with the spices. Add the lentils and mix to blend together.

4 Add the water to the lentil mixture, reduce the heat to low, and cook for 20–25 minutes.

5 When the lentils are cooked thoroughly, add the salt and stir gently to mix well.

6 Transfer the onion lentils to a serving dish. Garnish with the chopped green chilies and fresh cilantro leaves, and serve immediately.

COOK'S TIP

Masoor dal are small, round, pale orange split lentils. They turn a pale yellow color when cooked.

Murkha Dal

In this dal recipe, the garlic is intended to burn in the base of the pan, and this flavor permeates the dish.

NUTRITIONAL INFORMATION

Calories 372	Sugars 7g
Protein 18g	Fat 16g
Carbohydrate ...42g	Saturates 10g

5 MINS   55 MINS

SERVES 4

INGREDIENTS

¼ cup butter

2 tsp black mustard seeds

1 onion, finely chopped

2 garlic cloves, finely chopped

1 tbsp grated fresh ginger

1 tsp turmeric

2 green chilies, seeded and
    finely chopped

1 cup red lentils

4 cups water

1¼ cups coconut milk

1 tsp salt

1 Melt the butter in a large heavy-bottomed saucepan over a moderate heat. Add the mustard seeds and cover the pan. When you can hear the seeds popping, add the onion, garlic, and grated ginger. Cook, uncovered, for about 7–8 minutes, until the onion is soft and the garlic is brown.

2 Stir in the turmeric and green chilies and cook for 1–2 minutes, until the chilies soften a little.

3 Add the lentils and cook, stirring frequently, for 2 minutes, until the lentils begin to turn translucent.

4 Stir in the water, coconut milk, and salt. Bring to a boil, then reduce the heat and simmer for 40 minutes, or until the desired consistency is reached. However, if you intend to reheat the dal later rather than eat it right away, cook it for only 30 minutes to allow for reheating time.

5 Transfer the dal to a warmed serving dish and serve immediately, while piping hot.

COOK'S TIP

There are many types of lentils used in India, but the two most common are red lentils and green or beige lentils. The red lentils are very useful, as they cook in a relatively short time to form a homogeneous mass. Green and beige lentils stay more separate when cooked.

Oil-Dressed Dal

This dal is given a baghaar (seasoned oil dressing), just before serving, of ghee, onion, and a combination of spicy seeds.

NUTRITIONAL INFORMATION

Calories 173   Sugars 3g
Protein ....8g   Fat 8g
Carbohydrate ...20g   Saturates 5g

 5 MINS   30 MINS

SERVES 4

I N G R E D I E N T S

5 tbsp masoor dal

4 tbsp moong dal

2 cups water

1 tsp finely chopped fresh ginger

1 tsp crushed garlic

2 red chilies, chopped

1 tsp salt

B A G H A A R

2 tbsp ghee

1 medium onion, sliced

1 tsp mixed mustard and onion seeds

1 Rinse the lentils thoroughly and place in a large saucepan. Pour over the water, stirring. Add the ginger, garlic, and red chilies and bring to a boil over a medium heat. Half cover with a lid and simmer for about 15–20 minutes, until they are soft enough to be mashed.

2 Mash the lentils and add more water if necessary to form a thick sauce.

3 Add the salt to the lentil mixture and stir well. Transfer the lentils to a heatproof serving dish.

4 Just before serving, melt the ghee in a small saucepan. Add the onion and fry over a medium heat, stirring frequently, for 5–8 minutes, until golden brown. Add the mustard and onion seeds and stir to mix well.

5 Pour the onion mixture over the lentils while still hot. Stir to mix thoroughly and serve the oil-dressed dal immediately.

COOK'S TIP

This dish makes a a very good accompaniment, especially for a dry curry. It also freezes well—simply reheat it in a saucepan or covered in the oven.

Tarka Dal

This is just one version of many dals that are served throughout India; as many people are vegetarian, they form a staple part of the diet.

NUTRITIONAL INFORMATION

Calories ....183 Sugars 4g
Protein ....8g Fat 8g
Carbohydrate ...22g Saturates 5g

 10 MINS   25 MINS

SERVES 4

INGREDIENTS

2 tbsp ghee

2 shallots, sliced

1 tsp yellow mustard seeds

2 garlic cloves, crushed

8 fenugreek seeds

½-inch piece of fresh ginger, grated

½ tsp salt

½ cup red lentils

1 tbsp tomato paste

2½ cups water

2 tomatoes, peeled and chopped

1 tbsp lemon juice

4 tbsp chopped cilantro

½ tsp chili powder

½ tsp garam masala

1 Heat half of the ghee in a large saucepan and add the shallots. Cook for 2–3 minutes over a high heat, then add the mustard seeds. Cover the pan until the seeds begin to pop.

2 Immediately remove the lid from the pan and add the garlic, fenugreek, ginger, and salt.

3 Stir once and add the lentils, tomato paste, and water. Bring to a boil, then lower the heat and simmer for 10 minutes.

4 Stir in the tomatoes, lemon juice, and cilantro and simmer for 4–5 minutes, until the lentils are tender.

5 Transfer to a serving dish. Heat the remaining ghee in a pan. Remove from the heat and stir in the garam masala and chili powder. Pour over the tarka dal; serve.

COOK'S TIP

The flavors in a dal can be altered to suit your particular taste; for example, for extra heat, add more chili powder or chilies, or add fennel seeds for a pleasant aniseed flavor.

Stir-fries & Sautés

Stir-frying is one of the most convenient and nutritious ways of cooking vegetarian food because ingredients are cooked quickly over a very high heat in very little oil. The

high heat seals in the natural juices and helps preserve nutrients. The short cooking time makes the vegetables more succulent and preserves texture as well as the natural flavor and color. A round-bottomed wok is ideal for stir-frying since it conducts and retains heat evenly and requires the use of less oil. You need a flat-bottomed pan for sautéing so that the food can be easily tossed and stirred. A brisk heat is essential so that the food turns golden brown and crisp.

Sauté of Summer Vegetables

The freshness of lightly cooked summer vegetables is enhanced by the aromatic flavor of a tarragon and white wine dressing.

NUTRITIONAL INFORMATION

Calories 217	Sugars 8g
Protein 2g	Fat 18g
Carbohydrate 9g	Saturates 9g

 10 MINS   10–15 MINS

SERVES 4

I N G R E D I E N T S

8 oz baby carrots, scrubbed

4½ oz string beans

2 zucchini, trimmed

1 bunch large green onions

1 bunch radishes

½ cup butter

2 tbsp light olive oil

2 tbsp white wine vinegar

4 tbsp dry white wine

1 tsp sugar

1 tbsp chopped tarragon

salt and pepper

tarragon sprigs, to garnish

1 Cut the carrots in half lengthwise, slice the beans and zucchini, and halve the green onions and radishes, so that all the vegetables are cut to even-size pieces.

2 Melt the butter in a large, heavy-bottomed skillet or wok. Add all the vegetables and fry them over a medium heat, stirring frequently, until they are tender, but still crisp and firm to the bite.

3 Heat the olive oil, vinegar, white wine, and sugar in a small saucepan over a low heat, stirring until the sugar has dissolved. Remove from the heat and add the chopped tarragon.

4 When the vegetables are just cooked, pour over the "dressing." Stir through, tossing the vegetables well to coat, and then transfer to a warmed serving dish. Garnish with sprigs of fresh tarragon and serve immediately.

Vegetable Curry

This colorful and interesting mixture of vegetables, cooked in a spicy sauce, is excellent served with pulao rice and naan bread.

NUTRITIONAL INFORMATION

Calories 421   Sugars 20g
Protein . . . . .12g   Fat 24g
Carbohydrate . . .42g   Saturates 3g

15 MINS   45 MINS

SERVES 4

INGREDIENTS

8 oz turnips or rutabaga

1 eggplant

12 oz new potatoes

8 oz cauliflower

8 oz mushrooms

1 large onion

8 oz carrots

6 tbsp vegetable ghee or oil

2 garlic cloves, crushed

2 inch piece of fresh ginger,
   finely chopped

1–2 fresh green chillies,
   seeded and chopped

1 tbsp paprika

2 tsp ground coriander

1 tbsp mild or medium curry powder
   or paste

1¾ cups vegetable stock

14 oz can chopped tomatoes

1 green bell pepper, seeded and sliced

1 tbsp cornstarch

1⅔ cup coconut milk

2–3 tbsp ground almonds

salt

cilantro sprigs, to garnish

1 Cut the turnips or rutabaga, eggplant, and potatoes into ½-inch cubes. Divide the cauliflower into small flowerets. Leave the mushrooms whole, or slice thickly if preferred. Slice the onion and carrots.

2 Heat the ghee or oil in a large saucepan. Add the onion, turnip or rutabaga, potato, and cauliflower and cook over a low heat, stirring frequently, for 3 minutes.

3 Add the garlic, ginger, chillies, paprika, ground coriander, and curry powder or paste and cook, stirring, for 1 minute.

4 Add the stock, tomatoes, eggplant, and mushrooms and season with salt. Cover and simmer, stirring occasionally, for about 30 minutes, or until tender. Add the green bell pepper and carrots, cover, and continue cooking for a further 5 minutes.

5 Blend the cornstarch with the coconut milk to a smooth paste and stir into the mixture. Add the ground almonds and simmer, stirring constantly, for 2 minutes. Season if necessary. Transfer the curry to serving plates and serve hot, garnished with sprigs of fresh cilantro.

Potato Curry

Very little meat is eaten in India, their diet being mainly vegetarian. This potato curry with added vegetables makes a very substantial main meal.

NUTRITIONAL INFORMATION

Calories 301   Sugars 10g
Protein . . . . .9g   Fat 12g
Carbohydrate . . .41g   Saturates 1g

15 MINS   45 MINS

SERVES 4

INGREDIENTS

4 tbsp vegetable oil

1½ lb potatoes,
    cut into large chunks

2 onions, quartered

3 garlic cloves, crushed

1 tsp garam masala

½ tsp turmeric

½ tsp ground cumin

½ tsp ground coriander

1 inch piece of fresh ginger, grated

1 fresh red chili, chopped

8 oz cauliflower flowerets

4 tomatoes, peeled and quartered

¾ cup frozen peas

2 tbsp chopped cilantro

1¼ cups vegetable stock

shredded cilantro, to garnish

COOK'S TIP

Use a large heavy-bottomed saucepan or skillet for this recipe to ensure that the potatoes are cooked thoroughly.

1 Heat the vegetable oil in a large heavy-bottomed saucepan or skillet. Add the potato chunks, onion, and garlic and fry over a low heat, stirring frequently, for 2–3 minutes.

2 Add the garam masala, turmeric, ground cumin, ground coriander, grated ginger, and chopped chili to the pan, mixing the spices into the vegetables. Fry over a low heat, stirring constantly, for 1 minute.

3 Add the cauliflower flowerets, tomatoes, peas, chopped cilantro, and vegetable stock to the curry mixture.

4 Cook the potato curry over a low heat for 30–40 minutes, or until the potatoes are tender and completely cooked through.

5 Garnish the potato curry with fresh cilantro and serve with plain boiled rice or warm Indian bread.

Red Curry with Cashews

This is a wonderfully quick dish to prepare. If you don't have time to prepare the curry paste, it can be bought ready-made.

NUTRITIONAL INFORMATION

Calories	274	Sugars	........5g
Protein	........10g	Fat	..........10g
Carbohydrate	...38g	Saturates	.......3g

25 MINS   15 MINS

SERVES 4

INGREDIENTS

1 cup coconut milk

1 kaffir lime leaf

¼ tsp light soy sauce

4 baby corn cobs,
   halved lengthwise

1¼ cups broccoli flowerets

4½ oz green beans, cut into
   2 inch pieces

¼ cup cashews

15 fresh basil leaves

1 tbsp chopped cilantro

1 tbsp chopped roast peanuts, to garnish

RED CURRY PASTE

7 fresh red chilies, halved, seeded,
   and blanched

2 tsp cumin seeds

2 tsp coriander seeds

1-inch piece Thai ginger (galangal),
chopped

½ stalk lemon grass, chopped

1 tsp salt

grated zest of 1 lime

4 garlic cloves, chopped

3 shallots, chopped

2 kaffir lime leaves, shredded

1 tbsp vegetable oil

1 To make the curry paste, grind all the ingredients together in a large mortar with a pestle or a grinder. Alternatively, process briefly in a food processor. The quantity of red curry paste is more than required for this recipe. However, it will keep for up to 3 weeks in a sealed container in the refrigerator.

2 Put a wok or large, heavy-bottomed skillet over a high heat, add 3 tablespoons of the red curry paste and stir until it gives off its aroma. Reduce the heat to medium.

3 Add the coconut milk, kaffir lime leaf, light soy sauce, baby corn cobs, broccoli flowerets, green beans, and cashews. Bring to a boil and simmer for about 10 minutes, until the vegetables are cooked, but still firm and crunchy.

4 Remove and discard the lime leaf and stir in the basil leaves and cilantro. Transfer to a warmed serving dish, garnish with peanuts, and serve immediately.

Pan Potato Cake

This tasty meal is made with sliced potatoes, tofu, and vegetables cooked in the pan from which it is served.

NUTRITIONAL INFORMATION

Calories 452	Sugars 6g	
Protein 17g	Fat 28g	
Carbohydrate ...35g	Saturates 13g	

 15 MINS   30 MINS

SERVES 4

I N G R E D I E N T S

1½ lb potatoes, unpeeled
  and sliced

1 carrot, diced

8 oz small broccoli flowerets

½ cup butter

2 tbsp vegetable oil

1 red onion, quartered

2 garlic cloves, crushed

6 oz tofu, diced

2 tbsp chopped sage

¾ cup grated sharp cheese

COOK'S TIP

Make sure that the mixture fills the whole width of your skillet to enable the layers to remain intact.

1 Cook the sliced potatoes in a large saucepan of boiling water for 10 minutes. Drain thoroughly.

2 Meanwhile, cook the carrot and broccoli flowerets in a separate pan of boiling water for 5 minutes. Drain with a slotted spoon.

3 Heat the butter and oil in a 9 inch skillet. Add the onion and garlic and fry over a low heat for 2-3 minutes. Add half of the potatoes slices to the skillet, covering the base of the skillet.

4 Cover the potato slices with the carrot, broccoli, and the tofu. Sprinkle with half of the sage and cover with the remaining potato slices. Sprinkle the grated cheese over the top.

5 Cook over a moderate heat for 8-10 minutes. Then place the skillet under a preheated medium broiler for 2-3 minutes, or until the cheese melts and browns.

6 Garnish with the remaining sage and serve immediately, straight from the skillet.

Kidney Bean Kiev

This is a vegetarian version of chicken Kiev—the bean patties are topped with garlic and herb butter and coated in breadcrumbs.

NUTRITIONAL INFORMATION

Calories ....688 Sugars 8g
Protein ....17g Fat 49g
Carbohydrate ...49g Saturates 20g

 25 MINS   20 MINS

SERVES 4

INGREDIENTS

GARLIC BUTTER

7 tbsp butter

3 garlic cloves, crushed

1 tbsp chopped parsley

BEAN PATTIES

1½ lb canned red kidney beans

1¼ cups fresh white breadcrumbs

2 tbsp butter

1 leek, chopped

1 celery stalk, chopped

1 tbsp chopped parsley

1 egg, beaten

salt and pepper

vegetable oil, for shallow frying

1 To make the garlic butter, put the butter, garlic, and parsley in a bowl and blend together with a wooden spoon. Place the garlic butter onto a sheet of baking parchment, roll into a cigar shape, and wrap in the baking parchment. Chill in the refrigerator until required.

2 Using a potato masher, mash the red kidney beans in a mixing bowl and stir in ¾ cup of the breadcrumbs until thoroughly blended.

3 Melt the butter in a heavy-bottomed skillet. Add the leek and celery and sauté over a low heat, stirring constantly, for 3–4 minutes.

4 Add the bean mixture to the pan, together with the parsley, season with salt and pepper to taste, and mix thoroughly. Remove the pan from the heat and set aside to cool slightly.

5 Divide the kidney bean mixture into 4 equal portions and shape them into ovals.

6 Slice the garlic butter into 4 pieces and place a slice in the center of each bean patty. With your hands, mold the bean mixture around the garlic butter to encase it completely.

7 Dip each bean patty into the beaten egg to coat and then roll in the remaining breadcrumbs.

8 Heat a little oil in a skillet and fry the patties, turning once, for 7–10 minutes. or until golden brown. Serve immediately.

Potato & Cauliflower Curry

Potatoes and cauliflower go very well together. Served with a dal and rice or bread, this dish makes a perfect vegetarian meal.

NUTRITIONAL INFORMATION

Calories ....426 Sugars 6g
Protein ....4g Fat 35g
Carbohydrate ...26g Saturates 4g

  10 MINS 25 MINS

SERVES 4

INGREDIENTS

⅔ cup vegetable oil

½ tsp white cumin seeds

4 dried red chilies

2 medium onions, sliced

1 tsp finely chopped fresh ginger

1 tsp crushed garlic

1 tsp chili powder

1 tsp salt

pinch of turmeric

3 medium potatoes, chopped

½ cauliflower, cut into small flowerets

2 green chilies (optional)

cilantro leaves

⅔ cup water

1 Heat the oil in a large heavy-bottomed saucepan. Add the white cumin seeds and dried red chilies to the pan, stirring to mix.

2 Add the onions to the pan and fry over a medium heat, stirring occasionally, for about 5–8 minutes, until golden brown.

3 Mix the ginger, garlic, chili powder, salt, and turmeric together. Add the spice mixture to the onions and stir-fry for about 2 minutes.

4 Add the potatoes and cauliflower to the pan and stir to coat thoroughly with the spice mixture. Reduce the heat and add the green chilies (if using), cilantro leaves, and water to the pan. Cover and simmer for about 10-15 minutes, until the vegetables are cooked through and tender.

5 Transfer the potato and cauliflower curry to warmed serving plates and serve immediately.

COOK'S TIP

Ground ginger is no substitute for the fresh root. It is less aromatic and flavorful and cannot be used in fried or sautéed dishes, as it burns easily at the high temperatures required.

Muttar Paneer

Paneer is a delicious fresh, soft cheese frequently used in Indian cooking. It is easily made at home, but must be made the day before it's required.

NUTRITIONAL INFORMATION

Calories	550	Sugars	........25g
Protein	........19g	Fat	.........39g
Carbohydrate	...33g	Saturates	......12g

 15 MINS   🕐 25 MINS

SERVES 6

I N G R E D I E N T S

⅔ cup vegetable oil

2 onions, chopped

2 garlic cloves, crushed

1-inch piece of fresh ginger, chopped

1 tsp garam masala

1 tsp ground turmeric

1 tsp chili powder

4 cups frozen peas

8 oz can diced tomatoes

½ cup vegetable stock

salt and pepper

2 tbsp chopped cilantro

P A N E E R

10 cups pasteurized whole milk

5 tbsp lemon juice

1 garlic clove, crushed (optional)

1 tbsp chopped cilantro

(optional)

1 To make the paneer, bring the milk to a rolling boil in a pan. Remove from the heat and stir in the lemon juice. Return to the heat for about 1 minute until the curds and whey separate. Remove from the heat. Line a strainer with double thickness of cheesecloth and pour the mixture through, adding the garlic and cilantro, if using. Squeeze all the liquid from the curds and leave to drain.

2 Transfer to a dish, cover with a plate and a heavy weight, and leave overnight in the refrigerator.

3 Cut the pressed paneer into small cubes. Heat the oil in a large skillet. Add the paneer and fry until golden on all sides. Remove from the pan and drain on paper towels.

4 Pour off some of the oil, leaving about 4 tablespoons in the pan. Add the onions, garlic, and ginger and fry gently, stirring frequently, for 5 minutes. Stir in the spices and fry gently for 2 minutes. Add the peas, tomatoes, and stock and season with salt and pepper. Cover and simmer, stirring occasionally, for 10 minutes, until the onion is tender. Add the fried paneer cubes and cook for another 5 minutes. Taste and adjust the seasoning, if necessary. Sprinkle with the cilantro and serve immediately.

Bubble & Squeak

This is a vegetarian version of the English dish, which is made with mashed potato and leftover greens cooked in meat fat in a pan.

NUTRITIONAL INFORMATION

Calories 301	Sugars 5g
Protein 11g	Fat 18g
Carbohydrate . . .24g	Saturates 2g

15 MINS   40 MINS

SERVES 4

I N G R E D I E N T S

1 lb russet potatoes, diced

8 oz Savoy cabbage, shredded

5 tbsp vegetable oil

2 leeks, chopped

1 garlic clove, crushed

8 oz tofu, cubed

salt and pepper

shredded cooked leek, to garnish

1 Cook the diced potatoes in a saucepan of lightly salted boiling water for 10 minutes, until tender. Drain and mash the potatoes.

2 Meanwhile, in a separate saucepan, blanch the cabbage in boiling water for 5 minutes. Drain well and add to the potato.

COOK'S TIP

This vegetarian version is a perfect main meal because the smoked tofu cubes added to the basic bubble and squeak mixture make it very substantial and nourishing.

3 Heat the oil in a heavy-bottomed skillet. Add the leeks and garlic and fry gently for 2–3 minutes. Stir into the potato and cabbage mixture.

4 Add the tofu and season well with salt and pepper. Cook over a moderate heat for 10 minutes.

5 Carefully turn the whole mixture over and continue to cook over a moderate heat for another 5-7 minutes, until crispy underneath. Serve immediately, garnished with shredded leek.

Tomato Curry

This vegetarian tomato curry is served topped with a few hard-cooked eggs. It is a lovely accompaniment to any Indian meal.

NUTRITIONAL INFORMATION

Calories 170   Sugars 3g
Protein . . . . .6g   Fat 15g
Carbohydrate . . . .3g   Saturates 2g

25 MINS   15 MINS

SERVES 4

I N G R E D I E N T S

14 oz can tomatoes

1 tsp finely chopped fresh ginger

1 tsp crushed garlic

1 tsp chili powder

1 tsp salt

½ tsp ground coriander

½ tsp ground cumin

4 tbsp oil

½ tsp onion seeds

½ tsp mustard seeds

½ tsp fenugreek seeds

pinch of white cumin seeds

3 dried red chilies

2 tbsp lemon juice

3 eggs, hard-boiled

fresh cilantro leaves, to garnish

1 Place the tomatoes in a large mixing bowl. Add the ginger, garlic, chili powder, salt, ground coriander, and ground cumin and blend well.

2 Heat the oil in a saucepan. Add the onion, mustard, fenugreek, and white cumin seeds, and the dried red chilies, and stir-fry for about 1 minute, until they give off their aroma. Remove the pan from the heat.

3 Add the tomato mixture to the spicy oil mixture and return the pan to the heat. Stir-fry for about 3 minutes, then reduce the heat and cook, half-covered with a lid, stirring frequently, for 7–10 minutes.

4 Sprinkle over 1 tablespoon of the lemon juice. Taste the curry and add the remaining lemon juice, if required.

5 Transfer the tomato curry to a warmed serving dish, set aside and keep warm until required.

6 Shell the hard-boiled eggs and cut them into quarters. Gently add them, yolk end downwards, to the tomato curry.

7 Garnish with fresh cilantro leaves and serve hot.

Cheese Potato Cakes

Make these tasty potato cakes for a quick and simple supper dish. Serve them with scrambled eggs if you're very hungry.

NUTRITIONAL INFORMATION

Calories ....766 Sugars 7g
Protein ....22g Fat 50g
Carbohydrate ...60g Saturates 20g

25 MINS   35 MINS

SERVES 4

INGREDIENTS

2 lb 4 oz potatoes

4 tbsp milk

¼ cup butter or margarine

2 leeks, finely chopped

1 onion, finely chopped

1½ cups grated sharp cheddar cheese

1 tbsp chopped parsley or chives

1 egg, beaten

2 tbsp water

1½ cups fresh white or
   brown breadcrumbs

vegetable oil, for shallow frying

salt and pepper

fresh flat-leaf parsley sprigs, to garnish

tossed salad greens, to serve

1 Cook the potatoes in lightly salted boiling water until tender. Drain and mash them with the milk and the butter or margarine.

2 Cook the leeks and onion in a small quantity of lightly salted boiling water for about 10 minutes until tender. Drain well.

3 In a large mixing bowl, combine the leeks and onion with the mashed potato, cheese, and parsley or chives. Season to taste with salt and pepper.

4 Beat together the egg and water in a shallow bowl. Sprinkle the breadcrumbs into a separate shallow bowl. Shape the potato mixture into 12 even-sized cakes, brushing each with the egg mixture, then coating all over with the breadcrumbs.

5 Heat the oil in a large skillet. Add the potato cakes, in batches if necessary, and fry over a low heat for about 2–3 minutes on each side, until light golden brown. Garnish with flat-leaf parsley and serve with salad greens.

Green Pumpkin Curry

The Indian pumpkin used in this curry is long and green and sold by weight. It can easily be bought from any Indian or Pakistani grocers.

NUTRITIONAL INFORMATION

Calories	347	Sugars	. . . . .6g
Protein	. . . . .2g	Fat	. . . . .34g
Carbohydrate	. . . .8g	Saturates	. . . . . . .4g

 10 MINS   30 MINS

SERVES 4

INGREDIENTS

150 ml/¼ pint/⅔ cup vegetable oil

2 medium-sized onions, sliced

½ tsp white cumin seeds

500 g/1 lb 2 oz green pumpkin, cubed

1 tsp dried mango powder

1 tsp finely chopped root ginger

1 tsp crushed garlic

1 tsp crushed red chilli

½ tsp salt

300 ml/½ pint/1¼ cups water

chapatis or naan bread,
    to serve

1 Heat the oil in a large heavy-based frying pan (skillet). Add the onions and cumin seeds and fry over a medium heat, stirring occasionally, for about 5 minutes, until the onions are a light golden brown colour.

2 Add the cubed pumpkin to the pan and stir-fry over a low heat for 3–5 minutes.

3 Mix the dried mango powder, ginger, garlic, chilli and salt together. Add the spice mixture to the pan, stirring well to combine with the vegetables.

4 Add the water, cover and cook over a low heat, stirring occasionally, for 10–15 minutes.

5 Transfer to serving plates and serve with chapatis or naan bread.

COOK'S TIP

Cumin seeds are popular with Indian cooks because of their warm, pungent flavour and aroma. The seeds are sold whole or ground, and are usually included as one of the flavourings in garam masala.

Okra Curry

This is a delicious dry bhujia (vegetarian curry) which should be served hot with chapatis. As okra is such a tasty vegetable it needs few spices.

NUTRITIONAL INFORMATION

Calories	.371	Sugars	.8g
Protein	.4g	Fat	.35g
Carbohydrate	.10g	Saturates	.4g

10 MINS   30 MINS

SERVES 4

INGREDIENTS

1 lb okra

⅔ cup oil

2 medium onions, sliced

3 green chilies, finely chopped

2 curry leaves

1 tsp salt

1 tomato, sliced

2 tbsp lemon juice

cilantro leaves

1 Rinse the okra and drain thoroughly. Using a sharp knife, chop and discard the ends of the okra. Cut the okra into 1 inch long pieces.

2 Heat the oil in a large, heavy-bottomed skillet. Add the onions, green chilies, curry leaves, and salt and mix together. Stir-fry the vegetables for 5 minutes.

3 Gradually add the okra, mixing in gently with a perforated spoon. Stir-fry the vegetable mixture over a medium heat for 12–15 minutes.

4 Add the sliced tomato to the pan and sprinkle over half the lemon juice. Taste and add more if required.

5 Garnish with cilantro leaves, cover, and simmer for another 3–5 minutes.

6 Transfer to warmed serving plates and serve hot.

COOK'S TIP

Okra, also called lady's fingers, have a remarkable glutinous quality which naturally thickens curries and casseroles.

Cashew Paella

Paella traditionally contains chicken and fish, but this recipe is packed with vegetables and nuts for a truly delicious and simple vegetarian dish.

NUTRITIONAL INFORMATION

Calories 406	Sugars 8g	
Protein 10g	Fat 22g	
Carbohydrate ...44g	Saturates 6g	

 15 MINS   35 MINS

SERVES 4

INGREDIENTS

2 tbsp olive oil

1 tbsp butter

1 red onion, chopped

1 cup arborio rice

1 tsp ground turmeric

1 tsp ground cumin

½ tsp chili powder

3 garlic cloves, crushed

1 green chili, sliced

1 green bell pepper, seeded and diced

1 red bell pepper, seeded and diced

2¾ oz baby corn cobs,
    halved lengthwise

2 tbsp pitted black olives

1 large tomato, seeded and diced

2 cups vegetable stock

¾ cup unsalted cashews

¼ cup frozen peas

2 tbsp chopped parsley

pinch of cayenne pepper

salt and pepper

herbs, to garnish

1 Heat the olive oil and butter in a large skillet or paella pan until the butter has melted.

2 Add the chopped onion to the pan and sauté over a medium heat, stirring constantly, for 2–3 minutes, until the onion has softened.

3 Stir in the rice, ground turmeric, ground cumin, chili powder, garlic, sliced chili, bell peppers, corn, black olives, and diced tomato and cook over a medium heat, stirring occasionally, for 1–2 minutes.

4 Pour in the stock and bring the mixture to a boil. Reduce the heat and cook, stirring constantly, for 20 minutes.

5 Add the cashews and peas and cook, stirring occasionally, for 5 minutes. Season to taste with salt and pepper and sprinkle with parsley and cayenne pepper. Transfer to warm serving plates, garnish, and serve immediately.

Egg Curry

This curry can be made very quickly. It can either be served as a side dish or, with parathas, as a light lunch.

NUTRITIONAL INFORMATION

Calories 189	Sugars 3g
Protein 7g	Fat 16g
Carbohydrate 4g	Saturates 3g

10 MINS   15 MINS

SERVES 4

I N G R E D I E N T S

4 tbsp vegetable oil

1 medium onion, sliced

1 fresh red chilli, finely chopped

½ tsp chilli powder

½ tsp fresh root ginger, finely chopped

½ tsp fresh garlic, crushed

4 medium eggs

1 firm tomato, sliced

fresh coriander (cilantro) leaves

parathas, to serve (optional)

1 Heat the oil in a large heavy-based saucepan. Add the sliced onion to the pan and fry over a medium heat, stirring occasionally, for about 5 minutes, until it is just softened and a light golden colour.

2 Lower the heat. Add the red chilli, chilli powder, chopped ginger and crushed garlic and fry over a low heat, stirring constantly, for about 1 minute.

3 Add the eggs and tomatoes to the pan and continue cooking, stirring to break up the eggs when they begin to cook, for 3–5 minutes.

4 Sprinkle over the fresh coriander (cilantro) leaves.

5 Transfer the egg curry to warm serving plates and serve hot with parathas, if you wish.

 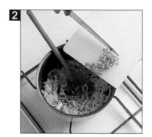 

COOK'S TIP

Both the leaves and finely chopped stems of coriander (cilantro) are used in Indian cooking, to flavour dishes and as edible garnishes. It has a very distinctive and pronounced taste.

Spicy Mixed Vegetable Curry

You can vary the vegetables used in this recipe according to personal preferences – experiment!

NUTRITIONAL INFORMATION

Calories 408   Sugars 20
Protein . . . . .11g   Fat 24g
Carbohydrate . . .39g   Saturates 3g

30 MINS   45 MINS

SERVES 4

INGREDIENTS

225 g/8 oz turnips or swede, peeled

1 aubergine (eggplant), leaf end trimmed

350 g/12 oz new potatoes, scrubbed

225 g/8 oz cauliflower

225 g/8 oz button mushrooms, wiped

1 large onion, peeled

225 g/8 oz carrots, peeled

6 tbsp vegetable ghee or oil

2 garlic cloves, peeled and crushed

5 cm/2 inch piece of ginger root, peeled
   and chopped

1-2 fresh green chillies, seeded and
   chopped

1 tbsp paprika

2 tsp ground coriander

1 tbsp mild or medium curry powder or
   paste

450 ml/16 fl oz/1¾ cups vegetable stock

400 g/14 oz can chopped tomatoes

salt

1 green (bell) pepper, seeded and sliced

1 tbsp cornflour (cornstarch)

150 ml/¼ pint/⅔cup coconut milk

2-3 tbsp ground almonds

coriander (cilantro) sprigs, to garnish

1 Using a sharp knife, cut the turnips or swede, aubergine (eggplant) and potatoes into 1 cm (½ inch) cubes.

2 Divide the cauliflower into small florets. Leave the mushrooms whole, or slice thickly. Slice the onion and carrots.

3 Heat the ghee or oil in a large saucepan, add the onion, turnip, potato and cauliflower and cook gently for 3 minutes, stirring frequently.

4 Add the garlic, ginger, chilli and spices and cook for 1 minute, stirring.

5 Add the stock, tomatoes, aubergine (eggplant) and mushrooms and season with salt. Cover and simmer gently for about 30 minutes or until tender, stirring occasionally. Add the green (bell) pepper, cover and continue cooking for a further 5 minutes.

6 Smoothly blend the cornflour (cornstarch) with the coconut milk and stir into the mixture. Add the ground almonds and simmer for 2 minutes, stirring all the time. Taste and adjust the seasoning, if necessary. Serve hot, garnished with coriander sprigs.

Fried Rice with Spicy Beans

This rice is really colorful and crunchy with the addition of corn and red kidney beans.

NUTRITIONAL INFORMATION

Calories ....363 Sugars 3g
Protein ....10g Fat 11g
Carbohydrate ...61g Saturates 2g

 10 MINS   25 MINS

SERVES 4

INGREDIENTS

3 tbsp sunflower oil

1 onion, finely chopped

1 cup long-grain white rice

1 green bell pepper, seeded and diced

1 tsp chili powder

2½ cups boiling water

3½ oz canned corn

8 oz canned red kidney beans

2 tbsp chopped fresh cilantro

1 Heat the sunflower oil in a large preheated wok.

2 Add the finely chopped onion to the wok and stir-fry for about 2 minutes or until the onion has softened.

COOK'S TIP

For perfect fried rice, the raw rice should ideally be soaked in a bowl of water for a short time before cooking to remove excess starch. Short-grain rice can be substituted for the long-grain rice.

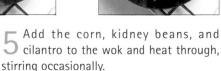

3 Add the long-grain rice, diced bell pepper, and chili powder to the wok and stir-fry for 1 minute.

4 Pour 2½ cups of boiling water into the wok. Bring to a boil, then reduce the heat and leave the mixture to simmer for 15 minutes.

5 Add the corn, kidney beans, and cilantro to the wok and heat through, stirring occasionally.

6 Transfer to a serving bowl and serve hot, scattered with extra cilantro, if wished.

Green Curry with Tempeh

Green curry paste will keep for up to three weeks in the refrigerator. Serve the curry over rice or noodles.

NUTRITIONAL INFORMATION

Calories 237	Sugars 4g	
Protein 16g	Fat 17g	
Carbohydrate 5g	Saturates 3g	

20 MINS   15–20 MINS

SERVES 4

INGREDIENTS

1 tbsp sunflower oil

6 oz marinated or plain tempeh, cut
   into diamonds

6 green onions, cut into 1 inch pieces

1⅔ cup coconut milk

grated zest of 1 lime

1¼ cup fresh basil leaves

¼ tsp liquid seasoning, such as Maggi

GREEN CURRY PASTE

2 tsp coriander seeds

1 tsp cumin seeds

1 tsp black peppercorns

4 large green chilies, seeded

2 shallots, quartered

2 garlic cloves,

2 tbsp chopped cilantro

grated zest of 1 lime

1 tbsp roughly chopped Thai ginger
   (galangal)

1 tsp ground turmeric

salt

2 tbsp oil

TO GARNISH

cilantro leaves

2 green chilies, thinly sliced

1 To make the green curry paste, grind together the coriander and cumin seeds and the peppercorns in a food processor or in a mortar with a pestle.

2 Blend the remaining ingredients together and add the ground spice mixture. Store in a clean, dry jar for up to 3 weeks in the refrigerator, or freeze in a suitable container.

3 Heat the oil in a wok or large, heavy skillet. Add the tempeh and stir over a high heat for about 2 minutes until sealed on all sides. Add the green onions and stir-fry for 1 minute. Remove the tempeh and green onions and reserve.

4 Put half the coconut milk into the wok or skillet and bring to a boil. Add 6 tablespoons of the curry paste and the lime zest, and cook for 1 minute, until fragrant. Add the reserved tempeh and green onions.

5 Add the remaining coconut milk and simmer for 7–8 minutes. Stir in the basil leaves and liquid seasoning. Leave to simmer for 1 minute before serving, garnished with cilantro leaves and chilies.

Potato Hash

This is a variation of beef hash, which was traditionally made with corned beef and leftovers, and served to seagoing New Englanders.

NUTRITIONAL INFORMATION

Calories	302	Sugars	.........5g
Protein	........15g	Fat	..........10g
Carbohydrate	...40g	Saturates	.......4g

 10 MINS 30 MINS

SERVES 4

INGREDIENTS

2 tbsp butter

1 red onion, halved and sliced

1 carrot, diced

1 oz green beans, halved

3 large potatoes, diced

2 tbsp all purpose flour

1¼ cups vegetable stock

8 oz tofu, diced

salt and pepper

chopped parsley, to garnish

1 Melt the butter in a large, heavy-bottomed skillet. Add the onion, carrot, green beans, and potatoes and fry over a fairly low heat, stirring constantly, for about 5–7 minutes, or until the vegetables begin to turn golden brown.

2 Add the flour to the skillet and cook, stirring constantly, for 1 minute. Gradually pour in the stock, stirring constantly.

3 Reduce the heat to low and simmer for 15 minutes, or until the potatoes are tender.

4 Add the diced tofu to the pan and cook for another 5 minutes. Season to taste with salt and pepper.

5 Sprinkle the chopped parsley over the top of the potato hash to garnish and then serve hot straight from the skillet.

COOK'S TIP

Hash is a term meaning to chop food into small pieces. Therefore a traditional hash dish is made from chopped fresh ingredients, such as bell peppers, onion, and celery.

Spinach & Cheese Curry

This vegetarian curry is full of protein and iron. Paneer is a type of cheese that you can easily make at home the day before it is needed.

NUTRITIONAL INFORMATION

Calories 578	Sugars 4g	
Protein 10g	Fat 58g	
Carbohydrate 4g	Saturates 7g	

20-30 MINS   25 MINS

SERVES 4

INGREDIENTS

1¼ cups vegetable oil

7 oz paneer, cubed (see page 237)

3 tomatoes, sliced

1 tsp ground cumin

1½ tsp ground chili powder

1 tsp salt

14 oz spinach

3 green chilies

pooris or boiled rice, to serve

1 Heat the oil in a large, heavy-bottomed skillet. Add the cubed paneer and fry, stirring occasionally, until golden brown.

2 Remove the paneer from the skillet with a perforated spoon and drain on paper towels.

3 Add the tomatoes to the remaining oil in the pan and stir-fry, breaking them up with a spoon, for 5 minutes.

4 Add the ground cumin, chili powder, and salt to the pan and mix together well to combine.

5 Add the spinach to the pan and stir-fry over a low heat for about 7–10 minutes until wilted.

6 Add the green chilies and return the paneer to the pan. Cook, stirring constantly, for another 2 minutes.

7 Transfer to warmed serving plates and serve immediately with pooris or plain boiled rice.

VARIATION

You could used frozen spinach in this recipe. It should be completely thawed and squeezed as dry as possible before using.

Potato Curry

Served hot with pooris or boiled rice, this curry makes an excellent brunch with mango chutney as the perfect accompaniment.

NUTRITIONAL INFORMATION

Calories	390	Sugars	.......0.7g
Protein	.........2g	Fat	.........34g
Carbohydrate	...19g	Saturates	.......4g

10 MINS   25 MINS

SERVES 4

I N G R E D I E N T S

3 medium potatoes

⅔ cup vegetable oil

1 tsp onion seeds

½ tsp fennel seeds

4 curry leaves

1 tsp ground cumin

1 tsp ground coriander

1 tsp chili powder

pinch of turmeric

1 tsp salt

1½ tsp dried mango powder

COOK'S TIP

Traditionally, Semolina Dessert (see page 501) is served to follow Potato Curry.

1 Peel and rinse the potatoes. Using a sharp knife, cut each potato into 6 slices.

2 Cook the potato slices in a saucepan of boiling water until just cooked, but not mushy (test by piercing with a sharp knife or a skewer). Drain and set aside until required.

3 Heat the vegetable oil in a separate, heavy-bottomed saucepan over a moderate heat. Reduce the heat and add the onion seeds, fennel seeds, and curry leaves and stir thoroughly.

4 Remove the pan from the heat and add the ground cumin, coriander, chili powder, turmeric, salt, and dried mango powder, stirring well to combine.

5 Return the pan to a low heat and fry the mixture, stirring constantly, for about 1 minute.

6 Pour this mixture over the cooked potatoes, mix together, and stir-fry over a low heat for about 5 minutes.

7 Transfer the potato curry to serving dishes and serve immediately.

Feta Cheese Patties

Grated carrots, zucchini, and feta cheese are combined with cumin seeds, poppy seeds, curry powder, and chopped fresh parsley.

NUTRITIONAL INFORMATION

Calories 217	Sugars 6g	
Protein 6g	Fat 16g	
Carbohydrate . . .12g	Saturates 7g	

15 MINS   20 MINS

SERVES 4

INGREDIENTS

2 large carrots

1 large zucchini

1 small onion

2 oz feta cheese

½ cup all-purpose flour

¼ tsp cumin seeds

½ tsp poppy seeds

1 tsp medium curry powder

1 tbsp chopped fresh parsley

1 egg, beaten

2 tbsp butter

2 tbsp vegetable oil

salt and pepper

herb sprigs, to garnish

1 Grate the carrots, zucchini, onion, and feta cheese coarsely, either by hand or process in a food processor.

2 Mix together the flour, cumin seeds, poppy seeds, curry powder, and parsley in a large bowl. Season to taste with salt and pepper.

3 Add the carrot mixture to the seasoned flour, tossing well to combine. Stir in the beaten egg.

4 Heat the butter and oil in a large, heavy-bottomed skillet. Place heaped tablespoonfuls of the carrot mixture in the pan, flattening them slightly with the back of the spoon. Fry gently for about 2 minutes on each side, until crisp and golden brown. Drain on paper towels and keep warm until all the mixture is used.

5 Serve immediately, garnished with sprigs of fresh herbs.

Green Bean & Potato Curry

You can use fresh or canned green beans for this semi-dry vegetable curry. Serve an oil-dressed dhal for contrasting flavours and colours.

NUTRITIONAL INFORMATION

Calories 690	Sugars 4g	
Protein 3g	Fat 69g	
Carbohydrate ...16g	Saturates 7g	

15 MINS   30 MINS

SERVES 4

INGREDIENTS

300 ml/½ pint/1¼ cups oil

1 tsp white cumin seeds

1 tsp mustard and onion seeds

4 dried red chillies

3 fresh tomatoes, sliced

1 tsp salt

1 tsp finely chopped root ginger

1 tsp crushed garlic

1 tsp chilli powder

200 g/7 oz green cut beans

2 medium potatoes, diced

300 ml/½ pint/1¼ cups water

coriander (cilantro) leaves, chopped

2 green chillies, finely chopped

boiled rice, to serve

COOK'S TIP

Mustard seeds are often fried in oil or ghee to bring out their flavour before being combined with other ingredients.

1 Heat the oil in a large, heavy-based saucepan. Lower the heat and add the white cumin seeds, mustard and onion seeds and dried red chillies to the saucepan, stirring well.

2 Add the tomatoes to the pan and stir-fry the mixture for 3–5 minutes.

3 Mix together the salt, ginger, garlic and chilli powder and spoon into the pan. Blend the mixture together.

4 Add the green beans and potatoes to the pan and stir-fry for about 5 minutes.

5 Add the water to the pan, reduce the heat to low and simmer for 10–15 minutes, stirring occasionally.

6 Garnish the green bean and potato curry with chopped coriander (cilantro) leaves and green chillies and serve hot with boiled rice.

Vegetable Medley

Serve this as a crisp and colorful dish, with pita bread, chapatis, or naan, or as an accompaniment to baked pasta dishes.

NUTRITIONAL INFORMATION

Calories	190	Sugars	........17g
Protein	.........7g	Fat	...........7g
Carbohydrate	...27g	Saturates	.......1g

15 MINS   10 MINS

SERVES 4

I N G R E D I E N T S

5½ oz young green beans

8 baby carrots

6 baby turnips

½ small cauliflower

2 tbsp vegetable oil

2 large onions, sliced

2 garlic cloves, finely chopped

1¼ cups plain yogurt

1 tbsp cornstarch

2 tbsp tomato paste

pinch of chili powder

salt

1 Trim the beans and snap them in half. Cut the carrots in half and the turnips in quarters. Divide the cauliflower into flowerets, discarding the thick stalk.

2 Steam the vegetables over boiling, salted water for 3 minutes, then turn them into a colander and plunge them immediately in a large bowl of cold water to prevent any more cooking.

3 Heat the oil in a pan and fry the onions over a medium heat until they are translucent. Stir in the garlic and cook for 1 minute.

4 Mix together the yogurt, cornstarch, and tomato paste to form a smooth paste. Stir this paste into the onions and cook for 1–2 minutes, until the sauce is thoroughly blended.

5 Drain the vegetables well, then gradually stir them into the sauce, taking care not to break them up. Season with salt and chili powder to taste, cover, and simmer over a low heat for 5 minutes, until the vegetables are just tender. Taste and adjust the seasoning if necessary. Serve immediately.

Sweet & Sour Vegetables

Serve this dish with plain noodles or fluffy white rice for a filling, and flavorsome meal.

NUTRITIONAL INFORMATION

Calories 401	Sugars 16g
Protein 14g	Fat 9g
Carbohydrate . . .70g	Saturates 2g

 10 MINS   15 MINS

SERVES 4

INGREDIENTS

1 tbsp peanut oil

2 garlic cloves, crushed

1 tsp grated fresh ginger

1¾ oz baby corn cobs

1¾ oz snow peas

1 carrot, cut into thin sticks

1 green bell pepper, seeded and cut
   into thin sticks

8 green onions

1¾ oz canned bamboo shoots

8 oz firm tofu, cubed

2 tbsp dry sherry or Chinese rice wine

2 tbsp rice vinegar

2 tbsp honey

1 tbsp light soy sauce

⅔ cup vegetable stock

1 tbsp cornstarch

noodles or boiled rice, to serve

1 Heat the oil in a preheated wok until almost smoking. Add the garlic and grated fresh ginger and cook over a medium heat, stirring frequently, for 30 seconds.

2 Add the baby corn cobs, snow peas, carrot and bell pepper sticks and stir-fry for about 5 minutes, or until the vegetables are tender, but still crisp.

3 Add the green onions, bamboo shoots, and tofu and cook for 2 minutes.

4 Stir in the sherry or Chinese rice wine, rice vinegar, honey, soy sauce, vegetable stock, and cornstarch and bring to a boil. Reduce the heat to low and simmer for 2 minutes, until heated through. Transfer to warmed serving dishes and serve immediately.

Vegetable Pasta Stir-Fry

East meets West in this delicious dish. Prepare all the vegetables and cook the pasta in advance, then the dish can be cooked in a few minutes.

NUTRITIONAL INFORMATION

Calories	383	Sugars	........18g
Protein	........14g	Fat	..........23g
Carbohydrate	...32g	Saturates	.......8g

20 MINS   30 MINS

SERVES 4

INGREDIENTS

4⅔ cups dried whole wheat pasta shells, or
    other short pasta shapes

1 tbsp olive oil

2 carrots, thinly sliced

4 oz baby corn cobs

3 tbsp peanut oil

1-inch piece fresh ginger,
    thinly sliced

1 large onion, thinly sliced

1 garlic clove, thinly sliced

3 celery stalks, thinly sliced

1 small red bell pepper, seeded and sliced
    into thin strips

1 small green bell pepper,
    seeded and sliced into thin strips

salt

steamed snow peas,
    to serve

SAUCE

1 tsp cornstarch

2 tbsp water

3 tbsp soy sauce

3 tbsp dry sherry

1 tsp honey

dash of hot pepper sauce (optional)

1 Cook the pasta in a large pan of boiling lightly salted water, adding the tablespoon of olive oil. When tender, but still firm to the bite, drain the pasta in a colander, return to the pan, cover, and keep warm.

2 Cook the carrots and baby corn cobs in boiling, salted water for 2 minutes. Drain in a colander, plunge into cold water to prevent any more cooking, and drain again.

3 Heat the peanut oil in a large skillet over medium heat. Add the ginger and stir-fry for 1 minute, to flavor the oil. Remove with a perforated spoon and discard.

4 Add the onion, garlic, celery, and bell peppers to the oil and stir-fry over a medium heat for 2 minutes. Add the carrots and baby corn cobs, and stir-fry for another 2 minutes, then stir in the reserved pasta.

5 Put the cornstarch in a small bowl and mix to a smooth paste with the water. Stir in the soy sauce, sherry, and honey.

6 Pour the sauce into the pan, stir well, and cook for 2 minutes, stirring once or twice. Taste the sauce and season with hot pepper sauce if wished. Serve with a steamed green vegetable, such as snow peas.

Casseroles & Bakes

Anyone who ever thought that vegetarian meals were dull will be proved wrong by the rich variety of dishes in this chapter. You will recognize influences from Mexican and Chinese cooking, but there are also  traditional stews and casseroles, as well as hearty bakes and roasts. They all make exciting meals, at any time of year, and for virtually any occasion. Don't be afraid to substitute your own personal favorite ingredients where appropriate. There is no reason why you cannot enjoy experimenting and adding your own touch to these imaginative ideas.

Lentil & Rice Casserole

This is a really hearty dish, perfect for cold days when a filling hot dish is just what you need.

NUTRITIONAL INFORMATION

Calories 312	Sugars 9g
Protein 20g	Fat 2g
Carbohydrate . . .51g	Saturates 0.4g

 15 MINS   40 MINS

SERVES 4

I N G R E D I E N T S

1 cup split red lentils

⅓ cup long grain white rice

5 cups vegetable stock

1 leek, cut into chunks

3 garlic cloves, crushed

14 oz can diced tomatoes

1 tsp ground cumin

1 tsp chili powder

1 tsp garam masala

1 red bell pepper, seeded and sliced

3½ oz small broccoli flowerets

8 baby corn cobs, halved lengthwise

1¾ oz green beans, halved

1 tbsp shredded basil

salt and pepper

fresh basil sprigs, to garnish

VARIATION

You can vary the rice in this recipe—use brown or wild rice, if you prefer.

1 Place the lentils, rice, and vegetable stock in a large flameproof casserole and cook over a low heat, stirring occasionally, for 20 minutes.

2 Add the leek, garlic, tomatoes, and their can juice, ground cumin, chili powder, garam masala, sliced bell pepper, broccoli, corn cobs, and green beans to the pan .

3 Bring the mixture to a boil, reduce the heat, cover, and simmer for another 10–15 minutes, or until the vegetables are tender.

4 Add the shredded basil and season with salt and pepper to taste.

5 Garnish with fresh basil sprigs and serve immediately.

Mushroom Vol-au-Vent

A simple mixture of creamy, tender mushrooms filling a crisp, rich pie shell, this dish will make an impression at any dinner party.

NUTRITIONAL INFORMATION

Calories 688	Sugars 2g	
Protein 10g	Fat 52g	
Carbohydrate ...45g	Saturates 22g	

🍞 25 MINS 🕐 50 MINS

SERVES 4

INGREDIENTS

1 lb 2 oz puff pastry, thawed if frozen

1 egg, beaten, for glazing

FILLING

2 tbsp butter or margarine

1 lb 10 oz mixed mushrooms, sliced

6 tbsp dry white wine

4 tbsp heavy cream

2 tbsp chopped chervil

salt and pepper

chervil sprigs, to garnish

1 Roll out the pastry on a lightly floured surface to an 8-inch square.

2 Using a sharp knife, mark a square 1-inch from the pastry edge, cutting halfway through the pastry.

3 Score the top in a diagonal pattern. Knock up the edges with a kitchen knife and put on a cookie sheet. Brush the top with beaten egg, taking care not to let the egg run into the cut. Bake in a preheated oven at 425°F for 35 minutes.

4 Cut out the central square. Discard the soft pastry inside the shell, leaving the base intact. Return to the oven, with the square, for 10 minutes.

5 Meanwhile, make the filling. Melt the butter or margarine in a skillet and stir-fry the mushrooms over a high heat for 3 minutes.

6 Add the wine and cook, stirring occasionally, for 10 minutes, until the mushrooms have softened. Stir in the cream and chervil and season to taste with salt and pepper.

7 Pile into the pastry shell. Top with the pastry square, garnish with sprigs of chervil, and serve.

Brazil Nut & Mushroom Pie

The mushrooms give this wholesome vegan pie a wonderful aromatic flavor. The pie can be frozen uncooked and baked from frozen.

NUTRITIONAL INFORMATION

Calories 530   Sugars 4g
Protein ....12g   Fat 38g
Carbohydrate ...38g   Saturates 8g

1 HOUR   50 MINS

SERVES 6

INGREDIENTS

PIE DOUGH

1¾ cups all-purpose whole wheat flour

⅓ cup margarine,
   cut into small pieces

4 tbsp water

soy milk, to glaze

FILLING

2 tbsp margarine

1 onion, chopped

1 garlic clove, finely chopped

4½ oz mushrooms, sliced

1 tbsp all-purpose flour

⅔ cup vegetable stock

6 oz Brazil nuts

1 tbsp tomato paste

2¾ oz fresh whole wheat breadcrumbs

2 tbsp chopped parsley

½ tsp pepper

1 To make the pie dough, place the flour in a mixing bowl and cut in the margarine with your fingertips until the mixture resembles fine breadcrumbs. Stir in the water and bring together to form a smooth dough. Knead lightly, then wrap and chill in the refrigerator for 30 minutes.

2 To make the filling, melt half of the margarine in a skillet. Add the onion, garlic, and mushrooms and fry over a medium heat, stirring occasionally, for 5 minutes, until softened. Add the flour and cook for 1 minute, stirring frequently. Gradually add the stock, stirring until the sauce is smooth and beginning to thicken. Chop the Brazil nuts. Stir in the tomato paste, nuts, breadcrumbs, parsley, and pepper. Set aside to cool slightly.

3 On a lightly floured work counter, roll out two-thirds of the pie dough and use to line an 8 inch loose-based flan pan or pie dish. Spread the filling in the pie shell. Brush the edges of the pie dough with soy milk. Roll out the remaining pie dough to fit the top of the pie. Seal the edges, make a slit in the top of the pie dough, and brush with soy milk to glaze.

4 Bake in a preheated oven at 400°F for 30–40 minutes, until golden brown. Serve immediately.

Almond & Sesame Nut Roast

Toasted almonds are combined with sesame seeds, rice, and vegetables in this tasty roast. Serve it with a delicious onion and mushroom sauce.

NUTRITIONAL INFORMATION

Calories	612	Sugars	.........7g
Protein	........22g	Fat	..........46g
Carbohydrate	...29g	Saturates	......13g

30–40 MINS   35 MINS

SERVES 4

INGREDIENTS

2 tbsp sesame or olive oil

1 small onion, finely chopped

¼ cup risotto rice

1¼ cups vegetable stock

1 large carrot, grated

1 large leek, finely chopped

2 tsp sesame seeds, toasted

¾ cup chopped almonds, toasted

½ cup ground almonds

¾ cup grated sharp cheddar cheese

2 eggs, beaten

1 tsp dried mixed herbs

salt and pepper

flat leaf parsley sprigs, to garnish

fresh vegetables, to serve

SAUCE

2 tbsp butter

1 small onion, finely chopped

1½ cups finely chopped mushrooms

¼ cup all-purpose flour

1½ cups vegetable stock

1 Heat the oil in a large skillet and fry the onion gently for 2–3 minutes. Add the rice and cook gently for 5–6 minutes, stirring frequently.

2 Add the stock, bring to a boil, lower the heat and simmer for 15 minutes, or until the rice is tender. Add a little extra water if necessary. Remove from the heat and transfer to a large mixing bowl.

3 Add the carrot, leek, sesame seeds, almonds, cheese, beaten egg, and herbs. Mix well and season with salt and pepper. Transfer the mixture to a greased 1 lb 2 oz loaf pan, leveling the surface.

Bake in a preheated oven at 350°F for 1 hour, until set and firm. Leave in the pan for 10 minutes.

4 To make the sauce, melt the butter in a small saucepan and fry the onion until dark golden brown. Add the mushrooms and cook for 2 minutes. Stir in the flour, cook gently for 1 minute, then gradually add the stock. Bring to a boil, stirring constantly, until thickened and blended. Season to taste.

5 Turn out the nut roast, slice and serve, garnished with parsley, with fresh vegetables, accompanied by the sauce.

Mexican Chili Corn Pie

This bake of corn and kidney beans, flavored with chili and fresh cilantro, is topped with crispy cheese cornbread.

NUTRITIONAL INFORMATION

Calories	.519	Sugars	17g
Protein	22g	Fat	22g
Carbohydrate	61g	Saturates	9g

 25 MINS   20 MINS

SERVES 4

I N G R E D I E N T S

1 tbsp corn oil

2 garlic cloves, crushed

1 red bell pepper, seeded and diced

1 green bell pepper, seeded and diced

1 celery stalk, diced

1 tsp hot chili powder

14 oz can chopped tomatoes

11½ oz can corn, drained

7½ oz can kidney beans,
    drained and rinsed

2 tbsp chopped cilantro

salt and pepper

cilantro sprigs, to garnish

tomato and avocado salad, to serve

T O P P I N G

⅔ cup cornmeal

1 tbsp all-purpose flour

½ tsp salt

2 tsp baking powder

1 egg, beaten

6 tbsp milk

1 tbsp corn oil

1 cup grated sharp cheddar cheese

1 Heat the oil in a large skillet and gently fry the garlic, bell peppers, and celery for 5–6 minutes until just softened.

2 Stir in the chili powder, tomatoes, corn, beans, and seasoning. Bring to a boil and simmer for 10 minutes. Stir in the cilantro and spoon into an ovenproof dish.

3 To make the topping, mix together the cornmeal, flour, salt, and baking powder. Make a well in the center, add the egg, milk, and oil, and beat until a smooth batter is formed.

4 Spoon over the bell pepper and corn mixture and sprinkle with the cheese. Bake in a preheated oven at 425°F for 25–30 minutes until golden and firm.

5 Garnish with cilantro sprigs and serve immediately with a tomato and avocado salad.

Vegetable Hot Pot

In this recipe, a variety of vegetables are cooked under a layer of potatoes, topped with cheese and cooked until golden brown.

  25 MINS   🕐 1 HOUR

SERVES 4

I N G R E D I E N T S

2 large potatoes, thinly sliced

2 tbsp vegetable oil

1 red onion, halved and sliced

1 leek, sliced

2 garlic cloves, crushed

1 carrot, cut into chunks

3½ oz broccoli flowerets

3½ oz cauliflower flowerets

2 small turnips, quartered

1 tbsp all-purpose flour

3 cups vegetable stock

⅔ cup dry cider or apple juice

1 apple, cored and sliced

2 tbsp chopped sage

pinch of cayenne pepper

½ cup grated cheddar cheese

salt and pepper

1 Cook the potato slices in a saucepan of boiling water for 10 minutes. Drain thoroughly and reserve.

2 Heat the oil in a flameproof casserole. Add the onion, leek, and garlic and sauté, stirring occasionally, for 2–3 minutes. Add the remaining vegetables and cook, stirring constantly, for another 3–4 minutes.

3 Stir in the flour and cook for 1 minute. Gradually add the stock and cider and bring to a boil. Add the apple, sage, and cayenne pepper and season well. Remove from the heat and transfer the vegetables to an ovenproof dish.

4 Arrange the potato slices on top of the vegetable mixture to cover.

5 Sprinkle the cheese on top of the potato slices and cook in a preheated oven at 375°F for 30–35 minutes or until the potato is golden brown and beginning to crispen around the edges. Serve immediately.

Spinach Crêpe Layer

Nutty-tasting buckwheat crêpes are combined with a cheese and spinach mixture and baked with a crispy topping.

NUTRITIONAL INFORMATION

Calories 467	Sugars 10g	
Protein 29g	Fat 26g	
Carbohydrate ...31g	Saturates 7g	

45 MINS · 1 HR 5 MINS

SERVES 4

I N G R E D I E N T S

1 cup buckwheat flour

1 egg, beaten

1 tbsp walnut oil

1¼ cups milk

2 tsp vegetable oil

FILLING

2 lb 4 oz young spinach leaves

2 tbsp water

1 bunch green onions, white
   and green parts, chopped

2 tsp walnut oil

1 egg, beaten

1 egg yolk

1 cup cottage cheese

½ tsp grated nutmeg

¼ cup grated sharp cheddar cheese

¼ cup walnut pieces

salt and pepper

1 Sift the flour into a bowl and add any husks that remain in the strainer.

2 Make a well in the center and add the egg and walnut oil. Gradually whisk in the milk to make a smooth batter. Leave to stand for 30 minutes.

3 To make the filling, wash the spinach and pack into a saucepan with the water. Cover tightly and cook on a high heat for 5–6 minutes, until soft.

4 Drain well and leave to cool. Gently fry the green onions in the walnut oil for 2–3 minutes, until just soft. Drain on paper towels and set aside.

5 Whisk the batter. Brush a small crêpe pan with oil, heat until hot, and pour in enough batter just to cover the base. Cook for 1–2 minutes, until set, flip over and cook for 1 minute, until golden on the underside. Transfer to a warmed plate. Repeat to make 8–10 crêpes, layering

them with baking parchment.

6 Chop the spinach and dry with paper towels. Mix with the green onions, beaten egg, egg yolk, cottage cheese, and nutmeg and season to taste with salt and pepper.

7 Layer the crêpes and spinach mixture on a cookie sheet lined with baking parchment, finishing with a crêpe. Sprinkle with cheddar cheese and bake in a preheated oven at 375°F for 20–25 minutes, until firm and golden. Sprinkle with the walnuts and serve immediately.

Winter Vegetable Casserole

This hearty supper dish is best served with plenty of warm crusty bread to mop up the delicious juices.

NUTRITIONAL INFORMATION

Calories 211	Sugars 6g
Protein 11g	Fat 6g
Carbohydrate . . .26g	Saturates 0.8g

10 MINS   40 MINS

SERVES 4

I N G R E D I E N T S

1 tbsp olive oil

1 red onion, halved and sliced

3 garlic cloves, crushed

8 oz spinach

1 fennel bulb, cut into eight

1 red bell pepper, seeded and cubed

1 tbsp all-purpose flour

1¾ cups vegetable stock

6 tbsp dry white wine

14 oz can garbanzo beans, drained

1 bay leaf

1 tsp ground coriander

½ tsp paprika

salt and pepper

fennel fronds, to garnish

1 Heat the olive oil in a large flameproof casserole. Add the onion and garlic and sauté over a low heat, stirring frequently, for 1 minute. Add the spinach and cook, stirring occasionally, for 4 minutes, or until wilted.

2 Add the fennel pieces and red bell pepper and cook, stirring constantly, for 2 minutes.

3 Stir in the flour and cook, stirring constantly, for 1 minute.

4 Add the vegetable stock, white wine, garbanzo beans, bay leaf, ground coriander, and paprika, cover, and simmer for 30 minutes. Season to taste with salt and pepper, garnish with fennel fronds and serve immediately straight from the casserole.

COOK'S TIP

Use other canned legumes or mixed beans instead of the garbanzo beans, if you prefer.

Potato & Cheese Soufflé

This soufflé is very simple to make, yet it has a delicious flavor and melts in the mouth. Choose three alternative cheeses, if preferred.

NUTRITIONAL INFORMATION

Calories 447	Sugars 1g	
Protein 22g	Fat 23g	
Carbohydrate ...41g	Saturates 11g	

 10 MINS 55 MINS

SERVES 4

I N G R E D I E N T S

2 tbsp butter

2 tsp all-purpose flour

2 lb russet potatoes

8 eggs, separated

¼ cup grated Gruyère cheese

¼ cup crumbled blue cheese

¼ cup grated sharp cheddar cheese

salt and pepper

1 Butter a 10-cup soufflé dish and dust with the flour. Set aside.

2 Cook the potatoes in a saucepan of boiling water until tender. Mash until very smooth and then transfer to a mixing bowl to cool.

3 Beat the egg yolks into the potato and stir in the Gruyère cheese, blue cheese, and cheddar, mixing well. Season to taste with salt and pepper.

4 Whisk the egg whites until standing in peaks, then gently fold them into the potato mixture with a metal spoon until fully incorporated.

5 Spoon the potato mixture into the prepared soufflé dish.

6 Cook in a preheated oven at 425°F for 35–40 minutes, until risin and set. Serve immediately.

COOK'S TIP

Insert a thin skewer into the center of the soufflé; it should come out clean when the soufflé is fully cooked through.

Winter Vegetable Cobbler

Seasonal fresh vegetables are casseroled with lentils, then topped with a ring of fresh cheese biscuits to make this tasty cobbler.

NUTRITIONAL INFORMATION

Calories 734	Sugars 22g	
Protein 27g	Fat 30g	
Carbohydrate ...96g	Saturates 16g	

20 MINS   40 MINS

SERVES 4

INGREDIENTS

1 tbsp olive oil

1 garlic clove, crushed

8 small onions, halved

2 celery stalks, sliced

8 oz rutabaga, chopped

2 carrots, sliced

½ small cauliflower, broken into flowerets

8 oz mushrooms, sliced

14 oz can diced tomatoes

¼ cup red lentils

2 tbsp cornstarch

3–4 tbsp water

1¼ cups vegetable stock

2 tsp Tabasco sauce

2 tsp chopped oregano

oregano sprigs, to garnish

TOPPING

2 cups self-rising flour

¼ cup butter

1 cup grated sharp cheddar cheese

2 tsp chopped oregano

1 egg, beaten

⅔ cup milk

salt

1 Heat the oil in a large saucepan. Fry the garlic and onions for 5 minutes. Add the celery, rutabaga, carrots, and cauliflower and fry for 2–3 minutes. Add the mushrooms, tomatoes, and lentils.

2 Mix the cornstarch and water and add to the pan with the stock, Tabasco, and oregano. Bring to a boil, stirring. Transfer to an ovenproof dish, cover, and bake in a preheated oven at 350°F for 20 minutes.

3 To make the topping, sift the flour and salt into a bowl. Rub in the butter, then stir in most of the cheese and the chopped herbs. Beat together the egg and milk and add enough to the dry ingredients to make a soft dough. Knead lightly, roll out to ½ inch thick and cut into 2 inch rounds.

4 Remove the dish from the oven and increase the temperature to 400°F. Arrange the rounds around the edge of the dish, brush with the remaining egg and milk, and sprinkle with the reserved cheese. Cook for another 10–12 minutes, until the topping is risen and golden. Garnish and serve.

Curry Turnovers

These turnovers, which are suitable for vegans, are a delicious combination of vegetables and spices. They can be eaten either hot or cold.

NUTRITIONAL INFORMATION

Calories 455	Sugars 5g
Protein 8g	Fat 27g
Carbohydrate ...48g	Saturates 5g

 1 HOUR   1 HOUR

SERVES 4

INGREDIENTS

2 cups all-purpose
   whole wheat flour

⅓ cup margarine,
   cut into small pieces

4 tbsp water

2 tbsp oil

8 oz diced root vegetables, such as
   potatoes, carrots, and parsnips

1 small onion, chopped

2 garlic cloves, finely chopped

½ tsp curry powder

½ tsp ground turmeric

½ tsp ground cumin

½ tsp wholegrain mustard

5 tbsp vegetable stock

soy milk, to glaze

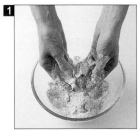  

1 Place the flour in a mixing bowl and cut in the margarine with your fingertips until the mixture resembles breadcrumbs. Stir in the water and bring together to form a soft dough. Wrap and set aside to chill in the refrigerator for 30 minutes.

2 To make the filling, heat the oil in a large saucepan. Add the diced root vegetables, chopped onion, and garlic and fry, stirring occasionally, for 2 minutes. Stir in all of the spices, turning the vegetables to coat them thoroughly. Fry the vegetables, stirring constantly, for 1 minute more.

3 Add the stock to the pan and bring to a boil. Cover and simmer, stirring occasionally, for about 20 minutes, until the vegetables are tender and the liquid has been absorbed. Leave to cool.

4 Divide the dough into 4 portions. Roll each portion into a 6-inch round. Place the filling on one half of each round.

5 Brush the edges of each round with soy milk, then fold over and press the edges together to seal. Place on a cookie sheet. Bake in a preheated oven at 400°F for 25–30 minutes until golden brown.

Creamy Baked Fennel

Fennel tastes fabulous in this creamy sauce, flavored with caraway seeds. A crunchy breadcrumb topping gives an interesting texture.

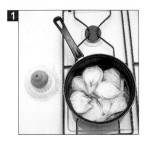

NUTRITIONAL INFORMATION

Calories 292	Sugars 5g	
Protein 10g	Fat 23g	
Carbohydrate ...12g	Saturates 14g	

10 MINS   45 MINS

SERVES 4

INGREDIENTS

2 tbsp lemon juice

2 fennel bulbs, thinly sliced

¼ cup butter, plus extra
  for greasing

¼ cup low-fat cream cheese

⅔ cup light cream

⅔ cup milk

1 egg, beaten

2 tsp caraway seeds

1 cup fresh white breadcrumbs

salt and pepper

parsley sprigs, to garnish

1 Bring a saucepan of water to a boil and add the lemon juice and fennel. Cook for 2–3 minutes to blanch, drain, and place in a greased ovenproof dish.

2 Beat the cream cheese in a bowl until smooth. Add the cream, milk, and beaten egg, and whisk together until combined. Season with salt and pepper and pour the mixture over the fennel.

3 Melt 1 tbsp of the butter in a small skillet and fry the caraway seeds gently for 1–2 minutes, until they release their aroma. Sprinkle them over the fennel.

4 Melt the remaining butter in a skillet. Add the breadcrumbs and fry over a low heat, stirring frequently, until lightly browned. Sprinkle them evenly over the surface of the fennel.

5 Place in a preheated oven at 350°F, and bake for 25–30 minutes, or until the fennel is tender. Serve immediately, garnished with sprigs of parsley.

Mushroom & Spinach Puffs

These pastry puffs, filled with garlic, mushrooms, and spinach are easy to make and simply melt in the mouth.

NUTRITIONAL INFORMATION

Calories	467	Sugars	.........4g
Protein	.........8g	Fat	..........38g
Carbohydrate	...24g	Saturates	......18g

 20 MINS   30 MINS

SERVES 4

INGREDIENTS

2 tbsp butter

1 red onion, halved and sliced

2 garlic cloves, crushed

3 cups sliced mushrooms,

6 oz baby spinach

pinch of nutmeg

4 tbsp heavy cream

8 oz puff pastry

1 egg, beaten

salt and pepper

2 tsp poppy seeds

1 Melt the butter in a skillet. Add the onion and garlic and sauté over a low heat, stirring, for 3–4 minutes, until the onion has softened.

2 Add the mushrooms, spinach, and nutmeg and cook over a medium heat, stirring occasionally, for 2–3 minutes.

3 Stir in the heavy cream, mixing thoroughly. Season with salt and pepper to taste and remove the pan from the heat.

4 Roll the pastry out on a lightly floured work counter and cut into four 6 inch rounds.

5 Put a quarter of the filling onto one half of each round and fold the pastry over to encase it. Press down to seal the edges and brush with the beaten egg. Sprinkle with the poppy seeds.

6 Place the pastries on a dampened cookie sheet and cook in a preheated oven at 400°F for 20 minutes, until risen and golden brown in color.

7 Transfer the mushroom and spinach puffs to warmed serving plates and serve immediately.

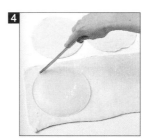

COOK'S TIP

The cookie sheet is moistened so that steam forms with the heat of the oven, which helps the pastry to rise and set.

Vegetable Cake

This is a savory version of a cheesecake with a layer of fried potatoes as a delicious base. Use frozen mixed vegetables for the topping, if liked.

NUTRITIONAL INFORMATION

Calories 502   Sugars 8g
Protein ....16g   Fat 31g
Carbohydrate ...41g   Saturates 14g

  20 MINS   45 MINS

SERVES 4

INGREDIENTS

BASE

2 tbsp vegetable oil, plus extra for brushing

4 large potatoes, thinly sliced

TOPPING

1 tbsp vegetable oil

1 leek, chopped

1 zucchini, grated

1 red bell pepper, seeded and diced

1 green bell pepper, seeded and diced

1 carrot, grated

2 tsp chopped parsley

1 cup full-fat cream cheese

¼ cup grated sharp cheese

2 eggs, beaten

salt and pepper

shredded cooked leek, to garnish

salad, to serve

1 Brush an 8 inch springform cake pan with oil.

2 To make the base, heat the oil in a skillet. Cook the potato slices until softened and browned. Drain on paper towels and place in the base of the pan.

3 To make the topping, heat the oil in a separate skillet. Add the leek and fry over a low heat, stirring frequently, for 3–4 minutes, until softened.

4 Add the zucchini, bell peppers, carrot, and parsley to the pan and cook over a low heat for 5–7 minutes, or until the vegetables have softened.

5 Meanwhile, beat the cheeses and eggs together in a bowl. Stir in the vegetables and season to taste with salt and pepper. Spoon the mixture evenly over the potato base.

6 Cook in a preheated oven at 375°F for 20–25 minutes, until the cake is set.

7 Remove the vegetable cake from the pan, transfer to a warm serving plate, garnish with shredded leek, and serve with a crisp salad.

Lentil & Vegetable Shells

These stuffed eggplants are delicious served hot or cold, topped with plain yogurt or cucumber raita.

NUTRITIONAL INFORMATION

Calories 386	Sugars 9g
Protein 14g	Fat 24g
Carbohydrate . . .30g	Saturates 3g

🍲 🍲 🍲

🥔 25 MINS   🕐 1 HOUR

SERVES 6

INGREDIENTS

1⅓ cup French lentils

3¾ cups water

2 garlic cloves, crushed

3 well-shaped eggplants

⅔ cup vegetable oil, plus
   extra for brushing

2 onions, chopped

4 tomatoes, chopped

2 tsp cumin seeds

1 tsp ground cinnamon

2 tbsp mild curry paste

1 tsp minced chili

2 tbsp chopped mint

salt and pepper

plain yogurt and
   mint sprigs, to serve

COOK'S TIP

Choose nice plump eggplants, rather than thin tapering ones, as they retain their shape better when filled and baked with a stuffing.

1 Rinse the lentils under cold running water. Drain and place in a saucepan with the water and garlic. Cover and simmer for 30 minutes.

2 Cook the eggplants in a saucepan of boiling water for 5 minutes. Drain, then plunge into cold water for 5 minutes. Drain again, then cut the eggplants in half lengthwise and scoop out most of the flesh and reserve, leaving a ½-inch thick border to form a shell.

3 Place the eggplant shells in a shallow greased ovenproof dish, brush with a little oil and sprinkle with salt and pepper. Cook in a preheated oven at 375°F for 10 minutes. Meanwhile, heat half the remaining oil in a skillet, add the onions and tomatoes, and fry gently for 5 minutes. Chop the reserved eggplant flesh, add to the pan with the spices, and cook gently for 5 minutes. Season with salt.

4 Stir in the lentils, most of the remaining oil, reserving a little for later, and the mint. Spoon the mixture into the shells. Drizzle with remaining oil and bake for 15 minutes. Serve hot or cold, topped with a spoonful of plain yogurt and mint sprigs.

Leek & Herb Soufflé

Hot soufflés look very impressive if served as soon as they come out of the oven, otherwise they will sink quite quickly.

NUTRITIONAL INFORMATION

Calories 182	Sugars 4g	
Protein 8g	Fat 15g	
Carbohydrate 5g	Saturates 2g	

15 MINS   50 MINS

SERVES 4

INGREDIENTS

12 oz baby leeks

1 tbsp olive oil

½ cup vegetable stock

½ cup walnuts

2 eggs, separated

2 tbsp chopped mixed herbs

2 tbsp plain yogurt

salt and pepper

1 Using a sharp knife, chop the leeks finely. Heat the oil in a skillet. Add the leeks and sauté over a medium heat, stirring occasionally, for 2–3 minutes.

2 Add the vegetable stock to the pan, lower the heat, and simmer gently for a further 5 minutes.

3 Place the walnuts in a food processor and process until finely chopped. Add the leek mixture to the nuts and process briefly to purée. Transfer to a mixing bowl.

4 Mix together the egg yolks, herbs, and yogurt until thoroughly combined. Pour the egg mixture into the leek mixture. Season with salt and pepper to taste and mix well.

5 In a separate mixing bowl, whisk the egg whites until firm peaks form.

6 Fold the egg whites into the leek mixture. Spoon the mixture into a lightly greased 3¾ cup soufflé dish and place on a warmed cookie sheet.

7 Cook in a preheated oven at 350°F for 35–40 minutes, or until risen and set. Serve the soufflé immediately.

COOK'S TIP

Placing the soufflé dish on a warm cookie sheet helps to cook the soufflé from the bottom, thus aiding its cooking and lightness.

Potato & Vegetable Gratin

Similar to a simple moussaka, this recipe is made up of layers of aubergine (eggplant), tomato and potato baked with a yogurt topping.

NUTRITIONAL INFORMATION

Calories 409	Sugars 17g	
Protein 28g	Fat 14g	
Carbohydrate ...45g	Saturates 3g	

 25 MINS 1¼ HOURS

SERVES 4

INGREDIENTS

500 g/1 lb 2 oz waxy potatoes, sliced

1 tbsp vegetable oil

1 onion, chopped

2 garlic cloves, crushed

500 g/1 lb 2 oz tofu (bean curd), diced

2 tbsp tomato purée (paste)

2 tbsp plain (all-purpose) flour

300 ml/½ pint/1¼ cups vegetable stock

2 large tomatoes, sliced

1 aubergine (eggplant), sliced

2 tbsp chopped fresh thyme

450 ml/16 fl oz/scant 2 cups natural
   (unsweetened) yogurt

2 eggs, beaten

salt and pepper

salad, to serve

VARIATION

You can use marinated or smoked tofu (bean curd) for extra flavour, if you wish.

1 Cook the sliced potatoes in a saucepan of boiling water for 10 minutes, until tender, but not breaking up. Drain and set aside.

2 Heat the oil in a frying pan (skillet). Add the onion and garlic and fry, stirring occasionally, for 2-3 minutes.

3 Add the tofu (bean curd), tomato purée (paste) and flour and cook for 1 minute. Gradually stir in the stock and bring to the boil, stirring. Reduce the heat and simmer for 10 minutes.

4 Arrange a layer of the potato slices in the base of a deep ovenproof dish.

Spoon the tofu (bean curd) mixture evenly on top. Layer the sliced tomatoes, then the aubergine (eggplant) and finally, the remaining potato slices on top of the tofu mixture, making sure that it is completely covered. Sprinkle with thyme.

5 Mix the yogurt and beaten eggs together in a bowl and season to taste with salt and pepper. Spoon the yogurt topping over the sliced potatoes to cover them completely.

6 Bake in a preheated oven, 190°C/ 375°F/Gas Mark 5, for about 35–45 minutes or until the topping is browned. Serve with a crisp salad.

Vegetable Jalousie

This is a really easy dish to make, but looks impressive. The mixture of vegetables gives the dish a wonderful color and flavor.

NUTRITIONAL INFORMATION

Calories	660	Sugars	.........7g
Protein	........11g	Fat	..........45g
Carbohydrate	...53g	Saturates	......15g

 25 MINS   ⏱ 45 MINS

SERVES 4

I N G R E D I E N T S

1 lb 2 oz puff pastry

1 egg, beaten

F I L L I N G

2 tbsp butter or margarine

1 leek, shredded

2 garlic cloves, crushed

1 red bell pepper, seeded and sliced

1 yellow bell pepper, seeded and sliced

½ cup sliced mushrooms

2¾ oz small asparagus spears

2 tbsp all-purpose flour

6 tbsp vegetable stock

6 tbsp milk

4 tbsp dry white wine

1 tbsp chopped oregano

salt and pepper

1 Melt the butter or margarine in a skillet and sauté the leek and garlic, stirring frequently, for 2 minutes. Add the remaining vegetables and cook, stirring, for 3–4 minutes.

2 Add the flour and cook for 1 minute. Remove the pan from the heat and stir in the vegetable stock, milk, and white wine. Return the pan to the heat and bring to a boil, stirring, until thickened.

Stir in the oregano and season with salt and pepper to taste.

3 Roll out half of the pastry on a lightly floured work counter to form a rectangle 15 x 6 inches.

4 Roll out the other half of the pastry to the same shape, but a little larger all round. Put the smaller rectangle on a cookie sheet lined with dampened baking parchment.

5 Spoon the filling evenly on top of the smaller rectangle, leaving a ½-inch clear margin around the edges.

6 Using a sharp knife, cut parallel diagonal slits across the larger rectangle to within 1 inch of each of the long edges.

7 Brush the edges of the smaller rectangle with beaten egg and place the larger rectangle on top, pressing the edges firmly together to seal.

8 Brush the whole jalousie with egg to glaze and bake in a preheated oven at 400°F for about 30–35 minutes, until risen and golden. Transfer to a warmed serving dish and serve immediately.

Indian Curry Feast

This vegetable curry is quick and easy to prepare and it tastes superb. A colorful Indian salad and mint raita make perfect accompaniments.

NUTRITIONAL INFORMATION

Calories 473	Sugars 18g
Protein 19g	Fat 9g
Carbohydrate ...84g	Saturates 1g

25–30 MINS   55 MINS

SERVES 4

INGREDIENTS

1 tbsp vegetable oil

2 garlic cloves, crushed

1 onion, chopped

3 celery stalks, sliced

1 apple, cored and chopped

1 tbsp medium-strength curry powder

1 tsp ground ginger

14 oz can garbanzo beans

4½ oz baby green beans, sliced

8 oz cauliflower, broken into flowerets

8 oz potatoes, cut into cubes

2 cups sliced mushrooms

2½ cups vegetable stock

1 tbsp tomato paste

1 oz golden raisins

1 cup basmati rice

1 tbsp garam masala

MINT RAITA

⅔ cup plain yogurt

1 tbsp chopped mint

1 Heat the oil in a large saucepan. Add the garlic, onion, celery, and apple and fry over a medium heat, stirring frequently, for 3–4 minutes. Add the curry powder and ginger, and cook gently for 1 more minute.

2 Drain the garbanzo beans and add to the onion mixture, together with the baby green beans, cauliflower, potatoes, mushrooms, stock, tomato paste, and golden raisins. Bring to a boil, then reduce the heat. Cover and simmer for 35–40 minutes.

3 Meanwhile, make the raita. Mix the yogurt and mint together. Transfer to a small serving bowl, then cover and chill in the refrigerator.

4 Cook the rice in a large saucepan of boiling, lightly salted water for about 12 minutes, or until just tender. Drain, rinse with boiling water, and drain again.

5 Just before serving, stir the garam masala into the curry. Divide between four warmed serving plates and serve with the rice. Garnish the raita with fresh mint and hand the bowl separately.

Italian Vegetable Tart

This mouthwateringly attractive tart is full of Mediterranean flavors—spinach, red bell peppers, ricotta cheese, and pine nuts.

NUTRITIONAL INFORMATION

Calories	488	Sugars 7g
Protein	........13g	Fat 40g
Carbohydrate	...21g	Saturates 19g

30 MINS   30 MINS

SERVES 6

INGREDIENTS

8 oz frozen phyllo pastry, thawed

½ cup butter, melted

12 oz frozen spinach, thawed

2 eggs

⅔ cup light cream

1 cup ricotta cheese

1 red bell pepper, seeded and
   sliced into strips

½ cup pine nuts

salt and pepper

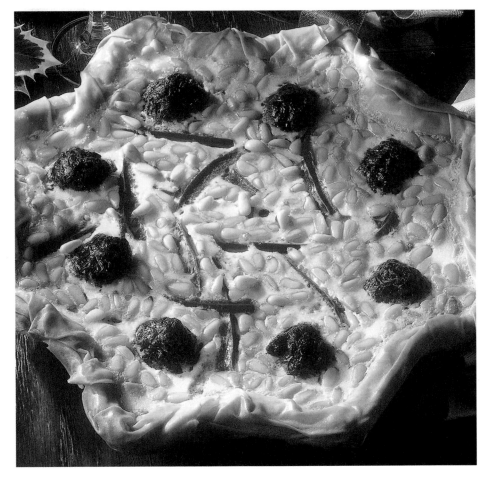

1 Use the sheets of phyllo pastry to line an 8 inch flan pan, brushing each layer with melted butter.

2 Put the spinach into a strainer or colander and squeeze out the excess moisture with the back of a spoon or your hand. Form the spinach into 8–9 small balls and arrange them in the prepared flan pan.

3 Beat the eggs, cream, and ricotta cheese together until thoroughly blended. Season to taste with salt and pepper and pour over the spinach.

4 Put the remaining butter into a saucepan. Add the red bell pepper strips and sauté over a low heat, stirring frequently, for about 4–5 minutes, until softened. Arrange the strips on the flan.

5 Scatter the pine nuts over the surface and bake in a preheated oven at 375°F for about 20–25 minutes, until the filling has set and the pastry is golden brown. Serve immediately or allow to cool completely and serve at room temperature.

VARIATION

If you do not like bell peppers, you could mushrooms instead. Wild mushrooms would be especially delicious. Add a few sliced sun-dried tomatoes for extra color and flavor.

Potato-Topped Lentil Bake

A wonderful mixture of red lentils, tofu, and vegetables is cooked beneath a crunchy potato topping for a really hearty meal.

NUTRITIONAL INFORMATION

Calories	627	Sugars	.........7g
Protein	........26g	Fat	..........30g
Carbohydrate	...66g	Saturates	......13g

🥔 10 MINS   🕐 1½ HOURS

SERVES 4

I N G R E D I E N T S

TOPPING

1½ lb russet potatoes, diced

2 tbsp butter

1 tbsp milk

½ cup chopped pecans

2 tbsp chopped thyme

thyme sprigs, to garnish

FILLING

1 cup red lentils

½ cup butter

1 leek, sliced

2 garlic cloves, crushed

1 celery stalk, chopped

4½ oz broccoli flowerets

6 oz tofu, cubed

2 tsp tomato paste

salt and pepper

VARIATION

You can use almost any combination of your favorite vegetables in this dish.

1 To make the topping, cook the potatoes in a saucepan of boiling water for 10–15 minutes, or until cooked through. Drain well, add the butter and milk, and mash thoroughly. Stir in the pecans and chopped thyme and set aside.

2 Cook the lentils in boiling water for 20–30 minutes, or until tender. Drain and set aside.

3 Melt the butter in a skillet. Add the leek, garlic, celery, and broccoli. Fry over a medium heat, stirring frequently, for 5 minutes, until softened. Add the tofu cubes. Stir in the lentils, together with the tomato paste. Season with salt and pepper to taste, then turn the mixture into the base of a shallow ovenproof dish.

4 Spoon the mashed potato on top of the lentil mixture, spreading to cover it completely.

5 Cook in a preheated oven at 400°F for about 30–35 minutes, or until the topping is golden. Garnish with sprigs of fresh thyme and serve hot.

Coconut Vegetable Curry

A mildly spiced, but richly flavored Indian-style dish full of different textures and flavors. Serve with naan bread to soak up the tasty sauce.

NUTRITIONAL INFORMATION

Calories	159	Sugars	.........8g
Protein	.........8g	Fat	...........6g
Carbohydrate	...19g	Saturates	.......1g

45 MINS   35 MINS

SERVES 6

INGREDIENTS

1 large eggplant,
    cut into 1-inch cubes

2 tbsp salt

2 tbsp vegetable oil

2 garlic cloves, crushed

1 fresh green chili,
    seeded and finely chopped

1 tsp grated fresh ginger

1 onion, finely chopped

2 tsp garam masala

8 cardamom pods

1 tsp ground turmeric

1 tbsp tomato paste

3 cups vegetable stock

1 tbsp lemon juice

8 oz potatoes, diced

8 oz small cauliflower flowerets

8 oz okra, trimmed

8 oz frozen peas

1⅔ cup coconut milk

salt and pepper

flaked coconut, to garnish

naan bread, to serve

1 Layer the eggplant in a bowl, sprinkling with salt as you go. Set aside for 30 minutes.

2 Rinse well under cold running water to remove all the salt. Drain and pat dry with paper towels. Set aside.

3 Heat the oil in a large saucepan. Add the garlic, chili, ginger, onion, and spices and fry over a medium heat, stirring occasionally, for 4–5 minutes, until lightly browned.

4 Stir in the tomato paste, stock, lemon juice, potatoes, and cauliflower and mix well. Bring to a boil, lower the heat, cover, and simmer for 15 minutes.

5 Stir in the eggplant, okra, peas, and coconut milk and season to taste with salt and pepper. Return to a boil and continue to simmer, uncovered, for another 10 minutes, or until tender. Remove and discard the cardamom pods.

6 Pile onto a warmed serving platter, garnish with flaked coconut, and serve immediately with naan bread.

Artichoke & Cheese Tart

Artichoke hearts are delicious to eat, as they are delicate in flavor and appearance. They are ideal for cooking in a cheese-flavored pastry shell.

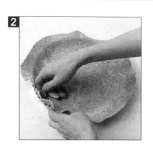

NUTRITIONAL INFORMATION

Calories	276	Sugars	.........3g
Protein	........10g	Fat	.........19g
Carbohydrate	...18g	Saturates	......10g

 15 MINS   30 MINS

SERVES 8

I N G R E D I E N T S

1¼ cups all-purpose
   whole wheat flour

2 garlic cloves, crushed

6 tbsp butter or margarine

3 tbsp water

salt and pepper

F I L L I N G

2 tbsp olive oil

1 red onion, halved and sliced

10 canned or fresh artichoke hearts

1 cup grated cheddar cheese

½ cup crumbled Gorgonzola cheese

2 eggs, beaten

1 tbsp chopped rosemary

⅔ cup milk

COOK'S TIP

Always roll pastry in one direction only to ensure an even thickness with no ridges. Do not press down on the dough; let the weight of a heavy rolling pin do the work for you.

1 To make the dough, sift the flour into a mixing bowl, add a pinch of salt and the garlic. Cut in the butter until the mixture resembles breadcrumbs. Stir in the water and bring the mixture together to form a dough.

2 Roll the dough out on a lightly floured work counter to fit an 8-inch flan pan. Prick the pastry with a fork.

3 Heat the oil in a skillet. Add the onion and sauté over a medium heat for 3 minutes. Add the artichoke hearts and cook, stirring frequently, for another 2 minutes.

4 Mix the cheeses with the beaten eggs, rosemary, and milk. Stir in the drained artichoke mixture and season to taste.

5 Spoon the artichoke and cheese mixture into the pastry shell and cook in a preheated oven at 400°F for 25 minutes or until cooked and set. Serve the flan hot or cold.

Potato-Topped Vegetables

This is a very colorful and nutritious dish, packed full of crunchy vegetables in a tasty white wine sauce.

NUTRITIONAL INFORMATION

Calories 413	Sugars 11g
Protein 19g	Fat 18g
Carbohydrate . . .41g	Saturates 11g

  20 MINS   1¼ HOURS

SERVES 4

I N G R E D I E N T S

1 carrot, diced

6 oz cauliflower flowerets

6 oz broccoli flowerets

1 fennel bulb, sliced

2¾ oz green beans, halved

2 tbsp butter

¼ cup all-purpose flour

⅔ cup vegetable stock

⅔ cup dry white wine

⅔ cup milk

6 oz mushrooms, quartered

2 tbsp chopped sage

TOPPING

4 potatoes, diced

2 tbsp butter

4 tbsp plain yogurt

4 tbsp grated Parmesan cheese

1 tsp fennel seeds

salt and pepper

1 Cook the carrot, cauliflower, broccoli, fennel, and beans in a large saucepan of boiling water for 10 minutes, until just tender. Drain the vegetables thoroughly and set aside.

2 Melt the butter in a saucepan. Stir in the flour and cook for 1 minute. Remove from the heat and stir in the stock, wine, and milk. Return to the heat and bring to a boil, stirring until thickened. Stir in the reserved vegetables, mushrooms and sage.

3 Meanwhile, make the topping. Cook the diced potatoes in a pan of boiling water for 10-15 minutes. Drain and mash with the butter, yogurt, and half the cheese. Stir in the fennel seeds.

4 Spoon the vegetable mixture into a 4 cup dish. Spoon the potato over the top and sprinkle with the remaining cheese. Cook in a preheated oven at 375°F for 30–35 minutes, or until golden. Serve hot.

Lentil Roast

The perfect dish to serve for Sunday lunch. Roast vegetables make a succulent accompaniment.

NUTRITIONAL INFORMATION

Calories	400	Sugars	. . . . .2g
Protein	. . . . .26g	Fat	. . . . .20g
Carbohydrate	. . .32g	Saturates	. . . . . .10g

15 MINS   1 HR 20 MINS

SERVES 6

INGREDIENTS

1 cup red lentils

2 cups vegetable stock

1 bay leaf

1 tbsp butter or

   margarine, softened

2 tbsp dried whole wheat breadcrumbs

2 cups grated sharp cheddar cheese

1 leek, finely chopped

4½ oz mushrooms, finely chopped

1½ cups fresh whole wheat breadcrumbs

2 tbsp chopped parsley

1 tbsp lemon juice

2 eggs, lightly beaten

salt and pepper

flat leaf parsley sprigs, to garnish

mixed roast vegetables, to serve

1 Put the lentils, stock and bay leaf in a saucepan. Bring to a boil, cover, and simmer gently for 15–20 minutes, until all the liquid is absorbed and the lentils have softened. Discard the bay leaf.

2 Base-line a 2 lb 4 oz-loaf pan with baking parchment. Grease with the butter or margarine and sprinkle with the dried breadcrumbs.

3 Stir the cheese, leek, mushrooms, fresh breadcrumbs, and parsley into the lentils.

4 Bind the mixture together with the lemon juice and eggs. Season with salt and pepper. Spoon into the prepared loaf pan and smooth the top.

5 Bake in a preheated oven at 375°F for about 1 hour, until golden.

6 Loosen the loaf with a metal spatula and turn onto a warmed serving plate. Garnish with parsley and serve sliced, with roast vegetables.

Chili Tofu

A tasty Mexican-style dish with a melt-in-the-mouth combination of tofu and avocado served with a tangy tomato sauce.

NUTRITIONAL INFORMATION

Calories 806   Sugars 20g
Protein . . . . .37g   Fat 54g
Carbohydrate . . .45g   Saturates 19g

30 MINS   35 MINS

SERVES 4

INGREDIENTS

½ tsp chili powder

1 tsp paprika

2 tbsp all-purpose flour

8 oz tofu, cut into ½-inch pieces

2 tbsp vegetable oil

1 onion, finely chopped

1 garlic clove, crushed

1 large red bell pepper, seeded and
   finely chopped

1 large ripe avocado

1 tbsp lime juice

4 tomatoes, peeled, seeded, and chopped

1 cup grated cheddar cheese

8 soft flour tortillas

⅔ cup sour cream

salt and pepper

cilantro sprigs, to garnish

pickled green jalapeño peppers, to serve

SAUCE

3¾ cups tomato sauce

3 tbsp chopped parsley

3 tbsp chopped cilantro

1 Mix the chili powder, paprika, flour, and salt and pepper on a plate and coat the tofu pieces.

2 Heat the oil in a skillet and gently fry the tofu for 3–4 minutes, until golden. Remove with a perforated spoon, drain on paper towels, and set aside.

3 Add the onion, garlic, and bell pepper to the oil and fry for 2–3 minutes, until just softened. Drain and set aside.

4 Halve the avocado, peel and remove the pit. Slice lengthwise, put in a bowl with the lime juice, and toss to coat.

5 Add the tofu and onion mixture and gently stir in the tomatoes and half the cheese. Spoon one-eighth of the filling down the center of each tortilla, top with sour cream and roll up. Arrange the tortillas in a shallow ovenproof dish in a single layer.

6 To make the sauce, mix together all the ingredients. Spoon the sauce over the tortillas, sprinkle with the remaining grated cheese and bake in a preheated oven at 375°F for 25 minutes, until golden and bubbling. Garnish with cilantro sprigs and serve immediately with pickled jalapeño peppers.

Spicy Potato Casserole

This is based on a Moroccan dish in which potatoes are spiced with cilantro and cumin and cooked in a lemon sauce.

NUTRITIONAL INFORMATION

Calories	338	Sugars	.........8g
Protein	.........5g	Fat	..........23g
Carbohydrate	...29g	Saturates	.......2g

15 MINS   35 MINS

SERVES 4

I N G R E D I E N T S

½ cup olive oil

2 red onions, cut into eight

3 garlic cloves, crushed

2 tsp ground cumin

2 tsp ground coriander

pinch of cayenne pepper

1 carrot, thickly sliced

2 small turnips, quartered

1 zucchini, sliced

1 lb 2 oz potatoes, thickly sliced

juice and zest of 2 large lemons

1¼ cups vegetable stock

2 tbsp chopped cilantro

salt and pepper

COOK'S TIP

Check the vegetables while they are cooking, as they may begin to stick to the pan. Add a little more boiling water or stock if necessary.

1 Heat the olive oil in a flameproof casserole. Add the onion and sauté over a medium heat, stirring frequently, for 3 minutes.

2 Add the garlic and cook for 30 seconds. Stir in the spices and cook, stirring constantly, for 1 minute.

3 Add the carrot, turnips, zucchini, and potatoes and stir to coat in the oil.

4 Add the lemon juice and zest and the vegetable stock. Season to taste with salt and pepper. Cover and cook over a medium heat, stirring occasionally, for 20–30 minutes, until tender.

5 Remove the lid, sprinkle in the cilantro, and stir well. Serve immediately.

Mushroom & Pine Nut Tarts

Different varieties of mushroom are becoming more widely available in supermarkets, so use this recipe to make the most of them.

NUTRITIONAL INFORMATION

Calories 494	Sugars 2g	
Protein 9g	Fat 35g	
Carbohydrate . . .38g	Saturates 18g	

🕑 15 MINS   🕑 20 MINS

SERVES 4

I N G R E D I E N T S

1 lb 2 oz phyllo pastry

½ cup butter, melted

1 tbsp hazelnut or walnut oil

¼ cup pine nuts

12 oz mixed mushrooms

2 tsp chopped parsley

1 cup soft goat cheese

salt and pepper

parsley sprigs to garnish

lettuce, tomatoes, cucumber, and
   green onions, to serve

1 Cut the sheets of phyllo pastry into pieces about 4 inches square and use them to line 4 individual tart pans, brushing each layer of pastry with melted butter. Line the pans with foil or baking parchment and dried baking beans. Bake in a preheated oven at 400°F for about 6–8 minutes, or until light golden brown.

2 Remove the tarts from the oven and carefully take out the foil or parchment and baking beans. Reduce the oven temperature to 350°F.

3 Put any remaining butter into a large saucepan with the hazelnut oil and fry the pine nuts gently until golden brown. Lift them out with a perforated spoon and drain on paper towels.

4 Add the mushrooms to the saucepan and cook them gently, stirring frequently, for about 4–5 minutes. Add the chopped parsley and season to taste with salt and pepper.

5 Spoon one-quarter of the goat cheese into the base of each cooked phyllo tart. Divide the mushrooms equally between them and scatter the pine nuts over the top.

6 Return the tarts to the oven for 5 minutes to heat through, and then serve them, garnished with sprigs of parsley. Serve with lettuce, tomatoes, cucumber, and green onions.

Layered Pies

These individual pies of layered potato, eggplant, and zucchini baked in a tomato sauce can be made ahead of time.

NUTRITIONAL INFORMATION

Calories	427	Sugars	........8g
Protein	........22g	Fat	.........21g
Carbohydrate	...41g	Saturates	.......8g

🍲 40 MINS   🕐 1 HR 20 MINS

SERVES 4

I N G R E D I E N T S

3 large potatoes, thinly sliced

1 small eggplant, thinly sliced

1 zucchini, sliced

3 tbsp vegetable oil

1 onion, diced

1 green bell pepper, seeded and diced

1 tsp cumin seeds

2 tbsp chopped basil

7 oz can diced tomatoes

6 oz mozzarella cheese, sliced

8 oz tofu, sliced

1 cup fresh white breadcrumbs

2 tbsp grated Parmesan cheese

salt and pepper

basil leaves, to garnish

1 Cook the sliced potatoes in a saucepan of boiling water for 5 minutes. Drain and set aside.

2 Put the eggplant slices on a plate, sprinkle with salt, and leave for 20 minutes. Meanwhile, blanch the zucchini in a saucepan of boiling water for 2-3 minutes. Drain and set aside.

3 Meanwhile, heat 2 tbsp of the oil in a skillet. Add the onion and fry over a low heat, stirring occasionally, for 2-3 minutes, until softened. Add the bell pepper, cumin seeds, basil, and canned tomatoes. Season to taste with salt and pepper and simmer for 30 minutes.

4 Rinse the eggplant slices and pat dry. Heat the remaining oil in a large skillet and fry the eggplant slices for 3-5 minutes, turning to brown both sides. Drain and set aside.

5 Arrange half of the potato slices in the base of 4 small loose-based flan pans. Cover with half of the zucchini slices, half of the eggplant slices, and half of the mozzarella slices. Lay the tofu on top and spoon over the tomato sauce. Repeat the layers of vegetables and cheese in the same order.

6 Mix the breadcrumbs and Parmesan together and sprinkle over the top. Cook in a preheated oven at 375°F for 25-30 minutes, or until golden. Garnish with basil leaves.

Green Vegetable Gougère

A tasty, simple supper dish of choux pastry and crisp green vegetables.
The choux pastry ring can be filled with all kinds of vegetables.

NUTRITIONAL INFORMATION

Calories	672	Sugars	.........6g
Protein	........19g	Fat	..........51g
Carbohydrate	...36g	Saturates	......14g

🥔 30 MINS   🕐 40 MINS

SERVES 4

INGREDIENTS

1¼ cups all-purpose flour

½ cup butter

1¼ cups water

4 eggs, beaten

¾ cup grated Gruyère cheese

1 tbsp milk

salt and pepper

FILLING

2 tbsp garlic and herb butter or margarine

2 tsp olive oil

2 leeks, shredded

8 oz green cabbage, finely shredded

2 cups bean sprouts

½ tsp grated lime zest

1 tbsp lime juice

celery salt and pepper

lime slices, to garnish

1 Sift the flour onto a piece of baking parchment. Cut the butter into dice and put in a saucepan with the water. Heat until the butter has melted.

2 Bring the butter and water to a boil, then pour in all the flour immediately.

Beat until the mixture becomes thick. Remove from the heat and beat until the mixture is glossy and comes away from the sides of the saucepan.

3 Transfer to a mixing bowl and cool for 10 minutes. Gradually beat in the eggs, a little at a time, making sure they are thoroughly incorporated after each addition. Stir in ½ cup of the cheese and season with salt and pepper.

4 Place spoonfuls of the mixture in a 9 inch circle on a dampened cookie sheet. Brush with milk and sprinkle with

the remaining cheese. Bake in a preheated oven at 425°F for 30–35 minutes, until golden and crisp. Transfer to a warmed serving plate.

5 Meanwhile, make the filling. Heat the butter or margarine and the oil in a large skillet and stir-fry the leeks and cabbage for 2 minutes. Add the bean sprouts, lime zest and juice, and stir-fry for 1 minute. Season to taste.

6 Pile into the center of the pastry ring. Garnish with lime slices and serve.

Baked Potatoes with Beans

Baked potatoes, topped with a tasty mixture of beans in a spicy sauce, provide a deliciously filling, high-fiber dish.

NUTRITIONAL INFORMATION

Calories ....378 Sugars 9g
Protein ....15g Fat 9g
Carbohydrate ...64g Saturates 1g

 15 MINS   1¼ HOURS

SERVES 6

INGREDIENTS

6 large potatoes

4 tbsp vegetable ghee or oil

1 large onion, chopped

2 garlic cloves, crushed

1 tsp ground turmeric

1 tbsp cumin seeds

2 tbsp mild or medium curry paste

12 oz cherry tomatoes

14 oz can black-eyed peas,
   drained and rinsed

14 oz can red kidney beans,
   drained and rinsed

1 tbsp lemon juice

2 tbsp tomato paste

⅔ cup water

2 tbsp chopped fresh mint or cilantro

salt and pepper

VARIATION

Instead of cutting the potatoes in half, cut a cross in each and squeeze gently to open out. Spoon some of the prepared filling into the cross and place any remaining filling to the side.

1 Scrub the potatoes and prick several times with a fork. Place in a preheated oven at 350°F and cook for 1–1¼ hours, or until the potatoes feel soft when gently squeezed.

2 About 20 minutes before the end of cooking time, prepare the topping. Heat the ghee or oil in a saucepan, add the onion, and cook over a low heat, stirring frequently, for 5 minutes. Add the garlic, turmeric, cumin seeds, and curry paste and cook gently for 1 minute.

3 Stir in the tomatoes, black-eyed peas and red kidney beans, lemon juice, tomato paste, water, and chopped mint. Season to taste with salt and pepper, then cover and simmer over a low heat, stirring frequently, for 10 minutes.

4 When the potatoes are cooked, cut them in half and mash the flesh lightly with a fork. Spoon the prepared bean mixture on top, place on warm serving plates, and serve immediately.

Vegetable & Tofu Strudels

These strudels look really impressive and are perfect if friends are coming around or for a more formal dinner party dish.

   25 MINS   30 MINS

SERVES 4

I N G R E D I E N T S

FILLING

2 tbsp vegetable oil

2 tbsp butter

⅓ cup potatoes, finely diced

1 leek, shredded

2 garlic cloves, crushed

1 tsp garam masala

½ tsp chili powder

½ tsp turmeric

1¾ oz okra, sliced

1¼ cups sliced mushrooms

2 tomatoes, diced

8 oz firm tofu, diced

12 sheets phyllo pastry

2 tbsp butter, melted

salt and pepper

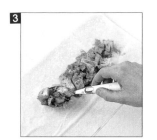

1 To make the filling, heat the oil and butter in a skillet. Add the potatoes and leek and fry, stirring constantly, for 2–3 minutes. Add the garlic and spices, okra, mushrooms, tomatoes, and tofu and season to taste with salt and pepper. Cook, stirring, for 5–7 minutes, or until tender.

2 Lay the pastry out on a cutting board and brush each individual sheet with melted butter. Place 3 sheets on top of one another; repeat to make 4 stacks.

3 Spoon a quarter of the filling along the center of each stack and brush the edges with melted butter. Fold the short edges in and roll up lengthwise to form a cigar shape. Brush the outside with melted butter. Place the strudels on a greased cookie sheet.

4 Cook in a preheated oven at 375°F for 20 minutes, or until golden brown and crisp. Transfer to a warm serving dish and serve immediately.

Four Cheese & Potato Layer

This is a quick dish to prepare and it can be left to cook in the oven without requiring any extra attention.

NUTRITIONAL INFORMATION

Calories 766	Sugars 14g	
Protein 44g	Fat 40g	
Carbohydrate . . .60g	Saturates 23g	

 25 MINS   45 MINS

SERVES 4

I N G R E D I E N T S

2 lb unpeeled potatoes,
 cut into wedges

2 tbsp butter

1 red onion, halved and sliced

2 garlic cloves, crushed

¼ cup all-purpose flour

2½ cups milk

14 oz can artichoke hearts, drained
 and halved

5½ oz frozen mixed
 vegetables, thawed

1 cup grated Gruyère cheese

1 cup grated sharp cheese

½ cup crumbled Gorgonzola cheese

⅓ cup grated Parmesan cheese

8 oz tofu, sliced

2 tbsp chopped thyme

salt and pepper

thyme sprigs, to garnish

1 Cook the potato wedges in a saucepan of boiling water for 10 minutes. Drain thoroughly.

2 Meanwhile, melt the butter in a saucepan. Add the sliced onion and garlic and fry over a low heat, stirring frequently, for 2-3 minutes.

3 Stir the flour into the pan and cook for 1 minute. Gradually add the milk and bring to a boil, stirring constantly.

4 Reduce the heat and add the artichoke hearts, mixed vegetables, half of each of the 4 cheeses, and the tofu to the pan, mixing well. Stir in the chopped thyme and season with salt and pepper to taste.

5 Arrange a layer of parboiled potato wedges in the base of a shallow ovenproof dish. Spoon the vegetable mixture over the top and cover with the remaining potato wedges. Sprinkle the rest of the 4 cheeses over the top.

6 Cook in a preheated oven at 400°F for 30 minutes or until the potatoes are cooked and the top is golden brown. Serve the bake garnished with fresh thyme sprigs.

Bread & Butter Savory

Quick, simple, nutritious and a pleasure to eat—what more could you ask for an inexpensive midweek meal?

NUTRITIONAL INFORMATION

Calories	472	Sugars	.........7g
Protein	........22g	Fat	..........33g
Carbohydrate	...25g	Saturates	......20g

  30 MINS 45 MINS

SERVES 4

I N G R E D I E N T S

¼ cup butter or margarine

1 bunch green onions, sliced

6 slices of white or brown bread,
   crusts removed

1½ cups grated sharp cheddar cheese

2 eggs

2 cups milk

salt and pepper

flat-leaf parsley sprigs, to garnish

1 Grease a 1½-quart ovenproof dish with a little of the butter or margarine.

2 Melt the remaining butter or margarine in a small saucepan. Add the green onions and fry over a medium heat, stirring occasionally, until softened and golden.

3 Meanwhile, cut the bread into triangles and place half of them in the base of the dish. Cover with the green onions and top with half the grated cheese.

4 Beat together the eggs and milk and season to taste with salt and pepper. Layer the remaining triangles of bread in the dish and carefully pour over the milk mixture. Leave to soak for 15–20 minutes.

5 Sprinkle the remaining cheese over the soaked bread. Bake in a preheated oven at 375°F for 35–40 minutes, until puffed up and golden brown. Garnish with flat-leaf parsley and serve immediately.

VARIATION

You can vary the vegetables used in this savory bake, depending on what you have on hand. Shallots, mushrooms, or tomatoes are all suitable.

Cauliflower Bake

The red of the tomatoes is a great contrast to the cauliflower and herbs, making this dish appealing to both the eye and the palate.

NUTRITIONAL INFORMATION

Calories	305	Sugars	.........9g
Protein	........15g	Fat	..........14g
Carbohydrate	...31g	Saturates	.......6g

10 MINS   40 MINS

SERVES 4

INGREDIENTS

1 lb 2 oz cauliflower, broken into flowerets

2 large potatoes, cubed

3½ oz cherry tomatoes

SAUCE

2 tbsp butter or margarine

1 leek, sliced

1 garlic clove, crushed

3 tbsp all-purpose flour

1¼ cups milk

¾ cup mixed grated cheese,
    such as cheddar, Parmesan,
    and Gruyère

½ tsp paprika

2 tbsp chopped flat-leaf parsley

salt and pepper

chopped parsley, to garnish

VARIATION

This dish could be made with broccoli instead of the cauliflower as an alternative.

1 Cook the cauliflower in a saucepan of boiling water for 10 minutes. Drain well and reserve. Meanwhile, cook the potatoes in a pan of boiling water for 10 minutes, drain, and reserve.

2 To make the sauce, melt the butter or margarine in a saucepan and sauté the leek and garlic for 1 minute. Stir in the flour and cook, stirring constantly, for 1 minute. Remove the pan from the heat and gradually stir in the milk, ½ cup of the cheese, the paprika, and parsley. Return the pan to the heat and bring to a boil, stirring constantly. Season with salt and pepper to taste.

3 Spoon the cauliflower into a deep ovenproof dish. Add the cherry tomatoes and top with the potatoes. Pour the sauce over the potatoes and sprinkle on the remaining cheese.

4 Cook in a preheated oven at 350°F for 20 minutes, or until the vegetables are cooked through and the cheese is golden brown and bubbling. Garnish and serve immediately.

White Nut Phyllo Packages

These crisp, buttery parcels, filled with nuts and pesto, would make an interesting and tasty family meal.

NUTRITIONAL INFORMATION

Calories	1100	Sugars	.........9g
Protein	........29g	Fat	..........80g
Carbohydrate	...73g	Saturates	......15g

 15 MINS   25 MINS

SERVES 4

I N G R E D I E N T S

3 tbsp butter or margarine

1 large onion, finely chopped

2¼ cups mixed white nuts,
  such as pine nuts, unsalted cashews,
  blanched almonds, unsalted peanuts,
  finely chopped

1½ cups fresh white breadcrumbs

½ tsp ground mace

1 egg, beaten

1 egg yolk

3 tbsp pesto sauce

2 tbsp chopped basil

½ cup butter or margarine, melted

16 sheets phyllo pastry

salt and pepper

basil sprigs to garnish

TO SERVE

cranberry sauce

steamed vegetables

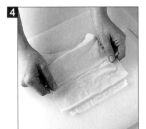

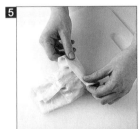

1 Melt the butter or margarine in a skillet and gently fry the onion for 2–3 minutes, until just softened but not browned.

2 Remove from the heat and stir in the nuts, two-thirds of the breadcrumbs, the mace, and beaten egg. Season to taste with salt and pepper. Set aside.

3 Place the remaining breadcrumbs in a bowl and stir in the egg yolk, pesto sauce, basil, and 1 tablespoon of the melted butter or margarine. Mix well.

4 Brush 1 sheet of phyllo with melted butter or margarine. Fold in half and brush again. Repeat with a second sheet and lay it on top of the first one so that it forms a cross.

5 Put one-eighth of the nut mixture in the center of the pastry. Top with one-eighth of the pesto mixture. Fold over the edges, brushing with more butter or margarine, to form a small package. Brush the top with butter or margarine and transfer to a cookie sheet. Make eight packages in the same way and brush with the remaining butter or margarine.

6 Bake in a preheated oven at 425°F for 15–20 minutes, until golden. Transfer to serving plates, garnish with basil sprigs, and serve with cranberry sauce and steamed vegetables.

Root Croustades

This colorful combination of grated root vegetables and mixed bell peppers would make a stunning dinner-party dish.

NUTRITIONAL INFORMATION

Calories .... .304   Sugars 17g
Protein .... .6g   Fat .... .19g
Carbohydrate ...28g   Saturates 3g

2½ HOURS   1¼ HOURS

SERVES 4

I N G R E D I E N T S

1 orange bell pepper

1 red bell pepper

1 yellow bell pepper

3 tbsp olive oil

2 tbsp red wine vinegar

1 tsp Dijon mustard

1 tsp liquid honey

salt and pepper

flat-leaf parsley sprigs, to garnish

green vegetables, to serve

C R O U S T A D E S

8 oz potatoes, coarsely grated

8 oz carrots, coarsely grated

12 oz celery root,
    coarsely grated

1 garlic clove, crushed

1 tbsp lemon juice

2 tbsp butter or
    margarine, melted

1 egg, beaten

1 tbsp vegetable oil

1 Place the bell peppers on a cookie sheet and bake in a preheated oven at 375°F for 35 minutes, turning after 20 minutes.

2 Cover with a dish towel and leave to cool for 10 minutes.

3 Peel the skin from the cooked bell peppers; cut in half and discard the seeds. Thinly slice the flesh into strips and place in a shallow dish.

4 Put the oil, vinegar, mustard, honey, and seasoning in a small screw-top jar and shake well to mix. Pour over the bell pepper strips, mix well and set aside to marinate for 2 hours.

5 To make the croustades, put the potatoes, carrots, and celery root in a mixing bowl and toss in the garlic and lemon juice.

6 Mix in the melted butter or margarine and the egg. Season to taste with salt and pepper. Divide the mixture into 8 and pile on to 2 cookie sheets lined with baking parchment, forming each into a 4-inch round. Brush with oil.

7 Bake in a preheated oven at 425°F for 30–35 minutes, until the croustades are crisp around the edges and golden. Carefully transfer to a warmed serving dish. Heat the bell peppers and the marinade for 2–3 minutes until warmed through. Spoon the bell peppers over the croustades, garnish with flat-leaf parsley, and serve immediately with green vegetables.

Spicy Potato & Nut Terrine

This delicious baked terrine has a base of mashed potato which is flavored with nuts, cheese, herbs, and spices.

NUTRITIONAL INFORMATION

Calories 1100	Sugars 13g
Protein 34g	Fat 93g
Carbohydrate . . .31g	Saturates 22g

🍲 15 MINS   🕐 1½ HOURS

SERVES 4

INGREDIENTS

8 oz russet potatoes, diced

8 oz pecan nuts

8 oz unsalted cashews

1 onion, finely chopped

2 garlic cloves, crushed

1½ cups diced mushrooms

2 tbsp butter

2 tbsp chopped mixed herbs

1 tsp paprika

1 tsp ground cumin

1 tsp ground coriander

4 eggs, beaten

½ cup full-fat cream cheese

⅔ cup grated Parmesan cheese

salt and pepper

SAUCE

3 large tomatoes, peeled, seeded, and chopped

2 tbsp tomato paste

⅓ cup red wine

1 tbsp red wine vinegar

pinch of sugar

1 Lightly grease a 2-lb loaf pan and line with baking parchment.

2 Cook the potatoes in a large pan of lightly salted boiling water for 10 minutes, or until cooked through. Drain and mash thoroughly.

3 Finely chop the pecan and cashews or process in a food processor. Mix the nuts with the onion, garlic, and mushrooms. Melt the butter in a skillet and cook the nut mixture for 5-7 minutes. Add the herbs and spices. Stir in the eggs, cheeses, and potatoes, and season to taste with salt and pepper.

4 Spoon the mixture into the prepared loaf pan, pressing down firmly. Cook in a preheated oven at 375°F for 1 hour, or until set.

5 To make the sauce, mix the tomatoes, tomato paste, wine, wine vinegar, and sugar in a pan and bring to a boil, stirring. Cook for 10 minutes, or until the tomatoes have reduced. Press the sauce through a strainer or process in a food processor for 30 seconds. Turn the terrine out of the pan onto a serving plate and cut into slices. Serve with the tomato sauce.

Vegetable Roast Wellington

This is a vegetarian version of the classic "Beef Wellington." Served with sherry sauce and roast vegetables, it is a tasty and impressive main dish.

NUTRITIONAL INFORMATION

Calories . . . . .821 Sugars 8g

Protein . . . . .23g Fat 51g

Carbohydrate . . .64g Saturates 10g

 20 MINS   45 MINS

SERVES 4

I N G R E D I E N T S

1 lb can garbanzo beans, drained

1 tsp yeast extract

1¼ cups chopped walnuts

1¼ cups fresh breadcrumbs

1 onion, finely chopped

1¼ cups mushrooms, sliced

⅓ cup canned corn, drained

2 garlic cloves, crushed

2 tbsp dry sherry

2 tbsp vegetable stock

1 tbsp chopped cilantro

8 oz puff pastry

1 egg, beaten

2 tbsp milk

salt and pepper

S A U C E

1 tbsp vegetable oil

1 leek, thinly sliced

4 tbsp dry sherry

⅔ cup vegetable stock

1 Process the garbanzo beans, yeast extract, nuts, and breadcrumbs in a food processor for 30 seconds. In a skillet, sauté the onion and mushrooms in their own juices for 3–4 minutes. Stir in the bean mixture, corn, and garlic. Add the sherry, stock, cilantro, and seasoning, and bind the mixture together. Remove from the heat and allow to cool.

2 Roll out the pastry out on a floured work counter to form a 14 x 12-inch-rectangle. Shape the garbanzo bean mixture into a loaf shape and wrap the pastry around it, sealing the edges. Place seam side down on a dampened cookie sheet and score the top in a criss-cross pattern. Mix the egg and milk and brush over the pastry. Cook in a preheated oven at 400°F for 25–30 minutes.

3 Heat the oil for the sauce in a pan and sauté the leek for 5 minutes. Add the sherry and stock and bring to a boil. Simmer for 5 minutes and serve the sauce with the roast.

Mushroom & Nut Crumble

A filling, tasty dish that is ideal for a warming family supper. The crunchy topping is flavored with three different types of nuts.

NUTRITIONAL INFORMATION

Calories 779	Sugars 5g
Protein 16g	Fat 59g
Carbohydrate . . .48g	Saturates 14g

🍲 20 MINS   🕐 55 MINS

SERVES 4

I N G R E D I E N T S

5 cups sliced mushrooms

5 cups sliced chestnut mushrooms, sliced

1¾ cups vegetable stock

¼ cup butter or margarine

1 large onion, finely chopped

1 garlic clove, crushed

½ cup all-purpose flour

4 tbsp heavy cream

2 tbsp chopped parsley

salt and pepper

herbs, to garnish

TOPPING

¾ cup rolled oats

¾ cup whole wheat flour

¼ cup ground almonds

¼ cup finely chopped walnuts

½ cup finely chopped unsalted
   shelled pistachios

1 tsp dried thyme

⅓ cup butter or margarine, softened

1 tbsp fennel seeds

1 Put the mushrooms and stock in a large saucepan, bring to a boil, cover, and simmer for 15 minutes, until tender. Drain, reserving the stock.

2 In another saucepan, melt the butter or margarine and fry the onion and garlic for 2–3 minutes, until just soft. Stir in the flour and cook for 1 minute.

3 Remove from the heat and gradually stir in the reserved mushroom stock. Return to the heat and cook, stirring, until thickened. Stir in the mushrooms, seasoning, cream, and parsley and spoon into a shallow ovenproof dish.

4 To make the topping, in a bowl, mix together the oatmeal, flour, nuts, thyme, and plenty of salt and pepper to taste.

5 Using a fork, mix in the butter or margarine until the topping resembles coarse breadcrumbs.

6 Sprinkle the topping mixture evenly over the mushrooms and then sprinkle with the fennel seeds. Bake in a preheated oven at 375°F for about 25–30 minutes, or until the topping is golden and crisp. Garnish with fresh herbs and serve immediately.

Baked Potatoes with Pesto

This is an easy, but very filling meal. The potatoes are baked until fluffy, then they are mixed with a tasty pesto filling and baked again.

NUTRITIONAL INFORMATION

Calories ....444 Sugars 3g
Protein ....10g Fat 28g
Carbohydrate ...40g Saturates 13g

10 MINS   1½ HOURS

SERVES 4

INGREDIENTS

4 baking potatoes, about 8 oz each

⅔ cup heavy cream

⅓ cup vegetable stock

1 tbsp lemon juice

2 garlic cloves, crushed

3 tbsp chopped basil

2 tbsp pine nuts

2 tbsp grated Parmesan cheese

1 Scrub the potatoes well and prick the skins with a fork. Rub a little salt into the skins and place on a cookie sheet.

2 Cook in a preheated oven at 375°F for 1 hour, or until the potatoes are cooked through and the skins are crisp.

3 Remove the potatoes from the oven and cut them in half lengthwise.

VARIATION

Add cream cheese or thinly sliced mushrooms to the mashed potato flesh in step 5, if you prefer.

Using a spoon, scoop the potato flesh into a mixing bowl, leaving a thin shell of potato inside the skins. Mash the potato flesh with a fork.

4 Meanwhile, mix the cream and stock in a saucepan and simmer over a low heat for about 8-10 minutes, or until reduced by half.

5 Stir in the lemon juice, garlic, and chopped basil and season to taste with salt and pepper. Stir the mixture into the mashed potato flesh, together with the pine nuts.

6 Spoon the mixture back into the potato shells and sprinkle the Parmesan cheese on top. Return the potatoes to the oven for 10 minutes, or until the cheese has browned. Serve.

Vegetable Toad-in-the-Hole

This dish can be cooked in a single large dish or in four individual popover pans.

NUTRITIONAL INFORMATION

Calories 313   Sugars 9g
Protein . . . . .9g   Fat 18g
Carbohydrate . . .31g   Saturates 7g

15 MINS   55 MINS

SERVES 4

INGREDIENTS

BATTER

¾ cup all-purpose flour

2 eggs, beaten

1 cup milk

2 tbsp wholegrain mustard

2 tbsp vegetable oil

FILLING

2 tbsp butter

2 garlic cloves, crushed

1 onion, cut into eight

2¾ oz baby carrots, halved lengthwise

1¾ oz green beans

⅓ cup canned corn, drained

2 tomatoes, seeded and cut into chunks

1 tsp wholegrain mustard

1 tbsp chopped mixed herbs

salt and pepper

1 To make the batter, sift the flour and a pinch of salt into a bowl. Beat in the eggs and milk to make a batter. Stir in the mustard and leave to stand.

2 Pour the oil into a shallow ovenproof dish and heat in a preheated oven at 400°F for 10 minutes.

3 To make the filling, melt the butter in a skillet and sauté the garlic and onion, stirring constantly, for 2 minutes. Cook the carrots and beans in a saucepan of boiling water for 7 minutes, or until tender. Drain well.

4 Add the corn and tomatoes to the skillet with the mustard and herbs.

Season well and add the carrots and beans.

5 Remove the dish from the oven and pour in the batter. Spoon the vegetables into the center, return to the oven, and cook for 30–35 minutes, until the batter has risen and set. Serve the vegetable toad-in-the-hole immediately.

Elizabethan Artichoke Pie

The filling of Jerusalem artichokes, grapes, onion, dates, and hard-boiled eggs is an unusual but delicious blend of flavors.

NUTRITIONAL INFORMATION

Calories ....136 Sugars 8g
Protein ....6g Fat 6g
Carbohydrate ...16g Saturates 3g

1¼ HOURS   55 MINS

SERVES 6

INGREDIENTS

12 oz Jerusalem artichokes

2 tbsp butter or margarine

1 onion, chopped

1–2 garlic cloves, crushed

4½ oz green seedless grapes, halved

⅓ cup dates, chopped coarsely

2 hard-boiled eggs, sliced

1 tbsp chopped fresh mixed herbs
    or 1 tsp dried herbs

4–6 tbsp light cream or plain yogurt

PIE DOUGH

3 cups all-purpose flour

pinch of salt

⅓ cup butter or margarine

⅓ cup white vegetable fat

4–6 tbsp cold water

beaten egg or milk, to glaze

1 To make the pie dough, sift the flour and salt into a bowl, cut in the butter or margarine and vegetable fat until the mixture resembles fine breadcrumbs, then add sufficient water to mix to a pliable dough. Knead lightly. Wrap in foil or plastic wrap and chill for 30 minutes.

2 Peel the artichokes, plunging them immediately into salted water to prevent discoloration. Drain, cover with fresh water, bring to a boil, and simmer for 10–12 minutes until just tender. Drain.

3 Heat the butter or margarine in a pan and fry the onion and garlic until soft but not colored. Remove from the heat and stir in the grapes and dates.

4 Roll out almost two-thirds of the pie dough and use to line an 8-inch pie dish. Slice the artichokes and arrange in the pie dish, cover with slices of egg and then with the onion mixture, seasoning, and herbs.

5 Roll out the remaining pie dough, dampen the edges, and use to cover the pie; press the edges firmly together, then trim and crimp. Roll out the trimmings and cut into narrow strips. Arrange a lattice over the top of the pie, dampening the strips to attach them.

6 Glaze with beaten egg or milk and make 2–3 slits in the lid. Bake in a preheated oven at 400°F for 40–50 minutes until golden. Gently heat the cream or yogurt and pour into the pie through the holes in the lid. Serve.

Nutty Harvest Loaf

This attractive and nutritious loaf is also utterly delicious. Served with a fresh tomato sauce, it can be eaten hot or cold with salad.

NUTRITIONAL INFORMATION

Calories	554	Sugars	........12g
Protein	........16g	Fat	..........37g
Carbohydrate	...43g	Saturates	......16g

 20 MINS   1HR 20 MINS

SERVES 4

I N G R E D I E N T S

2 tbsp butter, plus extra

   for greasing

1 lb russet potatoes, diced

1 onion, chopped

2 garlic cloves, crushed

1 cup unsalted peanuts

1⅓ cups fresh white breadcrumbs

1 egg, beaten

2 tbsp chopped cilantro

⅔ cup vegetable stock

1 cup sliced mushrooms

1¾ oz sun-dried tomatoes, sliced

salt and pepper

S A U C E

⅔ cup crème fraîche or sour cream

2 tsp tomato paste

2 tsp honey

2 tbsp chopped cilantro

1 Grease a 1 lb loaf pan. Cook the potatoes in a saucepan of boiling water for 10 minutes, until cooked through. Drain well, mash, and set aside.

2 Melt half of the butter in a skillet. Add the onion and garlic and fry gently for 2–3 minutes, until soft. Finely chop the nuts or process them in a food processor for 30 seconds with the breadcrumbs.

3 Mix the chopped nuts and breadcrumbs into the potatoes with the egg, cilantro, and vegetable stock. Stir in the onion and garlic and mix well.

4 Melt the remaining butter in the skillet, add the sliced mushrooms, and cook for 2–3 minutes.

5 Press half of the potato mixture into the base of the loaf pan. Spoon the mushrooms on top and sprinkle with the sun-dried tomatoes. Spoon the remaining potato mixture on top and smooth the surface. Cover with foil and bake in a preheated oven at 350°F for 1 hour, or until firm to the touch.

6 Meanwhile, mix the sauce ingredients together. Cut the nutty harvest loaf into slices and serve with the sauce.

Roast Bell Pepper Tart

This tastes truly delicious, the flavor of roasted vegetables being entirely different from that of boiled or fried.

NUTRITIONAL INFORMATION

Calories 237
Sugars 3g
Protein 6g
Fat 15g
Carbohydrate . . .20g
Saturates 4g

25 MINS   40 MINS

SERVES 8

INGREDIENTS

TART DOUGH

1½ cups all-purpose flour

pinch of salt

6 tbsp butter or margarine

2 tbsp green pitted olives,
    finely chopped

3 tbsp cold water

FILLING

1 red bell pepper

1 green bell pepper

1 yellow bell pepper

2 garlic cloves, crushed

2 tbsp olive oil

1 cup grated mozzarella cheese

2 eggs

⅔ cup milk

1 tbsp chopped basil

salt and pepper

1 To make the tart dough, sift the flour and salt into a bowl. Cut in the butter or margarine until the mixture resembles breadcrumbs. Add the olives and cold water, bringing the mixture together to form a dough.

2 Roll the dough out on a floured work counter and use to line an 8-inch loose-based flan pan. Prick the base with a fork and leave to chill.

3 Cut all the bell peppers in half lengthwise, seed, and place them, skin side up, on a cookie sheet. Mix the garlic and oil and brush over the bell peppers. Cook in a preheated oven at 400°F for 20 minutes, or until beginning to char slightly. Let the bell peppers cool slightly and thinly slice. Arrange in the base of the tart shell, layering with the mozzarella.

4 Beat the egg and milk and add the basil. Season and pour over the bell peppers. Put the tart on a cookie sheet and return to the oven for 20 minutes, or until set. Serve hot or cold.

Spinach Roulade

A delicious savory roll, stuffed with mozzarella and broccoli. Serve as a main course or as an appetizer, in which case it would easily serve six.

NUTRITIONAL INFORMATION

Calories ....287 Sugars 8g
Protein ....23g Fat 12g
Carbohydrate ....8g Saturates 6g

15 MINS   25 MINS

SERVES 4

INGREDIENTS

1 lb 2 oz small spinach leaves

2 tbsp water

4 eggs, separated

½ tsp ground nutmeg

salt and pepper

1¼ cups tomato sauce, to serve

FILLING

6 oz small broccoli flowerets

¼ cup freshly grated Parmesan cheese

1½ cups grated mozzarella cheese

1 Wash the spinach and pack, still wet, into a large saucepan. Add the water. Cover with a tight-fitting lid and cook over a high heat for 4–5 minutes, until reduced and soft. Drain thoroughly, squeezing out excess water. Chop finely and pat dry.

2 Mix the spinach with the egg yolks, seasoning, and nutmeg. Whisk the egg whites until very frothy but not too stiff, and fold into the spinach mixture.

3 Grease and line a 13 x 9-inch jelly roll pan. Spread the mixture in the pan and smooth the surface. Bake in a preheated oven at 425°F for about 12–15 minutes, until firm to the touch and golden.

4 Meanwhile, cook the broccoli flowerets in lightly salted boiling water for 4–5 minutes, until just tender. Drain and keep warm.

5 Sprinkle Parmesan on a sheet of baking parchment. Turn the base onto it and peel away the lining paper. Sprinkle with mozzarella and top with broccoli.

6 Hold one end of the paper and roll up the spinach base like a jelly roll. Heat the sugocasa and spoon onto warmed serving plates. Slice the roulade and place on top of the sugocasa.

Cauliflower & Broccoli Flan

This really is a tasty flan. The flan shell may be made ahead of time and frozen until needed.

NUTRITIONAL INFORMATION

Calories 252	Sugars 3g
Protein 7g	Fat 16g
Carbohydrate ...22g	Saturates 5g

🍧 15 MINS   🕐 50 MINS

SERVES 8

I N G R E D I E N T S

FLAN DOUGH

1½ cups all-purpose flour

pinch of salt

½ tsp paprika

1 tsp dried thyme

6 tbsp margarine

3 tbsp water

FILLING

3½ oz cauliflower flowerets

3½ oz broccoli flowerets

1 onion, cut into eight

2 tbsp butter or margarine

1 tbsp all-purpose flour

6 tbsp vegetable stock

½ cup milk

¾ cup grated cheddar cheese,

salt and pepper

paprika, to garnish

1 To make the flan dough, sift the flour and salt into a bowl. Add the paprika and thyme and cut in the margarine. Stir in the water and bind to form a dough.

2 Roll out the dough on a floured work counter and use to line a 7-inch loose-based flan pan. Prick the base with a fork and line with baking parchment. Fill with dried baking beans and bake in a preheated oven at 375°F for 15 minutes. Remove the parchment and beans and return the flan shell to the oven for 5 minutes.

3 To make the filling, cook the vegetables in a pan of lightly salted boiling water for 10–12 minutes, until tender. Drain and reserve.

4 Melt the butter in a pan. Add the flour and cook, stirring constantly, for 1 minute. Remove from the heat, stir in the stock and milk, and return to the heat. Bring to a boil, stirring, and add ½ cup of the cheese. Season to taste with salt and pepper.

5 Spoon the cauliflower, broccoli, and onion into the flan shell. Pour over the sauce and sprinkle with the cheese. Return to the oven for 10 minutes, until the cheese is bubbling. Dust with paprika, garnish, and serve.

Cheese & Potato Braid

This bread has a delicious cheese and garlic flavor, and is best eaten straight from the oven, as soon as it is the right temperature.

NUTRITIONAL INFORMATION

Calories ....387 Sugars 1g
Protein ....13g   Fat 8g
Carbohydrate ...70g   Saturates 4g

2½ HOURS   55 MINS

SERVES 8

INGREDIENTS

6 oz mealy potatoes, diced

2 x ¼ oz envelopes easy blend active
   dry yeast

6 cups white bread flour

2 cups vegetable stock

2 garlic cloves, minced

2 tbsp chopped rosemary

1 cup grated Swiss cheese

1 tbsp vegetable oil

1 tbsp salt

1 Lightly grease and flour a baking sheet. Cook the potatoes in a pan of boiling water for 10 minutes, or until soft. Drain and mash.

2 Transfer the mashed potatoes to a large mixing bowl, stir in the yeast, flour, and stock, and mix to form a smooth dough. Add the garlic, rosemary, and ¾ cup of the cheese and knead the dough for 5 minutes. Make a hollow in the dough, pour in the oil and knead the dough again.

3 Cover the dough and leave it to rise in a warm place for 1½ hours, or until doubled in size.

4 Knead the dough again and divide it into 3 equal portions. Roll each portion into a sausage shape about 14 inch long.

5 Press one end of each of the sausage shapes firmly together, then carefully braid the dough, without breaking it, and fold the remaining ends under, sealing them firmly.

6 Place the braid on the baking sheet, cover, and leave to rise for 30 minutes.

7 Sprinkle the remaining cheese over the top of the braid and cook in a preheated oven, 375°F, for 40 minutes, or until the base of the loaf sounds hollow when tapped. Serve warm.

Garlic & Sage Bread

This freshly made bread is an ideal accompaniment to salads and soups and is suitable for vegans.

NUTRITIONAL INFORMATION

Calories 141	Sugars 2g
Protein 6g	Fat 0.8g
Carbohydrate . . .30g	Saturates 0.1g

2¼ HOURS   30 MINS

SERVES 6

I N G R E D I E N T S

2 cups brown bread flour

1 x ¼-oz package active dry yeast

3 tbsp chopped sage

2 tsp sea salt

3 garlic cloves, finely chopped

1 tsp honey

⅔ cup tepid water

1 Grease a cookie sheet. Sift the flour into a large mixing bowl and stir in the bran remaining in the strainer.

2 Stir in the yeast, sage, and half of the sea salt. Reserve 1 teaspoon of the chopped garlic for sprinkling and stir the rest into the bowl. Add the honey, together with the tepid water, and mix to form a dough.

COOK'S TIP

Roll the dough into a long sausage and then curve it into a circular shape.

3 Turn the dough out onto a lightly floured surface and knead it for about 5 minutes.

4 Place the dough in a greased bowl, cover, and leave to rise in a warm place for 1½ hours or until doubled in size.

5 Knead the dough again for a few minutes, shape it into a circle (see Cook's Tip) and place on the cookie sheet.

6 Cover and leave to rise for another 30 minutes, or until springy to the touch. Sprinkle with the rest of the sea salt and garlic.

7 Bake in a preheated oven at 400°F for 25–30 minutes. Transfer to a cooling rack to cool completely before serving.

Sweet Potato Bread

This is a great tasting loaf, colored light orange by the sweet potato. Added sweetness from the honey is offset by the tangy orange zest.

NUTRITIONAL INFORMATION

Calories .... .267	Sugars 7g	
Protein 4g	Fat 9g	
Carbohydrate ...45g	Saturates 4g	

🍠 1½ HOURS   🕐 1¼ HOURS

SERVES 8

I N G R E D I E N T S

8 oz sweet potatoes, diced

⅔ cup tepid water

2 tbsp honey

2 tbsp vegetable oil

3 tbsp orange juice

⅓ cup semolina

2 cups white bread flour

1x ¼-oz package active dry yeast

1 tsp ground cinnamon

grated zest of 1 orange

¼ cup butter

1 Lightly grease a 1½-lb loaf pan. Cook the sweet potatoes in a saucepan of boiling water for about 10 minutes, or until soft. Drain well and mash until smooth.

2 Meanwhile, mix the water, honey, oil, and orange juice together in a large mixing bowl.

3 Add the mashed sweet potatoes, semolina, three-quarters of the flour, the yeast, ground cinnamon, and grated orange zest and mix thoroughly to form a dough. Leave to stand for about 10 minutes.

4 Cut the butter into small pieces and knead it into the dough with the remaining flour. Knead for about 5 minutes, until the dough is smooth.

5 Place the dough in the prepared loaf pan. Cover and leave in a warm place to rise for 1 hour, or until it has doubled in size.

6 Cook the loaf in a preheated oven at 375°F for 45–60 minutes, or until the base sounds hollow when tapped. Serve the bread warm, cut into slices.

Barbecues

Barbecues don't have to be meat feasts; there are lots of vegetarian options, too. Throughout this chapter you will find imaginative and delicious recipes that will really spice up your barbecue. The recipes provide plenty of protein—either from cheese, beans, or tofu. And because they contain lots of vegetables, they supply important vitamins,

minerals, and carbohydrates. Some preparation is needed before the barbecue starts. For instance, some foods need marinating, or threading onto skewers, but with a little forward planning you will find plenty of time to relax with your guests and enjoy your barbecue.

Tasty Barbecue Sauce

Just the thing for brushing onto vegetable kabobs and burgers, this sauce is easy and quick to make.

NUTRITIONAL INFORMATION

Calories 100   Sugars 9g
Protein . . . . .1g   Fat 6g
Carbohydrate . . .10g   Saturates 1g

 5 MINS   40 MINS

SERVES 4

INGREDIENTS

2 tbsp butter or margarine

1 garlic clove, crushed

1 onion, finely chopped

14 oz can diced tomatoes

1 tbsp dark brown sugar

1 tsp hot chili sauce

1–2 gherkins

1 tbsp capers, drained

salt and pepper

1 Melt the butter or margarine in a saucepan and fry the garlic and onion for 8–10 minutes, until well browned.

2 Add the diced tomatoes, sugar, and chili sauce. Bring to a boil, then reduce the heat and simmer gently for 20–25 minutes, until thick and pulpy.

COOK'S TIP

To make sure that the sauce has a good color, it is important to brown the onions really well to begin with. When fresh tomatoes are cheap and plentiful, they can be used instead of canned ones. Peel and chop 1 lb 2 oz.

3 Chop the gherkins and capers finely. Add to the sauce, stirring to mix. Cook the sauce over a low heat for 2 minutes.

4 Taste the sauce and season with a little salt and pepper to taste. Use as a baste for vegetarian kabobs and burgers, or as an accompaniment to other grilled food.

Citrus & Herb Marinades

Choose one of these marinades to give a marvelous flavor to grilled food. The nutritional information is for Orange & Marjoram only.

 20 MINS   0 MINS

SERVES 4

I N G R E D I E N T S

ORANGE & MARJORAM

1 orange

½ cup olive oil

4 tbsp dry white wine

4 tbsp white wine vinegar

1 tbsp snipped chives

1 tbsp chopped marjoram

salt and pepper

THAI-SPICED LIME

1 lemon grass stalk

finely grated zest and juice of 1 lime

4 tbsp sesame oil

2 tbsp light soy sauce

pinch of ground ginger

1 tbsp chopped cilantro

salt and pepper

BASIL & LEMON

finely grated zest of 1 lemon

4 tbsp lemon juice

1 tbsp balsamic vinegar

2 tbsp red wine vinegar

2 tbsp virgin olive oil

1 tbsp chopped oregano

1 tbsp chopped basil

salt and pepper

1 To make the Orange & Marjoram marinade, remove the peel from the orange with a zester, or grate it finely, then squeeze the juice.

2 Mix the orange zest and juice with all the remaining ingredients in a small bowl, whisking together to combine. Season with salt and pepper.

3 To make the Thai-spiced Lime marinade, bruise the lemon grass by crushing it with a rolling pin. Mix the remaining ingredients together in a small bowl and add the lemon grass.

4 To make the Basil & Lemon marinade, whisk all the ingredients together in a small bowl. Season to taste with salt and pepper.

5 Keep the marinades covered with plastic wrap or store them in screw-top jars, ready for using as marinades or bastes.

Three Favorite Dressings

You can rely on any of these dressings to bring out the best in your salads. The nutritional information is for the Mustard & Vinegar dressing only.

NUTRITIONAL INFORMATION

Calories 245	Sugars 0.5g	
Protein 0g	Fat 27g	
Carbohydrate ...0.5g	Saturates 4g	

 45 MINS   0 MINS

SERVES 4

I N G R E D I E N T S

WHOLEGRAIN MUSTARD & CIDER VINEGAR

½ cup olive oil

4 tbsp cider vinegar

2 tsp wholegrain mustard

½ tsp sugar

salt and pepper

GARLIC & PARSLEY

1 small garlic clove

1 tbsp parsley

⅔ cup light cream

4 tbsp plain yogurt

1 tsp lemon juice

pinch of sugar

salt and pepper

RASPBERRY & HAZELNUT

4 tbsp raspberry vinegar

4 tbsp light olive oil

4 tbsp hazelnut oil

½ tsp sugar

2 tsp chopped chives

salt and pepper

1 To make the Wholegrain Mustard & Cider Vinegar Dressing, whisk all the ingredients together in a small bowl.

2 To make the Garlic & Parsley Dressing, crush the garlic clove and finely chop the parsley.

3 Mix the garlic and parsley with the remaining ingredients. Whisk together until combined, then cover and chill for 30 minutes.

4 To make the Raspberry & Hazelnut Vinaigrette, whisk all the ingredients together until combined.

5 Keep the dressings covered with plastic wrap or sealed in screw-top jars. Chill until ready for use.

Mixed Vegetables

The wonderful aroma of vegetables as they are charbroiled over hot coals will set the tastebuds tingling.

NUTRITIONAL INFORMATION

Calories 155   Sugars 6g
Protein . . . . .2g   Fat 12g
Carbohydrate . . . .7g   Saturates 7g

 10 MINS   25 MINS

SERVES 6

INGREDIENTS

8 baby eggplants

4 zucchini

2 red onions

4 tomatoes

salt and pepper

1 tsp balsamic vinegar, to serve

BASTE

6 tbsp butter

2 tsp walnut oil

2 garlic cloves, chopped

4 tbsp dry white wine or cider

1 To prepare the vegetables, cut the eggplants in half. Trim and cut the zucchini in half lengthwise. Thickly slice the onion and halve the tomatoes.

2 Season all of the vegetables with salt and pepper to taste.

3 To make the baste, melt the butter with the oil in a saucepan. Add the garlic and cook gently for 1–2 minutes. Remove the pan from the heat and stir in the wine or cider.

4 Add the vegetables to the pan and toss them in the baste mixture. You may need to do this in several batches to make sure that all of the vegetables are coated evenly.

5 Remove the vegetables from the baste mixture, reserving any excess baste. Place the vegetables on an oiled rack over medium hot coals. Grill the vegetables for 15–20 minutes, basting with the reserved baste mixture and turning once or twice during cooking.

6 Transfer the vegetables to warm serving plates and serve immediately, sprinkled with balsamic vinegar.

Roasted Vegetables

Rosemary branches can be used as brushes for basting and as skewers.
Soak the rosemary skewers well in advance to cut down preparation time.

NUTRITIONAL INFORMATION

Calories	16	Sugars	.........3g
Protein	.........1g	Fat	..........0.3g
Carbohydrate	....3g	Saturates	.......0g

 8¹/₂ HOURS 10 MINS

SERVES 6

I N G R E D I E N T S

1 small red cabbage

1 head fennel

1 orange bell pepper, diced 1½-inches

1 eggplant, halved and sliced
   into ½-inch pieces

2 zucchini, sliced thickly
   diagonally

olive oil, for brushing

6 rosemary twigs, about 6 inches
   long, soaked in water for 8 hours

salt and pepper

1 Put the red cabbage on its side on a chopping board and cut through the middle of its stem and heart. Divide each piece into four, each time including a bit of the stem in the slice to hold it together.

VARIATION

Fruit skewers are a deliciously quick and easy dessert. Thread pieces of banana, mango, peach, strawberry, apple, and pear onto soaked wooden skewers and cook over the dying embers. Brush with sugar syrup toward the end of cooking.

2 Prepare the fennel in the same way as the red cabbage.

3 Blanch the red cabbage and fennel in boiling water for 3 minutes, then drain well.

4 With a wooden skewer, pierce a hole through the middle of each piece of vegetable.

5 On to each rosemary twig, thread a piece of orange bell pepper, fennel, red cabbage, eggplant, and zucchini, pushing the rosemary through the holes.

6 Brush liberally with olive oil and season with plenty of salt and pepper.

7 Cook over a hot barbecue for 8–10 minutes, turning occasionally. Serve at once.

Cheeseburgers in Buns

Soy mince and seasonings combine to make these tasty vegetarian burgers, which are topped with cheese.

NUTRITIONAL INFORMATION

Calories 551	Sugars 4g	
Protein 29g	Fat 24g	
Carbohydrate . . .57g	Saturates 5g	

🖐 🖐

🍲 1¼ HOURS   ⏰ 10 MINS

SERVES 4

INGREDIENTS

⅔ cup dehydrated soy mince (TVP)

1¼ cups vegetable stock

1 small onion, finely chopped

1 cup all-purpose flour

1 egg, beaten

1 tbsp chopped herbs

1 tbsp or soy sauce

2 tbsp vegetable oil

4 burger buns

4 cheese slices

salt and pepper

TO GARNISH

Tasty Barbecue Sauce (see page 310)

dill pickle

tomato slices

TO SERVE

lettuce, cucumber, & green onion salad

1 Put the soy mince into a large bowl. Pour over the vegetable stock and leave to soak for about 15 minutes, until it has been absorbed.

2 Add the onion, flour, beaten egg, and chopped herbs and mix thoroughly. Stir in the or soy sauce and season to taste with salt and pepper, stirring to mix again.

3 Form the mixture into 8 burgers. Cover and chill until ready to cook.

4 Brush the burgers with oil and grill over hot coals, turning once. Allow about 5 minutes on each side.

5 Split the buns and top with a burger. Lay a cheese slice on top and garnish with tasty barbecue sauce, dill pickle, and tomato slices. Serve with a salad made with lettuce, green onions, and sliced cucumber.

Grilled Bean Pot

Cook this tasty vegetable casserole conventionally on the stove, then keep it piping hot over the barbecue.

NUTRITIONAL INFORMATION

Calories 381   Sugars 17g
Protein . . . . .21g   Fat 19g
Carbohydrate . . .34g   Saturates 3g

 10 MINS   1 HOUR

SERVES 4

I N G R E D I E N T S

¼ cup butter or margarine

1 large onion, chopped

2 garlic cloves, crushed

2 carrots, sliced

2 celery stalks, sliced

1 tbsp paprika

2 tsp ground cumin

14 oz can of diced tomatoes

15 oz can of mixed beans,
    rinsed and drained

⅔ cup vegetable stock

1 tbsp molasses

12 oz TVP or soy cubes

salt and pepper

crusty French bread, to serve

VARIATION

If you prefer, cook the casserole in a preheated oven at 375°F from step 3, but keep the dish covered. Instead of mixed beans you could use just one type of canned beans.

1 Melt the butter or margarine in a large flameproof casserole and fry the onion and garlic over a medium heat, stirring occasionally, for about 5 minutes, until golden brown.

2 Add the carrots and celery and cook, stirring occasionally, for another 2 minutes, then stir in the paprika and ground cumin.

3 Add the tomatoes and beans. Pour in the stock and add the sugar or molasses. Bring to a boil, then reduce the heat and simmer, uncovered, stirring occasionally, for 30 minutes.

4 Add the mycoprotein or soy cubes to the casserole, cover, and cook, stirring occasionally, for 20 minutes more.

5 Season to taste, then transfer the casserole to the grill, setting it to one side to keep hot.

6 Ladle onto plates and serve with crusty French bread.

Corn & Parsley Butter

There are a number of ways of grilling corn on the cob. Leaving on the husks protects the tender kernels.

NUTRITIONAL INFORMATION

Calories ....178 Sugars 7g

Protein ....2g Fat 11g

Carbohydrate ...19g Saturates 7g

10 MINS   30 MINS

SERVES 4

INGREDIENTS

4 corn cobs, with husks

½ cup butter

1 tbsp chopped parsley

1 tsp chopped chives

1 tsp chopped thyme

grated zest of 1 lemon

salt and pepper

1 To prepare the corn, peel back the husks and remove the silks.

2 Fold back the husks and secure them in place with string, if necessary.

3 Blanch the cobs in a large saucepan of boiling water for about 5 minutes. Remove the cobs with a perforated spoon and drain thoroughly.

4 Grill the cobs over medium hot coals for about 20–30 minutes, turning frequently.

5 Meanwhile, soften the butter and beat in the parsley, chives, thyme, and lemon zest and season with salt and pepper to taste.

6 Transfer the cobs to serving plates, remove the string, if used, and pull back the husks. Serve with a generous portion of herb butter.

COOK'S TIP

If you are unable to get fresh corn cobs, cook frozen ones on the grill. Spread some of the herb butter onto a double thickness of foil. Wrap the corn in the foil and grill among the coals for 20–30 minutes.

Filled Baked Potatoes

Cook these potatoes conventionally, wrap them in foil, and keep warm at the edge of the barbecue, ready to fill with inspired mixtures.

NUTRITIONAL INFORMATION

Calories 564	Sugars 14g	
Protein 21g	Fat 29g	
Carbohydrate ...58g	Saturates 18g	

 15 MINS   ⏱ 1 HR 5 MINS

SERVES 4

I N G R E D I E N T S

4 large or 8 medium baking potatoes

paprika or chili powder, or chopped herbs,
    to garnish

MEXICAN RELISH

8 oz can corn, drained

½ red bell pepper, seeded and diced

2-inch piece of cucumber,
    finely chopped

½ tsp chili powder

salt and pepper

CHEESE & CHIVES

½ cup cream cheese

½ cup plain fresh cheese

4½ oz blue cheese, cut into cubes

1 celery stalk, finely chopped

2 tsp snipped chives

celery salt and pepper

SPICY MUSHROOMS

2 tbsp butter or margarine

8 oz mushrooms

⅔ cup plain yogurt

1 tbsp tomato paste

2 tsp mild curry powder

salt and pepper

1 Scrub the potatoes and prick them with a fork. Bake in a preheated oven at 400°F for about 1 hour, until just tender.

2 To make the Mexican Relish, put half the corn into a bowl. Process the remainder into a blender or food processor for 10–15 seconds, or chop and mash roughly by hand. Add the processed corn to the corn kernels with the bell pepper, cucumber, and chili powder. Season to taste with salt and pepper.

3 To make the Cheese & Chives filling, mix the cream cheese and fresh cheese together until smooth. Add the blue cheese, celery, and chives. Season with celery salt and pepper.

4 To make the Spicy Mushrooms, melt the butter or margarine in a small skillet. Add the mushrooms and cook gently for 3–4 minutes. Remove from the heat and stir in the yogurt, tomato paste, and curry powder. Season to taste with salt and pepper.

5 Wrap the cooked potatoes in foil and keep warm at the edge of the grill. Serve the fillings sprinkled with paprika or chili powder, or herbs.

Tofu Skewers

Tofu is full of protein, vitamins, and minerals, and it develops a fabulous flavor when marinated in garlic and herbs.

NUTRITIONAL INFORMATION

Calories	149	Sugars	.........5g
Protein	........13g	Fat	...........9g
Carbohydrate	....5g	Saturates	.......1g

  45 MINS   15 MINS

SERVES 4

INGREDIENTS

12 oz tofu

1 red bell pepper

1 yellow bell pepper

2 zucchini

8 mushrooms

slices of lemon, to garnish

MARINADE

grated zest and juice of ½ lemon

1 garlic clove, crushed

½ tsp rosemary, chopped

½ tsp chopped thyme

1 tbsp walnut oil

1 To make the marinade, combine the lemon zest and juice, garlic, rosemary, thyme, and oil in a shallow dish.

2 Drain the tofu, pat it dry on paper towels, and cut it into squares with a sharp knife. Add to the marinade and toss to coat thoroughly. Set aside to marinate for 20–30 minutes.

3 Meanwhile, seed the bell peppers and cut the flesh into 1-inch pieces. Blanch in a saucepan of boiling water for 4 minutes, refresh in cold water, and drain.

4 Using a citrus stripper or swivel vegetable peeler, remove strips of peel from the zucchini. Cut the zucchini into 1-inch chunks.

5 Remove the tofu from the marinade, reserving the marinade for basting. Thread the tofu onto 8 skewers, alternating with the bell peppers, zucchini, and button mushrooms.

6 Grill the skewers over medium hot coals for about 6 minutes, turning and basting with the marinade.

7 Transfer the skewers to serving plates, garnish with lemon slices, and serve.

Nutty Rice Burgers

Serve these burgers in toasted sesame seed rolls. If you wish, add a slice of cheese to top the burger at the end of cooking.

NUTRITIONAL INFORMATION

Calories 517	Sugars 5g
Protein 16g	Fat 26g
Carbohydrate ...59g	Saturates 6g

1¼ HOURS   30 MINS

SERVES 6

I N G R E D I E N T S

1 tbsp sunflower oil

1 small onion, finely chopped

1½ cups finely chopped mushrooms

8 cups cooked brown rice

2 cups breadcrumbs

¾ cup chopped walnuts

1 egg

2 tbsp brown fruity sauce

dash of Tabasco sauce

salt and pepper

oil, to baste

6 individual cheese slices (optional)

TO SERVE

6 sesame seed rolls

slices of onion

slices of tomato

COOK'S TIP

It is quicker and more economical to use leftover rice to make these burgers. However, if you are cooking the rice for this dish you will need to use 1 cup uncooked rice.

1 Heat the oil in a large saucepan and fry the onions for 3–4 minutes, until they just begin to soften. Add the mushrooms and cook for 2 minutes more.

2 Remove the pan from the heat and mix the cooked rice, breadcrumbs, walnuts, egg, and both the sauces into the vegetables. Season to taste with salt and pepper and mix well.

3 Shape the mixture into 6 burgers, pressing the mixture together with your fingers. Set aside to chill in the refrigerator for at least 30 minutes.

4 Grill the burgers on an oiled rack over medium coals for 5–6 minutes on each side, turning once and frequently basting with oil.

5 If liked, top the burgers with a slice of cheese 2 minutes before the end of the cooking time. Grill the onion and tomato slices for 3–4 minutes until they are just beginning to color.

6 Toast the sesame seed rolls at the side of the grill. Serve the burgers in the rolls, together with the grilled onions and tomatoes.

Curried Kabobs

Warmed Indian bread is served with grilled vegetable kabobs, which are brushed with a curry-spiced yogurt baste.

NUTRITIONAL INFORMATION

Calories 396   Sugars 11g
Protein ....13g   Fat 13g
Carbohydrate ...60g   Saturates 0.3g

🍖 30 MINS   🕐 25–30 MINS

SERVES 4

I N G R E D I E N T S

naan bread, to serve

mint sprigs, to garnish

YOGURT BASTE

⅔ cup plain yogurt

1 tbsp chopped mint or 1 tsp dried mint

1 tsp ground cumin

1 tsp ground coriander

½ tsp chili powder

pinch of turmeric

pinch of ground ginger

salt and pepper

KABOBS

8 small new potatoes

1 small eggplant

1 zucchini, cut into chunks

8 mushrooms

8 small tomatoes

1 To make the spiced yogurt baste, mix together the yogurt, mint, cumin, coriander, chili powder, turmeric, and ginger. Season to taste with salt and pepper. Cover and chill.

2 Cook the potatoes in boiling water until just tender.

3 Meanwhile, chop the eggplant into chunks and sprinkle them liberally with salt. Set aside for 10–15 minutes to extract the bitter juices. Rinse thoroughly and drain them well. Drain the potatoes.

4 Thread the potatoes, eggplant, zucchini, mushrooms, and tomatoes alternately onto 4 skewers.

5 Place the skewers in a shallow dish and brush with the yogurt baste, coating them evenly. Cover and chill until ready to cook.

6 Wrap the naan bread in foil and place toward one side of the grill to warm through.

7 Cook the kabobs over the grill, basting with any remaining spiced yogurt, until they begin to char slightly. Serve with the warmed naan bread, garnished with mint sprigs.

Spicy Sweet Potato Slices

Serve these as an accompaniment to other grilled dishes or with a spicy dip as appetizers while the main dishes are being cooked.

NUTRITIONAL INFORMATION

Calories ....178 Sugars 0.8g
Protein ....2g Fat 6g
Carbohydrate ...32g Saturates 0.7g

 10 MINS   25 MINS

SERVES 4

I N G R E D I E N T S

1 lb sweet potatoes

2 tbsp sunflower oil

1 tsp chili sauce

salt and pepper

1 Bring a large pan of water to a boil, add the sweet potatoes and parboil them for 10 minutes. Drain thoroughly and transfer to a cutting board.

2 Peel the potatoes and cut them into thick slices.

3 Mix together the sunflower oil, chili sauce, and salt and pepper to taste in a small bowl.

COOK'S TIP

For a simple spicy dip combine ²/₃ cup sour cream with ¹/₂ teaspoon of sugar, ¹/₂ teaspoon of Dijon mustard and salt and pepper to taste. Leave to chill until required.

4 Brush the spicy mixture liberally over one side of the potatoes. Place the potatoes, oil side down, over medium hot coals and grill for 5–6 minutes.

5 Lightly brush the tops of the potatoes with the oil, turn them over, and grill for a 5 minutes more, or until crisp and golden.

6 Transfer the potatoes to a warm serving dish and serve immediately.

Bean Burgers

These tasty patties are ideal for a barbecue in the summer, but they are equally delicious cooked indoors at any time of year.

15 MINS   1 HR 5 MINS

SERVES 6

I N G R E D I E N T S

½ cup dried garbanzo beans

½ cup dried black-eyed peas

6 tbsp vegetable oil

1 large onion, finely chopped

1 tsp yeast extract

¾ cup grated carrot

1½ cups fresh whole wheat breadcrumbs

2 tbsp whole wheat flour

salt and pepper

B A R B E C U E   S A U C E

½ tsp chili powder

1 tsp celery salt

2 tbsp light brown sugar

2 tbsp red wine vinegar

2 tbsp Worcestershire sauce

3 tbsp tomato paste

dash of Tabasco sauce

T O   S E R V E

6 whole wheat rolls, toasted

mixed salad

baked potato fries

1 Place the beans in separate saucepans, cover with water, and bring to a boil. Cover and simmer the garbanzo beans for 40 minutes and the black-eyed peas for 50 minutes, until tender. Drain and rinse well.

2 Transfer to a mixing bowl and lightly mash together with a potato masher or fork. Set aside.

3 Heat 1 tablespoon of the oil in a skillet and gently fry the onion for 3–4 minutes, until softened. Mix into the beans with the yeast extract, grated carrot, breadcrumbs, and seasoning. Mix together well.

4 With wet hands, divide the mixture into 6 and form into burgers 3½ inches in diameter. Put the flour on a plate and use to coat the burgers.

5 To make the sauce, mix all the ingredients together until well blended.

6 Cook the burgers on a medium hot grill for 3–4 minutes on each side, brushing with the remaining oil from time to time. Put the burgers in the toasted rolls and serve with a mixed salad, fries, and a spoonful of the barbecue sauce.

Turkish Kabobs

A spicy garbanzo bean sauce is served with grilled colorful vegetable kabobs.

NUTRITIONAL INFORMATION

Calories	303	Sugars	........13g
Protein	........13g	Fat	.........15g
Carbohydrate	...30g	Saturates	.......2g

  20 MINS   20 MINS

SERVES 4

I N G R E D I E N T S

S A U C E

4 tbsp olive oil

3 garlic cloves, crushed

1 small onion, finely chopped

15 oz can garbanzo beans, rinsed
   and drained

1¼ cups plain yogurt

1 tsp ground cumin

½ tsp chili powder

lemon juice

salt and pepper

K A B O B S

1 eggplant

1 red bell pepper, seeded

1 green bell pepper, seeded

4 plum tomatoes

1 lemon, cut into wedges

8 small fresh bay leaves

olive oil, for brushing

1 To make the sauce, heat the olive oil in a small skillet. Add the garlic and onion and fry over a medium heat, stirring occasionally, for about 5 minutes, until the onion is softened and golden brown.

2 Put the garbanzo beans and yogurt into a blender or food processor and add the cumin, chili powder, and onion mixture. Process for about 15 seconds, until smooth. Alternatively, mash the garbanzo beans with a potato masher and stir in the yogurt, ground cumin, chili powder, and onion.

3 Place the garbanzo bean mixture in a bowl and season to taste with lemon juice, salt, and pepper. Cover and chill until ready to serve.

4 To prepare the kabobs, cut the vegetables into large chunks and thread them onto 4 skewers, placing a bay leaf and lemon wedge at both ends of each kabob.

5 Brush the kabobs with olive oil and cook them over the grill, turning frequently, for 5–8 minutes. Heat the garbanzo bean sauce and serve with the kabobs.

Pumpkin Parcels with Chili

This spicy side dish is perfect for a Halloween party, although it is equally delicious on a summer evening, too.

NUTRITIONAL INFORMATION

Energy	118	Sugar 3g
Protein	.........1g	Fat 11g
Carbohydrates	....4g	Saturates 4g

 10 MINS   25–30 MINS

SERVES 4

INGREDIENTS

1 lb 9 oz pumpkin or squash

2 tbsp sunflower oil

2 tbsp butter

½ tsp chili sauce

grated zest of 1 lime

2 tsp lime juice

1 Halve the pumpkin or squash and scoop out the seeds. Rinse the seeds and reserve. Cut the pumpkin into thin wedges and peel.

2 Heat the oil and butter together in a large saucepan, stirring constantly, until melted. Stir in the chili sauce, lime zest and juice.

3 Add the pumpkin or squash and seeds to the pan and toss to coat all over in the flavored butter.

4 Divide the mixture between 4 double thickness sheets of foil. Fold over the foil to enclose the pumpkin or squash mixture completely.

5 Grill the foil packages over hot coals for 15–25 minutes, or until the pumpkin or squash is tender.

6 Transfer the foil packages to warm serving plates. Open the packages at the table and serve immediately.

VARIATION

Add 2 teaspoons of curry paste to the oil instead of the lime and chili. Use butternut squash when pumpkin is not available.

Cheese & Onion Baguettes

Part-baked baguettes are split and filled with a tasty cheese and onion mixture, then wrapped in foil, and cooked over the grill.

NUTRITIONAL INFORMATION

Calories 715	Sugars 5g
Protein 21g	Fat 41g
Carbohydrate . . .70g	Saturates 25g

15 MINS   20 MINS

SERVES 4

I N G R E D I E N T S

4 part-baked baguettes

2 tbsp tomato relish

¼ cup butter

8 green onions, finely chopped

½ cup cream cheese

1 cup grated cheddar cheese

1 tsp snipped chives

pepper

TO SERVE

tossed salad

herbs

1 Split the part-baked baguettes in half lengthwise, without cutting right through. Spread a little tomato relish on each split baguette.

2 Melt the butter in a skillet and add the green onions. Fry them over a medium heat, stirring frequently, for 5 minutes, until softened and golden. Remove from the heat and set aside to cool slightly.

3 Beat the cream cheese in a mixing bowl to soften it. Mix in the green onions, with any remaining butter. Add the grated cheese and snipped chives and mix well. Season to taste with pepper.

4 Divide the cheese mixture between the baguettes, spread it over the cut surfaces, and sandwich the baguettes together again. Wrap each baguette tightly in foil.

5 Heat the baguettes over the barbecue for about 10–15 minutes, turning them occasionally. Peel back the foil to check that they are cooked and if the cheese mixture has melted. Serve with tossed salad and garnished with fresh herbs.

COOK'S TIP

If there's no room on the barbecue, and you want to eat these at the same time as the rest of the food, bake them in a preheated oven at 400°F for 15 minutes.

Vegetarian Sausages

The delicious cheese flavor will make these sausages a hit with vegetarians who do not need to feel left out when it comes to a barbecue.

NUTRITIONAL INFORMATION

Calories 213	Sugars 4g	
Protein 8g	Fat 12g	
Carbohydrate . . .19g	Saturates 4g	

🥘 50 MINS   🕐 25 MINS

MAKES 8

INGREDIENTS

1 tbsp sunflower oil

1 small onion, finely chopped

¾ cup finely chopped mushrooms

½ red bell pepper,
  seeded and finely diced

14 oz can cannellini beans, rinsed
  and drained

2 cups fresh breadcrumbs

1 cup grated cheddar cheese

1 tsp dried mixed herbs

1 egg yolk

seasoned all-purpose flour

oil, to baste

TO SERVE

bread rolls

fried onion slices

1 Heat the oil in a saucepan. Add the onion, mushrooms, and bell peppers and fry over a low heat, stirring frequently, for 5 minutes, or until softened.

2 Mash the cannellini beans in a large mixing bowl with a potato masher. Add the onion, mushroom, and bell pepper mixture, the breadcrumbs, grated cheddar, herbs, and egg yolk, and mix together well.

3 Press the mixture together with your fingers and shape into 8 sausages. Roll each sausage in the seasoned flour to coat evenly. Set aside to chill in the refrigerator for at least 30 minutes.

4 Grill the sausages on a sheet of oiled foil set over medium coals for 15–20 minutes, turning and basting frequently with oil, until golden.

5 Split a bread roll down the middle and insert a layer of fried onions. Place the sausage in the roll and serve.

Sidekick Vegetables

Colorful vegetables are grilled over hot coals to make this unusual hot salad, which is served with a spicy chili sauce on the side.

NUTRITIONAL INFORMATION

Calories 224	Sugars 14g	
Protein 4g	Fat 15g	
Carbohydrate ...21g	Saturates 2g	

 15 MINS   30 MINS

SERVES 4

INGREDIENTS

1 red bell pepper, seeded

1 orange or yellow bell pepper, seeded

2 zucchini

2 corn cobs

1 eggplant

olive oil, for brushing

chopped thyme, rosemary, and parsley

salt and pepper

lime or lemon wedges, to serve

DRESSING

2 tbsp olive oil

1 tbsp sesame oil

1 garlic clove, crushed

1 small onion, finely chopped

1 celery stalk, finely chopped

1 small green chili, seeded and chopped

4 tomatoes, diced

2-inch piece of cucumber, chopped

1 tbsp tomato paste

1 tbsp lime or lemon juice

1 To make the dressing, heat the olive and sesame oils together in a saucepan or skillet. Add the garlic and onion, and fry over a low heat for about 3 minutes, until softened.

2 Add the celery, chili, and tomatoes to the pan and cook, stirring frequently, for 5 minutes.

3 Stir in the cucumber, tomato paste, and lime or lemon juice, and simmer over a low heat for 8–10 minutes, until thick and pulpy. Season to taste with salt and pepper.

4 Cut the vegetables into thick slices and brush with a little olive oil.

5 Cook the vegetables over the hot coals of the grill for about 5–8 minutes, sprinkling them with salt and pepper and fresh herbs as they cook, and turning once.

6 Divide the vegetables between 4 serving plates and spoon some of the dressing onto the side. Serve immediately, sprinkled with a few more chopped herbs and accompanied by the lime or lemon wedges.

Stuffed Tomatoes

These grilled tomato cups are filled with a delicious Greek-style combination of herbs, nuts, and raisins.

NUTRITIONAL INFORMATION

Calories 156	Sugars 10g	
Protein 3g	Fat 7g	
Carbohydrate ...22g	Saturates 0.7g	

 40 MINS   10 MINS

MAKES 8

INGREDIENTS

4 large tomatoes

4½ cups cooked rice

8 green onions, chopped

3 tbsp chopped mint

2 tbsp chopped parsley

3 tbsp pine nuts

3 tbsp raisins

2 tsp olive oil

salt and pepper

1 Cut the tomatoes in half, then scoop out the seeds and discard.

2 Stand the tomatoes upside down on absorbent paper towels for a few moments in order for the juices to drain out.

3 Turn the tomatoes the right way up and sprinkle the insides with salt and pepper to taste.

4 Mix together the rice, green onions, mint, parsley, pine nuts, and raisins. Spoon the mixture into the tomato cups.

5 Drizzle a little olive oil over the top, then, handling them carefully, grill the tomatoes on an oiled rack over medium hot coals for about 10 minutes,

until they are tender.

6 Transfer the tomatoes to serving plates and serve immediately.

COOK'S TIP

Tomatoes are a popular vegetable to grill or broil, and can be quickly cooked. Try broiling slices of large tomato and slices of onion brushed with a little oil and topped with sprigs of fresh herbs.

Stuffed Grape Leaves

A wonderful combination of cream cheese, chopped dates, ground almonds, and lightly fried nuts is encased in grape leaves.

NUTRITIONAL INFORMATION

Calories ....459 Sugars 8g
Protein ....12g Fat 42g
Carbohydrate ....9g Saturates 20g

 25 MINS   15 MINS

SERVES 4

I N G R E D I E N T S

1¼ cups cream cheese

¼ cup ground almonds

2 tbsp dates, pitted and chopped

2 tbsp butter

¼ cup slivered almonds

12–16 grape leaves

salt and pepper

grilled baby corn cobs, to serve

T O   G A R N I S H

rosemary sprigs

tomato wedges

1 Beat the cream cheese in a large bowl until smooth. Add the ground almonds and chopped dates, and mix together thoroughly. Season to taste with salt and pepper.

2 Melt the butter in a small skillet. Add the slivered almonds and fry over a very low heat, stirring constantly, for 2–3 minutes, until golden brown. Remove from the heat and set aside to cool for a few minutes.

3 Mix the fried almonds into the cream cheese mixture, stirring well to combine thoroughly.

4 Soak the grape leaves in water to remove some of the saltiness, if specified on the pack. Drain them, lay them out on a work counter, and spoon an equal amount of the cream cheese mixture onto each one. Fold over the leaves to enclose the filling.

5 Wrap the grape leaves in foil, 1 or 2 per foil package. Place over the grill to heat through for about 8–10 minutes, turning once. Serve with grilled baby corn cobs, and garnish with sprigs of rosemary and tomato wedges.

Garlic Potato Wedges

Serve this tasty potato dish with grilled kabobs, bean burgers, or vegetarian sausages.

NUTRITIONAL INFORMATION

Calories ....257 Sugars 1g
Protein ....3g Fat 16g
Carbohydrate ...26g Saturates 5g

 10 MINS   30-35 MINS

SERVES 4

I N G R E D I E N T S

3 large baking potatoes, scrubbed

4 tbsp olive oil

2 tbsp butter

2 garlic cloves, chopped

1 tbsp chopped rosemary

1 tbsp chopped parsley

1 tbsp chopped thyme

salt and pepper

1 Bring a large pan of water to a boil, add the potatoes, and parboil them for 10 minutes. Drain the potatoes, refresh under cold water, and then drain them again thoroughly.

2 Transfer the potatoes to a cutting board. When the potatoes are cold enough to handle, cut them into thick wedges, but do not peel.

3 Heat the oil and butter in a small pan together with the garlic. Cook gently until the garlic begins to brown, then remove the pan from the heat.

4 Stir the herbs and salt and pepper to taste into the mixture in the pan.

5 Brush the herb mixture all over the potato wedges.

6 Grill the potatoes over hot coals for 10–15 minutes, brushing liberally with any of the remaining herb and butter mixture, or until the potato wedges are just tender.

7 Transfer the garlic potato wedges to a warm serving plate and serve as an appetizer or as a side dish.

COOK'S TIP

You may find it easier to grill these potatoes in a hinged rack or in a specially designed grill roasting pan.

Marinated Kabobs

These tofu and mushroom kabobs are marinated in a lemon, garlic, and herb mixture so that they soak up a delicious flavor.

NUTRITIONAL INFORMATION

Calories 192   Sugars 0.5g
Protein . . . . .11g   Fat 16g
Carbohydrate . . . .1g   Saturates 2g

2¼ HOURS   6 MINS

SERVES 4

INGREDIENTS

1 lemon

1 garlic clove, crushed

4 tbsp olive oil

4 tbsp white wine vinegar

1 tbsp chopped herbs, such as rosemary, parsley, and thyme

10½ oz tofu

12 oz mushrooms

salt and pepper

herbs, to garnish

TO SERVE

tossed salad

cherry tomatoes, halved

1 Finely grate the zest from the lemon and squeeze out the juice.

2 Add the garlic, olive oil, vinegar, and chopped herbs to the lemon zest and juice, mixing well. Season to taste with salt and pepper.

3 Slice the tofu into large chunks with a sharp knife. Thread the pieces onto metal or wooden skewers, alternating them with the mushrooms.

4 Place the kabobs in a shallow dish and pour over the marinade. Cover and chill in the refrigerator for 1–2 hours, turning the kabobs in the marinade from time to time.

5 Cook the kabobs on a medium hot grill, frequently brushing them with the marinade and turning often, for about 6 minutes until cooked through and golden brown.

6 Transfer to warm serving plates, garnish with fresh herbs, and serve with tossed salad and cherry tomatoes.

Chunky Italian Slices

The flavor of charbroiled eggplant is hard to beat. The nutritional information includes the pesto dressing.

NUTRITIONAL INFORMATION

Calories	318	Sugars	.........1g
Protein	.........4g	Fat	..........33g
Carbohydrate	....1g	Saturates	.......6g

  20 MINS   10 MINS

SERVES 4

I N G R E D I E N T S

1 large eggplant

3 tbsp olive oil

1 tsp sesame oil

salt and pepper

P E S T O

1 garlic clove

¼ cup pine nuts

½ cup fresh basil leaves

2 tbsp grated Parmesan cheese

6 tbsp olive oil

salt and pepper

C U C U M B E R S A U C E

⅔ cup plain yogurt

2-inch piece of cucumber

½ tsp mint sauce

1 Remove the stalk from the eggplant, then cut it lengthwise into 8 thin slices.

2 Lay the slices on a plate or board and sprinkle them liberally with salt to remove the bitter juices. Leave to stand.

3 Meanwhile, prepare the baste. Combine the olive and sesame oils, season with pepper, and set aside.

4 To make the pesto, process the garlic, pine nuts, basil, and cheese in a food processor until finely chopped. With the machine running, gradually add the oil in a thin stream. Season to taste.

5 To make the minty cucumber sauce, place the yogurt in a mixing bowl. Remove the seeds from the cucumber and finely dice the flesh. Stir into the yogurt with the mint sauce.

6 Rinse the eggplant slices and pat them dry with absorbent paper towels. Baste with the oil mixture and grill over hot coals for about 10 minutes, turning once. The eggplant should be golden and tender.

7 Transfer the eggplant slices to serving plates and serve with either the cucumber sauce or the pesto.

Corn on the Cob

Corn on the cob is available nearly all year round, and it can be grilled with the husk on or off.

NUTRITIONAL INFORMATION

Calories	99	Sugars	.........2g
Protein	.........4g	Fat	..........2g
Carbohydrate	...17g	Saturates	.....0.3g

 25 MINS   30–40 MINS

SERVES 6

INGREDIENTS

4–6 corn cobs

oil for brushing

TO SERVE

butter (optional)

salt (optional)

1 Soak the cobs in hot water for 20 minutes. Drain them thoroughly.

2 If the cobs have no green leaves, brush with oil and cook over a hot grill for 30 minutes, brushing occasionally with the oil and turning often.

COOK'S TIP

While you are grilling the corn cobs, you may like to flavor it with oils or herbs. Try tucking some rosemary, cilantro, or thyme inside the husk for a deliciously aromatic flavor.

3 If your cobs have green leaves, tear off all but the last two layers and brush with oil.

4 Cook over a hot grill for 40 minutes, brushing with oil once or twice and turning occasionally.

5 Serve hot, without the husks. If you like, add butter and season with salt to taste.

Roast Leeks

Use a good-quality French or Italian olive oil for this deliciously simple yet sophisticated vegetable accompaniment.

NUTRITIONAL INFORMATION

Calories	71	Sugars	. . . . .2g
Protein	. . . . .2g	Fat	. . . . .6g
Carbohydrate	. . . .3g	Saturates	. . . . . . .1g

 5 MINS   ⧖ 7 MINS

SERVES 6

INGREDIENTS

4 leeks

3 tbsp olive oil

2 tsp balsamic vinegar

sea salt and pepper

1 Cut the leeks in half lengthwise, making sure that you hold the knife straight, so that the leek is held together by the root. Brush each leek liberally with the olive oil.

2 Cook over a hot grill for 6–7 minutes, turning once.

3 Remove the leeks from the grill and brush lightly with the balsamic vinegar.

4 Season to taste with salt and pepper and serve hot or warm.

Colorful Kabobs

Brighten up a barbecued meal with these colorful vegetable kabobs. They are basted with an aromatic flavored oil.

NUTRITIONAL INFORMATION

Calories 131	Sugars 7g
Protein 2g	Fat 11g
Carbohydrate 8g	Saturates 2g

 15 MINS   15 MINS

SERVES 4

I N G R E D I E N T S

1 red bell pepper, seeded

1 yellow bell pepper, seeded

1 green bell pepper, seeded

1 small onion

8 cherry tomatoes

3½ oz wild mushrooms

S E A S O N E D   O I L

6 tbsp olive oil

1 garlic clove, crushed

½ tsp mixed dried herbs

1 Cut the bell peppers into 1 inch pieces.

2 Peel the onion and cut it into wedges, leaving the root end just intact to help keep the wedges together.

COOK'S TIP

To make walnut sauce, process 1 cup of walnuts in a food processor to a smooth paste. With the machine running, add ²/₃ cup heavy cream and 1 tbsp olive oil. Season to taste with salt and pepper.

3 Thread the bell peppers, onion wedges, tomatoes, and mushrooms on to skewers, alternating the colors of the bell peppers.

4 To make the seasoned oil, mix together the olive oil, garlic, and mixed herbs in a small bowl. Brush the mixture liberally over the kabobs.

5 Grill the kabobs over medium hot coals for 10–15 minutes, brushing with the seasoned oil and turning the skewers frequently.

6 Transfer the vegetable kabobs to warm serving plates. Serve the kabobs immediately with walnut sauce (see Cook's Tip, below), if you wish.

Filled Pita Breads

Pita, or pocket, breads are warmed over the hot coals, then split and filled with a Greek salad tossed in a fragrant rosemary dressing.

NUTRITIONAL INFORMATION

Calories 456	Sugars 4g
Protein 13g	Fat 25g
Carbohydrate ...49g	Saturates 7g

 15 MINS   10 MINS

SERVES 4

INGREDIENTS

½ iceberg lettuce, roughly chopped

2 large tomatoes, cut into wedges

3-inch piece of cucumber,
  cut into chunks

¼ cup pitted black olives

4½ oz feta cheese

4 pita breads

DRESSING

6 tbsp olive oil

3 tbsp red wine vinegar

1 tbsp crushed rosemary

½ tsp sugar

salt and pepper

1 To make the salad, combine the lettuce, tomatoes, cucumber, and black olives.

2 Cut the feta cheese into chunks and add to the salad. Toss gently.

3 To make the dressing, whisk together the olive oil, red wine vinegar, rosemary, and sugar. Season to taste with salt and pepper. Place in a small saucepan or heatproof bowl and heat gently or place over the grill to just warm through.

4 Wrap the pita breads tightly in foil and place over the hot grill for 2–3 minutes, turning once, to warm through.

5 Unwrap the breads and split them open. Fill with the Greek salad mixture and drizzle over the warm dressing. Serve immediately.

COOK'S TIP

Substitute different herbs for the rosemary—either oregano or basil would make a delicious alternative. Pack plenty of the salad into the pita breads—they taste much better when they are full to bursting!

Salads

A salad makes a refreshing accompaniment or side dish, but can also make a substantial main course meal. Salads are also a very good source of vitamins and minerals; always use the freshest possible ingredients for maximum flavor and texture. Salads are quick to "rustle up" and good for times when you need to prepare a meal-in-a

moment and have to use pantry ingredients. A splash of culinary inspiration and you will find that you have prepared a fantastic salad that you had no idea was lurking in your kitchen! Experiment with new ingredients in order to add taste and interest to ordinary salads. The only limit is your imagination!

Mexican Salad

This is a colourful salad with a Mexican theme, using beans, tomatoes, and avocado. The chili dressing adds a little kick.

NUTRITIONAL INFORMATION

Calories 307
Sugars 7g
Protein 5g
Fat 26g
Carbohydrate . . .13g
Saturates 5g

10-15 MINS   0 MINS

SERVES 4

INGREDIENTS

leaf lettuce

2 ripe avocados

2 tsp lemon juice

4 medium tomatoes

1 onion

2 cups mixed canned beans, drained

DRESSING

4 tbsp olive oil

drop of chili oil

2 tbsp garlic wine vinegar

pinch of sugar

pinch of chili powder

1 tbsp chopped parsley

COOK'S TIP

The lemon juice is sprinkled onto the avocados to prevent discoloration when in contact with the air. For this reason the salad should be prepared, assembled, and served quite quickly.

 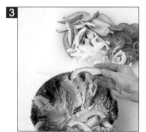 

1 Line a large serving bowl with the lettuce leaves.

2 Using a sharp knife, cut the avocados in half and remove the pits. Thinly slice the flesh and sprinkle with the lemon juice.

3 Thinly slice the tomatoes and onion and push the onion out into rings. Arrange the avocado, tomatoes, and onion around the salad bowl, leaving a space in the center.

4 Spoon the beans into the center of the salad and whisk the dressing ingredients together. Pour the dressing over the salad and serve.

Goat Cheese Salad

A delicious hot salad of melting goat cheese over sliced tomato and basil on a base of hot ciabatta bread.

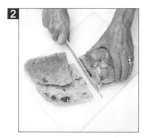

NUTRITIONAL INFORMATION

Calories	379	Sugars	.........3g
Protein	........15g	Fat	..........23g
Carbohydrate	...30g	Saturates	......10g

 10 MINS   6 MINS

SERVES 4

I N G R E D I E N T S

3 tbsp olive oil

1 tbsp white wine vinegar

1 tsp black olive paste

1 garlic clove, crushed

1 tsp chopped fresh thyme

1 ciabatta (Italian bread) loaf

4 small tomatoes

12 fresh basil leaves

2 x 4½ oz logs goat cheese

TO SERVE

mixed salad greens, including
  arugula and radicchio

1 Mix the oil, vinegar, olive paste, garlic, and thyme together in a screw-top jar and shake vigorously.

2 Cut the ciabatta in half horizontally then in half vertically to make 4 pieces.

3 Drizzle some of the dressing over the bread, then arrange the tomatoes and basil leaves on the top.

4 Cut each roll of goat cheese into 6 slices and places 3 slices on each piece of ciabatta.

5 Brush with some of the dressing and bake in a preheated oven at 450°F for 5–6 minutes until turning brown at the edges.

6 Pour the remaining dressing over the salad greens and serve with the baked bread.

COOK'S TIP

Many French goat cheeses are widely available. Those labelled *chèvre* or *pur chèvre* are made purely from goat milk. The goat milk in *mi-chèvre* cheeses is mixed with up to 75 percent cow's milk.

Green & White Salad

This potato, arugula, and apple salad is flavored with creamy, salty goat cheese—perfect with salad greens.

NUTRITIONAL INFORMATION

Calories	282	Sugars	........10g
Protein	.........8g	Fat	..........17g
Carbohydrate	...26g	Saturates	.......5g

  15 MINS   20 MINS

SERVES 4

INGREDIENTS

2 large potatoes, unpeeled and sliced

2 green apples, diced

1 tsp lemon juice

¼ cup walnut pieces

4½ oz goat cheese, cubed

2–3 bunches arugula leaves

salt and pepper

DRESSING

2 tbsp olive oil

1 tbsp red wine vinegar

1 tsp honey

1 tsp fennel seeds

COOK'S TIP

Serve this salad immediately to prevent the apple from discoloring. Alternatively, prepare all of the other ingredients ahead of time and add the apple at the last minute.

1 Cook the potatoes in a pan of boiling water for 15 minutes, until tender. Drain and set aside to cool. Transfer the cooled potatoes to a serving bowl.

2 Toss the diced apples in the lemon juice, drain, and stir them into the cold potatoes.

3 Add the walnut pieces, cheese cubes, and arugula leaves, then toss the salad to mix.

4 In a small bowl, whisk the dressing ingredients together until well combined and pour the dressing over the salad. Serve immediately.

Moroccan Salad

Couscous is a type of semolina made from durum wheat. It is wonderful in salads because it takes up the flavor of the dressing.

NUTRITIONAL INFORMATION

Calories 195   Sugars 15g
Protein ....8g   Fat 2g
Carbohydrate ...40g   Saturates 0.3g

30–35 MINS   0 MINS

SERVES 6

INGREDIENTS

2 cups couscous

1 bunch scallions, finely chopped

1 small green bell pepper, seeded and chopped

4-inch piece of cucumber, chopped

6 oz can garbanzo beans, rinsed and drained

⅔ cup golden raisins or raisins

2 oranges

salt and pepper

mint sprigs, to garnish

lettuce leaves, to serve

DRESSING

finely grated zest of 1 orange

1 tbsp chopped fresh mint

⅔ cup plain yogurt

1 Put the couscous into a bowl and cover with boiling water. Leave it to soak for about 15 minutes to swell the grains, then stir gently with a fork to separate them.

2 Add the scallions, green bell pepper, cucumber, garbanzo beans, and golden raisins or raisins to the couscous, stirring to combine. Season well with salt and pepper.

3 To make the dressing, place the orange zest, mint, and yogurt in a bowl and mix together until well combined. Pour over the couscous mixture and stir to mix well.

4 Using a sharp serrated knife, remove the peel and pith from the oranges. Cut the flesh into segments, removing all the membrane.

5 Arrange the lettuce leaves on 4 serving plates. Divide the couscous mixture between the plates and arrange the orange segments on top. Garnish with sprigs of fresh mint and serve.

Salad with Yogurt Dressing

This is a very quick and refreshing salad, using a whole range of colorful ingredients, which make it look as good as it tastes.

NUTRITIONAL INFORMATION

Calories	100	Sugars	8g
Protein	3g	Fat	6g
Carbohydrate	8g	Saturates	1g

 20 MINS   0 MINS

SERVES 4

INGREDIENTS

2¾ oz cucumber, cut into thin sticks

6 green onions, halved

2 tomatoes, seeded and cut into eight

1 yellow bell pepper, cut into strips

2 celery stalks, cut into strips

4 radishes, quartered

1 bunch arugula

1 tbsp chopped mint, to serve

DRESSING

2 tbsp lemon juice

1 garlic clove, crushed

⅔ cup plain yogurt

2 tbsp olive oil

salt and pepper

1 Mix the cucumber, green onions, tomatoes, bell pepper, celery, radishes, and arugula together in a large serving bowl.

2 To make the dressing, stir the lemon juice, garlic, plain yogurt, and olive oil together. Season well with salt and pepper.

3 Spoon the dressing over the salad and toss to mix.

4 Sprinkle the salad with chopped mint and serve.

COOK'S TIP

Do not toss the dressing into the salad until just before serving, otherwise it will turn soggy.

Mexican Potato Salad

The flavors of Mexico are echoed in this dish where potato slices are topped with tomatoes and chilies, and served with guacamole.

NUTRITIONAL INFORMATION

Calories 260   Sugars 6g
Protein . . . . .6g   Fat 9g
Carbohydrate . . .41g   Saturates 2g

20 MINS   20 MINS

SERVES 4

INGREDIENTS

4 large potatoes, sliced

1 ripe avocado

1 tsp olive oil

1 tsp lemon juice

1 garlic clove, crushed

1 onion, chopped

2 large tomatoes, sliced

1 green chili, chopped

1 yellow bell pepper, seeded and sliced

2 tbsp chopped cilantro

salt and pepper

lemon wedges, to garnish

1 Cook the potato slices in a saucepan of boiling water for 10–15 minutes, or until tender. Drain and set aside to cool.

2 Meanwhile, cut the avocado in half and remove the pit. Mash the avocado flesh with a fork (you could also scoop the avocado flesh from the 2 halves using a spoon and then mash it).

3 Add the olive oil, lemon juice, garlic, and chopped onion to the avocado flesh and stir to mix. Cover the bowl with clear plastic wrap, to minimize discoloration, and set aside.

4 Mix the tomatoes, chili, and yellow bell pepper together and transfer to a salad bowl with the potato slices.

5 Arrange the avocado mixture on top of the salad and sprinkle with the cilantro. Season to taste with salt and pepper and serve garnished with lemon wedges.

VARIATION

You can omit the green chili from this salad if you do not like hot dishes.

Mixed Bean Salad

You can use a mixture of any canned beans in this crunchy, very filling salad.

NUTRITIONAL INFORMATION

Calories	198	Sugars	.........6g
Protein	........10g	Fat	...........6g
Carbohydrate	...26g	Saturates	.......1g

30 MINS   15–20 MINS

SERVES 8

INGREDIENTS

14 oz can garbanzo beans, drained

14 oz can red kidney beans, drained

14 oz can lima beans, drained

1 small red onion, thinly sliced

6 oz green beans, trimmed

1 red bell pepper, halved and seeded

salt

DRESSING

4 tbsp olive oil

2 tbsp sherry vinegar

2 tbsp lemon juice

1 tsp light brown sugar

1 tsp chili sauce (optional)

VARIATION

Use any combination of beans in this salad. For a distinctive flavor, add 1 teaspoon of curry paste instead of the chili sauce.

1 Put the canned beans in a large mixing bowl. Add the sliced onion and mix together.

2 Cut the green beans in half and cook in lightly salted boiling water for about 8 minutes until just tender. Refresh under cold water and drain again. Add to the mixed beans and onions.

3 Place the bell pepper halves, cut side down, on a broiler rack and cook until the skin blackens and chars. Leave to cool slightly then pop them into a plastic bag for about 10 minutes. Peel away the skin from the bell peppers and discard. Roughly chop the bell pepper flesh and add it to the beans.

4 To make the dressing, place the oil, sherry vinegar, lemon juice, sugar, and chili sauce (if using) in a screw-top jar and shake vigorously.

5 Pour the dressing over the mixed bean salad and toss well. Leave to chill in the refrigerator until required.

 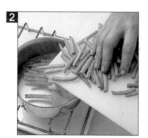 

Middle Eastern Salad

This attractive-looking salad can be served with a couple of vegetable kabobs for a delicious light lunch or an informal supper.

NUTRITIONAL INFORMATION

Calories	163	Sugars	........12g
Protein	.........8g	Fat	...........3g
Carbohydrate	...27g	Saturates	.....0.4g

  15 MINS · 0 MINS

SERVES 4

I N G R E D I E N T S

14 oz can garbanzo beans

4 carrots

1 bunch green onions

1 medium cucumber

½ tsp salt

½ tsp pepper

3 tbsp lemon juice

1 red bell pepper, sliced

1 Drain the garbanzo beans and place them in a large salad bowl.

2 Using a sharp knife, thinly slice the carrots. Cut the green onions into small pieces. Thickly slice the cucumber and then cut the slices into quarters.

3 Add the carrot slices, green onions, and cucumber to the garbanzo beans and mix.

4 Season to taste with the salt and pepper and sprinkle with the lemon juice. Toss the salad ingredients together gently, using 2 serving spoons.

5 Using a sharp knife, thinly slice the red bell pepper. Arrange the slices of red bell pepper decoratively on top of the

garbanzo bean salad. Serve the salad immediately or chill in the refrigerator and serve when required.

VARIATION

This salad would also be delicious made with *ful medames*, a brown fava bean used in Egyptian dishes. If they are not available canned, use 1 cup dried, soaked for 5 hours and then simmered for 2½ hours.

Green Vegetable Salad

This salad uses lots of green-colored ingredients, which look and taste wonderful with the minty yogurt dressing.

NUTRITIONAL INFORMATION

Calories 50   Sugars 6g
Protein ....4g   Fat 1g
Carbohydrate ....6g   Saturates 0.4g

 10–15 MINS   10 MINS

SERVES 4

I N G R E D I E N T S

2 zucchini, cut into sticks

3½ oz green beans, cut into three

1 green bell pepper, seeded and cut
   into strips

2 celery stalks, sliced

1 bunch watercress

D R E S S I N G

¾ cup plain yogurt

1 garlic clove, crushed

2 tbsp chopped mint

pepper

COOK'S TIP

The salad must be served as soon as the yogurt dressing has been added—the dressing will start to separate if kept for any length of time.

1 Cook the zucchini and green beans in a saucepan of salted boiling water for 7–8 minutes. Drain and set aside to cool completely.

2 Mix the zucchini and green beans with the bell pepper, celery, and watercress in a large serving bowl.

3 To make the dressing, mix together the plain yogurt, garlic, and chopped mint in a bowl. Season with pepper to taste.

4 Spoon the dressing onto the salad and serve immediately.

Sweet Potato & Nut Salad

Pecans with their slightly bitter flavor are mixed with sweet potatoes to make a sweet and sour salad with an interesting texture.

NUTRITIONAL INFORMATION

Calories . . . . . . .330 Sugars 5g
Protein . . . . .4g Fat 20g
Carbohydrate . . .36g Saturates 2g

25 MINS   10 MINS

SERVES 4

INGREDIENTS

1 lb 2 oz sweet potatoes, diced

2 celery stalks, sliced

4½ oz celery root, grated

2 green onions, sliced

½ cup pecans, chopped

2 heads Belgian endive, separated

1 tsp lemon juice

thyme sprigs, to garnish

DRESSING

4 tbsp vegetable oil

1 tbsp garlic wine vinegar

1 tsp soft light brown sugar

2 tsp chopped thyme

1 Cook the sweet potatoes in a large saucepan of boiling water for 5 minutes, until tender. Drain thoroughly and set aside to cool.

2 When cooled, stir in the celery, celery root, green onions, and pecans.

3 Line a salad plate with the Belgian endive leaves and sprinkle with lemon juice.

4 Spoon the sweet potato mixture into the center of the leaves.

5 In a small bowl, whisk the dressing ingredients together.

6 Pour the dressing over the salad and serve immediately, garnished with fresh thyme sprigs.

COOK'S TIP

Sweet potatoes do not store as well as ordinary potatoes. It is best to store them in a cool, dark place (not the refrigerator) and use within 1 week of purchase.

Warm Goat Cheese Salad

This delicious salad combines soft goat cheese with walnut halves, served on a bed of tossed salad greens.

NUTRITIONAL INFORMATION

Calories	408	Sugars	.........8g
Protein	.........9g	Fat	..........38g
Carbohydrate	....8g	Saturates	.......8g

 5 MINS   5 MINS

SERVES 4

I N G R E D I E N T S

¾ cup walnut halves

mixed salad greens

4½ oz soft goat cheese

snipped chives, to garnish

D R E S S I N G

6 tbsp walnut oil

3 tbsp white wine vinegar

1 tbsp honey

1 tsp Dijon mustard

pinch of ground ginger

salt and pepper

1 To make the dressing, whisk together the walnut oil, wine vinegar, honey, mustard, and ginger in a small saucepan. Season to taste with salt and pepper.

2 Heat the dressing gently, stirring occasionally, until warm. Add the walnut halves and continue to heat for 3–4 minutes.

3 Arrange the salad greens on 4 serving plates and place spoonfuls of goat cheese on top. Lift the walnut halves from the dressing with a perforated spoon, and scatter them over the salads.

4 Transfer the warm dressing to a small jug. Sprinkle chives over the salads and serve with the dressing.

VARIATION

You could also use a ewe-milk cheese, such as feta, in this recipe for a sharper flavor.

Gado Gado

This is a well-known and very popular Indonesian salad of mixed vegetables with a peanut dressing.

NUTRITIONAL INFORMATION

Calories 392	Sugars 8g	
Protein 9g	Fat 35g	
Carbohydrate 11g	Saturates 5g	

🍴 10 MINS 🕐 25 MINS

SERVES 4

INGREDIENTS

1 cup shredded green cabbage

3½ oz green beans,
    cut into three

3½ oz carrots, cut into thin sticks

3½ oz cauliflower flowerets

3½ oz bean sprouts

DRESSING

½ cup vegetable oil

1 cup unsalted peanuts

2 garlic cloves, crushed

1 small onion, finely chopped

½ tsp chili powder

½ tsp light brown sugar

2 cups water

juice of ½ lemon

salt

sliced green onions, to garnish

1 Cook the vegetables separately in a saucepan of salted boiling water for 4–5 minutes, drain well, and chill.

2 To make the dressing, heat the oil in a skillet and fry the peanuts, tossing frequently, for 3–4 minutes.

3 Remove from the pan with a perforated spoon and drain on absorbent paper towels. Process the peanuts in a food processor or crush with a rolling pin until a fine mixture is formed.

4 Pour all but 1 tablespoon of the oil from the pan and fry the garlic and onion for 1 minute. Add the chili powder, sugar, a pinch of salt, and the water and bring to a boil.

5 Stir in the peanuts. Reduce the heat and simmer for 4–5 minutes. until the sauce thickens. Add the lemon juice and set aside to cool.

6 Arrange the vegetables in a serving dish and spoon the peanut dressing into the center. Garnish and serve.

Three-Bean Salad

Fresh baby green beans are combined with soybeans and red kidney beans in a chive and tomato dressing to make a tasty salad.

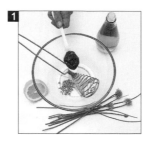

NUTRITIONAL INFORMATION

Calories ....276 Sugars 7g
Protein ....18g Fat 15g
Carbohydrate ...18g Saturates 4g

 15 MINS   10 MINS

SERVES 6

I N G R E D I E N T S

3 tbsp olive oil

1 tbsp lemon juice

1 tbsp tomato paste

1 tbsp light malt vinegar

1 tbsp chopped chives

6 oz thin green beans

14 oz can soybeans,
    rinsed and drained

14 oz can red kidney beans, rinsed
    and drained

2 tomatoes, chopped

4 green onions, chopped

4½ oz feta cheese, cut into cubes

salt and pepper

mixed salad greens, to serve

chopped chives, to garnish

1 Put the olive oil, lemon juice, tomato paste, malt vinegar, and chopped chives into a large bowl and whisk together well until thoroughly combined. Set aside.

2 Cook the green beans in boiling, lightly salted water for 4–5 minutes, until just cooked. Drain, refresh under cold running water, and drain again. Pat dry with paper towels.

3 Add the green beans, soybeans, and red kidney beans to the dressing, stirring to mix.

4 Add the tomatoes, green onions, and feta cheese to the bean mixture, tossing gently to coat in the dressing. Season well with salt and pepper.

5 Arrange the mixed salad greens on 6 serving plates. Pile the bean salad onto the plates and garnish with chopped chives.

Potato & Radish Salad

The radishes and the herb and mustard dressing give this colorful salad a mild mustard flavor that compliments the potatoes perfectly.

NUTRITIONAL INFORMATION

Calories 140	Sugars 3g	
Protein 3g	Fat 6g	
Carbohydrate ...20g	Saturates 1g	

  50 MINS   20 MINS

SERVES 4

INGREDIENTS

1 lb 2 oz new potatoes, scrubbed
  and halved

½ cucumber, thinly sliced

2 tsp salt

1 bunch radishes, thinly sliced

DRESSING

1 tbsp Dijon mustard

2 tbsp olive oil

1 tbsp white wine vinegar

2 tbsp mixed chopped herbs

1 Cook the potatoes in a saucepan of boiling water for 10–15 minutes, or until tender. Drain and set aside to cool.

2 Meanwhile, spread out the cucumber slices on a plate and sprinkle with the salt. Leave to stand for 30 minutes, then rinse under cold running water and pat dry with paper towels.

3 Arrange the cucumber and radish slices on a serving plate in a decorative pattern and pile the cooked potatoes in the center of the slices.

  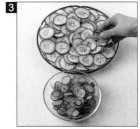

4 In a small bowl, mix all the dressing ingredients together, whisking until thoroughly combined. Pour the dressing over the salad, tossing well to coat all of the ingredients. Chill in the refrigerator before serving.

COOK'S TIP

The cucumber adds not only color, but also a freshness to the salad. It is salted and left to stand to remove the excess water, which would make the salad soggy. Wash the cucumber well to remove all of the salt, before adding to the salad.

Three-Way Potato Salad

Small new potatoes, served warm in a delicious dressing. The nutritional information is for the potato salad with the curry dressing only.

15–20 MINS   20 MINS

SERVES 4

I N G R E D I E N T S

1 lb 2 oz new potatoes (for each
   dressing)

herbs, to garnish

LIGHT CURRY DRESSING

1 tbsp vegetable oil

1 tbsp medium curry paste

1 small onion, chopped

1 tbsp mango chutney, chopped

6 tbsp plain yogurt

3 tbsp light cream

2 tbsp mayonnaise

salt and pepper

1 tbsp light cream, to garnish

VINAIGRETTE DRESSING

6 tbsp hazelnut or walnut oil

3 tbsp cider vinegar

1 tsp wholegrain mustard

1 tsp sugar

few basil leaves, torn

PARSLEY CREAM

⅔ cup sour cream

3 tbsp light mayonnaise

4 green onions, finely chopped

1 tbsp chopped fresh parsley

1 To make the Light Curry Dressing, heat the vegetable oil in a saucepan, add the curry paste and onion, and fry, stirring frequently, until the onion is soft. Remove from the heat and set aside to cool slightly.

2 Mix together the mango chutney, yogurt, cream, and mayonnaise. Add the curry mixture and blend together. Season with salt and pepper.

3 To make the Vinaigrette Dressing, whisk the oil, vinegar, mustard, sugar, and basil together in a small jug or bowl. Season with salt and pepper.

4 To make the Parsley Cream, combine the mayonnaise, sour cream, green onions, and parsley, mixing well. Season with salt and pepper.

5 Cook the potatoes in lightly salted boiling water until just tender. Drain well and set aside to cool for 5 minutes, then add the chosen dressing, tossing to coat. Serve garnished with fresh herbs, spooning a little light cream onto the potatoes if you have used the curry dressing.

Red Cabbage & Pear Salad

Red cabbage is much underused—it is a colorful and tasty ingredient that is perfect with such fruits as pears and apples.

NUTRITIONAL INFORMATION

Calories	143	Sugars	........14g
Protein	.........2g	Fat	..........9g
Carbohydrate	...15g	Saturates	.......1g

 15 MINS   0 MINS

SERVES 4

INGREDIENTS

4 cups finely shredded
  red cabbage

2 pears, cored and thinly sliced

4 green onions, sliced

1 carrot, grated

chives, to garnish

DRESSING

4 tbsp pear juice

1 tsp wholegrain mustard

3 tbsp olive oil

1 tbsp garlic wine vinegar

1 tbsp chopped chives

salt and pepper

1 Put the cabbage, pears, and green onions in a bowl and mix together.

2 Line a serving dish with lettuce leaves and spoon the cabbage and pear mixture into the center.

3 Sprinkle the carrot into the center of the cabbage to form a domed pile.

4 To make the dressing, mix together the pear juice, wholegrain mustard, olive oil, garlic wine vinegar, and chives. Season to taste with salt and pepper.

5 Pour the dressing over the salad, garnish, and serve immediately.

COOK'S TIP

Mix the salad just before serving to prevent the color from the red cabbage bleeding into the other ingredients.

Potato & Banana Salad

This hot fruity salad combines sweet potato and fried bananas with colorful mixed bell peppers, tossed in a honey-based dressing.

NUTRITIONAL INFORMATION

Calories	424	Sugars	........29g
Protein	.........5g	Fat	..........17g
Carbohydrate	...68g	Saturates	.......8g

 15 MINS   20 MINS

SERVES 4

I N G R E D I E N T S

1 lb 2 oz sweet potatoes, diced

4 tbsp butter

1 tbsp lemon juice

1 garlic clove, crushed

1 red bell pepper, seeded and diced

1 green bell pepper, seeded and diced

2 bananas, thickly sliced

2 thick slices white bread, crusts
   removed, diced

salt and pepper

D R E S S I N G

2 tbsp honey

2 tbsp chopped chives

2 tbsp lemon juice

2 tbsp olive oil

1 Cook the sweet potatoes in a saucepan of boiling water for 10–15 minutes, until tender. Drain thoroughly and reserve.

2 Meanwhile, melt the butter in a skillet. Add the lemon juice, garlic, and bell peppers and cook, stirring constantly for 3 minutes.

3 Add the banana slices to the pan and cook for 1 minute. Remove the bananas from the pan with a perforated spoon and stir into the potatoes.

4 Add the bread cubes to the skillet and cook, stirring frequently, for 2 minutes, until they are golden brown on all sides.

5 Mix the dressing ingredients together in a small saucepan and heat until the honey is runny.

6 Spoon the potato mixture into a serving dish and season to taste with salt and pepper. Pour the dressing over the potatoes and sprinkle the croûtons over the top. Serve immediately.

COOK'S TIP

Use firm, slightly under-ripe bananas in this recipe since they will not turn soft and mushy when fried.

Marinated Vegetable Salad

Lightly steamed vegetables taste superb served slightly warm in a marinade of olive oil, white wine, vinegar, and fresh herbs.

NUTRITIONAL INFORMATION

Calories	114	Sugars	. . . . .4g
Protein	. . . . .3g	Fat	. . . . .9g
Carbohydrate	. . . .5g	Saturates	. . . . . . .1g

 10 MINS   10 MINS

SERVES 6

I N G R E D I E N T S

6 oz baby carrots

2 celery hearts, cut into 4 pieces

4½ oz sugar snap peas or snow peas

1 fennel bulb, sliced

6 oz small asparagus spears

1½ tbsp sunflower seeds

dill sprigs, to garnish

D R E S S I N G

4 tbsp olive oil

4 tbsp dry white wine

2 tbsp white wine vinegar

1 tbsp chopped dill

1 tbsp chopped parsley

salt and pepper

1 Put the carrots, celery, sugar snap peas or snow peas, fennel, and asparagus into a steamer and cook over gently boiling water until just tender. It is important that they retain a little "bite."

2 Meanwhile, make the dressing. Mix together the olive oil, wine, vinegar, and chopped herbs, whisking until thoroughly combined. Season to taste with salt and pepper.

3 When the vegetables are cooked, transfer them to a serving dish and pour over the dressing immediately. The hot vegetables will absorb the flavor of the dressing as they cool.

4 Spread out the sunflower seeds on a cookie sheet and toast them under a preheated broiler for 3-4 minutes or until lightly browned. Sprinkle the toasted sunflower seeds over the vegetables.

5 Serve the salad while the vegetables are still slightly warm, garnished with sprigs of fresh dill.

Melon & Strawberry Salad

This refreshing fruit-based salad is perfect for a hot summer's day and would go well with barbecued food.

NUTRITIONAL INFORMATION

Calories 112   Sugars 22g
Protein . . . . .5g   Fat 1g
Carbohydrate . . .22g   Saturates 0.3g

15 MINS   0 MINS

SERVES 4

INGREDIENTS

½ iceberg lettuce, shredded

1 small honeydew melon

1½ cups sliced strawberries

2-inch piece of cucumber, thinly sliced

mint sprigs to garnish

DRESSING

1 cup plain yogurt

2-inch piece of cucumber, peeled

a few mint leaves

½ tsp finely grated lime or lemon zest

pinch of sugar

3–4 ice cubes

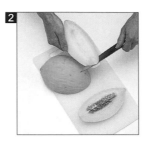  

1 Arrange the shredded lettuce on 4 serving plates.

VARIATION

Omit the ice cubes in the dressing if you prefer, but make sure that the ingredients are well-chilled. This will ensure that the finished dressing is really cool.

2 Cut the melon lengthwise into quarters. Scoop out the seeds and cut through the flesh down to the skin at 1 inch intervals. Cut the melon close to the skin and detach the flesh.

3 Place the chunks of melon on the beds of lettuce with the strawberries and cucumber slices.

4 To make the dressing, put the yogurt, cucumber, mint leaves, lime or lemon zest, sugar, and ice cubes into a blender or food processor. Blend together for about 15 seconds, until smooth. Alternatively, chop the cucumber and mint finely, crush the ice cubes, and combine with the other ingredients.

5 Serve the salad with a little dressing poured over it. Garnish with sprigs of fresh mint.

Multicolored Salad

The beet adds a rich color to this dish, tinting the potato an appealing pink. Mixed with cucumber, it is a really vibrant salad.

NUTRITIONAL INFORMATION

Calories 174	Sugars 8g
Protein 4g	Fat 6g
Carbohydrate ...27g	Saturates 1g

 15-20 MINS 20 MINS

SERVES 4

INGREDIENTS

1 lb 2 oz potatoes, diced

4 small cooked beets, sliced

½ small cucumber, thinly sliced

2 large dill pickles, sliced

1 red onion, halved and sliced

dill sprigs, to garnish

DRESSING

1 garlic clove, crushed

2 tbsp olive oil

2 tbsp red wine vinegar

2 tbsp chopped fresh dill

salt and pepper

1 Cook the diced potatoes in a saucepan of boiling water for about 15 minutes, or until just tender. Drain and set aside to cool.

2 When cool, mix the potato and beets together in a bowl and set aside.

3 To make the dressing, whisk together the garlic, olive oil, vinegar, and dill and season to taste with salt and pepper.

4 When ready to serve, line a large serving platter with the slices of cucumber, dill pickles, and red onion.

Spoon the potato and beet mixture into the center of the platter.

5 Pour the dressing over the salad and serve immediately, garnished with fresh dill sprigs.

VARIATION

Line the salad platter with 2 heads of Belgian endive, separated into leaves, and arrange the cucumber, dill pickle, and red onion slices on top of the leaves.

Carrot & Nut Coleslaw

This simple salad has a dressing made from poppy seeds pan-fried in sesame oil to bring out their flavor and aroma.

NUTRITIONAL INFORMATION

Calories 220	Sugars 7g
Protein 4g	Fat 19g
Carbohydrate ...10g	Saturates 3g

  15 MINS   5–10 MINS

SERVES 4

I N G R E D I E N T S

1 large carrot, grated

1 small onion, finely chopped

2 celery stalks, chopped

¼ small hard green cabbage, shredded

1 tbsp chopped parsley

4 tbsp sesame oil

½ tsp poppy seeds

½ cup cashews

2 tbsp white wine vinegar or cider vinegar

salt and pepper

parsley sprigs, to garnish

1 In a large salad bowl, mix together the carrot, onion, celery, and cabbage. Stir in the chopped parsley and season to taste with salt and pepper.

2 Heat the sesame oil in a saucepan with a lid. Add the poppy seeds and cover the pan. Cook over a medium-high heat until the seeds start to make a popping sound. Remove from the heat and set aside to cool.

3 Spread out the cashews on a cookie sheet. Place them under a medium-hot broiler and toast until lightly browned, being careful not to burn them. Leave to cool.

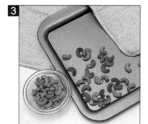

4 Add the vinegar to the oil and poppy seeds, then pour the dressing over the carrot mixture. Add the cooled cashews. Toss together to coat well.

5 Garnish the salad with sprigs of fresh parsley and serve immediately.

Hot Salad

This quickly-made dish is ideal for a cold winter's night. Serve with crusty bread, freshly made rolls, or garlic bread.

  10 MINS   10 MINS

SERVES 4

I N G R E D I E N T S

½ medium-sized cauliflower

1 green bell pepper

1 red bell pepper

½ cucumber

4 carrots

2 tbsp butter

salt and pepper

crusty bread, rolls, or garlic bread,
    to serve

D R E S S I N G

3 tbsp olive oil

1 tbsp white wine vinegar

1 tbsp light soy sauce

1 tsp sugar

salt and pepper

1 Cut the cauliflower into small flowerets, using a sharp knife. Seed the bell peppers and cut the flesh into thin slices. Cut the cucumber into thin slices. Thinly slice the carrots lengthwise.

2 Melt the butter in a large heavy-bottomed saucepan. Add the cauliflower, bell peppers, cucumber, and carrots and fry over a medium heat, stirring constantly, for 5-7 minutes, until tender, but still firm to the bite. Season

with salt and pepper. Lower the heat, cover with a lid, and simmer for 3 minutes.

3 Meanwhile, make the dressing. Whisk together all the ingredients until thoroughly combined.

4 Transfer the vegetables to a serving dish, pour over the dressing, toss to mix well and serve immediately.

VARIATION

You can replace the vegetables in this recipe with those of your choice, such as broccoli, green onions, and zucchini.

Melon & Mango Salad

A little freshly grated fresh ginger mixed with creamy yogurt and honey makes a perfect dressing for this refreshing melon salad.

NUTRITIONAL INFORMATION

Calories 189   Sugars 30g
Protein . . . . .5g   Fat 7g
Carbohydrate . . .30g   Saturates 1g

 15-20 MINS 0 MINS

SERVES 4

INGREDIENTS

1 cantaloupe melon

½ cup black grapes, halved
   and seeded

½ cup seedless green grapes

1 large mango

1 bunch of watercress

iceberg lettuce leaves, shredded

2 tbsp olive oil

1 tbsp cider vinegar

1 passion fruit

salt and pepper

DRESSING

¾ cup thick plain yogurt

1 tbsp honey

1 tsp grated fresh ginger

1 First, make the dressing for the melon. Mix together the yogurt, honey, and ginger in a small bowl, stirring to combine.

2 Halve the melon and scoop out the seeds. Slice, peel, and cut into chunks. Mix with the grapes.

3 Slice the mango on each side of its large flat pit. On each mango half, slash the flesh into a criss-cross pattern down to, but not through, the skin. Push the skin from underneath to turn the mango halves inside out. Now remove the flesh and add to the melon mixture.

4 Arrange the watercress and lettuce on 4 serving plates. Make the dressing for the salad greens. Whisk together the olive oil and cider vinegar and season to taste with salt and pepper. Drizzle the dressing over the watercress and lettuce.

5 Divide the melon mixture equally between the 4 plates and spoon over the yogurt dressing. Scoop the seeds out of the passion fruit and sprinkle them over the salads. Serve immediately.

COOK'S TIP

Grated fresh ginger gives a marvelous flavor to this recipe, but if you can't get fresh ginger, substitute ½ teaspoon of ground ginger instead.

Broiled Salad

The vegetables for this dish are best prepared well ahead of time and chilled in the refrigerator before serving.

NUTRITIONAL INFORMATION

Calories ....230 Sugars 10g
Protein ....2g Fat 20g
Carbohydrate ....11g Saturates 3g

  1¹/₄ HOURS 🕐 10 MINS

SERVES 4

I N G R E D I E N T S

1 zucchini, sliced

1 yellow bell pepper, seeded and sliced

1 eggplant, sliced

1 fennel bulb, cut into eight

1 red onion, cut into eight

16 cherry tomatoes

3 tbsp olive oil

1 garlic clove, crushed

rosemary sprigs, to garnish

D R E S S I N G

4 tbsp olive oil

2 tbsp balsamic vinegar

2 tsp chopped rosemary

1 tsp Dijon mustard

1 tsp honey

2 tsp lemon juice

1 Spread out the slices of zucchini, bell pepper, eggplant, fennel, onion and the tomatoes on a large cookie sheet.

2 Mix together the oil and garlic and brush all over the vegetables. Cook under a medium-hot broiler for 10 minutes, until tender and just beginning to char. Remove from the heat and set aside to cool.

3 When cool, spoon the vegetables into a serving bowl and gently mix.

4 Whisk together the dressing ingredients until thoroughly combined and pour over the vegetables. Cover and chill in the refrigerator for 1 hour.

5 Garnish the salad with rosemary sprigs and serve.

COOK'S TIP

This dish could also be served warm—heat the dressing in a pan over a low heat and then pour over the vegetables.

Grapefruit & Coconut Salad

This salad is quite deceptive—it is, in fact, surprisingly filling, even though it looks very light.

NUTRITIONAL INFORMATION

Calories	.201	Sugars	.13g
Protein	.3g	Fat	.15g
Carbohydrate	...14g	Saturates	.9g

 10 MINS   ⏲ 10 MINS

SERVES 4

I N G R E D I E N T S

1 cup grated coconut

2 tsp light soy sauce

2 tbsp lime juice

2 tbsp water

2 tsp sunflower oil

1 garlic clove, halved

1 onion, finely chopped

2 large ruby grapefruits, peeled
   and segmented

1½ cups alfalfa sprouts

1 Toast the coconut in a dry skillet over a low heat, stirring constantly, for about 3 minutes, or until golden brown. Transfer the toasted coconut to a bowl.

2 Add the light soy sauce, lime juice, and water to the toasted coconut and mix together well.

3 Heat the oil in a saucepan and fry the garlic and onion until soft. Stir the onion into the coconut mixture. Remove and discard the garlic.

4 Divide the grapefruit segments between 4 plates. Sprinkle each with a quarter of the alfalfa sprouts and spoon over a quarter of the coconut mixture.

  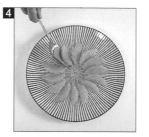

COOK'S TIP

Alfalfa sprouts can be bought in trays or packs from most supermarkets, but you can easily grow your own, if you like to have a constant and cheap supply.

Alfalfa & Spinach Salad

This is a really refreshing salad that must be assembled just before serving to prevent everything being colored by the beet.

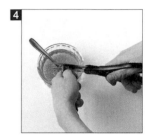

NUTRITIONAL INFORMATION

Calories	139	Sugars	.........7g
Protein	.........2g	Fat	...........11g
Carbohydrate	....8g	Saturates	.......2g

 10 MINS 0 MINS

SERVES 4

INGREDIENTS

3½ oz baby spinach

1⅓ cups alfalfa sprouts

2 celery stalks, sliced

4 cooked beets, cut into 8

DRESSING

4 tbsp olive oil

4½ tsp garlic wine vinegar

1 garlic clove, crushed

2 tsp honey

1 tbsp chopped chives

1 Place the spinach and alfalfa sprouts in a large bowl and mix together.

2 Add the celery to the bowl and mix together well.

3 Toss in the beets and mix until well combined.

4 To make the dressing, mix the oil, wine vinegar, garlic, honey, and chopped chives.

5 Pour the dressing over the salad, toss well, and serve immediately.

VARIATION

Add the segments of 1 large orange to the salad to make it even more colorful and refreshing. Replace the garlic wine vinegar with a different flavored oil such as chili or herb, if you prefer.

Potato, Bean, & Apple Salad

Use any mixture of beans you have at hand in this recipe, but the wider the variety, the more colorful the salad.

NUTRITIONAL INFORMATION

Calories 183   Sugars 8g
Protein ....6g   Fat 7g
Carbohydrate ...26g   Saturates 1g

  20 MINS   20 MINS

SERVES 4

INGREDIENTS

8 oz new potatoes, scrubbed
    and quartered

8 oz mixed canned beans, drained
    and rinsed

1 red apple, diced and tossed in
    1 tbsp lemon juice

1 yellow bell pepper, seeded and diced

1 shallot, sliced

½ fennel bulb, sliced

lettuce leaves

DRESSING

1 tbsp red wine vinegar

2 tbsp olive oil

½ tbsp mustard

1 garlic clove, crushed

2 tsp chopped fresh thyme

VARIATION

Use Dijon or wholegrain
mustard for a different flavor.

1 Cook the quartered potatoes in a saucepan of boiling water for 15 minutes, until tender. Drain and transfer to a mixing bowl.

2 Add the mixed beans to the potatoes, together with the apple, bell pepper, shallots, and fennel. Mix well, taking care not to break up the cooked potatoes.

3 To make the dressing, whisk all the dressing ingredients together until thoroughly combined, then pour it over the potato salad.

4 Line a serving plate or salad bowl with the lettuce leaves and spoon the potato mixture into the center. Serve immediately.

Garden Salad

This chunky salad includes tiny new potatoes tossed in a minty dressing, and has a mustard dip for dunking.

NUTRITIONAL INFORMATION

Calories 227	Sugars 6g	
Protein 4g	Fat 17g	
Carbohydrate ...16g	Saturates 4g	

15–20 MINS   20 MINS

SERVES 8

INGREDIENTS

1 lb 2 oz tiny new potatoes

8 oz broccoli flowerets

4½ oz sugar snap peas or snow peas

2 large carrots

4 celery stalks

1 yellow or orange bell pepper, seeded

1 bunch green onions

1 head Belgian endive

DRESSING

3 tbsp olive oil

1 tbsp white wine vinegar

1 tsp wholegrain mustard

2 tbsp chopped mint

MUSTARD DIP

6 tbsp sour cream

3 tbsp thick mayonnaise

2 tsp balsamic vinegar

1½ tsp grainy mustard

½ tsp creamed horseradish

pinch of brown sugar

salt and pepper

1 Cook the potatoes in boiling salted water for about 10 minutes, until just tender. While they cook, combine the dressing ingredients.

2 Drain the potatoes thoroughly, add to the dressing while hot, toss well, and set aside until cold, giving them an occasional stir.

3 To make the dip, combine the sour cream, mayonnaise, vinegar, mustard, horseradish, and sugar and season to taste with salt and pepper. Transfer to a small serving bowl, cover, and refrigerate until ready to serve.

4 Cut the broccoli into bite-sized flowerets and blanch for 2 minutes in boiling water. Drain and toss immediately in cold water; drain thoroughly.

5 Blanch the sugar snap peas in boiling water for 1 minute. Drain, rinse in cold water, and drain again.

6 Cut the carrots and celery into thin sticks about 2½ x ½ inches. Slice the bell pepper or cut it into small cubes. Cut off some of the green parts of the green onions and separate the endive leaves.

7 Arrange the vegetables attractively in a fairly shallow bowl with the potatoes piled up in the center. Serve accompanied with the mustard dip.

Side Dishes

The main aim of the recipes in this chapter is to complement the main course recipes found throughout the rest of this book. The side dishes include a range of different vegetable dishes—you will be amazed at the variety! Try potatoes flavored with exotic saffron and mustard, or green beans full of the sun-drenched flavors

of Greece. Whatever the main course, you are sure to find a suitable side dish among the wealth of recipes in this chapter. They are all perfect for elaborate dinner parties, or for simple family meals. You could even use some of them for a snack or a light meal on its own. The choice is yours!

Spicy Potatoes & Onions

Masala aloo are potatoes cooked in spices and onions. Semi-dry when cooked, they make an excellent accompaniment to almost any curry.

NUTRITIONAL INFORMATION

Calories 313   Sugars 5g
Protein . . . . .2g   Fat 25g
Carbohydrate . . .21g   Saturates 3g

 10-15 MINS   10 MINS

SERVES 4

I N G R E D I E N T S

6 tbsp vegetable oil

2 medium-sized onions,
   finely chopped

1 tsp finely chopped
   fresh ginger

1 tsp crushed garlic

1 tsp chili powder

1½ tsp ground cumin

1½ tsp ground coriander

1 tsp salt

14 oz can new potatoes

1 tbsp lemon juice

B A G H A A R

3 tbsp oil

3 dried red chilies

½ tsp onion seeds

½ tsp mustard seeds

½ tsp fenugreek seeds

T O   G A R N I S H

fresh cilantro leaves

1 green chili, finely chopped

1 Heat the oil in a large, heavy-bottomed saucepan. Add the onions and fry, stirring, until golden brown. Reduce the heat, add the ginger, garlic, chili powder, ground cumin, ground coriander, and salt and stir-fry for about 1 minute. Remove the pan from the heat and set aside until required.

2 Drain the water from the potatoes. Add the potatoes to the onion mixture and spice mixture and heat through. Sprinkle over the lemon juice and mix well.

3 To make the baghaar, heat the oil in a separate pan. Add the red chilies, onion seeds, mustard seeds, and fenugreek seeds and fry until the seeds turn a shade darker. Remove the pan from the heat and pour the baghaar over the potatoes.

4 Garnish with cilantro leaves and chilies, then serve.

Seasonal Vegetables

These vegetables are ideal for a special occasion, such as Christmas Day. Do not start cooking them too early; they take only a little time to cook.

NUTRITIONAL INFORMATION

Calories ....434 Sugars 20g
Protein ....7g Fat 19g
Carbohydrate ...62g Saturates 5g

 20 MINS   1 HR 40 MINS

SERVES 8

INGREDIENTS

CRISPY ROAST POTATOES

4 lb 8 oz potatoes

vegetable oil, for roasting

salt

HONEY-GLAZED CARROTS

2 lb 4 oz carrots

1 tbsp honey

2 tbsp butter

2 tsp sesame seeds, toasted

SPICED WINTER CABBAGE

1 hard green cabbage

2 apples, peeled, cored,
  and chopped

few drops of lemon juice

2 tbsp butter

freshly grated nutmeg

salt

1 To make Crispy Roast Potatoes, peel the potatoes and cut them into large, even-sized chunks. Put them into a large saucepan of cold water with ½ tsp salt. Bring to the boil, and then reduce the heat. Cover and simmer for about 8–10 minutes to parboil them. Drain thoroughly.

2 Heat about ⅔ cup vegetable oil in a large roasting pan until very hot. Add the potatoes, basting thoroughly. Roast in a preheated oven at 400°F for about 1 hour, basting occasionally, until crisp and golden brown.

3 To make Honey-glazed Carrots, cut the carrots into a saucepan and barely cover with water. Add the honey and butter. Cook, uncovered, for about 15 minutes, until the liquid has just evaporated and the carrots are glazed. Serve in a warmed dish, sprinkled with toasted sesame seeds.

4 To maked Spiced Winter Cabbage, shred the cabbage just before cooking it to retain the vitamins. Add the chopped apples and lemon juice, and cook in a small amount of water in a covered saucepan over a medium heat for about 6 minutes. Drain thoroughly. Season to taste with salt and add the butter, tossing to melt. Transfer to a warmed serving dish, sprinkle with freshly grated nutmeg, and serve immediately.

Baby Cauliflowers

Whole baby cauliflowers coated with a red Leicester cheese and poppy-seed sauce are cooked to perfection in the microwave.

NUTRITIONAL INFORMATION

Calories ....173 Sugars 6g
Protein ....8g Fat 11g
Carbohydrate ...10g Saturates 6g

30 MINS   15 MINS

SERVES 4

I N G R E D I E N T S

4 cloves

½ onion

½ carrot

1 bouquet garni

1 cup milk

4 baby cauliflowers

3 tbsp water

1 tbsp butter

2 tbsp all-purpose flour

½ cup grated red Leicester or
  cheddar cheese

1 tbsp poppy seeds

pinch of paprika

salt and pepper

parsley to garnish

1 Stick the cloves into the onion. Place in a bowl with the carrot, bouquet garni, and milk. Heat on HIGH power for 2¹/₂–3 minutes. Leave to stand for 20 minutes to allow the flavors to infuse.

2 Trim the base and leaves from the cauliflowers and scoop out the stem using a small sharp knife, leaving the cauliflowers intact. Place the cauliflowers upside down in a large dish. Add the water, cover, and cook on HIGH power for 5 minutes, until just tender. Leave to stand for 2–3 minutes.

3 Put the butter in a bowl and cook on HIGH power for 30 seconds, until melted. Stir in the flour. Cook on HIGH power for 30 seconds.

4 Strain the milk into a jug, discarding the vegetables. Gradually add to the flour and butter, beating well between each addition. Cover and cook on HIGH power for 3 minutes, stirring every 30 seconds after the first minute, until the sauce has thickened.

5 Stir the cheese and poppy seeds into the sauce and season with salt and pepper to taste. Cover and cook on HIGH power for 30 seconds.

6 Drain the cauliflowers and arrange on a plate or in a shallow dish. Pour over the sauce and sprinkle with a little paprika. Cook on HIGH power for 1 minute to reheat. Serve garnished with fresh parsley.

Dry Split Okra

This is an unusual way of cooking this delicious vegetable. The dish is dry when cooked, and should be served hot with chapatis and a dal.

NUTRITIONAL INFORMATION

Calories	190	Sugars	........4g
Protein	........3g	Fat	.........18g
Carbohydrate	....5g	Saturates	.......2g

 10 MINS 20 MINS

SERVES 4

I N G R E D I E N T S

1 lb 2 oz okra

⅔ cup vegetable oil

½ cup dried onions

2 tsp dried mango powder

1 tsp ground cumin

1 tsp chili powder

1 tsp salt

1 Prepare the okra by cutting the ends off and discarding them. Carefully split the okra down the middle without cutting through completely.

2 Heat the oil in a large saucepan. Add the dried onions and fry until crisp.

3 Remove the onions from the pan with a perforated spoon and drain thoroughly on paper towels. When cool enough to handle, roughly tear the dried onions and place in a large bowl.

4 Add the dried mango powder, ground cumin, chili powder, and salt to the dried onions and blend well together.

5 Spoon the onion and spice mixture into the split okra.

6 Re-heat the oil in the saucepan. Gently add the okra to the hot oil

and cook over a low heat for about 10–12 minutes.

7 Transfer the cooked okra to a serving dish and serve immediately.

COOK'S TIP

Ground cumin has a warm, pungent aromatic flavor and is used extensively in Indian cooking. It is a good pantry standby.

Baked Celery with Cream

This dish is topped with breadcrumbs for a crunchy topping, underneath which is hidden a creamy celery and pecan mixture.

NUTRITIONAL INFORMATION

Calories	237	Sugars	.........5g
Protein	.........7g	Fat	..........19g
Carbohydrate	....11g	Saturates	.......7g

 15 MINS   40 MINS

SERVES 4

INGREDIENTS

1 head of celery

½ tsp ground cumin

½ tsp ground coriander

1 garlic clove, crushed

1 red onion, thinly sliced

½ cup pecan halves

⅔ cup vegetable stock

⅔ cup light cream

1 cup fresh whole wheat breadcrumbs

⅓ cup grated Parmesan cheese

salt and pepper

celery leaves, to garnish

COOK'S TIP

Once grated, Parmesan cheese quickly loses its "bite" so it is best to grate only the amount you need for the recipe. Wrap the rest tightly in foil and it will keep for several months in the refrigerator.

1 Trim the celery and cut into thin sticks. Place the celery in an ovenproof dish, together with the ground cumin, coriander, garlic, red onion, and pecans.

2 Mix the stock and cream together and pour over the vegetables. Season with salt and pepper to taste.

3 Mix the breadcrumbs and cheese together and sprinkle over the top to cover the vegetables.

4 Cook in a preheated oven at 400°F for 40 minutes, or until the vegetables are tender and the top crispy. Garnish with celery leaves and serve immediately.

Sweet Hot Carrots & Beans

Take care not to overcook the vegetables in this tasty dish—they are definitely at their best served tender-crisp.

NUTRITIONAL INFORMATION

Calories	268	Sugars	........16g
Protein	.........5g	Fat	..........19g
Carbohydrate	...19g	Saturates	.......3g

10 MINS · 15 MINS

SERVES 4

INGREDIENTS

1 lb 2 oz young carrots

8 oz green beans

1 bunch green onions

4 tbsp vegetable ghee or oil

1 tsp ground cumin

1 tsp ground coriander

3 cardamom pods, split and seeds removed

2 whole dried red chilies

2 garlic cloves, crushed

1–2 tsp honey

1 tsp lime or lemon juice

½ cup unsalted, toasted cashews

1 tbsp chopped cilantro
   or parsley

salt and pepper

slices of lime or lemon and cilantro sprigs,
   to garnish

1 Cut the carrots lengthwise into quarters and then in half crossways if very long. Top and tail the beans. Cut the green onions into 2-inch pieces.

2 Cook the carrots and beans in a saucepan of boiling, salted water for 5–6 minutes, until tender-crisp. Drain.

3 Heat the ghee or oil in a large skillet, add the green onions, carrots, beans, cumin, ground coriander, cardamom seeds, and whole dried chilies. Cook gently, stirring frequently, for 2 minutes.

4 Stir in the garlic, honey, and lemon or lime juice and continue cooking, stirring occasionally, for another 2 minutes. Season to taste with salt and pepper. Remove and discard the chilies.

5 Sprinkle the vegetables with the cashews and chopped cilantro, mix together lightly. Serve immediately, garnished with lime or lemon slices and cilantro sprigs.

Pommes Anna

This is a classic potato dish, which may be left to cook unattended while the rest of the meal is being prepared, so it is ideal with stews.

NUTRITIONAL INFORMATION

Calories 237   Sugars 1g
Protein ....4g   Fat 13g
Carbohydrate ...29g   Saturates 8g

15 MINS   2 HOURS

SERVES 4

INGREDIENTS

¼ cup butter, melted

1½ lb potatoes

4 tbsp chopped mixed herbs

salt and pepper

chopped fresh herbs, to garnish

1 Brush a shallow 4-cup ovenproof dish with a little of the melted butter.

2 Slice the potatoes thinly and pat dry with paper towels.

3 Arrange a layer of potato slices in the prepared dish until the base is covered. Brush with a little butter and sprinkle with a quarter of the chopped mixed herbs. Season to taste.

4 Continue layering the potato slices, brushing each layer with melted butter and sprinkling with herbs, until they are all used up.

5 Brush the top layer of potato slices with butter, cover the dish, and cook in a preheated oven at 375°F for 1½ hours.

6 Invert onto a warm ovenproof platter and return to the oven for another 25–30 minutes, until golden brown. Serve immediately, garnished with fresh herbs.

COOK'S TIP

Make sure that the potatoes are sliced very thinly so that they are almost transparent. This will ensure that they cook thoroughly.

Kashmiri Spinach

This is an imaginative way to serve spinach, which adds a little zip to it. It is a very simple dish, which will complement almost any curry.

NUTRITIONAL INFORMATION

Calories	81	Sugars	. . . . .2g
Protein	. . . . .4g	Fat	. . . . .7g
Carbohydrate	. . . .2g	Saturates	. . . . . . .1g

 5 MINS   25 MINS

SERVES 4

I N G R E D I E N T S

1 lb 2 oz spinach, or chard or
  baby leaf spinach

2 tbsp mustard oil

¼ tsp garam masala

1 tsp yellow mustard seeds

2 green onions, sliced

1 Remove the tough stalks from the spinach.

2 Heat the mustard oil in a preheated wok or large heavy-bottomed skillet until it smokes. Add the garam masala and mustard seeds. Cover the pan quickly—you will hear the mustard seeds popping inside.

3 When the popping has ceased, remove the cover, add the green onions and spinach. Cook, stirring constantly, until the spinach has wilted.

4 Continue cooking the spinach, uncovered, over a medium heat for 10–15 minutes, until most of the water has evaporated. If using frozen spinach, it will not need to cook for so long—cook it until most of the water has evaporated.

5 Remove the spinach and green onions with a perforated spoon, draining off

any remaining liquid. (This dish is nicer to eat when it is served as dry as possible.)

6 Transfer to a warmed serving dish and serve immediately, while it is still piping hot.

COOK'S TIP

Mustard oil is made from mustard seeds and is very fiery when raw. However, when it is heated to this smoking stage, it loses a lot of the fire and takes on a delightful sweet quality.

Sweet & Sour Vegetables

This is a dish of Persian origin, not Chinese as it sounds. Eggplant is fried and mixed with tomatoes, mint, sugar, and vinegar.

NUTRITIONAL INFORMATION

Calories . . . . .218 Sugars 12g
Protein . . . . .3g Fat 17g
Carbohydrate . . .14g Saturates 3g

45 MINS   30 MINS

SERVES 4

INGREDIENTS

2 large eggplants

6 tbsp olive oil

4 garlic cloves, crushed

1 onion, cut into eight

4 large tomatoes, seeded and chopped

3 tbsp chopped mint

⅔ cup vegetable stock

4 tsp brown sugar

2 tbsp red wine vinegar

1 tsp chili flakes

salt and pepper

1 Using a sharp knife, cut the eggplants into cubes. Put them in a colander, sprinkle with plenty of salt, and leave to stand for 30 minutes. Rinse thoroughly under cold running water to remove all traces of the salt and drain thoroughly. This process removes all the bitter juices from the eggplants. Pat dry with absorbent paper towels.

2 Heat the oil in a large, heavy-bottomed skillet.

3 Add the eggplant and sauté over a medium heat, stirring, for 1–2 minutes, until beginning to color.

4 Stir in the garlic and onion wedges and cook, stirring constantly, for a further 2–3 minutes.

5 Stir in the tomatoes, mint, and vegetable stock. Lower the heat, cover with a lid, and simmer for about 15–20 minutes, or until the eggplant is tender.

6 Add the brown sugar, red wine vinegar, and chili flakes, then season with salt and pepper according to taste and cook for another 2–3 minutes, stirring constantly.

7 Transfer to a warmed serving dish, garnish the eggplant with fresh mint sprigs, and serve immediately.

Zucchini Curry

This delicious curry is spiced with fenugreek seeds, which have a beautiful aroma and a distinctive taste.

NUTRITIONAL INFORMATION

Calories 188   Sugars 5g
Protein ....3g   Fat 17g
Carbohydrate ....6g   Saturates 2g

🥘 20 MINS   🕐 15 MINS

SERVES 4

INGREDIENTS

6 tbsp vegetable oil

1 medium onion, finely chopped

3 fresh green chilies, finely chopped

1 tsp finely chopped fresh ginger

1 tsp crushed garlic

1 tsp chili powder

1 lb 2 oz zucchini, thinly sliced

2 tomatoes, sliced

fresh cilantro leaves,
    plus extra to garnish

2 tsp fenugreek seeds

chapatis, to serve

1 Heat the oil in a large, heavy-bottomed skillet.

2 Add the onion, fresh green chilies, ginger, garlic, and chili powder to the pan, stirring well to combine.

3 Add the sliced zucchini and the sliced tomatoes to the pan and stir-fry over a medium heat, for 5-7 minutes.

4 Add the cilantro leaves and fenugreek seeds to the zucchini mixture in the pan and stir-fry over a medium heat for 5 minutes, until the vegetables are tender.

5 Remove the pan from the heat and transfer the zucchini and fenugreek seed mixture to serving dishes. Garnish and serve hot with chapatis

VARIATION

You could use coriander seeds instead of the fenugreek seeds, if you prefer.

Chili Roast Potatoes

Small new potatoes are scrubbed and boiled in their skins, before being coated in a chili mixture and roasted to perfection in the oven.

NUTRITIONAL INFORMATION

Calories 178	Sugars 2g
Protein 2g	Fat 11g
Carbohydrate ...18g	Saturates 1g

5-10 MINS   30 MINS

SERVES 4

INGREDIENTS

1 lb 2 oz small new potatoes,
  scrubbed

⅔ cup vegetable oil

1 tsp chili powder

½ tsp caraway seeds

1 tsp salt

1 tbsp chopped basil

1 Cook the potatoes in a saucepan of boiling water for 10 minutes, then drain thoroughly.

2 Pour a little of the oil into a shallow roasting pan to coat the base. Heat the oil in a preheated oven at 400°F for 10 minutes. Add the potatoes to the pan and brush them with the hot oil.

3 In a small bowl, mix together the chili powder, caraway seeds, and salt. Sprinkle the mixture over the potatoes, turning to coat them all over.

4 Add the remaining oil to the pan and roast in the oven for about 15 minutes, or until the potatoes are cooked through.

5 Using a perforated spoon, remove the potatoes from the the oil, draining them well, and transfer them to a warmed serving dish. Sprinkle the chopped basil over the top and serve immediately.

VARIATION

Use any other spice of your choice, such as curry powder or paprika, for a variation in flavor.

Broccoli with Fluffy Eggs

Broccoli or cauliflower flowerets in a mustard sauce are topped with an egg yolk set in whisked egg white and finished off with grated cheese.

NUTRITIONAL INFORMATION

Calories	733	Sugars	........11g
Protein	........43g	Fat	..........53g
Carbohydrate	...23g	Saturates	......25g

🍲 10 MINS 🕐 15 MINS

SERVES 1

I N G R E D I E N T S

1½ cups broccoli or
  cauliflower flowerets

1 tbsp butter or margarine

2 tbsp all-purpose flour

⅔ cup milk

1 tbsp wholegrain mustard

dash of lemon juice

¾ cup grated sharp cheddar cheese

1 large egg, separated

salt and pepper

paprika, to garnish

1 Cook the broccoli or cauliflower in boiling lightly salted water for about 3–4 minutes, until tender, but still crisp.

2 Meanwhile, melt the butter or margarine in a small saucepan. Stir in the flour and cook, stirring constantly, for 1 minute. Gradually add the milk and bring to a boil, stirring constantly until thickened. Season to taste with salt and pepper. Stir in the mustard and lemon juice and simmer for 1–2 minutes.

3 Remove the sauce from the heat and stir in two-thirds of the grated cheese until melted.

4 Drain the broccoli or cauliflower very thoroughly and place on an ovenproof plate or dish. Pour the cheese sauce over the vegetables.

5 Whisk the egg white until very stiff and season lightly. Pile the egg white on top of the broccoli or cauliflower and make a well in the center.

6 Drop the egg yolk into the well in the egg white and sprinkle with the remaining cheese. Place under a preheated moderate broiler for 3–4 minutes, until the meringue is lightly browned and the cheese has melted. Serve immediately, sprinkled with paprika.

Spicy Lentils & Spinach

This is quite a filling accompaniment, so should be served with a fairly light main course.

NUTRITIONAL INFORMATION

Calories 340	Sugars 6g
Protein 21g	Fat 14g
Carbohydrate ...34g	Saturates 2g

 2 HRS 5 MINS 25 MINS

SERVES 4

INGREDIENTS

1¼ cups green split peas

2 lb spinach

4 tbsp vegetable oil

1 onion, halved and sliced

1 tsp grated fresh ginger

1 tsp ground cumin

½ tsp chili powder

½ tsp ground coriander

2 garlic cloves, crushed

1¼ cups vegetable stock

salt and pepper

fresh cilantro sprigs and
    lime wedges, to garnish

COOK'S TIP

Once the split peas have been added, stir occasionally to prevent them from sticking to the base of the pan.

1 Rinse the peas under cold running water. Transfer to a mixing bowl, cover with cold water and set aside to soak for 2 hours. Drain well.

2 Meanwhile, cook the spinach in a large saucepan, in just the water clinging to its leaves after washing, for 5 minutes until wilted. Drain well and roughly chop.

3 Heat the oil in a large saucepan and add the onion, spices, and garlic. Sauté, stirring constantly, for 2–3 minutes.

4 Add the peas and spinach and stir in the stock. Cover and simmer for 10–15 minutes, or until the peas are cooked and the liquid has been absorbed. Season with salt and pepper to taste, garnish, and serve.

Potatoes Dauphinois

This is a classic potato dish of layered potatoes, cream, garlic, onion, and cheese. Serve with bakes and casseroles.

NUTRITIONAL INFORMATION

Calories	580	Sugars	.........5g
Protein	........10g	Fat	..........46g
Carbohydrate	...34g	Saturates	......28g

25 MINS   1½ HOURS

SERVES 4

I N G R E D I E N T S

1 tbsp butter

1½ lb potatoes, sliced

2 garlic cloves, crushed

1 red onion, sliced

¾ cup grated Gruyère cheese

1¼ cups heavy cream

salt and pepper

1 Lightly grease a 4-cup shallow ovenproof dish with the butter.

2 Arrange a single layer of potato slices in the base of the prepared dish.

3 Top the potato slices with half the garlic, half the sliced red onion and one-third of the grated Gruyère cheese. Season to taste with a little salt and pepper.

4 Repeat the layers in exactly the same order, finishing with a layer of potatoes topped with grated cheese.

5 Pour the cream over the top of the potatoes and cook in a preheated oven at 350°F for 1½ hours, or until the potatoes are cooked through and the top

is browned and crispy. Serve immediately, straight from the dish.

COOK'S TIP

There are many versions of this classic potato dish, but the different recipes always contain heavy cream, making it a rich and very filling side dish or accompaniment. This recipe must be cooked in a shallow dish so there is plenty of crispy topping.

Steamed Vegetables

Serve these vegetables in their paper packages to retain the juices. The result is truly delicious.

NUTRITIONAL INFORMATION

Calories	64	Sugars	......9g
Protein	......2g	Fat	......0.5g
Carbohydrate	...12g	Saturates	.....0.1g

  25 MINS 20 MINS

SERVES 4

I N G R E D I E N T S

1 carrot, cut into sticks

1 fennel bulb, sliced

3½ oz zucchini, sliced

1 red bell pepper, seeded and sliced

4 small onions, halved

8 tbsp vermouth

4 tbsp lime juice

grated zest of 1 lime

pinch of paprika

4 sprigs tarragon

salt and pepper

tarragon sprigs, to garnish

COOK'S TIP

Vermouth is a fortified white wine flavored with various herbs and spices. It its available in both sweet and dry forms.

1 Place all of the vegetables in a large bowl and mix well.

2 Cut 4 large squares of baking parchment and place a quarter of the vegetables in the center of each. Bring the sides of the paper up and pinch together to make an open package.

3 Mix together the vermouth, lime juice, grated lime zest, and paprika and pour a quarter of the mixture into each package. Season to taste with salt and pepper and add a tarragon sprig to each. Fold and pinch the tops of the packages firmly together to seal, enclosing the vegetables completely.

4 Place the packages in a steamer, cover, and cook for 15–20 minutes, or until the vegetables are tender. Garnish and serve immediately.

Brindil Bhaji

This is one of the most delicious of the Indian bhaji dishes, and has a wonderful sweet spicy flavor.

 20 MINS   ⏱ 20 MINS

SERVES 4

I N G R E D I E N T S

1 lb 2 oz eggplant

2 tbsp vegetable ghee

1 onion, thinly sliced

2 garlic cloves, sliced

1 inch piece of fresh ginger, grated

½ tsp ground turmeric

1 dried red chili

½ tsp salt

14 oz can tomatoes

1 tsp garam masala

fresh cilantro sprigs,
    to garnish

1 Cut the eggplant slices into finger-width strips.

2 Heat the ghee in a saucepan. Add the onion and cook over a medium heat, stirring constantly, for 7–8 minutes, until very soft.

3 Add the garlic and eggplant strips, increase the heat, and cook for 2 minutes.

4 Stir in the ginger, turmeric, chili, salt, and tomatoes, together with their can juices. Use the back of a wooden spoon to break up the tomatoes. Simmer, uncovered, for 15–20 minutes, until the eggplant is very soft.

5 Stir in the garam masala. Simmer for 4–5 minutes more.

6 Transfer the brindil bhaji to a warmed serving plate, garnish with fresh cilantro sprigs, and serve immediately.

VARIATION

Other vegetables can be used instead of the eggplant. Try zucchini, potatoes, or bell peppers, or any combination of these vegetables, using the same sauce.

Vegetables in Saffron Sauce

Here is a quick and simple, delicately spiced, and delicious way to cook eggplant and onion.

NUTRITIONAL INFORMATION

Calories	350	Sugars	.......14g
Protein	.........3g	Fat	.........31g
Carbohydrate	...15g	Saturates	......14g

🍲 25 MINS   🕐 20 MINS

SERVES 4

I N G R E D I E N T S

pinch of saffron strands,
   finely crushed

1 tbsp boiling water

1 large eggplant

3 tbsp vegetable oil

1 large onion, coarsely chopped

2 garlic cloves, crushed

1-inch piece of fresh
   ginger, chopped

1½ tbsp mild or medium curry paste

1 tsp cumin seeds

⅔ cup heavy cream

⅔ cup strained plain yogurt

2 tbsp mango chutney,
   chopped if necessary

salt and pepper

COOK'S TIP

You will find that yogurt adds a creamy texture and pleasant tartness to this sauce. If you are worried about it curdling on heating, add a tablespoonful at a time and stir it in well before adding another.

1 Place the saffron in a small bowl, add the boiling water and set aside to infuse for 5 minutes. Cut the eggplant lengthwise into quarters, then into ½-inch thick slices.

2 Heat the oil in a large skillet, add the onion, and cook gently for 3 minutes. Stir in the eggplant, garlic, ginger, curry paste, and cumin and cook gently for 3 minutes.

3 Stir in the saffron water, cream, yogurt, and chutney and cook, stirring frequently, for 8–10 minutes, until the eggplant is cooked through and tender. Season with salt and pepper to taste and serve hot.

Gingered Potatoes

This is a simple spicy dish which is ideal with a plain main course.
The cashews and celery add extra crunch.

NUTRITIONAL INFORMATION

Calories	325	Sugars 1g
Protein	.........5g	Fat 21g
Carbohydrate	...30g	Saturates 9g

 20 MINS   30 MINS

SERVES 4

I N G R E D I E N T S

1½ lb potatoes, cubed

2 tbsp vegetable oil

2 inch piece of fresh ginger, grated

1 fresh green chili, chopped

1 celery stalk, chopped

¼ cup cashews

few strands of saffron

3 tbsp boiling water

¼ cup butter

celery leaves, to garnish

1 Cook the potatoes in a saucepan of boiling water for 10 minutes, then drain thoroughly.

2 Heat the oil in a heavy-bottomed skillet and add the potatoes. Cook over a medium heat, stirring constantly, for 3-4 minutes.

3 Add the grated ginger, chili, celery, and cashews and cook for 1 minute.

4 Meanwhile, place the saffron strands in a small bowl. Add the boiling water and set aside to soak for 5 minutes.

5 Add the butter to the pan, lower the heat, and stir in the saffron mixture. Cook over a low heat for 10 minutes, or until the potatoes are tender.

6 Transfer to a warm serving dish, garnish the gingered potatoes with the celery leaves, and serve immediately.

COOK'S TIP

Use a non-stick, heavy-bottomed skillet because the potato mixture is fairly dry and may stick to an ordinary pan.

Greek Green Beans

This dish contains many Greek flavors, such as lemon, garlic, oregano, and olives, for a really flavorful recipe.

NUTRITIONAL INFORMATION

Calories 115   Sugars 4g
Protein . . . . .6g   Fat 4g
Carbohydrate . . .15g   Saturates 0.6g

 5 MINS   1 HR 5 MINS

SERVES 4

INGREDIENTS

14 oz can navy beans, drained

1 tbsp olive oil

3 garlic cloves, crushed

2 cups vegetable stock

1 bay leaf

2 sprigs oregano

1 tbsp tomato paste

juice of 1 lemon

1 small red onion, chopped

1 oz pitted black olives, halved

salt and pepper

1 Put the navy beans in a large flameproof casserole.

2 Add the olive oil and crushed garlic and cook over a moderate heat, stirring occasionally, for 4–5 minutes, or until the garlic is beginning to color.

3 Add the stock, bay leaf, oregano, tomato paste, lemon juice, and red onion, cover, and simmer for about 1 hour, or until the sauce has thickened.

4 Stir in the olives, season with salt and pepper to taste, and serve.

COOK'S TIP

This dish may be made ahead of time and served cold, but not chilled, with crusty bread, if preferred.

Curried Okra

Okra, also known as bhindi and ladies' fingers, is a favorite Indian vegetable. It is now sold in many supermarkets.

NUTRITIONAL INFORMATION

Calories ....156 Sugars 5g
Protein ....5g Fat 12g
Carbohydrate ....6g Saturates 2g

 10 MINS   20 MINS

SERVES 4

I N G R E D I E N T S

1 lb 2 oz fresh okra

4 tbsp vegetable ghee or oil

1 bunch green onions, sliced

2 garlic cloves, crushed

2-inch piece of fresh
    ginger, chopped

1 tsp minced chili

1½ tsp ground cumin

1 tsp ground coriander

1 tsp ground turmeric

8 oz can diced tomatoes

⅔ cup vegetable stock

salt and pepper

1 tsp garam masala

chopped cilantro,
    to garnish

1 Wash the okra, trim off the stalks, and pat dry. Heat the ghee or oil in a large pan, add the green onions, garlic, ginger, and chili and fry over a low heat, stirring frequently, for 1 minute.

2 Stir in the spices and fry gently for 30 seconds, then add the tomatoes, stock, and okra. Season with salt and pepper to taste and simmer, stirring and turning the mixture occasionally, for about 15 minutes, until the okra is cooked, but still a little crisp.

3 Sprinkle with the garam masala, taste and adjust the seasoning, if necessary. Transfer to a warm serving dish, garnish with the chopped cilantro, and serve hot.

COOK'S TIP

If preferred, slice the okra into rings, add to the mixture (step 2), cover and cook until tender-crisp, stirring occasionally. When you buy fresh okra, make sure that the pods are not shrivelled or do not have any brown spots.

Potato Crumble

This is a delicious way to liven up mashed potato by topping it with a crumble mixture flavored with herbs, mustard, and onion.

NUTRITIONAL INFORMATION

Calories	.451	Sugars	.5g
Protein	.13g	Fat	.19g
Carbohydrate	.60g	Saturates	.12g

 25 MINS   30 MINS

SERVES 4

INGREDIENTS

2 lb russet potatoes, diced

2 tbsp butter

2 tbsp milk

½ cup grated sharp
  cheese or blue cheese

CRUMBLE TOPPING

3 tbsp butter

1 onion, cut into chunks

1 garlic clove, crushed

1 tbsp wholegrain mustard

3 cups fresh whole wheat breadcrumbs

2 tbsp chopped parsley

salt and pepper

1 Cook the potatoes in a pan of lightly salted boiling water for 10 minutes, or until cooked through.

2 Meanwhile, make the crumble topping. Melt the butter in a skillet. Add the onion, garlic, and mustard and fry over a medium heat, stirring constantly, for 5 minutes, until the onion has softened.

3 Put the breadcrumbs in a mixing bowl and stir in the fried onion and chopped parsley. Season to taste with salt and pepper.

4 Drain the potatoes thoroughly and place them in another mixing bowl. Add the butter and milk, then mash until smooth. Stir in the grated cheese while the potato is still hot.

5 Spoon the mashed potato into a shallow ovenproof dish and sprinkle with the crumble topping.

6 Cook in a preheated oven at 400°F for 10–15 minutes, until the crumble topping is golden brown and crunchy. Serve immediately.

COOK'S TIP

For extra crunch, add freshly cooked vegetables, such as celery and bell peppers, to the mashed potato in step 4.

Fried Cauliflower

A dry dish flavored with a few herbs, this is a very versatile accompaniment to curries and rice dishes.

NUTRITIONAL INFORMATION

Calories ....135 Sugars 3g
Protein ....4g Fat 12g
Carbohydrate ....4g Saturates 1g

 5 MINS   20 MINS

SERVES 4

I N G R E D I E N T S

4 tbsp vegetable oil

½ tsp onion seeds

½ tsp mustard seeds

½ tsp fenugreek seeds

4 dried red chilies

1 small cauliflower, cut into small flowerets

1 tsp salt

1 green bell pepper, seeded and diced

1 Heat the oil in a large, heavy-bottomed saucepan over a moderate heat.

2 Add the onion seeds, mustard seeds, fenugreek seeds, and the dried red chilies to the pan, stirring to mix.

3 Reduce the heat and gradually add all of the cauliflower and the salt to the pan. Stir-fry the mixture for 7–10 minutes, thoroughly coating the cauliflower in the spices.

4 Add the diced green bell pepper to the pan and stir-fry the over a low heat for 3–5 minutes.

5 Transfer the spicy fried cauliflower to a warmed serving dish and serve hot.

Lemon Beans

Use a variety of beans if possible, although this recipe is perfectly acceptable with just one type of bean.

NUTRITIONAL INFORMATION

Calories 285	Sugars 6g	
Protein 9g	Fat 19g	
Carbohydrate ...18g	Saturates 6g	

 5 MINS   20 MINS

SERVES 4

INGREDIENTS

2 lb mixed green beans, such as
    fava beans, green beans, and
    string beans

5 tbsp butter or margarine

4 tsp all-purpose flour

1¼ cups vegetable stock

5 tbsp dry white wine

6 tbsp light cream

3 tbsp chopped mixed herbs

2 tbsp lemon juice

grated zest of 1 lemon

salt and pepper

VARIATION

Use lime zest and juice instead of lemon for an alternative citrus flavor. Replace the light cream with plain yogurt for a healthier version of this dish.

1 Cook the beans in a saucepan of boiling salted water for 10 minutes, or until tender. Drain and place in a warmed serving dish.

2 Meanwhile, melt the butter in a saucepan. Add the flour and cook, stirring constantly, for 1 minute. Remove the pan from the heat and gradually stir in the stock and wine. Return the pan to the heat and bring to a boil, stirring.

3 Remove the pan from the heat once again and stir in the light cream, mixed herbs, lemon juice, and zest. Season with salt and pepper to taste. Pour the sauce over the beans, mixing well. Serve immediately.

Spanish Potatoes

This type of dish is usually served as part of a Spanish *tapas*, and is delicious with salad or a simply cooked main course dish.

NUTRITIONAL INFORMATION

Calories	176	Sugars	.........9g
Protein	.........5g	Fat	...........6g
Carbohydrate	...27g	Saturates	.......1g

20 MINS   35 MINS

SERVES 4

I N G R E D I E N T S

2 tbsp olive oil

1 lb 2 oz small new potatoes, halved

1 onion, halved and sliced

1 green bell pepper, seeded and
   cut into strips

1 tsp chili powder

1 tsp prepared mustard

1¼ cups strained tomatoes

1¼ cups vegetable stock

salt and pepper

chopped parsley, to garnish

1 Heat the olive oil in a large heavy-bottomed skillet. Add the halved new potatoes and the sliced onion and cook, stirring frequently, for 4–5 minutes, until the onion slices are soft and translucent.

2 Add the green bell pepper strips, chili powder, and mustard to the pan and cook for 2–3 minutes more.

3 Stir the strained tomatoes and the vegetable stock into the pan and bring to a boil. Reduce the heat and simmer for about 25 minutes, or until the potatoes are tender.

4 Transfer the potatoes to a warmed serving dish. Sprinkle the parsley over the top and serve immediately. Alternatively, leave the Spanish potatoes to cool completely and serve cold, at room temperature.

COOK'S TIP

In Spain, tapas are traditionally served with a glass of chilled sherry or some other aperitif.

Okra Bhaji

This is a very mild-tasting, rich curry, which would be an ideal accompaniment to a tomato-based main-course curry.

NUTRITIONAL INFORMATION

Calories 173	Sugars 11g
Protein 6g	Fat 11g
Carbohydrate ...13g	Saturates 5g

 25 MINS   35 MINS

SERVES 4

INGREDIENTS

1 tbsp sunflower oil

1 tsp black mustard seeds

1 tsp cumin seeds

1 tsp coriander seeds, ground

½ tsp turmeric

1 green chili, seeded and finely chopped

1 red onion, finely sliced

2 garlic cloves, crushed

1 orange bell pepper, seeded and
   thinly sliced

1 lb 2 oz okra, trimmed and blanched

1 cup vegetable juice

⅔ cup light cream

1 tbsp lemon juice

salt

COOK'S TIP

Okra, or lady's fingers, have a unique glutinous quality which, when they are added to curries and casseroles, disperses in the sauce and thickens it wonderfully—and naturally!

1 Heat the oil in a preheated wok or large heavy-bottomed skillet. Add the mustard seeds and cover the pan until they start to pop. Stir in the cumin seeds, ground coriander, turmeric, and chili. Stir constantly for 1 minute, until the spices are giving off their aroma.

2 Add the onion, garlic, and bell pepper, and cook, stirring frequently, for about 5 minutes, until soft.

3 Add the okra to the pan and combine all the ingredients thoroughly.

4 Pour in the vegetable juice, bring to a boil, and cook over a high heat, stirring occasionally, for 5 minutes.

5 When most of the liquid has evaporated, check the seasoning.

6 Add the cream, bring to a boil again and continue to cook the mixture over a high heat for about 12 minutes, until almost dry.

7 Sprinkle over the lemon juice and serve immediately.

Carrot & Orange Bake

Poppy seeds add texture and flavor to this recipe and counteract the slightly sweet flavor of the carrots.

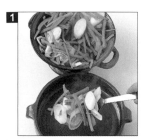

NUTRITIONAL INFORMATION

Calories	138	Sugars	........31g
Protein	.........2g	Fat	...........1g
Carbohydrate	...32g	Saturates	.....0.2g

20 MINS   40 MINS

SERVES 4

INGREDIENTS

1½ lb carrots, cut into thin strips

1 leek, sliced

1¼ cups fresh orange juice

2 tbsp honey

1 garlic clove, crushed

1 tsp mixed spice

2 tsp chopped thyme

1 tbsp poppy seeds

salt and pepper

thyme sprigs and orange zest,
   to garnish

1 Cook the carrots and leek in a saucepan of boiling lightly salted water for 5–6 minutes. Drain well and transfer to a shallow ovenproof dish until required.

2 Mix together the orange juice, honey, garlic, mixed spice, and thyme and pour the mixture over the vegetables. Season with salt and pepper to taste.

3 Cover the dish and cook in a preheated oven at 350°F for 30 minutes, or until the vegetables are tender.

4 Remove the lid and sprinkle with poppy seeds. Transfer to a warmed serving dish, garnish with fresh thyme sprigs and orange zest, and serve.

COOK'S TIP

Lemon or lime juice could be used instead of the orange juice, if you prefer. Garnish with lemon or lime zest.

Palak Paneer

Paneer, curd cheese, figures widely on Indian menus. It is combined with all sorts of ingredients, but most popularly with spinach and vegetables.

NUTRITIONAL INFORMATION

Calories 287	Sugars 7g
Protein 12g	Fat 18g
Carbohydrate ...22g	Saturates 11g

20 MINS   40 MINS

SERVES 6

INGREDIENTS

2 tbsp vegetable ghee

1 onion, sliced

1 garlic clove, crushed

1 dried red chili

1 tsp ground turmeric

1 lb 2 oz potatoes, cut into
   1-inch cubes

14 oz can tomatoes, drained

⅔ cup water

8 oz fresh spinach

2 cups curd cheese, cut into
   1-inch cubes

1 tsp garam masala

1 tbsp chopped cilantro

1 tbsp chopped parsley

salt and pepper

naan bread, to serve

VARIATION

Fresh Italian pecorino cheese can be used as a substitute for Indian paneer.

1 Heat the ghee in a saucepan. Add the onion and cook over a low heat, stirring frequently, for 10 minutes, until very soft. Add the garlic and chili and cook for a further 5 minutes.

2 Add the turmeric, salt, potatoes, canned tomatoes, and water and bring to a boil.

3 Simmer for 10–15 minutes, until the potatoes are cooked.

4 Stir in the spinach, cheese cubes, garam masala, cilantro, and parsley to taste.

5 Simmer for another 5 minutes and season well. Serve with naan bread.

Mixed Vegetables

This is one of the best Indian vegetarian recipes. You can make it with any vegetables you choose, but the combination below is ideal.

NUTRITIONAL INFORMATION

Calories 785   Sugars 20g
Protein ....6g   Fat 70g
Carbohydrate ...35g   Saturates 7g

25 MINS   45 MINS

SERVES 4

INGREDIENTS

1¼ cups vegetable oil

1 tsp mustard seeds

1 tsp onion seeds

½ tsp white cumin seeds

3–4 curry leaves, chopped

1 lb 2 oz onions, finely chopped

3 medium tomatoes, chopped

½ red and ½ green bell pepper, seeded
   and sliced

1 tsp finely chopped fresh ginger

1 tsp crushed garlic

1 tsp chili powder

¼ tsp turmeric

1 tsp salt

2 cups water

2 medium potatoes, cut into pieces

½ cauliflower, cut into small flowerets

4 medium carrots, sliced

3 fresh green chilies, finely chopped

cilantro leaves

1 tbsp lemon juice

1 Heat the oil in a large saucepan. Add the mustard, onion, and white cumin seeds, together with the curry leaves, and fry until they turn a shade darker.

2 Add the onions to the pan and fry over a medium heat, stirring frequently, until golden brown.

3 Add the tomatoes and bell peppers and stir-fry for about 5 minutes.

4 Add the ginger, garlic, chili powder, turmeric, and salt and mix well.

5 Add 1¼ cups of the water, cover, and simmer, stirring occasionally, for 10–12 minutes.

6 Add the potatoes, cauliflower, carrots, green chilies, and cilantro leaves and stir-fry for about 5 minutes.

7 Add the remaining ⅔ cup of water and the lemon juice, stirring to combine. Cover and simmer, stirring occasionally, for 15 minutes .

8 Transfer the mixed vegetables to serving plates and serve immediately.

Cheese & Potato Layer Bake

This really is a great side dish, perfect for serving with main meals cooked in the oven.

NUTRITIONAL INFORMATION

Calories	295	Sugars	.........5g
Protein	........13g	Fat	..........17g
Carbohydrate	...24g	Saturates	......11g

 20 MINS   1½ HOURS

SERVES 4

INGREDIENTS

1 lb 2 oz potatoes

1 leek, sliced

3 garlic cloves, crushed

½ cup grated cheddar cheese

½ cup grated mozzarella cheese

⅓ cup grated Parmesan cheese

2 tbsp chopped parsley

⅔ cup light cream

⅔ cup milk

salt and pepper

chopped flat-leaf parsley, to garnish

1 Cook the potatoes in a saucepan of boiling salted water for 10 minutes. Drain well.

2 Cut the potatoes into thin slices. Arrange a layer of potatoes in the base of an ovenproof dish. Layer with a little of the leek, garlic, cheeses, and parsley. Season to taste.

3 Repeat the layers until all of the ingredients have been used, finishing with a layer of cheese. Mix the cream and milk together, season with salt and pepper to taste, and pour over the potato layers.

4 Cook in a preheated oven at 325°F for 1–1¼ hours, or until the cheese is golden brown and bubbling and the potatoes are cooked through and tender.

5 Garnish with chopped fresh flat-leaf parsley and serve immediately.

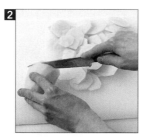  

COOK'S TIP

Potatoes make a very good basis for a vegetable accompaniment. They are a good source of complex carbohydrate and contain a number of vitamins. From the point of view of flavor, they combine well with a vast range of other ingredients.

Spinach & Cauliflower Bhaji

This excellent vegetable dish goes well with most Indian food—and it is simple and quick-cooking, too.

NUTRITIONAL INFORMATION

Calories . . . . .212 Sugars 12g
Protein . . . . .10g Fat 13g
Carbohydrate . . .14g Saturates 2g

 10 MINS   25 MINS

SERVES 4

I N G R E D I E N T S

1 cauliflower

1 lb 2 oz fresh spinach, washed,
  or 8 oz frozen spinach, thawed

4 tbsp vegetable ghee or oil

2 large onions, coarsely chopped

2 garlic cloves, crushed

1-inch piece of fresh
  ginger, chopped

1¼ tsp cayenne pepper,
  or to taste

1 tsp ground cumin

1 tsp ground turmeric

2 tsp ground coriander

14 oz can diced tomatoes

1¼ cups vegetable stock

salt and pepper

1 Divide the cauliflower into small flowerets, discarding the hard central stalk. Trim the stalks from the spinach leaves. Heat the ghee or oil in a large saucepan, add the onions and cauliflower flowerets, and fry over a low heat, stirring frequently, for about 3 minutes.

2 Add the garlic, ginger, and spices and cook gently, stirring occasionally, for 1 minute. Stir in the tomatoes and the vegetable stock and season to taste with salt and pepper. Bring to a boil, cover, reduce the heat and simmer gently for 8 minutes.

3 Add the spinach to the pan, stirring and turning to wilt the leaves. Cover and simmer gently, stirring frequently, for about 8–10 minutes, until the spinach and the cauliflower is tender. Transfer to a warmed serving dish and serve hot.

COOK'S TIP

When buying cauliflower, look for firm, white heads with no discoloration or signs of wilting.

Long Beans with Tomatoes

Indian meals often need some green vegetables to complement the spicy dishes and to set off the rich sauces.

NUTRITIONAL INFORMATION

Calories	76	Sugars 3g
Protein	. . . . .2g	Fat 6g
Carbohydrate	. . . .4g	Saturates 3g

 15 MINS   25 MINS

SERVES 6

INGREDIENTS

1 lb 2 oz green beans, cut into
  2-inch lengths

2 tbsp vegetable ghee

1-inch piece of fresh ginger, grated

1 garlic clove, crushed

1 tsp turmeric

½ tsp cayenne

1 tsp ground coriander

4 tomatoes, peeled, seeded, and diced

⅔ cup vegetable stock

1 Blanch the beans briefly in boiling water, drain, refresh under cold running water, and drain again.

2 Melt the ghee in a large saucepan over a moderate heat. Add the grated ginger and crushed garlic, stir, and add the turmeric, cayenne, and ground coriander. Stir over a low heat for about 1 minute, until fragrant.

3 Add the diced tomatoes, tossing them until they are thoroughly coated in the spice mix.

4 Add the vegetable stock to the pan, bring to a boil and cook over a medium-high heat, stirring occasionally, for about 10 minutes, until the sauce has thickened.

5 Add the beans, reduce the heat to moderate, and heat through, stirring constantly, for 5 minutes.

6 Transfer to a warmed serving dish and serve immediately.

COOK'S TIP

Ginger graters are an invaluable piece of equipment to have when cooking Indian food. These small flat graters, made of either bamboo or china, can be held directly over the pan while you grate.

Soufaléd Cheesy Potato Fries

These small potato chunks are mixed in a creamy cheese sauce and fried in oil until deliciously golden brown.

NUTRITIONAL INFORMATION

Calories	.614	Sugars	.2g
Protein	.12g	Fat	.46g
Carbohydrate	.40g	Saturates	.18g

20 MINS 25 MINS

SERVES 4

I N G R E D I E N T S

2 lb potatoes, cut
    into chunks

⅔ cup heavy cream

¾ cup grated Gruyère cheese

pinch of cayenne pepper

2 egg whites

oil, for deep-frying

salt and pepper

chopped flat-leaf parsley and grated
    cheese, to garnish

1 Cook the potatoes in a saucepan of boiling lightly salted water for about 10 minutes. Drain thoroughly and pat dry with absorbent paper towels. Set aside until required.

2 Mix the heavy cream and Gruyère cheese in a large bowl. Stir in the cayenne pepper and season with salt and pepper to taste.

3 Whisk the egg whites until stiff peaks form. Gently fold into the cheese mixture until fully incorporated.

4 Add the cooked potatoes, turning to coat thoroughly in the mixture.

5 Heat the oil for deep-frying to 350°F or until a cube of bread browns in 30 seconds. Remove the potatoes from the cheese mixture with a perforated spoon and cook in the oil, in batches, if necessary, for 3–4 minutes, or until golden.

6 Transfer the potatoes to a warmed serving dish and garnish with parsley and grated cheese. Serve immediately.

VARIATION

Add other flavorings, such as grated nutmeg or curry powder, to the cream and cheese.

Easy Cauliflower & Broccoli

Whole baby cauliflowers are used in this recipe. Try to find them if you can; if not, use large bunches of flowerets.

NUTRITIONAL INFORMATION

Calories 433	Sugars 2g	
Protein 8g	Fat 44g	
Carbohydrate 3g	Saturates 9g	

 10 MINS   20 MINS

SERVES 4

INGREDIENTS

2 baby cauliflowers

8 oz broccoli

salt and pepper

SAUCE

8 tbsp olive oil

4 tbsp butter or margarine

2 tsp grated fresh ginger

juice and zest of 2 lemons

5 tbsp chopped cilantro

5 tbsp grated cheddar cheese

1 Using a sharp knife, cut the cauliflowers in half and the broccoli into very large flowerets.

2 Cook the cauliflower and broccoli in a saucepan of boiling salted water for 10 minutes. Drain well, transfer to a shallow ovenproof dish, and keep warm until required.

3 To make the sauce, put the oil and butter or margarine in a pan and heat gently until the butter melts. Add the grated fresh ginger, lemon juice, lemon zest, and cilantro and simmer for 2–3 minutes, stirring occasionally.

4 Season the sauce with salt and pepper to taste, then pour over the vegetables in the dish and sprinkle the cheese on top.

5 Cook under a preheated hot broiler for 2–3 minutes, or until the cheese is bubbling and golden. Leave to cool for 1–2 minutes and then serve.

COOK'S TIP

Lime or orange could be used instead of the lemon for a fruity and refreshing sauce.

Saffron-flavored Potatoes

Saffron is made from the dried stigma of the crocus and is native to Greece. It is very expensive, but only a very small amount is needed.

NUTRITIONAL INFORMATION

Calories 197	Sugars 4g
Protein 4g	Fat 6g
Carbohydrate ...30g	Saturates 1g

 25 MINS   40 MINS

SERVES 4

INGREDIENTS

1 tsp saffron strands

6 tbsp boiling water

1½ lb potatoes, unpeeled and
    cut into wedges

1 red onion, cut into 8 wedges

2 garlic cloves, crushed

1 tbsp white wine vinegar

2 tbsp olive oil

1 tbsp wholegrain mustard

5 tbsp vegetable stock

5 tbsp dry white wine

2 tsp chopped rosemary

salt and pepper

1 Place the saffron strands in a small bowl and pour over the boiling water. Set aside to soak for about 10 minutes.

2 Place the potatoes in a roasting pan, together with the red onion wedges and crushed garlic.

3 Add the vinegar, oil, mustard, vegetable stock, white wine, rosemary, and saffron water to the potatoes and onion in the pan. Season to taste with salt and pepper.

4 Cover the roasting pan with foil and bake in a preheated oven at 400°F for 30 minutes.

5 Remove the foil and cook the potatoes for another 10 minutes until crisp, browned, and cooked through. Serve hot.

COOK'S TIP

Turmeric may be used instead of saffron to provide the yellow color in this recipe. However, it is worth using saffron, if possible, for the lovely nutty flavor it gives a dish.

Eggplant Bhaji

The panch poran spice mix used here is one of the many traditional spice mixes used in Indian cooking and originated in the Bengal state.

NUTRITIONAL INFORMATION

Calories	170	Sugars	4g
Protein	2g	Fat	17g
Carbohydrate	4g	Saturates	2g

 5 MINS   25 MINS

SERVES 4

I N G R E D I E N T S

2 tbsp mustard oil

4 tbsp sunflower oil

1 tsp panch poran spice mix
(see Cook's Tip p.414)

6 baby eggplants,
quartered, or 2 eggplants,
cut into 1-inch cubes

¼ tsp cayenne

1 tsp coriander seeds, ground

½ tsp turmeric

7 oz can of diced tomatoes
in juice

½ tsp sugar

2 tsp lime juice

salt

1 Heat the mustard oil in a wok or large skillet until it just starts to smoke. Reduce the heat and add the sunflower oil. Add the panch poran mix to the pan, stir once, and add all the eggplant.

2 Add the cayenne, coriander, and turmeric, and stir over a high heat for 2–3 minutes, until the eggplant is sealed on all sides.

3 Add the chopped tomatoes, together with their can juices, to the pan and bring to a boil.

4 Simmer for 15 minutes, or until the bhaji is nearly dry. Stir once or twice. Remove from the heat and stir in the sugar, a pinch of salt, and the lime juice.

5 Transfer to a warmed serving dish, and serve immediately.

COOK'S TIP

Most Asian cooks do not salt eggplant. The eggplants available for most of the year are so fresh that they do not have any bitter juices, especially the plump, shiny ones that have been left on the plant until they are sweet.

Candied Sweet Potatoes

A taste of the Caribbean is introduced in this recipe, where sweet potatoes are cooked with sugar and lime with a dash of brandy.

NUTRITIONAL INFORMATION

Calories 348	Sugars 21g
Protein 3g	Fat 9g
Carbohydrate . . .67g	Saturates 6g

 15 MINS   25 MINS

SERVES 4

I N G R E D I E N T S

1½ lb sweet potatoes, sliced

3 tbsp butter

1 tbsp lime juice

½ cup soft dark brown sugar

1 tbsp brandy

grated zest of 1 lime

lime wedges, to garnish

1 Cook the sweet potatoes in a saucepan of boiling water for about 5 minutes. Test the potatoes have softened by pricking with a fork. Remove the sweet potatoes with a perforated spoon and drain thoroughly.

2 Melt the butter in a large skillet. Add the lime juice and brown sugar and heat gently, stirring, to dissolve the sugar.

3 Stir the sweet potatoes and the brandy into the sugar and lime juice mixture. Cook over a low heat for about 10 minutes or until the potato slices are cooked through.

4 Sprinkle the lime zest over the top of the sweet potatoes and mix well.

5 Transfer the candied sweet potatoes to a serving plate. Garnish with lime wedges and serve immediately.

COOK'S TIP

Sweet potatoes have a pinkish skin and either white, yellow, or orange flesh. It doesn't matter which type is used for this dish.

Spicy Corn

This dish is an ideal accompaniment to a wide range of Indian dishes and would also go well with a Western-style casserole.

NUTRITIONAL INFORMATION

Calories	162	Sugars	.........6g
Protein	.........2g	Fat	...........11g
Carbohydrate	...15g	Saturates	.......7g

 10 MINS   10 MINS

SERVES 4

I N G R E D I E N T S

1 cup canned or
   frozen corn

1 tsp ground cumin

1 tsp crushed garlic

1 tsp ground coriander

1 tsp salt

2 fresh green chilies

1 medium onion, finely chopped

3 tbsp unsalted butter

4 red chilies, crushed

½ tsp lemon juice

fresh cilantro leaves

1 Thaw or drain the corn, if using canned corn, and set aside.

2 Place the ground cumin, garlic, ground coriander, salt, 1 fresh green chili, and the onion in a mortar or a food processor and grind to form a smooth paste.

3 Heat the butter in a large skillet. Add the onion and spice mixture to the pan and fry over a medium heat, stirring occasionally, for about 5–7 minutes.

4 Add the crushed red chilies to the mixture in the pan and stir to combine.

5 Add the corn to the pan and stir-fry for a 2 minutes more.

6 Add the remaining green chili, lemon juice, and the fresh cilantro leaves to the pan, stirring occasionally to combine.

7 Transfer the spicy corn mixture to a warm serving dish. Garnish with fresh cilantro and serve hot.

COOK'S TIP

Coriander is available ground or as seeds and is one of the essential ingredients in Indian cooking. Coriander seeds are often dry roasted before use to develop their flavor.

Potatoes & Peas

This quick and easy-to-prepare Indian dish can be served either as an accompaniment or on its own with chapatis.

NUTRITIONAL INFORMATION

Calories	434	Sugars	.........6g
Protein	.........5g	Fat	..........35g
Carbohydrate	...28g	Saturates	.......4g

  15 MINS   25 MINS

SERVES 4

I N G R E D I E N T S

⅔ cup oil

3 medium onions, sliced

1 tsp crushed garlic

1 tsp finely chopped fresh ginger

1 tsp chili powder

½ tsp turmeric

1 tsp salt

2 fresh green chilies, finely chopped

1¼ cups water

3 medium potatoes

1 cup peas

cilantro leaves and chopped red
   chilies, to garnish

1 Heat the oil in a large, heavy-bottomed skillet.

2 Add the onions to the skillet and fry, stirring occasionally, until the onions are golden brown.

3 Mix together the garlic, ginger, chili powder, turmeric, salt, and fresh green chilies. Add the spice mixture to the onions in the pan.

4 Stir in ⅔ cup of the water, cover, and cook until the onions are cooked through.

5 Meanwhile, cut the potatoes into six slices each, using a sharp knife.

6 Add the potato slices to the mixture in the pan and stir-fry for 5 minutes.

7 Add the peas and the remaining ⅔ cup of the water to the pan, cover, and cook for 7–10 minutes.

8 Transfer the potatoes and peas to serving plates and serve, garnished with fresh cilantro leaves.

COOK'S TIP

Turmeric is an aromatic root which is dried and ground to produce the distinctive bright yellow-orange powder used in many Indian dishes. It has a warm, aromatic smell and a full, somewhat musty taste.

Vegetable Galette

This is a dish of eggplant and zucchini layered with a quick tomato sauce and melted cheese.

NUTRITIONAL INFORMATION

Calories 412   Sugars 12g
Protein . . . . .13g   Fat 34g
Carbohydrate . . .13g   Saturates 11g

  40 MINS   1¼ HOURS

SERVES 4

INGREDIENTS

2 large eggplants, sliced

4 zucchini, sliced

2 x 14 oz cans diced
   tomatoes, drained

2 tbsp tomato paste

2 garlic cloves, crushed

4 tbsp olive oil

1 tsp sugar

2 tbsp chopped basil

olive oil, for frying

8 oz mozzarella cheese, sliced

salt and pepper

basil leaves, to garnish

1 Put the eggplant slices in a colander and sprinkle with salt. Leave to stand for 30 minutes, then rinse well under cold water and drain. Thinly slice the zucchini.

2 Meanwhile, put the tomatoes, tomato paste, garlic, olive oil, sugar, and chopped basil into a pan and simmer for 20 minutes, or until reduced by half. Season to taste with salt and pepper.

3 Heat 2 tablespoons of olive oil in a large skillet and cook the eggplant slices for 2–3 minutes until just beginning to brown. Remove from the pan.

4 Add another 2 tablespoons of oil to the pan and fry the zucchini slices until browned.

5 Lay half of the eggplant slices in the base of an ovenproof dish. Top with half of the tomato sauce and the zucchini and then half of the mozzarella.

6 Repeat the layers and bake in a preheated oven at 350°F for 45–50 minutes, or until the vegetables are tender. Garnish with basil leaves and serve.

Spiced Potatoes & Spinach

This is a classic Indian accompaniment for many different curries or plainer main vegetable dishes. It is very quick to cook.

NUTRITIONAL INFORMATION

Calories	176	Sugars 4g
Protein	. . . . .6g	Fat 9g
Carbohydrate	. . .18g	Saturates 1g

 10 MINS   20–25 MINS

SERVES 4

I N G R E D I E N T S

3 tbsp vegetable oil

1 red onion, sliced

2 garlic cloves, crushed

½ tsp chili powder

2 tsp ground coriander

1 tsp ground cumin

⅔ cup vegetable stock

10½ oz potatoes, diced

1 lb 2 oz baby spinach

1 red chili, sliced

salt and pepper

1 Heat the oil in a heavy-bottomed skillet. Add the onion and garlic and sauté over a medium heat, stirring occasionally, for 2–3 minutes.

2 Stir in the chili powder, ground coriander and cumin and cook, stirring constantly, for another 30 seconds.

3 Add the vegetable stock, diced potatoes, and spinach and bring to a boil. Reduce the heat, cover the skillet, and simmer for about 10 minutes, or until the potatoes are cooked through and tender.

4 Uncover, season to taste with salt and pepper, add the chili, and cook for 2–3 minutes more. Transfer to a warmed serving dish and serve immediately.

COOK'S TIP

Besides adding extra color to a dish, red onions have a sweeter, less pungent flavor than other varieties.

Tamarind Chutney

A mouth-watering chutney which is extremely popular all over India and served with various vegetarian snacks, particularly with samosas.

NUTRITIONAL INFORMATION

Calories	8	Sugars	.........1g
Protein	........0.3g	Fat	..........0.3g
Carbohydrate	....1g	Saturates	.......0g

 10 MINS   0 MINS

SERVES 6

INGREDIENTS

2 tbsp tamarind paste

5 tbsp water

1 tsp chili powder

½ tsp ground ginger

½ tsp salt

1 tsp sugar

finely chopped cilantro leaves,
 to garnish

COOK'S TIP

Vegetable dishes are often given a sharp, sour flavor with the addition of tamarind. This is made from the semi-dried, compressed pulp of the tamarind tree. You can buy bars of the pungent-smelling pulp in Indian and oriental food markets.

1 Place the tamarind paste in a medium-size mixing bowl.

2 Gradually add the water to the tamarind paste, gently whisking with a fork to form a smooth, runny paste.

3 Add the chili powder and the ginger to the mixture and blend well.

4 Add the salt and the sugar and mix well.

5 Transfer the chutney to a serving dish and garnish with the cilantro.

Curried Roast Potatoes

This is the kind of Indian-inspired dish that would fit easily into any Western menu, or how about serving with a curry instead of rice?

NUTRITIONAL INFORMATION

Calories	297	Sugars 2g
Protein	.........3g	Fat 19g
Carbohydrate	...30g	Saturates 12g

 5 MINS   30-35 MINS

SERVES 4

I N G R E D I E N T S

2 tsp cumin seeds

2 tsp coriander seeds

6 tbsp butter

1 tsp ground turmeric

1 tsp black mustard seeds

2 garlic cloves, crushed

2 dried red chilies

1 lb 10 oz baby new potatoes

1 Grind the cumin and coriander seeds together in a mortar with a pestle or spice grinder. Grinding them fresh like this captures all of the flavor before it has a chance to dry out.

2 Melt the butter gently in a roasting pan and add the turmeric, mustard seeds, garlic and chilies, and the ground cumin and coriander seeds. Stir well to combine evenly. Place in a preheated oven at 400°F for 5 minutes.

3 Remove the pan from the oven—the spices should be very fragrant at this stage—and add the potatoes. Stir well so that the butter and spice mix coats the potatoes completely.

4 Return to the oven and bake for 20-25 minutes. Stir occasionally to make sure that the potatoes are coated evenly. Test the potatoes with a skewer—if they drop off the end of the skewer when lifted, they are done. Transfer to a serving dish and serve immediately.

COOK'S TIP

Baby new potatoes are now available all year round from supermarkets. However, they are not essential for this recipe. Red or white old potatoes can be substituted, cut into 1-inch cubes. You can also try substituting parsnips, carrots, or turnips, cut into 1-inch cubes.

Colcannon

This is an old Irish recipe, usually served with a piece of bacon, but it is equally delicious with a vegetarian main course dish.

NUTRITIONAL INFORMATION

Calories	102	Sugars	........4g
Protein	.........4g	Fat	..........4g
Carbohydrate	...14g	Saturates	.......2g

 20 MINS   ⏱ 20 MINS

SERVES 4

INGREDIENTS

8 oz green cabbage, shredded

5 tbsp milk

8 oz russet potatoes, diced

1 large leek, chopped

pinch of grated nutmeg

1 tbsp butter, melted

salt and pepper

1 Cook the shredded cabbage in a saucepan of boiling salted water for 7–10 minutes. Drain thoroughly and set aside.

2 Meanwhile, in a separate saucepan, bring the milk to a boil and add the potatoes and leek. Reduce the heat and simmer for 15–20 minutes, or until they are cooked through.

3 Stir in the grated nutmeg and thoroughly mash the potatoes and leek together.

4 Add the drained cabbage to the mashed potato and leek mixture and mix well.

5 Spoon the mixture into a warmed serving dish, making a hollow in the center with the back of a spoon.

6 Pour the melted butter into the hollow and serve the colcannon immediately.

COOK'S TIP

There are many different varieties of cabbage, which produce hearts at varying times of year, so you can be sure of being able to make this delicious cabbage dish all year round.

Fried Eggplant

This makes a good alternative to a raita. The eggplant is fried until crisp, then given a *baghaar*, or seasoned oil dressing.

NUTRITIONAL INFORMATION

Calories 215	Sugars 4g	
Protein 3g	Fat 21g	
Carbohydrate 5g	Saturates 2g	

 5 MINS 15 MINS

SERVES 4

INGREDIENTS

¾ cup plain yogurt

5 tbsp water

1 tsp salt

1 medium eggplant

⅔ cup oil

1 tsp white cumin seeds

6 dried red chilies

1 Place the yogurt in a bowl and beat with a fork.

2 Add the water and salt to the yogurt and mix well.

3 Using a sharp knife, slice the eggplant thinly.

4 Heat the oil in a large, heavy-bottomed skillet. Add the eggplant slices and fry, in batches if necessary, over a medium heat, turning occasionally, until they begin to turn crisp. Remove from the pan, drain on paper towels, transfer to a serving plate, and keep warm.

5 When all of the eggplant slices have been fried, lower the heat, and add the white cumin seeds and the dried red chilies to the pan. Cook, stirring constantly, for 1 minute.

6 Spoon the yogurt on top of the eggplants, then pour over the white cumin and red chili mixture. Serve immediately.

COOK'S TIP

Rich in protein and calcium, yogurt plays an important part in Indian cooking. It is used as a marinade, as a creamy flavoring in curries and sauces, and as a cooling accompaniment to hot dishes.

Bombay Potatoes

Although virtually unknown in India, this dish is a very popular item on Indian restaurant menus in other parts of the world.

NUTRITIONAL INFORMATION

Calories . . . . .307 Sugars 9g
Protein . . . . .9g Fat 9g
Carbohydrate . . .51g Saturates 5g

 5 MINS   1 HR 10 MINS

SERVES 4

I N G R E D I E N T S

2 lb 4 oz potatoes

2 tbsp vegetable ghee

1 tsp panch poran spice mix

3 tsp ground turmeric

2 tbsp tomato paste

1¼ cups plain yogurt

salt

chopped cilantro, to garnish

1 Put the whole potatoes into a large saucepan of salted cold water, bring to a boil, then simmer until the potatoes are just cooked, but not tender; the time depends on the size of the potato, but an average-sized one should take about 15 minutes.

COOK'S TIP

Panch poran spice mix can be bought from Asian or Indian food markets, or make your own from equal quantities of cumin seeds, fennel seeds, mustard seeds, nigella seeds, and fenugreek seeds.

2 Heat the ghee in a saucepan over a medium heat and add the panch poran, turmeric, tomato paste, yogurt, and salt. Bring to a boil and simmer, uncovered, for 5 minutes.

3 Drain the potatoes and cut each one into 4 pieces. Add the potatoes to the pan, cover, and cook briefly. Transfer to an ovenproof casserole, cover, and cook in a preheated oven at 350°F for about 40 minutes, or until the potatoes are tender and the sauce has thickened a little.

4 Sprinkle with chopped cilantro and serve immediately.

Eggplant Bake

This is an unusual dish, in that the eggplant is first baked in the oven, then cooked in a saucepan.

NUTRITIONAL INFORMATION

Calories	....	140
Protein	....	3g
Carbohydrate	....	6g

Sugars	....	5g
Fat	....	12g
Saturates	....	1g

 10 MINS   55 MINS

SERVES 4

INGREDIENTS

2 medium eggplants

4 tbsp vegetable oil

1 medium onion, sliced

1 tsp white cumin seeds

1 tsp chili powder

1 tsp salt

3 tbsp plain yogurt

½ tsp mint sauce

mint leaves, to garnish

1 Rinse the eggplants under cold running water and pat thoroughly dry with absorbent paper towels.

2 Place the eggplants side by side in an ovenproof dish or roasting pan. Bake in a preheated oven at 325°F for 45 minutes. Remove the baked eggplants from the oven and set aside to cool.

3 Using a teaspoon, scoop out the eggplant flesh and set aside.

4 Heat the oil in a heavy-bottomed saucepan over a low heat. Add the onion and cumin seeds and fry, stirring constantly, for 1–2 minutes.

5 Add the chili powder, salt, plain yogurt, and mint sauce to the pan and stir well to mix.

6 Add the eggplant flesh to the onion and yogurt mixture and fry over a medium heat, stirring constantly, for 5–7 minutes, or until all of the liquid has been absorbed and the mixture is quite dry.

7 Transfer the eggplant and yogurt mixture to a warmed serving dish and garnish with fresh mint leaves. Serve immediately.

Potatoes Lyonnaise

In this classic French recipe, sliced potatoes are cooked with onions to make a delicious accompaniment to a main meal.

NUTRITIONAL INFORMATION

Calories	.277	Sugars	.4g
Protein	.5g	Fat	.12g
Carbohydrate	.40g	Saturates	.4g

 10 MINS 25 MINS

SERVES 6

I N G R E D I E N T S

2 lb 12 oz potatoes

4 tbsp olive oil

2 tbsp butter

2 onions, sliced

2–3 garlic cloves, crushed (optional)

salt and pepper

chopped parsley, to garnish

1 Slice the potatoes into ¼-inch slices. Put in a large saucepan of lightly salted water and bring to a boil. Cover and simmer gently for about 10–12 minutes, until just tender. Avoid boiling too rapidly or the potatoes will break up and lose their shape. When cooked, drain well.

COOK'S TIP

If the potatoes blacken slightly as they are boiling, add a spoonful of lemon juice to the cooking water.

2 While the potatoes are cooking, heat the oil and butter in a very large skillet. Add the onions and garlic, if using, and fry over a medium heat, stirring frequently, until the onions are softened.

3 Add the cooked potato to the skillet and cook with the onions, carefully stirring occasionally, for about 5–8 minutes until the potatoes are browned.

4 Season to taste with salt and pepper. Sprinkle over the chopped parsley to serve. If wished, transfer the potatoes and onions to a large ovenproof dish and keep warm in a low oven until ready to serve.

Cauliflower & Spinach Curry

The contrast in color in this recipe makes it very appealing to the eye, especially as the cauliflower is lightly colored with yellow turmeric.

NUTRITIONAL INFORMATION

Calories 228	Sugars 6g
Protein 8g	Fat 18g
Carbohydrate 8g	Saturates 2g

 10 MINS   25 MINS

SERVES 4

I N G R E D I E N T S

1 medium cauliflower

6 tbsp vegetable oil

1 tsp mustard seeds

1 tsp ground cumin

1 tsp garam masala

1 tsp turmeric

2 garlic cloves, crushed

1 onion, halved and sliced

1 green chili, sliced

1 lb 2 oz spinach

5 tbsp vegetable stock

1 tbsp chopped cilantro

salt and pepper

cilantro sprigs, to garnish

1 Break the cauliflower into small flowerets.

2 Heat the oil in a deep flameproof casserole dish. Add the mustard seeds and cook until they begin to pop.

3 Stir in the remaining spices, the garlic, onion, and chili and cook, stirring constantly, for 2–3 minutes.

4 Add the cauliflower, spinach, vegetable stock, chopped cilantro, and seasoning and cook over a gentle heat for 15 minutes, or until the cauliflower is tender. Uncover the dish and boil for 1 minute to thicken the juices.

5 Transfer to a warmed serving dish, garnish with cilantro sprigs, and serve.

COOK'S TIP

Mustard seeds are used throughout India and are particularly popular in southern vegetarian cooking. They are fried in oil first to bring out their flavor before the other ingredients are added.

Caramelized New Potatoes

This simple recipe is best served with a plainly cooked main course because it is fairly sweet and has delicious juices.

NUTRITIONAL INFORMATION

Calories	289	Sugars	........18g
Protein	.........3g	Fat	..........13g
Carbohydrate	...43g	Saturates	.......8g

 5 MINS   20 MINS

SERVES 4

I N G R E D I E N T S

1½ lb new potatoes, scrubbed

4 tbsp dark brown sugar

¼ cup butter

1 tbsp orange juice

1 tbsp chopped fresh parsley or
   cilantro

salt and pepper

orange zest curls, to garnish

1 Cook the new potatoes in a saucepan of boiling water for 10 minutes, or until almost tender. Drain thoroughly.

2 Melt the sugar in a large, heavy-bottomed skillet over a low heat, stirring constantly.

3 Add the butter and orange juice to the pan, stirring the mixture constantly as the butter melts.

4 Add the potatoes to the orange and butter mixture and continue to cook, turning the potatoes frequently until they are completely coated in the caramel.

5 Sprinkle the chopped parsley or cilantro over the potatoes and season according to taste with salt and pepper.

6 Transfer the caramelized new potatoes to a serving dish and garnish with the orange zest. Serve immediately.

VARIATION

Lemon or lime juices may be used instead of the orange juice, if preferred. In addition, garnish the finished dish with pared lemon or lime zest, if preferred.

Mango Chutney

Everyone's favorite chutney, this has a sweet and sour taste. It is best made well ahead of time and stored for at least 2 weeks before use.

NUTRITIONAL INFORMATION

Calories 2819	Sugars 731g
Protein 12g	Fat 2g
Carbohydrate . .734g	Saturates 1g

 10-15 MINS 1 HR 5 MINS

MAKES 1 QUANTITY

INGREDIENTS

2 lb 4 oz mangoes

4 tsp salt

2½ cups water

2⅓ cups sugar

2 cups vinegar

2 tsp finely chopped fresh ginger

2 tsp crushed garlic

2 tsp chili powder

2 cinnamon sticks

½ cup raisins

½ cup dates, pitted

1 Using a sharp knife, peel, halve, and pit the mangoes. Cut the mango flesh into cubes. Place the mango flesh in a large bowl. Add the salt and water and leave overnight. Drain the liquid from the mangoes and set aside.

2 Bring the sugar and vinegar to a boil in a large saucepan over a low heat, stirring constantly.

3 Gradually add the mango cubes, stirring to coat them in the mixture.

4 Add the ginger, garlic, chili powder, cinnamon sticks, raisins, and dates, and bring to a boil again, stirring occasionally. Reduce the heat and cook for about 1 hour, or until the mixture thickens. Remove from the heat and set aside to cool.

5 Remove the cinnamon sticks from the chutney and discard.

6 Spoon the chutney into clean dry jars and cover tightly with lids. Leave in a cool place for the flavors to develop fully.

COOK'S TIP

When choosing mangoes, select ones that are shiny with unblemished skins. To test if they are ripe, gently cup the mango in your hand and squeeze—it should give slightly to the touch if it is ready for eating.

Fried Spiced Potatoes

Deliciously good and a super accompaniment to almost any main course dish, although rather high in calories!

NUTRITIONAL INFORMATION

Calories 430	Sugars 7g
Protein 4g	Fat 35g
Carbohydrate . . .26g	Saturates 11g

 15 MINS   🕐 30 MINS

SERVES 6

I N G R E D I E N T S

2 onions, quartered

2-inch piece of fresh ginger,
    finely chopped

2 garlic cloves

2–3 tbsp mild or medium curry paste

4 tbsp water

1 lb 10 oz new potatoes

vegetable oil, for deep frying

3 tbsp vegetable ghee or oil

⅔ cup strained plain yogurt

⅔ cup heavy cream

3 tbsp chopped mint

salt and pepper

½ bunch green onions, chopped,
    to garnish

1 Place the onions, ginger, garlic, curry paste, and water in a blender or food processor and process until smooth, scraping down the sides of the machine and processing again, if necessary.

2 Cut the potatoes into quarters—the pieces need to be about 1 inch in size—and pat dry with absorbent paper towels. Heat the oil in a deep fryer to 350°F or until a cube of bread browns in 30 seconds and fry the potatoes, in batches, for about 5 minutes or until golden brown, turning frequently. Remove from the pan and drain on paper towels.

3 Heat the ghee or oil in a large skillet, add the curry and onion mixture, and fry gently, stirring constantly, for 2 minutes. Add the yogurt, cream and 2 tablespoons of mint and mix well.

4 Add the fried potatoes and stir until coated in the sauce. Cook, stirring frequently, for another 5–7 minutes, or until heated through and sauce has thickened. Season with salt and pepper to taste and sprinkle with the remaining mint and sliced green onions. Serve immediately.

COOK'S TIP

When buying new potatoes, look for the freshest you can find. The skin should be beginning to rub off. Cook them as soon after purchase as possible, but if you have to store them, keep them in a cool, dark well-ventilated place.

Potatoes with Almonds

This oven-cooked dish has a subtle creamy, almond flavor and a pale yellow color as a result of being cooked with turmeric.

NUTRITIONAL INFORMATION

Calories 531	Sugars 6g
Protein 7g	Fat 46g
Carbohydrate . . .24g	Saturates 23g

5 MINS   40-45 MINS

SERVES 4

I N G R E D I E N T S

2 large potatoes, unpeeled and sliced

1 tbsp vegetable oil

1 red onion, halved and sliced

1 garlic clove, crushed

½ cup slivered almond

½ tsp turmeric

1¼ cups heavy cream

2 bunches arugula

salt and pepper

1 Cook the sliced potatoes in a saucepan of boiling water for 10 minutes. Drain thoroughly.

2 Heat the vegetable oil in a heavy-bottomed skillet. Add the onion and garlic and fry over a medium heat, stirring frequently, for 3–4 minutes.

3 Add the almonds, turmeric, and potato slices to the skillet and cook, stirring constantly, for 2–3 minutes. Stir in the arugula.

4 Transfer the potato and almond mixture to a shallow ovenproof dish. Pour the heavy cream over the top and season with salt and pepper.

5 Cook in a preheated oven at 375°F for 20 minutes, or until the potatoes are cooked through. Transfer to a warmed serving dish and serve immediately.

Herby Potatoes & Onions

Fried potatoes are a classic favorite; here they are given extra flavor by frying them in butter with onion, garlic, and herbs.

NUTRITIONAL INFORMATION

Calories	.413	Sugars	.4g
Protein	.5g	Fat	.26g
Carbohydrate	.42g	Saturates	.17g

 10 MINS   50 MINS

SERVES 4

INGREDIENTS

2 lb potatoes, cut into cubes

½ cup butter

1 red onion, cut into 8 wedges

2 garlic cloves, crushed

1 tsp lemon juice

2 tbsp chopped thyme

salt and pepper

1 Cook the cubed potatoes in a saucepan of boiling water for 10 minutes. Drain thoroughly.

2 Melt the butter in a large, heavy-bottomed skillet and add the red onion wedges, garlic, and lemon juice. Cook, stirring constantly for 2–3 minutes.

3 Add the potatoes to the pan and mix well to coat in the butter mixture.

COOK'S TIP

Keep checking the potatoes and stirring throughout the cooking time to make sure that they do not burn or stick to the base of the skillet.

4 Reduce the heat, cover, and cook for 25–30 minutes, or until the potatoes are golden brown and tender.

5 Sprinkle the chopped thyme over the top of the potatoes and season.

6 Transfer to a warm serving dish and serve immediately.

Spicy Indian Potatoes

The potato is widely used in Indian cooking and there are many variations of spicy potatoes.

NUTRITIONAL INFORMATION

Calories ....173 Sugars 6g
Protein ....7g Fat 9g
Carbohydrate ...18g Saturates 1g

15 MINS   40 MINS

SERVES 6

INGREDIENTS

½ tsp coriander seeds

1 tsp cumin seeds

4 tbsp vegetable oil

2 cardamom pods

½-inch piece of fresh ginger, grated

1 red chili, chopped

1 onion, chopped

2 garlic cloves, crushed

1 lb 2 oz new potatoes, quartered

⅔ cup vegetable stock

1½ lb spinach, chopped

4 tbsp plain yogurt

salt

1 Grind the coriander and cumin seeds using a pestle and mortar.

2 Heat the oil in a skillet. Add the ground coriander and cumin seeds to the pan, together with the cardamom pods and ginger, and cook for about 2 minutes.

3 Add the chopped chili, onion, and garlic to the pan. Cook, stirring frequently, for 2 minutes more.

4 Add the potatoes to the pan, together with the vegetable stock. Cook gently, stirring occasionally, for 30 minutes, or until the potatoes are cooked through.

5 Add the spinach to the pan and cook for 5 minutes more.

6 Remove the pan from the heat and stir in the yogurt. Season with salt and pepper to taste. Transfer the potatoes and spinach to a warmed serving dish and serve immediately.

VARIATION

Use frozen spinach instead of fresh spinach, if you prefer. Thaw the frozen spinach and drain it thoroughly before adding it to the dish, otherwise it will turn soggy.

Pooris

Although pooris are deep-fried, they are very light. The nutritional information supplied is for each poori.

NUTRITIONAL INFORMATION

Calories 165   Sugars 0.7g
Protein ....3g   Fat 10g
Carbohydrate ...17g   Saturates 1g

 35 MINS   15–20 MINS

MAKES 10

I N G R E D I E N T S

1½ cups whole wheat flour,
    ata, or chapati flour

½ tsp salt

⅔ cup water

2½ cups vegetable oil

1 Place the flour and salt in a large mixing bowl and stir to combine.

2 Make a well in the center of the flour. Gradually pour in the water and mix together to form a dough, adding more water if necessary.

3 Knead the dough until it is smooth and elastic and set aside in a warm place to rise for about 15 minutes.

4 Divide the dough into about 10 equal portions and with lightly oiled or floured hands pat each into a smooth ball.

5 On a lightly oiled or floured work counter, roll out each ball to form a thin round.

6 Heat the oil in a deep skillet. Deep-fry the rounds, in batches, turning once, until golden brown in color.

7 Remove the pooris from the pan and drain. Serve hot.

COOK'S TIP

You can serve pooris either piled one on top of the other or spread out in a layer on a large serving platter so that they remain puffed up.

Naan Bread

There are many ways of making naan bread, but this recipe is very easy to follow. Naan bread should be served immediately after cooking.

NUTRITIONAL INFORMATION

Calories ....152 Sugars 1g
Protein ....3g Fat 7g
Carbohydrate ...20g Saturates 4g

2¼ HOURS   10 MINS

SERVES 8

I N G R E D I E N T S

1 tsp sugar

1 tsp fresh yeast

⅔ cup warm water

1½ cups all-purpose flour

1 tbsp ghee

1 tsp salt

4 tbsp unsalted butter

1 tsp poppy seeds

1 Put the sugar and yeast in a small bowl or jug together with the warm water and mix thoroughly until the yeast has completely dissolved. Set aside for about 10 minutes, or until the mixture is frothy.

2 Place the flour in a large mixing bowl. Make a well in the center of the flour, add the ghee and salt, and pour in the yeast mixture. Mix thoroughly to form a dough, using your hands and adding more water if required.

3 Turn the dough out onto a floured work counter and knead for about 5 minutes, or until smooth.

4 Return the dough to the bowl, cover, and set aside to rise in a warm place for 1½ hours, or until doubled in size.

5 Turn the dough out onto a floured surface and knead for another 2 minutes. Break off small balls with your hand and pat them into rounds about 5 inches in diameter and ½-inch thick.

6 Place the dough rounds on a greased sheet of foil and broil under a very hot preheated broiler for 7–10 minutes, turning twice and brushing with the butter and sprinkling with the poppy seeds.

7 Serve warm immediately, or keep wrapped in foil until required.

Spinach Pooris

These little nibbles are very satisfying to make and they will still be little puffballs when you get to the table.

NUTRITIONAL INFORMATION

Calories . . . . . . .368 Sugars 3g
Protein . . . . .6g Fat 25g
Carbohydrate . . .33g Saturates 3g

 1 HOUR   10 MINS

SERVES 6

INGREDIENTS

1 cup whole wheat flour

1 cup all-purpose flour

½ tsp salt

2 tbsp vegetable oil

½ cup chopped spinach,
   fresh or frozen, blanched, puréed, and all
   excess water squeezed out

¼ cup water

oil, for deep-frying

RELISH

2 tbsp chopped mint

2 tbsp plain yogurt

½ red onion, sliced and rinsed

½ tsp cayenne pepper

1 Sift the flours and salt together into a bowl. Drizzle over the oil and rub in with the fingertips until the mixture resembles fine breadcrumbs.

2 Add the spinach and water, and stir in to make a stiff dough. Turn out and knead for 10 minutes until smooth. Form the dough into a ball. Put into an oiled bowl, turn to coat, cover with plastic wrap, and set aside for 30 minutes.

3 Meanwhile make the relish. Combine the mint, yogurt, and onion, transfer to a serving bowl, and sift the cayenne over the top.

4 Knead the dough again and divide into 12 small balls. Remove 1 ball and keep the rest covered. Roll this ball out into a 5-inch circle.

5 Put the oil into a wok or wide skillet to a depth of 1 inch. Heat it until a haze appears. It must be very hot.

6 Have ready a plate lined with paper towels. Put 1 poori on the surface of the oil—if it sinks, it should rise up immediately and sizzle; if it doesn't, the oil isn't hot enough. Keep the poori submerged in the oil, using the back of a fish slice or a perforated spoon. The poori will puff up immediately. Turn it over and cook the other side for 5–10 seconds.

7 As soon as the poori is cooked, remove and drain on paper towels. Repeat with the remaining balls of dough.

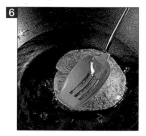

Parathos

These triangular shaped breads are so easy to make and are the perfect addition to most Indian meals. Serve hot, spread with a little butter.

NUTRITIONAL INFORMATION

Calories	127	Sugars	.......0.5g
Protein	.........3g	Fat	..........4g
Carbohydrate	...22g	Saturates	.....0.4g

 50 MINS　　🕐 10 MINS

SERVES 6

I N G R E D I E N T S

¾ cup all-purpose
　whole wheat flour

¾ cup all-purpose flour

pinch of salt

1 tbsp vegetable oil, plus extra for greasing

⅓ cup tepid water

1 Place the flours and the salt in a bowl. Drizzle 1 tablespoon of oil over the flour, add the tepid water, and mix to form a soft dough, adding a little more water, if necessary. Knead on a lightly floured work counter until smooth, then cover and leave for 30 minutes.

2 Knead the dough on a floured work counter and divide into 6 equal pieces. Shape each one into a ball. Roll out on a floured counter to a 6-inch round and brush very lightly with oil.

3 Fold in half, and then in half again to form a triangle. Roll out to form a 7-inch triangle (when measured from point to center top), dusting with extra flour as necessary.

4 Brush a large, heavy-bottomed skillet with a little oil and heat until hot, then add one or two parathas and cook for about 1–1½ minutes. Brush the surfaces

very lightly with oil, then turn and cook the other sides for 1½ minutes until completely cooked through.

5 Place the cooked parathos on a plate and cover with foil, or place between the folds of a clean dish cloth to keep warm, while you are cooking the remainder in the same way, greasing the pan between cooking each batch.

VARIATION

For added flavor, try brushing the parathos with a garlic- or chilli-flavored oil as they are cooking.

Peshwari Naan

A tandoor oven throws out a ferocious heat; this bread is traditionally cooked on its side wall, where the heat is slightly less intense.

NUTRITIONAL INFORMATION

Calories	420	Sugars	........13g
Protein	........11g	Fat	..........9g
Carbohydrate	...77g	Saturates	.......3g

 3¾ HOURS   30 MINS

SERVES 6

INGREDIENTS

¼ cup warm water

pinch of sugar

½ tsp active dry yeast

4 cups bread flour

½ tsp salt

¼ cup plain yogurt

2 tart apples, peeled, cored, and diced

⅓ cup golden raisins

½ cup slivered almonds

1 tbsp cilantro leaves

2 tbsp grated coconut

1 Combine the water and sugar in a bowl and sprinkle over the yeast. Leave for 5–10 minutes, until the yeast has dissolved and the mixture is foamy.

2 Put the flour and salt into a bowl and make a well in the center. Add the yeast mixture and yogurt. Draw in the flour until it is all absorbed. Mix together, adding enough tepid water to form a soft dough. Turn out on to a floured board and knead for 10 minutes, until smooth. Put into an oiled bowl, cover, and leave for 3 hours in a warm place.

3 Line the broiler pan with foil, shiny side up.

4 Put the apples into a saucepan with a little water. Bring to a boil, mash them down, reduce the heat, and simmer for 20 minutes, mashing occasionally.

5 Divide the dough into 4 pieces and roll each piece out to an 8-inch oval. Pull one end out into a teardrop shape, about ¼ inch thick. Lay on a floured work counter and prick the dough all over with a fork.

6 Brush both sides of the bread with oil. Place under a preheated broiler at the highest setting. Cook for 3 minutes, turn the bread over, and cook for another 3 minutes. It should have dark brown spots all over.

7 Spread a teaspoonful of the apple purée all over the bread, then sprinkle over a quarter of the golden raisins, the slivered almonds, the cilantro leaves, and the coconut. Repeat with the remaining 3 ovals of dough.

Mixed Bell Pepper Pooris

These pooris are easy to make and so good to eat served with a scrumptious topping of spicy mixed bell peppers and yogurt.

NUTRITIONAL INFORMATION

Calories .... .386   Sugars 6g
Protein .... .5g   Fat .... .32g
Carbohydrate ...21g   Saturates 4g

55 MINS   15 MINS

SERVES 6

I N G R E D I E N T S

POORIS

1 cup all-purpose whole wheat flour

1 tbsp vegetable ghee or oil

pinch of salt

5 tbsp hot water

vegetable oil, for shallow frying

cilantro sprigs, to garnish

plain yogurt, to serve

TOPPING

4 tbsp vegetable ghee or oil

1 large onion, quartered and thinly sliced

½ red bell pepper, seeded and thinly sliced

½ green bell pepper, seeded and
  thinly sliced

¼ eggplant, cut lengthwise into 6
  wedges and thinly sliced

1 garlic clove, crushed

1-inch piece of fresh
  ginger, chopped

½–1 tsp minced chili

2 tsp mild or medium curry paste

8 oz can diced tomatoes

salt

1 To make the pooris, put the flour in a bowl with the ghee or oil and salt. Add hot water and mix to form a fairly soft dough. Knead gently, cover with a damp cloth, and leave for 30 minutes.

2 Meanwhile, prepare the topping. Heat the ghee or oil in a large saucepan. Add the onion, bell peppers, eggplant, garlic, ginger, chili, and curry paste and fry gently for 5 minutes. Stir in the tomatoes and salt to taste and simmer gently, uncovered, for 5 minutes, stirring occasionally until the sauce thickens. Remove from the heat.

3 Knead the dough on a floured work counter and divide into 6. Roll each piece to a round about 6 inches in diameter. Cover each one as you finish rolling to prevent drying out.

4 Heat about ½ inch oil in a large skillet. Add the pooris, one at a time, and fry for about 15 seconds on each side, until puffed and golden, turning frequently. Drain on paper towels and keep warm while you are cooking the remainder in the same way.

5 Reheat the vegetable mixture. Place a poori on each serving plate and top with the vegetable mixture. Add a spoonful of yogurt to each, garnish with the cilantro sprigs, and serve.

Lightly Fried Bread

This is perfect with egg dishes and vegetable curries. Allow 2 portions of bread per person. The nutritional information is for each portion.

NUTRITIONAL INFORMATION

Calories 133	Sugars 1g
Protein 3g	Fat 7g
Carbohydrate ...17g	Saturates 4g

  35 MINS   20-25 MINS

MAKES 10

I N G R E D I E N T S

1½ cups whole wheat, ata, or chapati flour

½ tsp salt

1 tbsp ghee

1¼ cups water

1 Place the flour and the salt in a large mixing bowl and mix to combine.

2 Make a well in the center of the flour. Add the ghee and cut in well. Gradually pour in the water and work to form a soft dough. Set the dough aside to rise for 10–15 minutes.

3 Carefully knead the dough for about 5–7 minutes. Divide the dough into about 10 equal portions.

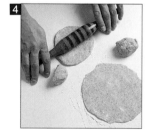

4 On a lightly floured surface, roll out each dough portion to form a flat pancake shape.

5 Using a sharp knife, lightly draw lines in a criss-cross pattern on each rolled-out dough portion.

6 Heat a heavy-bottomed skillet. Gently place the dough portions, one by one, into the pan.

7 Cook the bread for about 1 minute, then turn over and spread with 1 teaspoon of ghee. Turn the bread over again and fry gently, moving it around the pan with a metal spatula, until golden. Turn the bread over once again, then remove from the pan and keep warm while you cook the remaining batches.

COOK'S TIP

In India, breads are cooked on a tava, a traditional flat griddle. A large skillet makes an adequate substitute.

Spicy Oven Bread

This is a Western-style bread with an Indian touch. It is very quick once the dough is made and is quite a rich mix and very tasty.

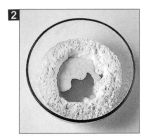

NUTRITIONAL INFORMATION

Calories 445	Sugars 1g
Protein 6g	Fat 26g
Carbohydrate . . .49g	Saturates 17g

1½ HOURS   10 MINS

SERVES 8

I N G R E D I E N T S

½ tsp active dry yeast

1¼ cups warm water

4 cups white flour

1 tsp salt

1 cup butter, melted and cooled

½ tsp garam masala

½ tsp coriander seeds, ground

1 tsp cumin seeds, ground

1 Mix the yeast with a little of the warm water until it starts to foam and is completely dissolved.

2 Put the flour and salt into a large bowl, make a well in the center, and add the yeast mixture, and ½ cup of the melted butter. Blend the yeast and butter together before drawing in the flour and kneading lightly. Add the water gradually until a firm dough is obtained; you may not need it all.

3 Turn the dough out onto a floured work counter and knead for about 10 minutes, until smooth and elastic. Put it into an oiled bowl and turn it over so that it is coated. Cover and leave in a warm place to rise for 30 minutes, until doubled in size. Alternatively, leave in the refrigerator overnight.

4 Knead the dough again and divide into 8 balls. Roll each one out to a 6-inch round. Place on a floured cookie sheet. Sprinkle with flour and leave for 20 minutes.

5 Mix the spices together with the remaining melted butter.

6 Brush each bread with the spice and butter mixture and cover with foil.

Place on the middle shelf of a preheated oven at 425°F for 5 minutes. Remove the foil, brush with the butter once again, and cook for another 5 minutes.

7 Remove from the oven and wrap in a clean dish cloth until ready to eat.

Desserts

Vegetarian or not, confirmed dessert lovers feel a meal is lacking if there isn't a tempting dessert to finish off. Desserts are often loaded with fat and sugar, but this chapter contains recipes that are light but still full of flavor so that you can enjoy a sweet treat without piling on the calories. A lot of the recipes contain fruit, which is

the perfect ingredient for healthy desserts that are still deliciously tempting. A few rich chocolate recipes are also included—they are particularly decadent, so that you can treat yourself now and again! Whatever the occasion, you are sure to find the perfect recipe in this chapter to satisfy every craving. Enjoy!

Chocolate Fudge Pudding

This pudding has a hidden surprise when cooked—it separates to give a rich chocolate sauce at the bottom of the dish.

NUTRITIONAL INFORMATION

Calories 397	Sugars 27g	
Protein 10g	Fat 25g	
Carbohydrate . . .36g	Saturates 5g	

 10 MINS   40 MINS

SERVES 4

I N G R E D I E N T S

4 tbsp margarine, plus extra
   for greasing

6 tbsp light brown sugar

2 eggs, beaten

1¼ cups milk

½ cup chopped walnuts

¼ cup all-purpose flour

2 tbsp unsweetened cocoa powder

icing sugar and unsweetened

cocoa powder, to dust

1 Lightly grease a 4-cup ovenproof dish.

2 Cream together the margarine and sugar in a large mixing bowl until fluffy. Beat in the eggs.

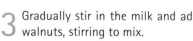
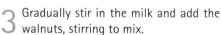
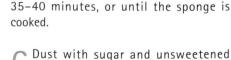

VARIATION

Add 1–2 tbsp brandy or rum to the mixture for a slightly alcoholic pudding, or 1–2 tbsp orange juice for a child-friendly version.

3 Gradually stir in the milk and add the walnuts, stirring to mix.

4 Sift the flour and cocoa powder into the mixture and fold in gently, with a metal spoon, until well mixed.

5 Spoon the mixture into the dish and cook in a preheated oven at 350°F for 35–40 minutes, or until the sponge is cooked.

6 Dust with sugar and unsweetened cocoa powder, and serve.

Date & Apricot Tart

There is no need to add any extra sugar to this filling because the dried fruit is naturally sweet. This tart is suitable for vegans.

45 MINS   50 MINS

SERVES 8

I N G R E D I E N T S

1¾ cups all-purpose
   whole wheat flour

½ cup mixed nuts, ground

⅓ cup margarine,
   cut into small pieces

4 tbsp water

1 cup dried apricots, chopped

1⅓ cups chopped pitted dates

2 cups apple juice

1 tsp ground cinnamon

grated zest of 1 lemon

soy custard, to serve (optional)

1 Place the flour and ground nuts in a mixing bowl and rub in the margarine with your fingertips until the mixture resembles breadcrumbs. Stir in the water and bring together to form a dough. Wrap the dough and chill in the refrigerator for 30 minutes.

2 Meanwhile, place the apricots and dates in a saucepan, together with the apple juice, cinnamon, and lemon zest. Bring to a boil, cover, and simmer over a low heat for about 15 minutes, until the fruit softens and can be mashed to a purée.

3 Reserve a small ball of pie dough for making lattice strips. On a lightly floured work counter, roll out the rest of the dough to form a round and use to line a 9-inch loose-based quiche pan.

4 Spread the fruit filling over the base of the pie dough. Roll out the reserved dough and cut into strips ½ inch wide. Cut the strips to fit the tart and twist them across the top of the fruit to form a decorative lattice pattern. Moisten the edges of the strips with water and seal them firmly around the rim.

5 Bake in a preheated oven at 400°F for 25–30 minutes, until golden brown. Cut into slices and serve immediately with soy custard, if using.

Coconut Cream Molds

Smooth, creamy, and refreshing—these tempting little custards are made with an unusual combination of coconut milk, cream, and eggs.

NUTRITIONAL INFORMATION

Calories 288   Sugar 24g
Protein . . . . .4g   Fat 20g
Carbohydrate . . .25g   Saturates 14g

  10 MINS   45 MINS

SERVES 8

INGREDIENTS

CARAMEL

½ cup granulated sugar

⅔ cup water

CUSTARD

1¼ cups water

3 oz creamed coconut, chopped

2 eggs

2 egg yolks

1½ tbsp sugar

1¼ cups light cream

sliced banana or slivers of fresh pineapple

1–2 tbsp freshly grated or
    shredded coconut

1 Have ready 8 small ovenproof dishes about ⅔-cup capacity. To make the caramel, place the granulated sugar and water in a saucepan and heat gently to dissolve the sugar, then boil rapidly, without stirring, until the mixture turns a rich golden brown.

2 Immediately remove the pan from the heat and dip the base into a bowl of cold water in order to stop it cooking. Quickly, but carefully, pour the caramel into the ovenproof dishes to coat the bases.

3 To make the custard, place the water in the same saucepan, add the coconut and heat, stirring constantly, until the coconut dissolves. Place the eggs, egg yolks, and sugar in a bowl and beat well with a fork. Add the hot coconut milk and stir well to dissolve the sugar. Stir in the cream and strain the mixture into a jug.

4 Arrange the dishes in a roasting pan and fill with enough cold water to come halfway up the sides of the dishes. Pour the custard mixture into the caramel-lined dishes, cover with baking parchment paper or foil and cook in a preheated oven at 300°F for about 40 minutes, or until set.

5 Remove the dishes, set aside to cool, and then chill overnight. To serve, run a knife around the edge of each dish and turn out onto a serving plate. Serve with slices of banana or slivers of fresh pineapple sprinkled with freshly grated or shredded coconut.

Raspberry Fool

This dish is very easy to make and can be prepared ahead of time and stored in the refrigerator until required.

NUTRITIONAL INFORMATION

Calories	288	Sugars	........19g
Protein	.........4g	Fat	..........22g
Carbohydrate	...19g	Saturates	......14g

1¼ HOURS   0 MINS

SERVES 4

I N G R E D I E N T S

1⅔ cups fresh raspberries

¼ cup icing sugar

1¼ cups crème fraîche,
    plus extra to decorate

½ tsp vanilla extract

2 egg whites

raspberries and lemon balm leaves,
    to decorate

1 Put the raspberries and icing sugar in a food processor or blender and process until smooth. Alternatively, press through a strainer with the back of a spoon.

2 Reserve 1 tablespoon per portion of crème fraîche for decorating.

3 Put the vanilla extract and remaining crème fraîche in a bowl and stir in the raspberry mixture.

4 Whisk the egg whites in a separate mixing bowl until stiff peaks form. Gently fold the egg whites into the raspberry mixture using a metal spoon, until fully incorporated.

5 Spoon the raspberry fool into individual serving dishes and chill for at least 1 hour. Decorate with the reserved crème fraîche, raspberries, and lemon balm leaves and serve.

COOK'S TIP

Although this dessert is best made with fresh raspberries in season, an acceptable result can be achieved with frozen raspberries, which are available from most supermarkets.

Cinnamon Pears

These spicy sweet pears are accompanied by a delicious melt-in-the-mouth cream, which is relatively low in fat.

NUTRITIONAL INFORMATION

Calories	190	Sugars 28g
Protein	.........6g	Fat 7g
Carbohydrate	...28g	Saturates 4g

 10 MINS   25 MINS

SERVES 4

INGREDIENTS

1 lemon

4 firm ripe pears

1¼ cups unsweetened apple juice

1 cinnamon stick, broken in half

mint leaves, to decorate

MAPLE RICOTTA CREAM

½ cup ricotta cheese

½ cup plain fromage frais

½ tsp ground cinnamon

½ tsp grated lemon zest

1 tbsp maple syrup

lemon zest, to decorate

1 Using a swivel vegetable peeler, remove the zest from the lemon and put in a non-stick skillet. Squeeze the lemon and pour the juice into a shallow bowl.

2 Peel, halve, and core the pears. Toss them in the lemon juice to prevent them from discoloring. Add them to the skillet and pour over the lemon juice remaining in the bowl.

3 Add the unsweetened apple juice and the cinnamon stick. Gently bring to a boil, then lower the heat and simmer for 10 minutes. Remove the pears using a perforated spoon, reserving the cooking juice. Put the pears in a warm heatproof serving dish, cover with foil, and keep warm in a low oven.

4 Return the pan to the heat, bring to a boil, then simmer for about 8–10 minutes, until reduced by half. Spoon over the pears.

5 To make the maple ricotta cream, mix together all the ingredients. Decorate with lemon zest and serve with the pears.

Almond Slices

A mouth-watering dessert that is sure to impress your guests, especially if it is served with whipped cream.

NUTRITIONAL INFORMATION

Calories 416   Sugars 37g
Protein . . . . .11g   Fat 26g
Carbohydrate . . .38g   Saturates 12g

 5 MINS   🕐 5 MINS

SERVES 8

I N G R E D I E N T S

3 eggs

½ cup ground almonds

1½ cups milk powder

1 cup sugar

½ tsp saffron strands

½ cup unsalted butter

1 tbsp slivered almonds

1 Beat the eggs together in a bowl and set aside.

2 Place the ground almonds, milk powder, sugar, and saffron in a large mixing bowl and stir to mix well.

3 Melt the butter in a small saucepan. Pour the melted butter over the dry ingredients and mix well until thoroughly combined.

4 Add the reserved beaten eggs to the mixture and stir to blend well.

5 Spread the mixture in a shallow 7–9-inch ovenproof dish and bake in a preheated oven at 325°F for 45 minutes. Test whether the cake is cooked through by piercing with the tip of a sharp knife or a skewer—it will come out clean if it is cooked thoroughly.

6 Cut the almond cake into slices. Decorate the almond slices with slivered almonds and transfer to serving plates. Serve hot or cold.

COOK'S TIP

These almond slices are best eaten hot, but they may also be served cold. They can be made a day or even a week ahead of time and re-heated. They also freeze beautifully.

Fruity Queen of Puddings

A scrumptious version of a classic British pudding, made here with fresh bananas and apricot jelly.

NUTRITIONAL INFORMATION

Calories 406	Sugars 60g
Protein 13g	Fat 7g
Carbohydrate ...77g	Saturates 3g

 30 MINS   1 HOUR

SERVES 4

INGREDIENTS

2 cups fresh white breadcrumbs

2½ cups milk

3 eggs

½ tsp vanilla extract

¼ cup sugar

2 bananas

1 tbsp lemon juice

3 tbsp apricot jelly

1 Sprinkle the breadcrumbs into a 4-cup ovenproof dish. Heat the milk until lukewarm, then pour it over the breadcrumbs.

2 Separate 2 of the eggs and beat the yolks with the remaining whole egg. Add to the dish with the vanilla extract and half the sugar, stirring well to mix. Allow to stand for 10 minutes.

COOK'S TIP

The meringue will have a soft, marshmallow-like texture, unlike a hard meringue which is cooked slowly for 2–3 hours, until dry. Always use a grease-free bowl and whisk for beating egg whites, otherwise they will not whip properly.

3 Bake in a preheated oven at 350°F for 40 minutes until set. Remove from the oven.

4 Slice the bananas and sprinkle with the lemon juice. Spoon the apricot jelly onto the pudding and spread out to cover the surface. Arrange the bananas on top of the apricot jelly.

5 Whisk the egg whites until stiff, then add the remaining sugar. Continue whisking until the meringue is very stiff and glossy.

6 Pile the meringue on top of the pudding, return to the oven, and cook for another 10–15 minutes, until set and golden brown. Serve immediately.

Chocolate Chip Ice Cream

This marvelous frozen dessert offers the best of both worlds, delicious chocolate chip cookies and a rich dairy-flavored ice.

NUTRITIONAL INFORMATION

Calories	238	Sugars	........23g
Protein	.........9g	Fat	..........10g
Carbohydrate	...30g	Saturates	.......4g

6 HOURS   5 MINS

SERVES 6

I N G R E D I E N T S

1¼ cups milk

1 vanilla bean

2 eggs

2 egg yolks

¼ cup sugar

1¼ cups plain yogurt

4½ oz chocolate chip cookies,
    broken into small pieces

1 Pour the milk into a small pan, add the vanilla bean and bring to a boil over a low heat. Remove from the heat, cover the pan and set aside to cool.

2 Beat the eggs and egg yolks in a double boiler or in a bowl set over a pan of simmering water. Add the sugar and continue beating until the mixture is pale and creamy.

3 Reheat the milk to simmering point and strain it over the egg mixture. Stir continuously until the custard is thick enough to coat the back of a spoon. Remove the custard from the heat and stand the pan or bowl in cold water to prevent any more cooking. Wash and dry the vanilla bean for future use.

4 Stir the yogurt into the cooled custard and beat until it is well blended. When the mixture is thoroughly cold, stir in the broken cookies.

5 Transfer the mixture to a chilled metal cake pan or plastic container, cover and freeze for 4 hours. Remove from the freezer every hour, transfer to a chilled bowl and beat vigorously to prevent ice crystals from forming then return to the freezer. Alternatively, freeze the mixture in an ice-cream maker, following the manufacturer's instructions.

6 To serve the ice cream, transfer it to the main part of the refrigerator for 1 hour. Serve in scoops.

Steamed Coffee Sponge

This steamed sponge is very light and is delicious served with a sweet chocolate sauce.

NUTRITIONAL INFORMATION

Calories	300	Sugars	........21g
Protein	.........8g	Fat	..........13g
Carbohydrate	...40g	Saturates	.......4g

🥘 10 MINS   🕐 1¼ HOURS

SERVES 4

INGREDIENTS

2 tbsp margarine

2 tbsp soft brown sugar

2 eggs

⅓ cup all-purpose flour

¾ tsp baking powder

6 tbsp milk

1 tsp coffee extract

SAUCE

1¼ cups milk

1 tbsp soft brown sugar

1 tsp unsweetened cocoa powder

2 tbsp cornstarch

1 Lightly grease a 2½ cup heatproof bowl. Cream the margarine and sugar until light and fluffy and beat in the eggs.

2 Gradually stir in the flour and baking powder and then the milk and coffee extract to make a smooth batter.

3 Spoon the mixture into the prepared heatproof bowl and cover with a pleated piece of baking parchment and then a pleated piece of foil, securing around the bowl with string. Place in a steamer or large pan and half-fill with boiling water. Cover and steam for 1–1¼ hours, or until cooked through.

4 To make the sauce, put the milk, soft brown sugar, and unsweetened cocoa powder in a pan and heat , stirring constantly, until the sugar dissolves. Blend the cornstarch with 4 tablespoons of cold water to make a smooth paste and stir into the pan. Bring to a boil, stirring constantly until thickened. Cook over a gentle heat for 1 minute.

5 Turn the steamed dessert out onto a warmed serving plate and spoon the sauce over the top. Serve immediately.

COOK'S TIP

The sponge is covered with pleated paper and foil to allow it to rise. The foil will react with the steam and therefore must not be placed directly against the sponge.

Toasted Tropical Fruit

Spear some chunks of exotic tropical fruits on kabob sticks,
sear them over the grill, and serve with this amazing chocolate dip.

NUTRITIONAL INFORMATION

Calories	435	Sugars	........60g
Protein	.........6g	Fat	...........11g
Carbohydrate	...68g	Saturates	.......6g

45 MINS   5 MINS

SERVES 4

I N G R E D I E N T S

DIP

4 squares dark chocolate, broken into
  pieces

2 tbsp light corn syrup

1 tbsp unsweetened cocoa powder

1 tbsp cornstarch

¾ cup milk

KABOBS

1 mango

1 papaya

2 kiwi fruit

½ small pineapple

1 large banana

2 tbsp lemon juice

⅔ cup white rum

1 Put all the ingredients for the chocolate dip into a heavy-bottomed saucepan. Heat over the grill or a low heat, stirring constantly, until thickened and smooth. Keep warm at the edge of the barbecue.

2 Slice the mango on each side of its large, flat pit. Cut the flesh into chunks, removing the peel. Halve, seed, and peel the papaya and cut it into chunks. Peel the kiwi and slice into chunks. Peel and cut the pineapple into chunks. Peel and slice the banana and dip the pieces in the lemon juice to prevent it from discoloring.

3 Thread the pieces of fruit alternately on to 4 wooden skewers. Place them in a shallow dish and pour over the rum. Leave to soak up the flavor of the rum for at least 30 minutes, until ready to grill.

4 Cook the kabobs over the hot coals, turning frequently, for about 2 minutes, until seared. Serve, accompanied by the hot chocolate dip.

Fruit Crumble

Any fruits in season can be used in this healthy pudding. It is suitable for vegans since it contains no dairy produce.

NUTRITIONAL INFORMATION

Calories ....426 Sugars 37g
Protein ....8g Fat 16g
Carbohydrate ...67g Saturates 4g

  10 MINS   30 MINS

SERVES 6

INGREDIENTS

6 dessert pears, peeled, cored,
   quartered, and sliced

1 tbsp crystallized ginger, chopped

1 tbsp molasses

2 tbsp orange juice

TOPPING

1½ cups all-purpose flour

⅓ cup margarine,
   cut into small pieces

¼ cup slivered almonds

⅓ cup rolled oats

1¾ oz molasses

soy custard, to serve

VARIATION

Stir 1 tsp ground apple spice into the crumble mixture in step 3 for added flavor, if you prefer.

1 Lightly grease a 4-cup ovenproof dish.

2 Prepare the pears. In a bowl, mix together the pears, ginger, molasses, and orange juice. Spoon the mixture into the prepared dish.

3 To make the topping, sift the flour into a mixing bowl and rub in the margarine with your fingertips until the mixture resembles fine breadcrumbs. Stir in the slivered almonds, oats, and molasses. Mix until well combined.

4 Sprinkle the topping evenly over the pear and ginger mixture in the dish.

5 Bake in a preheated oven at 375°F for 30 minutes, until the topping is golden and the fruit tender. Serve with soy custard, if using.

Rice & Banana Brûlée

Take a can of rice pudding, flavor it with orange zest, preserved ginger, raisins, and sliced bananas and top with a brown sugar glaze.

NUTRITIONAL INFORMATION

Calories	509	Sugars	........98g
Protein	.........9g	Fat	...........6g
Carbohydrate	...112g	Saturates	.......4g

5 MINS   5 MINS

SERVES 2

INGREDIENTS

14 oz can creamed rice pudding

grated zest of ½ orange

2 pieces crystallized ginger,
  finely chopped

2 tsp ginger syrup from the jar

¼ cup raisins

1–2 bananas

1–2 tsp lemon juice

4–5 tbsp brown crystal sugar

1 Empty the can of rice pudding into a bowl and mix in the grated orange zest, ginger, ginger syrup, and raisins.

2 Cut the bananas diagonally into slices, toss in the lemon juice to prevent them from discoloring, drain, and divide between 2 individual flameproof dishes.

3 Spoon the rice mixture in an even layer over the bananas so the dishes are almost full.

4 Sprinkle an even layer of sugar over the rice in each dish.

5 Place the dishes under a preheated moderate broiler and heat until the sugar melts, taking care the sugar does not burn.

6 Set aside to cool until the caramel sets, then chill in the refrigerator until ready to serve. Tap the caramel with the back of a spoon to break it.

COOK'S TIP

Canned rice pudding is very versatile and is delicious heated with orange segments and grated apples added. Try it served cold with grated chocolate and mixed chopped nuts stirred through it.

Indian Bread Pudding

This, the Indian equivalent of the English bread and butter pudding, is usually cooked for special occasions.

NUTRITIONAL INFORMATION

Calories 445   Sugars 43g
Protein . . . . .10g   Fat 20g
Carbohydrate . . .60g   Saturates 11g

20 MINS   25 MINS

SERVES 6

INGREDIENTS

6 medium slices bread

5 tbsp ghee (preferably pure)

¾ cup sugar

1¼ cups water

3 green cardamoms, without husks

2½ cups milk

¾ cup evaporated milk or
   khoya (see Cook's Tip)

½ tsp saffron threads

heavy cream, to serve (optional)

TO DECORATE

8 pistachios, soaked,
   peeled, and chopped

chopped almonds

2 leaves varq (silver leaf) (optional)

COOK'S TIP

To make khoya, bring 3¾ cups milk to a boil in a large, heavy saucepan. Reduce the heat and boil, stirring occasionally, for 35-40 minutes, until reduced to a quarter of its volume and resembling a sticky dough.

1 Cut the bread slices into quarters. Heat the ghee in a large, heavy-bottomed skillet. Add the bread slices and fry, turning once, until a crisp golden brown color. Place the fried bread in the base of a heatproof dish and set aside.

2 To make a syrup, place the sugar, water and cardamom seeds in a saucepan and bring to a boil over a medium heat, stirring constantly, until the sugar has dissolved. Boil until the syrup thickens. Pour the syrup over the fried bread.

3 Put the milk, evaporated milk or khoya (see Cook's Tip), and the saffron in a separate saucepan and bring to a boil over a low heat. Simmer until the it has halved in volume. Pour the mixture over the syrup-coated bread.

4 Decorate with the pistachios, chopped almonds, and varq (if using). Serve the bread pudding with cream, if liked.

Apple Fritters

These apple fritters are coated in a light, spiced batter and deep-fried until crisp and golden. Serve warm with an unusual almond sauce.

NUTRITIONAL INFORMATION

Calories 438   Sugars 15g
Protein ....6g   Fat 32g
Carbohydrate ...35g   Saturates 4g

 15 MINS

15 MINS

SERVES 4

I N G R E D I E N T S

¾ cup all-purpose flour

pinch of salt

½ tsp ground cinnamon

¾ cup warm water

4 tsp vegetable oil

2 egg whites

2 eating apples, peeled

vegetable or sunflower oil,
    for deep-frying

sugar and cinnamon,
    to decorate

S A U C E

⅔ cup plain yogurt

½ tsp almond extract

2 tsp honey

1 Sift the flour and salt together into a large mixing bowl.

2 Add the cinnamon and mix well. Stir in the warm water and vegetable oil to make a smooth batter.

3 Whisk the egg whites until stiff peaks form and fold into the batter.

4 Using a sharp knife, cut the apples into chunks and dip the pieces of apple into the batter to coat.

5 Heat the oil for deep-frying to 350°F or until a cube of bread browns in 30 seconds. Fry the apple pieces, in batches if necessary, for about 3–4 minutes until light golden brown and puffy.

6 Remove the apple fritters from the oil with a perforated spoon and drain on paper towels.

7 Mix together the sugar and cinnamon and sprinkle over the fritters.

8 Mix the sauce ingredients in a serving bowl and serve with the fritters.

Frozen Citrus Soufflés

These delicious desserts are a refreshing way to end a meal. They can be made ahead of time and kept in the freezer until required.

NUTRITIONAL INFORMATION

Calories 364	Sugars 27g	
Protein 11g	Fat 24g	
Carbohydrate ...27g	Saturates 14g	

🍲 35 MINS   🕐 0 MINS

SERVES 4

I N G R E D I E N T S

1 tbsp vegetarian gelatin

6 tbsp very hot water

3 eggs, separated

⅓ cup sugar

finely grated zest and juice of 1 lemon,
   ½ lime, and ½ orange

⅔ cup heavy cream

½ cup plain fresh cheese

thin lemon, lime, and orange slices,
   to decorate

1 Tie parchment paper collars around 4 individual soufflé or ramekin dishes or around 1 large (6-inch diameter) soufflé dish.

2 Sprinkle the gelatin into the very hot (not boiling) water, stirring well to disperse. Leave to stand for 2–3 minutes, stirring occasionally, to give a completely clear liquid. Leave to cool for 10–15 minutes.

3 Meanwhile, whisk the egg yolks and sugar, using a hand-held electric mixer or eggbeater until very pale and light in texture. Add the zest and juice from the fruits, mixing well. Stir in the cooled gelatin liquid, making sure that it is thoroughly incorporated.

4 Put the cream in a large chilled bowl and whip until it holds its shape. Stir the fresh cheese and then add it to the cream, mixing it in gently. Fold the cream mixture into the citrus mixture, using a large metal spoon.

5 Using a clean whisk, beat the egg whites in a clean bowl until stiff, and then gently fold them into the citrus mixture, using a metal spoon.

6 Pour the mixture into the prepared dishes, almost to the top of their collars. Allow some room for the mixture to expand on freezing. Transfer the dishes to the freezer and open-freeze for about 2 hours, until frozen.

7 Remove from the freezer 10 minutes before serving. Peel away the parchment collars carefully and decorate with the slices of lemon, lime, and orange.

Almond Sherbet

It is best to use whole almonds rather than ready-ground almonds for this dish because they give it a better texture.

NUTRITIONAL INFORMATION

Calories	836	Sugars 33g
Protein	........29g	Fat 65g
Carbohydrate	...36g	Saturates 7g

3¾ HOURS   0 MINS

SERVES 2

INGREDIENTS

2 cups whole almonds

2 tbsp sugar

1¼ cups milk

1¼ cups water

1 Put the almonds in a bowl, cover with water, and set aside to soak for at least 3 hours or preferably overnight.

2 Using a sharp knife, chop the almonds into small pieces. Grind to a fine paste in a food processor or in a mortar with a pestle.

3 Add the sugar to the almond paste and grind once again to form a very fine paste.

4 Add the milk and water and mix thoroughly, preferably in a blender or food processor.

5 Transfer the almond sherbet to a large serving dish.

6 Chill the almond sherbet in the refrigerator for about 30 minutes. Stir it well just before serving.

Warm Currants in Cassis

Crème de cassis is a blackcurrant-based liqueur which comes from France and is an excellent flavoring for fruit dishes.

NUTRITIONAL INFORMATION

Calories	202	Sugars	........35g
Protein	.........2g	Fat	..........6g
Carbohydrate	...35g	Saturates	.......4g

   10 MINS 10 MINS

SERVES 4

I N G R E D I E N T S

3 cups blackcurrants

2 cups redcurrants

4 tbsp sugar

grated zest and juice of 1 orange

2 tsp arrowroot flour

2 tbsp crème de cassis

whipped cream, to serve

1 Using a fork, strip the currants from their stalks and put in a saucepan.

2 Add the sugar and orange zest and juice, and heat gently until the sugar has dissolved. Bring to a boil, then simmer gently for 5 minutes.

3 Strain the currants and place in a bowl. Return the juice to the pan. Blend the arrowroot with a little water to a smooth paste and mix into the juice. Bring to a boil over a medium heat and cook until thickened.

4 Set aside to cool slightly, then stir in the crème de cassis.

5 Serve in individual dishes with whipped cream.

Lime Cheesecakes

These cheesecakes are flavored with lime and mint, and set on a base of crushed graham crackers mixed with chocolate.

NUTRITIONAL INFORMATION

Calories 696   Sugars 44g
Protein ....18g   Fat 40g
Carbohydrate ...70g   Saturates 22g

3 HOURS   5 MINS

SERVES 2

INGREDIENTS

BASE

2 tbsp butter

1 square dark chocolate

1½ cups crushed graham crackers

FILLING

finely grated zest of 1 lime

⅓ cup creamed cottage cheese

⅓ cup low-fat cream cheese

1 mint sprig, very finely
   chopped (optional)

1 tsp vegetarian gelatin

1 tbsp lime juice

1 egg yolk

3 tbsp sugar

TO DECORATE

whipped cream

kiwi fruit slices

mint sprigs

1 Grease 2 fluted, preferably loose-based 4½-inch flan pans thoroughly. To make the base, melt the butter and chocolate in a heatproof bowl over a pan of gently simmering water, or melt in a microwave set on HIGH power for about 1 minute. Stir until smooth.

2 Stir the crushed graham crackers evenly through the melted chocolate and then press into the bases of the flan pans, leveling the surface. Chill until set.

3 To make the filling, put the grated lime zest and cheeses into a bowl and beat until smooth and evenly blended, then beat in the mint, if using.

4 Dissolve the gelatin in the lime juice in a heatproof bowl over a pan of simmering water or in a microwave set on HIGH power for about 30 seconds.

5 Beat the egg yolk and sugar together until creamy and fold into the cheese mixture, followed by the dissolved gelatin. Pour over the base and chill until set.

6 To serve, remove the cheesecakes carefully from the flan pans. Decorate with whipped cream, slices of kiwi, and mint sprigs.

Chocolate Mousse

This is a light and fluffy mousse with a subtle hint of orange. It is wickedly delicious served with a fresh fruit sauce.

NUTRITIONAL INFORMATION

Calories 164	Sugars 24g	
Protein 5g	Fat 5g	
Carbohydrate ...25g	Saturates 3g	

2¼ HOURS   5 MINS

SERVES 8

INGREDIENTS

4 squares dark chocolate, melted

1¼ cups plain yogurt

⅔ cup quark cheese

4 tbsp sugar

1 tbsp orange juice

1 tbsp brandy

1½ tsp vegetarian gelatin

9 tbsp cold water

2 large egg whites

coarsely grated dark and white chocolate
    and orange zest, to decorate

1 Put the melted chocolate, yogurt, quark cheese, sugar, orange juice, and brandy in a food processor and process for 30 seconds. Transfer the mixture to a large bowl.

COOK'S TIP

For a quick fruit sauce, process a can of mandarin segments in natural juice in a food processor and press through a strainer. Stir in 1 tablespoon honey and serve with the mousse.

2 Sprinkle the gelatin over the water and stir until dissolved.

3 In a pan, bring the gelatin and water to a boil for 2 minutes. Cool slightly, then stir into the chocolate.

4 Whisk the egg whites until stiff peaks form and fold into the chocolate mixture using a metal spoon.

5 Line a 1 lb 2 oz-loaf pan with plastic wrap. Spoon the mousse into the pan. Chill in the refrigerator for 2 hours, until set. Invert the mousse onto a serving plate, decorate, and serve.

Quick Syrup Sponge

You won't believe your eyes when you see just how quickly this light-as-air steamed sponge cooks in the microwave!

NUTRITIONAL INFORMATION

Calories 650	Sugars 60g	
Protein 10g	Fat 31g	
Carbohydrate . . .89g	Saturates 7g	

 15 MINS   ⏲ 5 MINS

SERVES 4

I N G R E D I E N T S

½ cup butter or margarine

4 tbsp light corn syrup

⅓ cup sugar

2 eggs

1 cup self-rising flour

1 tsp baking powder

about 2 tbsp warm water

custard, to serve

1 Grease a 1½-quart heatproof bowl with a small amount of the butter or margarine. Spoon the syrup into the bowl.

2 Cream the remaining butter or margarine with the sugar until light and fluffy. Gradually add the eggs, beating well between each addition.

3 Sift the flour and baking powder together, then fold into the creamed mixture using a large metal spoon. Add enough water to give a soft, dropping consistency. Spoon into the bowl and level the surface.

4 Cover with plastic wrap, leaving a small space to allow air to escape. Microwave on HIGH power for 4 minutes, then remove from the

microwave and allow the sponge to stand for 5 minutes, while it continues to cook.

5 Invert the sponge out onto a serving plate. Serve with custard.

COOK'S TIP

This sponge can be steamed conventionally. Cover it with a piece of pleated baking parchment and a piece of pleated foil. Place in a saucepan, add boiling water, and steam for 1½ hours.

Mixed Fruit Crumble

In this crumble, tropical fruits are flavored with ginger and coconut, for something a little different and very tasty.

NUTRITIONAL INFORMATION

Calories	602	Sugars	........51g
Protein	.........6g	Fat	..........29g
Carbohydrate	...84g	Saturates	......11g

 10 MINS 50 MINS

SERVES 4

I N G R E D I E N T S

2 mangoes, sliced

1 papaya, seeded and sliced

8 oz fresh pineapple, cubed

1½ tsp ground ginger

½ cup margarine

½ cup light brown sugar

1½ cups all-purpose flour

1 cup shredded coconut,
   plus extra to decorate

1 Place the fruit in a pan with ½ tsp of the ginger, 2 tbsp of the margarine, and ¼ cup of the sugar. Cook over a low heat for 10 minutes, until the fruit softens. Spoon the fruit into the base of a shallow ovenproof dish.

2 Mix the flour and remaining ginger together. Cut in the remaining

margarine until the mixture resembles fine breadcrumbs. Stir in the remaining sugar and the coconut and spoon over the fruit to cover completely.

3 Cook the crumble in a preheated oven at 350°F for about 40 minutes, or until the top is crisp. Decorate and serve.

VARIATION

Use other fruits, such as plums, apples, or blackberries, as a fruit base and add chopped nuts to the topping instead of the coconut.

Saffron-Spiced Rice Pudding

This rich pudding is cooked in milk delicately flavored with saffron, then mixed with dried fruit, almonds, and cream before baking.

NUTRITIONAL INFORMATION

Calories 339	Sugars 28g
Protein 9g	Fat 16g
Carbohydrate ...41g	Saturates 9g

 5 MINS   1 HOUR

SERVES 4

I N G R E D I E N T S

2½ cups creamy whole milk

several pinches of saffron threads, finely crushed (see Cook's Tip)

¼ cup short grain rice

1 cinnamon stick or piece of cassia bark

¼ cup sugar

¼ cup seedless raisins or golden raisins

¼ cup dried apricots, chopped

1 egg, beaten

5 tbsp light cream

11 tbsp butter, diced

2 tbsp slivered almonds

freshly grated nutmeg, for sprinkling

cream, for serving (optional)

1 Place the milk and crushed saffron in a non-stick saucepan and bring to a boil. Stir in the rice and cinnamon stick, reduce the heat, and simmer very gently, uncovered, stirring frequently, for 25 minutes, until tender.

2 Remove the pan from the heat. Remove and discard the cinnamon stick from the rice mixture. Stir in the sugar, raisins, or golden raisins and dried apricots, then beat in the egg, cream, and diced butter.

3 Transfer the mixture to a greased ovenproof pie or flan dish, sprinkle with the almonds and freshly grated nutmeg to taste. Cook in a preheated oven at 350°F for 25–30 minutes, until mixture is set and lightly golden. Serve hot with extra cream, if wished.

COOK'S TIP

For a slightly stronger flavor, place the saffron threads on a small piece of aluminum foil and toast them lightly under a hot broiler for a few moments and then crush between your fingers and thumb.

Christmas Shortbread

Make this wonderful shortbread and then give it the Christmas touch by cutting it into shapes with seasonal cookie cutters.

NUTRITIONAL INFORMATION

Calories 162   Sugars 10g
Protein . . . . .1g   Fat 9g
Carbohydrate . . .21g   Saturates 6g

🧊 45 MINS   🕐 15 MINS

MAKES 24

I N G R E D I E N T S

½ cup sugar

1 cup butter

3 cups all-purpose
    flour, sifted

pinch of salt

TO DECORATE

½ cup icing sugar

edible silver balls

candied cherries

1 Beat the sugar and butter together in a large bowl until combined (thorough creaming is not necessary).

2 Sift in the flour and salt and work together to form a stiff dough. Transfer to a lightly floured work counter. Knead lightly for a few moments until smooth, but avoid overhandling. Chill in the refrigerator for 10–15 minutes.

3 Roll out the dough on a lightly floured work counter and cut into shapes with small Christmas cookie cutters, such as bells, stars, and angels. Place on greased cookie sheets.

4 Bake the cookies in a preheated oven at 350°F for 10–15 minutes, until pale golden brown. Leave on the cookie sheets for 10 minutes, then transfer to cooling racks to cool completely.

5 Mix the icing sugar with a little water to make a frosting, and use to frost the cookies. Decorate with silver balls, and tiny pieces of candied cherries. Store in an airtight container or wrap the cookies individually in cellophane, tie with colored ribbon or string, and then hang them on the Christmas tree as edible decorations.

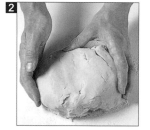  

Passion Cake

Decorating this moist, rich carrot cake with sugared flowers lifts it into the celebration class. It is a perfect choice for Easter.

NUTRITIONAL INFORMATION

Calories 506   Sugars 40g
Protein . . . . .10g   Fat 27g
Carbohydrate . . .60g   Saturates 4g

 15 MINS   1½ HOURS

SERVES 10

INGREDIENTS

⅔ cup corn oil

¾ cup sugar

4 tbsp plain yogurt

3 eggs, plus 1 extra yolk

1 tsp vanilla extract

1 cup walnut pieces, chopped

6 oz carrots, grated

1 banana, mashed

1½ cups all-purpose flour

½ cup fine oatmeal

1 tsp baking soda

1 tsp baking powder

1 tsp ground cinnamon

½ tsp salt

FROSTING

generous ½ cup cream cheese

4 tbsp plain yogurt

¾ cup icing sugar

1 tsp grated lemon zest

2 tsp lemon juice

DECORATION

primroses and violets

1 egg white, lightly beaten

3 tbsp sugar

1 Grease and line a 9-inch round cake pan. Beat together the oil, sugar, yogurt, eggs, egg yolk, and vanilla extract. Beat in the chopped walnuts, grated carrot, and banana.

2 Sift together the remaining ingredients and gradually beat into the mixture.

3 Pour the mixture into the pan and level the surface. Bake in a preheated oven at 350°F for 1½ hours, or until firm. To test, insert a fine skewer into the center: it should come out clean. Leave to cool in the pan for 15 minutes, then invert onto a cooling rack.

4 To make the frosting, beat together the cream cheese and yogurt. Sift in the icing sugar and stir in the lemon zest and juice. Spread over the top and sides of the cake.

5 To prepare the decoration, dip the flowers quickly in the beaten egg white, then sprinkle with sugar to cover the surface completely. Place well apart on baking parchment. Leave in a warm, dry place for several hours until they are dry and crisp. Arrange the flowers in a pattern on top of the cake.

Indian Vermicelli Pudding

Indian vermicelli (seviyan), which is very fine, is delicious cooked in milk and ghee. Muslims make this for a religious festival called Eid.

NUTRITIONAL INFORMATION

Calories	397	Sugars	........42g
Protein	........11g	Fat	..........17g
Carbohydrate	...54g	Saturates	.......8g

 5 MINS   20 MINS

SERVES 6

I N G R E D I E N T S

¼ cup pistachios (optional)

¼ cup slivered almonds

3 tbsp ghee

1½ cups seviyan (Indian vermicelli)

3¾ cups milk

¾ cup evaporated milk

8 tbsp sugar

6 dried dates, pitted

1 Soak the pistachios (if using) in a bowl of water for at least 3 hours. Peel the pistachios and mix them with the slivered almonds. Chop the nuts finely and set aside.

2 Melt the ghee in a large saucepan and lightly fry the seviyan (Indian

vermicelli). Reduce the heat immediately (the seviyan will turn golden brown very quickly so be careful not to burn it), and if necessary remove the pan from the heat (do not worry if some bits are a little darker than others).

3 Add the milk to the seviyan (Indian vermicelli) and bring to a boil over a low heat, taking care that it does not boil over.

4 Add the evaporated milk, sugar, and dates to the mixture in the pan. Simmer over a low heat, uncovered, stirring occasionally, for about 10 minutes. When the consistency starts to thicken, pour the pudding into a warmed serving bowl.

5 Decorate the pudding with the chopped pistachios and slivered almonds.

COOK'S TIP

You will find seviyan (Indian vermicelli) in Indian food markets. This dessert can be served warm or cold.

Bread & Butter Pudding

There are many versions of this English recipe, but this one has added marmalade and grated apples for a really rich and unique taste.

NUTRITIONAL INFORMATION

Calories	427	Sugars	........63g
Protein	.........9g	Fat	..........13g
Carbohydrate	...74g	Saturates	.......7g

 45 MINS   1 HOUR

SERVES 6

I N G R E D I E N T S

about ¼ cup butter, softened

4–5 slices white or brown bread

4 tbsp chunky orange marmalade

grated zest of 1 lemon

½–¾ cup raisins or golden raisins

¼ cup chopped mixed candied fruit peel

1 tsp ground cinnamon or mixed apple
 spice

1 cooking apple, peeled,
 cored, and coarsely grated

½ cup light brown sugar

3 eggs

2 cups milk

2 tbsp brown sugar

1 Use the butter to grease an ovenproof dish and to spread on the slices of bread, then spread the bread with the marmalade.

2 Place a layer of bread in the base of the dish and sprinkle with the lemon zest, half the raisins or golden raisins, half the mixed candied peel, half the spice, all of the apple, and half the light brown sugar.

3 Add another layer of bread, cutting so it fits the dish.

4 Sprinkle over most of the remaining raisins or golden raisins and the remaining peel, spice, and light brown sugar, sprinkling it evenly over the bread. Top with a final layer of bread, again cutting to fit the dish.

5 Lightly beat together the eggs and milk and then carefully strain the mixture over the bread in the dish. If time allows, set aside to stand for 20–30 minutes.

6 Sprinkle the top of the pudding with the brown sugar and scatter over the remaining raisins or golden raisins and cook in a preheated oven at 400°F for 50–60 minutes, until risen and golden brown. Serve immediately, or allow to cool and then serve cold.

Fruit & Nut Loaf

This loaf is like a fruit bread which may be served warm or cold, perhaps spread with a little margarine or butter or topped with jam (jelly).

NUTRITIONAL INFORMATION

Calories . . . . . . .354 Sugars 36g
Protein . . . . .8g Fat 9g
Carbohydrate . . .64g Saturates 1.2g

 35 MINS   40 MINS

SERVES 6

INGREDIENTS

225 g/8 oz/1¾ cups white bread flour,
    plus extra for dusting

½ tsp salt

1 tbsp margarine, plus extra for greasing

2 tbsp light brown sugar

100 g/3½ oz/⅔ cup sultanas (golden raisins)

50 g/1¾ oz/¼ cup ready-to-eat
    dried apricots, chopped

50 g/1¾ oz/½ cup chopped hazelnuts

2 tsp easy-blend dried (active dry) yeast

6 tbsp orange juice

6 tbsp natural (unsweetened) yogurt

2 tbsp strained apricot jam (jelly)

VARIATION

You can vary the nuts according to whatever you have at hand – try chopped walnuts or almonds.

1 Sift the flour and salt into a mixing bowl. Add the margarine and rub in with the fingertips. Stir in the sugar, sultanas (golden raisins), apricots, nuts and yeast.

2 Warm the orange juice in a saucepan, but do not allow to boil.

3 Stir the warm orange juice into the flour mixture, together with the natural (unsweetened) yogurt and bring the mixture together to form a dough.

4 Knead the dough on a lightly floured surface for 5 minutes, until smooth and elastic. Shape into a round and place on a lightly greased baking tray (cookie sheet). Cover with a clean tea towel (dish cloth) and leave to rise in a warm place until doubled in size.

5 Cook the loaf in a preheated oven, 220°C/425°F/Gas Mark 7, for 35–40 minutes, until cooked through. Transfer to a wire rack and brush with the apricot jam. Leave to cool before serving.

Apricot Brûlée

Serve this melt-in-the-mouth dessert with crisp baked meringues for an extra-special occasion.

NUTRITIONAL INFORMATION

Calories 307	Sugars 38g
Protein 5g	Fat 16g
Carbohydrate . . .38g	Saturates 9g

 2¼ HOURS 35 MINS

SERVES 6

INGREDIENTS

⅔ cup unsulphured dried apricots

⅔ cup orange juice

4 egg yolks

2 tbsp sugar

⅔ cup plain yogurt

⅔ cup heavy cream

1 tsp vanilla extract

½ cup brown sugar

meringues, to serve (optional)

1 Place the apricots and orange juice in a bowl and set aside to soak for at least 1 hour. Pour into a small pan, bring slowly to a boil, and simmer for 20 minutes. Process in a blender or food processor or chop very finely and push through a strainer.

2 Beat together the egg yolks and sugar until the mixture is light and fluffy. Place the yogurt in a small pan, add the cream and vanilla, and bring to a boil over a low heat.

3 Pour the yogurt mixture over the eggs, beating all the time, then transfer to the top of a double boiler or place the bowl over a pan of simmering water. Stir until the custard thickens. Divide the apricot mixture between 6 ramekins and carefully pour on the custard. Cool, then chill in the refrigerator at least 1 hour.

4 Sprinkle the brown crystal sugar evenly over the custard and place under a preheated broiler until the sugar caramelizes. Set aside to cool. To serve the brûlée, crack the hard caramel topping with the back of a tablespoon.

Spiced Steamed Pudding

Steamed puddings are irresistible on a winter's day, but the texture of this pudding is so light it can be served throughout the year.

NUTRITIONAL INFORMATION

Calories 488	Sugars 56g
Protein 5g	Fat 19g
Carbohydrate . . .78g	Saturates 4g

🍮 15 MINS   🕐 1½ HOURS

SERVES 6

I N G R E D I E N T S

2 tbsp light corn syrup, plus extra
    to serve

½ cup butter or margarine

generous ½ cup

2 eggs

1½ cups self-rising flour

¾ tsp ground cinnamon or apple spice

grated zest of 1 orange

1 tbsp orange juice

½ cup golden raisins

5 tbsp crystallized ginger,
    finely chopped

1 apple, peeled, cored, and
    coarsely grated

1 Thoroughly grease a 3³/₄-cup heatproof bowl. Put the light corn syrup into the bowl.

2 Cream the butter or margarine and sugar together until very light and fluffy and pale in color. Beat in the eggs, one at a time, following each with a spoonful of the flour.

3 Sift the remaining flour with the cinnamon or apple spice and fold into the mixture, followed by the orange zest and juice. Fold in the golden raisins, then the ginger and apple.

4 Turn the mixture into the bowl and level the top. Cover with a piece of pleated greased baking parchment, tucking the edges under the rim of the bowl.

5 Cover with a sheet of pleated foil. Tie securely in place with string, with a piece of string tied over the top of the bowl for a handle to make it easy to lift out of the saucepan.

6 Put the bowl into a saucepan half-filled with boiling water, cove, and steam for 1½ hours, adding more boiling water to the pan as necessary during cooking.

7 To serve the pudding, remove the foil and parchment, invert the pudding and its sauce onto a warmed serving plate and serve immediately.

Pistachio Dessert

An attractive-looking dessert, especially when decorated, this is another dish that can be prepared ahead of time.

NUTRITIONAL INFORMATION

Calories 676	Sugars 98g	
Protein 15g	Fat 27g	
Carbohydrate ...98g	Saturates 9g	

 15 MINS   10 MINS

SERVES 6

I N G R E D I E N T S

3¾ cups water

2 cups pistachios

1¾ cups dried whole milk powder

2⅓ cups sugar

2 cardamoms, with seeds crushed

2 tbsp rosewater

a few threads of saffron

TO DECORATE

¼ cup slivered almonds

mint leaves

1 Put about 2½ cups water in a saucepan and bring to a boil. Remove the pan from the heat and soak the pistachios in this water for about 5 minutes. Drain the pistachios thoroughly and remove the skins.

2 Process the pistachios in a food processor or grind in a mortar with a pestle.

3 Add the dried milk powder to the ground pistachios and mix well.

4 To make the syrup, place the remaining water and the sugar in a pan and heat gently. When the liquid begins to thicken, add the cardamom seeds, rosewater, and saffron.

5 Add the syrup to the pistachio mixture and cook, stirring constantly, for about 5 minutes, until the mixture thickens. Set the mixture aside and to cool slightly.

6 Once cool enough to handle, roll the mixture into balls in the palms of your hands. Decorate with the slivered almonds and fresh mint leaves and leave to set before serving.

COOK'S TIP

It is best to buy whole pistachio nuts and grind them yourself, rather than using packs of ready-ground nuts. Freshly ground nuts have the best flavor because grinding releases their natural oils.

Upside-down Cake

This recipe shows how a classic favorite can be adapted for vegans by using vegetarian margarine and oil instead of butter and eggs.

NUTRITIONAL INFORMATION

Calories 354
Sugars 31g
Protein 3g
Fat 15g
Carbohydrate . . .56g
Saturates 2g

 15 MINS   50 MINS

SERVES 6

I N G R E D I E N T S

¼ cup vegan margarine,
 cut into small pieces, plus extra
 for greasing

15 oz can unsweetened pineapple
 pieces, drained and juice reserved

4 tsp cornstarch

¼ cup soft brown sugar

½ cup water

zest of 1 lemon

S P O N G E

¼ cup sunflower oil

⅓ cup soft brown sugar

⅔ cup water

1¼ cups all-purpose flour

2 tsp baking powder

1 tsp ground cinnamon

1 Grease a deep 7-inch cake pan. Mix the reserved juice from the pineapple with the cornstarch until it forms a smooth paste. Put the paste in a saucepan with the sugar, margarine, and water and stir over a low heat until the sugar has dissolved. Bring to a boil and simmer for 2–3 minutes, until thickened. Set aside to cool slightly.

2 To make the sponge, place the oil, sugar, and water in a saucepan. Heat gently until the sugar has dissolved; do not allow it to boil. Remove from the heat and leave to cool. Sift the flour, baking powder, and ground cinnamon into a mixing bowl. Pour over the cooled sugar syrup and beat well to form a batter.

3 Place the pineapple pieces and lemon zest on the base of the prepared pan and pour over 4 tablespoons of the pineapple syrup. Spoon the sponge batter on top.

4 Bake in a preheated oven at 350°F for 35–40 minutes, until set and a fine metal skewer inserted into the center comes out clean. Invert onto a plate, leave to stand for 5 minutes, then remove the pan. Serve with the remaining syrup.

Baked Semolina Pudding

Succulent plums simmered in orange juice and apple spice complement this rich and creamy semolina pudding perfectly.

NUTRITIONAL INFORMATION

Calories	304	Sugars	........32g
Protein	.........9g	Fat	..........12g
Carbohydrate	...43g	Saturates	.......4g

🍰 5 MINS   🕐 45 MINS

SERVES 4

I N G R E D I E N T S

2 tbsp butter or margarine

2½ cups milk

finely pared zest and juice of 1 orange

⅓ cup semolina

pinch of grated nutmeg

2 tbsp sugar

1 egg, beaten

TO SERVE

butter

grated nutmeg

SPICED PLUMS

8 oz plums, halved and pitted

⅔ cup orange juice

2 tbsp sugar

½ tsp ground apple spice

1 Grease a 4 cup ovenproof dish with a little of the butter or margarine. Put the milk, the remaining butter or margarine, and the orange zest in a saucepan. Sprinkle in the semolina and heat until boiling, stirring constantly. Simmer gently for 2–3 minutes. Remove from the heat.

2 Add the nutmeg, orange juice, and sugar to the semolina mixture, stirring well. Add the egg and stir to mix.

3 Transfer the mixture to the prepared dish and bake in a preheated oven at 375°F for about 30 minutes, until lightly browned.

4 To make the spiced plums, put the plums, orange juice, sugar, and spice into a saucepan and simmer gently for about 10 minutes, until just tender. Set aside to cool slightly.

5 Top the semolina pudding with butter and grated nutmeg, and serve with the spiced plums.

Cherry Clafoutis

This is a hot dessert that is simple and quick to put together. Try the batter with other fruits. Apricots and plums are particularly delicious.

NUTRITIONAL INFORMATION

Calories . . . . .261 Sugars 24g
Protein . . . . .10g Fat 6g
Carbohydrate . . .40g Saturates 3g

 10 MINS 40 MINS

SERVES 6

I N G R E D I E N T S

1 cup all-purpose flour

4 eggs, lightly beaten

2 tbsp sugar

pinch of salt

2½ cups milk

butter, for greasing

1 lb 2 oz black cherries,
    fresh or canned, pitted

3 tbsp brandy

1 tbsp sugar, to decorate

1 Sift the flour into a large mixing bowl. Make a well in the center and add the eggs, sugar, and salt. Gradually, draw in the flour from around the edges and whisk.

2 Pour in the milk and whisk the batter thoroughly until very smooth.

3 Thoroughly grease a 7½-cup ovenproof serving dish with butter and pour in about half of the batter.

4 Spoon over the cherries and pour the remaining batter over the top. Sprinkle the brandy over the batter.

5 Bake in a preheated oven at 350°F for 40 minutes, until risen and golden.

6 Remove from the oven and sprinkle over the sugar just before serving. Serve warm.

Sweet Saffron Rice

This is a traditional Indian dessert, which is quick and easy to make and looks very impressive, especially decorated with pistachios.

NUTRITIONAL INFORMATION

Calories 460   Sugars 57g
Protein ....4g   Fat 9g
Carbohydrate ...97g   Saturates 5g

 5 MINS   35 MINS

SERVES 4

INGREDIENTS

1 cup basmati rice

1 cup sugar

1 pinch saffron threads

1¼ cups water

2 tbsp vegetable ghee

3 cloves

3 cardamoms

2 tbsp golden raisins

TO DECORATE

a few pistachios (optional)

silver leaf (optional) (see p. 471)

1 Rinse the rice twice and bring to a boil in a saucepan of water, stirring constantly. Remove the pan from the heat when the rice is half-cooked, drain the rice thoroughly, and set aside.

2 In a separate saucepan, boil the sugar and saffron in the water, stirring constantly, until the syrup thickens. Set the syrup aside until required.

3 In another saucepan, heat the ghee, cloves, and cardamoms, stirring occasionally. Remove the pan from the heat.

4 Return the rice to a low heat and stir in the golden raisins.

5 Pour the syrup over the rice mixture and stir to mix.

6 Pour the ghee mixture over the rice and simmer over a low heat for about 10–15 minutes. Check to see whether the rice is cooked. If it is not, add a little boiling water, cover, and continue to simmer until tender.

7 Serve warm, decorated with pistachios and silver leaf, if desired.

COOK'S TIP

Basmati rice is the "prince of rices" and comes from the Himalayan foothills. Its name means fragrant and it has a superb texture and flavor.

Traditional Apple Pie

This apple pie has a double crust and can be served either hot or cold. The apples can be flavored with other spices or grated citrus zest.

NUTRITIONAL INFORMATION

Calories	577	Sugars	........36g
Protein	.........6g	Fat	..........28g
Carbohydrate	...80g	Saturates	.......9g

 55 MINS 50 MINS

SERVES 6

INGREDIENTS

1 lb 10 oz–2 lb 4 oz cooking

  apples, peeled, cored, and sliced

½ cup brown or white sugar, plus

extra for sprinkling

½–1 tsp ground cinnamon, apple spice, or

  ground ginger

1–2 tbsp water

PIE DOUGH

3 cups all-purpose flour

pinch of salt

6 tbsp butter or margarine

⅓ cup shortening

about 6 tbsp cold water

beaten egg or milk, for glazing

1 To make the pie dough, sift the flour and salt into a mixing bowl. Add the butter or margarine and shortening and rub in with the fingertips until the mixture resembles fine breadcrumbs. Add the water and gather the mixture together into a dough. Wrap the dough and chill for 30 minutes.

2 Roll out almost two-thirds of the pie dough thinly and use to line a 8–9-inch-deep pie plate or shallow pie pan.

3 Mix the apples with the sugar and spice and pack into the pie shell; the filling can come up above the rim. Add the water if liked, particularly if the apples are a dry variety.

4 Roll out the remaining pie dough to form a lid. Dampen the edges of the pie rim with water and position the lid, pressing the edges firmly together. Trim and crimp the edges.

5 Use the trimmings to cut out leaves or other shapes to decorate the top of the pie, dampen, and attach. Glaze the top of the pie with beaten egg or milk, make 1–2 slits in the top, and put the pie on a cookie sheet.

6 Bake in a preheated oven at 425°F for 20 minutes, then reduce the temperature to 350°F and cook for about 30 minutes, until the pastry is a light golden brown. Serve hot or cold, sprinkled with sugar.

Lemon & Lime Syllabub

This dessert is rich but absolutely delicious. It is not, however, for the calorie conscious as it contains a high proportion of cream.

NUTRITIONAL INFORMATION

Calories 403	Sugars 16g	
Protein 2g	Fat 36g	
Carbohydrate ...16g	Saturates 22g	

  4¼ HOURS 0 MINS

SERVES 4

INGREDIENTS

¼ cup sugar

grated zest and juice of
  1 small lemon

grated zest and juice of
  1 small lime

¼ cup Marsala or medium sherry

1¼ cups heavy cream

lime and lemon zest,
  to decorate

1 Put the sugar, lemon juice, and zest, lime juice and zest, and sherry in a bowl, mix well, and set aside to infuse for 2 hours.

2 Add the cream to the fruit juice mixture and whisk until it just holds its shape.

3 Spoon the mixture into 4 tall serving glasses and chill in the refrigerator for 2 hours.

4 Decorate with lime and lemon zest and serve.

Fruity Pancake Bundles

This unusual pancake is filled with a sweet cream, flavored with ginger, nuts, and apricots, and served with a raspberry and orange sauce.

NUTRITIONAL INFORMATION

Calories 610   Sugars 60g
Protein . . . . .19g   Fat 20g
Carbohydrate . . .94g   Saturates 5g

 15 MINS   35 MINS

SERVES 2

I N G R E D I E N T S

BATTER

½ cup all-purpose flour

pinch of salt

¼ tsp ground cinnamon

1 egg

generous ½ cup milk

shortening, for frying

FILLING

1½ tsp all-purpose flour, sifted

1½ tsp cornstarch

1 tbsp sugar

1 egg

⅔ cup milk

¼ cup chopped nuts

¼ cup dried apricots, chopped

1 piece crystallized ginger,
  finely chopped

SAUCE

3 tbsp raspberry preserve

4½ tsp orange juice

finely grated zest of ¼ orange

1 To make the batter, sift the flour, salt, and cinnamon into a bowl and make a well in the center. Add the egg and beat in the flour and milk gradually until smooth.

2 Melt a little shortening in a medium skillet. Pour in batter to cover the base thinly. Cook for 2 minutes until golden, then cook the other side for about 1 minute, until browned. Set aside and make a second pancake.

3 For the filling, beat together the flour, cornstarch, sugar, and egg. Heat the milk gently in a pan, then beat 2 tablespoons of it into the flour mixture. Transfer to the saucepan and cook gently, stirring constantly until thick. Remove from the heat, cover with baking parchment to prevent a skin forming, and leave to cool.

4 Beat the nuts, apricots, and ginger into the cooled mixture and put a heaped tablespoonful in the center of each pancake. Gather and squeeze the edges together to make a bundle. Place in an ovenproof dish in a preheated oven at 350°F for 15–20 minutes, until hot but not too brown.

5 To make the sauce, melt the preserve gently with the orange juice, then strain. Return to a clean pan with the orange zest and heat through. Serve with the pancakes.

Indian Rice Pudding

This rice pudding is cooked in a saucepan over a low heat, rather than in the oven, and is a less sweet version than many conventional recipes.

NUTRITIONAL INFORMATION

Calories . . . . . . .152 Sugars 23g
Protein . . . . .5g Fat 3g
Carbohydrate . . .29g Saturates 1g

  10 MINS   30 MINS

SERVES 10

I N G R E D I E N T S

¼ cup basmati rice

5 cups milk

8 tbsp sugar

silver leaf or chopped pistachios,
  to decorate

1 Rinse the rice and place in a large saucepan. Add 2½ cups of the milk and bring to a boil over a very low heat. Cook, stirring occasionally, until the milk has been completely absorbed by the rice.

2 Remove the pan from the heat. Mash the rice, making swift, round movements in the pan, for at least 5 minutes, until all of the lumps have been removed.

3 Gradually add the remaining 2½ cups milk. Bring to a boil over a low heat, stirring occasionally.

4 Add the sugar and continue to cook, stirring constantly, for 7–10 minutes, or until the mixture is quite thick in consistency.

5 Transfer the rice pudding to a heatproof serving bowl. Decorate with varq (silver leaf) or chopped pistachios, and serve on its own or with pooris.

COOK'S TIP

Varq is edible silver that is used to decorate elaborate dishes prepared for special occasions and celebrations in India. It is pure silver that has been beaten until it is wafer thin. It comes with a backing paper that is peeled off as the varq is laid on the cooked food.

Potato & Nutmeg Scones

Making these scones with mashed potato gives them a slightly different texture from traditional scones, but they are just as delicious.

NUTRITIONAL INFORMATION

Calories 178	Sugars 8g
Protein 4g	Fat 5g
Carbohydrate ...30g	Saturates 3g

  15 MINS   30 MINS

MAKES 6

INGREDIENTS

8 oz russet potatoes, diced

1 cup all-purpose flour

1½ tsp baking powder

½ tsp grated nutmeg

⅓ cup golden raisins

1 egg, beaten

¼ cup heavy cream

2 tsp light brown sugar

1 Line and lightly grease a cookie sheet.

2 Cook the diced potatoes in a saucepan of boiling water for 10 minutes, or until soft. Drain thoroughly and mash the potatoes.

COOK'S TIP

For extra convenience, make a batch of scones ahead of time and open-freeze them. Thaw thoroughly and warm in a moderate oven when ready to serve.

3 Transfer the mashed potatoes to a large mixing bowl and stir in the flour, baking powder, and grated nutmeg, mixing well to combine.

4 Stir in the golden raisins, beaten egg, and cream, and then beat the mixture thoroughly with a spoon until completely smooth.

5 Shape the mixture into 8 rounds ¾ inch thick and put on the cookie sheet.

6 Cook in a preheated oven at 400°F for about 15 minutes, or until the scones have risen and are golden. Sprinkle with sugar and serve warm and spread with butter.

Chocolate Bread Pudding

This chocolate pudding is served with hot fudge sauce, making it the most delicious way to use up bread that is slightly stale.

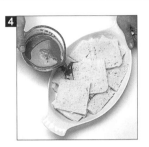

NUTRITIONAL INFORMATION

Calories ....633 Sugars 50g
Protein ....18g Fat 29g
Carbohydrate ...79g Saturates 11g

 2¼ HOURS 45 MINS

SERVES 4

INGREDIENTS

6 thick slices white bread, crusts removed

2 cups milk

6 oz can evaporated milk

2 tbsp unsweetened cocoa powder

2 eggs

2 tbsp dark brown sugar

1 tsp vanilla extract

icing sugar, for dusting

HOT FUDGE SAUCE

2 squares dark chocolate,
  broken into pieces

1 tbsp unsweetened cocoa powder

2 tbsp light corn syrup

¼ cup butter or margarine

2 tbsp dark brown sugar

⅔ cup milk

1 tbsp cornstarch

1 Grease a shallow ovenproof dish. Cut the bread into squares and layer them in the dish.

2 Put the milk, evaporated milk, and unsweetened cocoa powder in a saucepan and heat gently, stirring occasionally, until lukewarm.

3 Whisk together the eggs, sugar, and vanilla extract. Add the warm milk mixture and beat well.

4 Pour into the prepared dish, making sure that all the bread is completely covered. Cover the dish with plastic wrap and chill in the refrigerator for 1–2 hours.

5 Bake the pudding in a preheated oven at 350°F for about 35–40 minutes, until set. Allow to stand for 5 minutes.

6 To make the sauce, put the chocolate, unsweetened cocoa powder, syrup, butter or margarine, sugar, milk, and cornstarch into a saucepan. Heat gently, stirring until smooth.

7 Dust the pudding with icing sugar and serve with the hot fudge sauce.

Carrot Dessert

This makes an impressive dinner-party dessert. It is best served warm, with cream, and can be made ahead of time because it freezes well.

NUTRITIONAL INFORMATION

Calories 509	Sugars 54g
Protein 8g	Fat 30g
Carbohydrate ...55g	Saturates 19g

 10 MINS   1 HOUR

SERVES 6

INGREDIENTS

3 lb 5 oz carrots

10 tbsp ghee

2½ pints milk

¾ cup evaporated milk or
   khoya (see page 446)

10 whole cardamoms, peeled and crushed

8–10 tbsp sugar

TO DECORATE

¼ cup pistachios, chopped

2 leaves varq (silver leaf) (optional)
   (see p.471)

1 Rinse, peel, and carefully grate the carrots.

2 Heat the ghee in a large, heavy saucepan.

COOK'S TIP

Pure ghee is best for this dessert, as it is rather special and tastes better made with pure ghee. However, if you are trying to limit your fat intake, use vegetable ghee instead.

3 Add the grated carrots to the ghee and stir-fry for 15–20 minutes, or until the moisture from the carrots has evaporated and the carrots have darkened in color.

4 Add the milk, evaporated milk or khoya, cardamoms, and sugar to the carrot mixture and continue to stir-fry for 30–35 minutes more, until it is a rich brownish-red color.

5 Transfer the carrot mixture to a large shallow dish.

6 Decorate with the pistachios and varq, if using, and serve immediately.

Barbecued Pineapple

Fresh pineapple slices are cooked on the grill, and brushed with a buttery fresh ginger and brown sugar baste.

NUTRITIONAL INFORMATION

Calories 461	Sugars 44g
Protein 5g	Fat 30g
Carbohydrate . . .45g	Saturates 20g

10 MINS   10 MINS

SERVES 4

INGREDIENTS

1 fresh pineapple

BUTTER

½ cup butter

½ cup light brown sugar

1 tsp finely grated fresh ginger

TOPPING

1 cup plain fromage frais

½ tsp ground cinnamon

1 tbsp light brown sugar

1 Prepare the fresh pineapple by cutting off the spiky top. Peel the pineapple with a sharp knife, remove the "eyes" and cut the flesh into thick slices.

2 To make the ginger-flavored butter, put the butter, sugar, and ginger into a small saucepan and heat gently until melted. Transfer to a heatproof bowl and keep warm at the side of the grill, ready for basting the fruit.

3 To prepare the topping, mix together the fresh cheese, cinnamon, and sugar. Cover and chill until ready to serve.

4 Barbecue the pineapple slices for about 2 minutes on each side, brushing them well with the ginger butter baste.

5 Serve the grilled pineapple with a little extra ginger butter sauce poured over. Top with a spoonful of the spiced fresh cheese.

VARIATION

If you prefer, substitute ½ teaspoon ground ginger for the grated fresh ginger. Light molasses sugar gives the best flavor, but you can use ordinary soft brown sugar instead. You can make this dessert indoors by cooking the pineapple under a hot broiler.

Chocolate Cheesecake

This cheesecake takes a little time to prepare and cook but is well worth the effort. It is quite rich and is good served with a little fresh fruit.

NUTRITIONAL INFORMATION

Calories 471   Sugars 20g
Protein . . . . .10g   Fat 33g
Carbohydrate . . .28g   Saturates 5g

15 MINS   1¼ HOURS

SERVES 12

I N G R E D I E N T S

¾ cup all-purpose flour

¾ cup ground almonds

¾ cup brown sugar

11 tbsp margarine

1½ lb firm tofu

¾ cup vegetable oil

½ cup orange juice

¾ cup brandy

6 tbsp unsweetened cocoa powder, plus
    extra to decorate

2 tsp almond extract

icing sugar and berries, to decorate

1 Put the flour, ground almonds, and 1 tablespoon of the sugar in a bowl and mix well. Cut in the margarine to form a dough.

2 Lightly grease and line the base of a 9-inch springform pan. Press the dough into the base of the pan to cover, pushing the dough right up to the edge of the pan.

3 Roughly chop the tofu and put in a food processor with the vegetable oil, orange juice, brandy, unsweetened cocoa powder, almond extract, and remaining sugar and process until smooth and creamy. Pour over the base in the pan and cook in a preheated oven at 325°F for 1–1¼ hours, or until set.

4 Leave to cool in the pan for 5 minutes, then remove from the pan and chill in the refrigerator. Dust with confectioners' sugar and unsweetened cocoa powder. Decorate with berries and serve.

COOK'S TIP

Cape gooseberries (ground cherries) make an attractive decoration for many desserts. Peel open the papery husks to expose the bright orange fruits.

Ginger & Apricot Alaskas

No ice cream in this Alaska, but a mixture of apples and apricots poached in orange juice enclosed in meringue.

NUTRITIONAL INFORMATION

Calories . . . . . . .442 Sugars 77g
Protein . . . . .7g Fat 9g
Carbohydrate . . .83g Saturates 3g

15 MINS   10 MINS

SERVES 2

I N G R E D I E N T S

2 slices rich, dark ginger cake,
  about ¾ inch thick

1–2 tbsp rum

1 apple

6 dried apricots, chopped

4 tbsp orange juice or water

1 tbsp slivered almonds

2 small egg whites

⅓ cup sugar

1 Place each slice of ginger cake on an ovenproof plate and sprinkle with the rum.

2 Quarter, core, and slice the apple into a small saucepan. Add the chopped apricots and orange juice or water, and simmer over a low heat for about 5 minutes, or until tender.

3 Stir the almonds into the fruit and spoon the mixture equally over the slices of soaked cake, piling it up in the center.

4 Whisk the egg whites until very stiff and dry, then whisk in the sugar, a little at a time, making sure the meringue has become stiff again before adding any more sugar.

5 Either pipe or spread the meringue over the fruit and cake, making sure that both are completely covered.

6 Place in a preheated oven at 400°F for 4–5 minutes, until golden brown. Serve hot.

VARIATION

A slice of vanilla, coffee, or chocolate ice cream can be placed on the fruit before adding the meringue, but this must be done at the last minute and the dessert must be eaten immediately after it is removed from the oven.

Stuffed Pooris

This is a very old family recipe from India. The pooris freeze well, so it pays to make a large quantity and re-heat them in the oven.

NUTRITIONAL INFORMATION

Calories 429   Sugars 22g
Protein ....9g   Fat 21g
Carbohydrate ...54g   Saturates 7g

6½ HOURS   1 HOUR

MAKES 10

INGREDIENTS

POORIS

1 cup coarse semolina

¾ cup all-purpose flour

½ tsp salt

4½ tsp ghee, plus extra for frying

⅔ cup milk

FILLING

8 tbsp channa dal

3¾ cups water

5 tbsp ghee

2 green cardamoms, peeled

4 cloves

8 tbsp sugar

2 tbsp ground almonds

½ tsp saffron threads

¼ cup golden raisins

1 To make the pooris, place the semolina, flour, and salt in a bowl and mix. Add the ghee and rub in with your fingertips. Add the milk and mix to form a dough. Knead the dough for 5 minutes, cover, and set aside for about 3 hours to rise. Knead the dough on a floured work counter for 15 minutes.

2 Roll out the dough until it measures 10 inches and divide into ten portions.

Roll out each of these into 5-inch rounds and set aside.

3 To make the filling, soak the chana dal for at least 3 hours. Place the dal in a pan and add 3 cups of the water. Bring to a boil over a medium heat until all of the water has evaporated and the dal is soft enough to be mashed into a paste.

4 Meanwhile, heat the ghee. Add the cardamom seeds and cloves. Lower the heat, add the dal paste, and stir for 5–7 minutes.

5 Fold in the sugar and almonds and cook, stirring constantly, for 10 minutes. Add the saffron and golden raisins and blend until thickened. Cook, stirring constantly, for 5 minutes.

6 Spoon the filling onto one half of each dough round. Dampen the edges with water and fold the other half over, pressing to seal.

7 Heat the ghee in a pan and fry the filled pooris over a low heat until golden. Drain on paper towels and serve immediately.

Summer Puddings

A wonderful mixture of summer fruits encased in slices of white bread which soak up all the deep red, flavorsome juices.

NUTRITIONAL INFORMATION

Calories	250	Sugars	........41g
Protein	.........4g	Fat	...........4g
Carbohydrate	...53g	Saturates	.......2g

 10 MINS   10 MINS

SERVES 6

I N G R E D I E N T S

vegetable oil or butter, for greasing

6–8 thin slices white bread, crusts removed

¾ cup sugar

1¼ cups water

2 cups strawberries

2½ cups raspberries

1¼ cups blackcurrants and/or redcurrants

¾ cup blackberries or loganberries

mint sprigs, to decorate

cream, to serve

1 Grease six ⅔-cup molds with butter or oil.

2 Line the molds with the bread, cutting it so it fits snugly.

3 Place the sugar in a saucepan with the water and heat gently, stirring frequently until dissolved, then bring to a boil and boil for 2 minutes.

4 Reserve 6 large strawberries for decoration. Add half the raspberries and the rest of the fruits to the syrup, cutting the strawberries in half if large, and simmer gently for a few minutes, until

beginning to soften but still retaining their shape.

5 Spoon the fruits and some of the liquid into molds. Cover with more slices of bread. Spoon a little juice around the sides of the molds so the bread is well soaked. Cover with a saucer and a heavy weight, leave to cool, then chill thoroughly, preferably overnight.

6 Process the remaining raspberries in a food processor or blender, or press through a non-metallic strainer. Add enough of the liquid from the fruits to give a coating consistency.

7 Invert onto serving plates and spoon the raspberry sauce over. Decorate with the mint sprigs and reserved strawberries, and serve with cream.

Fruit Brûlée

This is a cheat's brûlée, in that yogurt is used to cover a base of fruit, before being sprinkled with sugar and broiled.

NUTRITIONAL INFORMATION

Calories	.311	Sugars	.48g
Protein	.7g	Fat	.11g
Carbohydrate	.48g	Saturates	.7g

1¼ HOURS   15 MINS

SERVES 4

INGREDIENTS

4 plums, pitted and sliced

2 cooking apples, peeled and sliced

1 tsp ground ginger

2½ cups thick plain yogurt

2 tbsp icing sugar, sifted

1 tsp almond extract

⅓ cup brown sugar

1 Put the plums and apples in a saucepan with 2 tablespoons of water and cook for 7–10 minutes, until tender, but not mushy. Set aside to cool, then stir in the ginger.

2 Using a perforated spoon, spoon the mixture into the base of a shallow serving dish.

  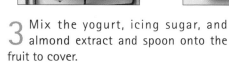

COOK'S TIP

Use any variety of fruit, such as mixed berries or mango pieces, for this dessert, but in that case, do not poach them.

3 Mix the yogurt, icing sugar, and almond extract and spoon onto the fruit to cover.

4 Sprinkle the brown crystal sugar over the top of the yogurt and cook under a hot broiler for 3–4 minutes, or until the sugar has dissolved and formed a crust.

5 Leave to chill in the refrigerator for 1 hour and serve.

Crêpes with Apples

The sharpness of the apples contrasts with the sweetness of the butterscotch sauce in this mouthwatering crêpe recipe.

NUTRITIONAL INFORMATION

Calories	543	Sugars 55g
Protein	.........8g	Fat 24g
Carbohydrate	...78g	Saturates 14g

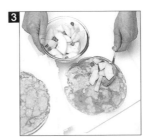

 15 MINS 45 MINS

SERVES 4

I N G R E D I E N T S

1 cup all-purpose flour

1 tsp finely grated lemon zest

1 egg

1¼ cups milk

1–2 tbsp vegetable oil

salt

pared lemon zest, to garnish

FILLING

8 oz apples, peeled, cored,
   and sliced

2 tbsp golden raisins

SAUCE

⅓ cup butter

3 tbsp light corn syrup

½ cup light brown sugar

1 tbsp rum or brandy (optional)

1 tbsp lemon juice

1 Sift the flour and salt into a large mixing bowl. Add the lemon zest, egg, and milk and whisk together to make a smooth batter.

2 Heat a little oil in a heavy-bottomed skillet. Make 8 thin pancakes, using extra oil as required. Stack the cooked pancakes, layering them with paper towels.

3 To make the filling, cook the apples with the golden raisins in a little water until soft. Divide the mixture evenly between the pancakes and roll up or fold into triangles. Arrange the pancakes in a buttered ovenproof dish and bake in a preheated oven at 325°F for 15 minutes, until warmed through.

4 To make the sauce, melt the butter, syrup and sugar together in a saucepan, stirring well. Add the rum or brandy, if using, and the lemon juice. Do not allow the mixture to boil.

5 Serve the pancakes on warm plates, with a little sauce poured over and garnished with lemon zest.

Banana & Mango Tart

Bananas and mangoes are a great combination of colors and flavors, especially when topped with toasted coconut chips.

NUTRITIONAL INFORMATION

Calories 235	Sugars 17g	
Protein 4g	Fat 10g	
Carbohydrate . . .35g	Saturates 5g	

   1¼ HOURS   5 MINS

SERVES 8

INGREDIENTS

PASTRY

8-inch baked tart shell

FILLING

2 small ripe bananas

1 mango, sliced

3½ tbsp cornstarch

6 tbsp brown sugar

1¼ cups soy milk

⅔ cup coconut milk

1 tsp vanilla extract

toasted coconut chips, to decorate

COOK'S TIP

Coconut chips are available in some supermarkets and most health food shops. It is worth using them as they look much more attractive and are not so sweet as shredded coconut.

1 Slice the bananas and arrange half in the baked tart shell with half of the mango pieces.

2 Put the cornstarch and sugar in a saucepan and mix together. Gradually, stir in the soy and coconut milks until combined and cook over a low heat, beating until the mixture thickens.

3 Stir in the vanilla extract, then pour the mixture over the fruit.

4 Top with the remaining fruit and toasted coconut chips. Chill in the refrigerator for 1 hour before serving.

Christmas Tree Clusters

Popcorn is the perfect snack to have around at Christmas. If wrapped in cellophane, these clusters make ideal decorations for the Christmas tree.

NUTRITIONAL INFORMATION

Calories 94	Sugars 14g
Protein 1g	Fat 4g
Carbohydrate . . .15g	Saturates 0.3g

10 MINS   10 MINS

MAKES 16

I N G R E D I E N T S

1 tbsp vegetable oil

1 oz popping corn

2 tbsp butter

4 tbsp light brown sugar

4 tbsp light corn syrup

¼ cup candied cherries, chopped

⅓ cup golden raisins
   or raisins

½ cup ground almonds

2 tbsp chopped almonds

½ tsp ground apple spice

1 To pop the corn, heat the oil in a large saucepan or in a popcorn pan. The oil is hot enough when a kernel spins around in the pan. Add the popping corn, cover tightly, and pop the corn over a medium-high heat, shaking the pan frequently.

2 Remove the pan from the heat and wait until the popping sound subsides.

3 Put the butter, sugar, and syrup into a large saucepan and heat gently, stirring frequently, to dissolve the sugar. Do not allow the mixture to boil. Remove from the heat once the sugar is dissolved.

4 Add the popped corn, candied cherries, golden raisins or raisins, ground and chopeed almonds, and apple spice to the syrup mixture, stirring well. Set aside to cool for a few minutes.

5 Shape the mixture into small balls. Set aside to cool completely, then wrap in cellophane and tie with colored ribbon or string and hang from the Christmas tree.

VARIATION

Omit the cherries, golden raisins, ground almonds, and apple spice and replace with ½ cup roughly chopped pecans and ½ tsp ground cinnamon to make Pecan Nut Clusters.

Sweet Potato Dessert

This unusual milky dessert is very easy to make and can be eaten either hot or cold.

NUTRITIONAL INFORMATION

Calories ....234 Sugars 23g
Protein ....5g Fat 3g
Carbohydrate ...51g Saturates 1g

 15 MINS   20 MINS

SERVES 10

INGREDIENTS

2 lb 4 oz sweet potatoes

3¾ cups milk

1¾ cups sugar

a few chopped almonds, to decorate

1 Using a sharp knife, peel the sweet potatoes. Rinse them and then cut them into slices.

2 Place the sweet potato slices in a large saucepan. Cover with 2½ cups milk and cook over a low heat until the sweet potato is soft enough to be mashed.

3 Remove the sweet potatoes from the heat and mash thoroughly until completely smooth.

4 Add the sugar and the remaining 1¼ cups milk to the mashed sweet

potatoes, and carefully stir to blend together.

5 Return the pan to the heat and simmer the mixture until it starts to thicken (it should reach the consistency of a creamy soup).

6 Transfer the sweet potato dessert to a serving dish.

7 Decorate with the chopped almonds and serve immediately.

COOK'S TIP

Sweet potatoes are longer than ordinary potatoes and have a pinkish or yellowish skin with yellow or white flesh. As their name suggests, they taste slightly sweet.

Giggle Cake

It's a mystery how this cake got its name—perhaps it's because it's easy to make and fun to eat.

NUTRITIONAL INFORMATION

Calories 493	Sugars 66g
Protein 6g	Fat 15g
Carbohydrate ...90g	Saturates 3g

25 MINS   1¼ HOURS

SERVES 8

INGREDIENTS

2 cups mixed dried fruit

½ cup butter or margarine

1 cup soft brown sugar

2 cups self-rising flour

pinch of salt

2 eggs, beaten

8 oz can chopped
   pineapple, drained

½ cup candied
   cherries, halved

1 Put the mixed dried fruit into a large bowl and cover with boiling water. Set aside to soak for 10–15 minutes, then drain well.

2 Put the butter or margarine and sugar into a large saucepan and heat gently until melted. Add the drained mixed dried fruit and cook over a low heat, stirring frequently, for 4–5 minutes. Remove from the heat and transfer to a mixing bowl. Set aside to cool.

3 Sift together the flour and salt into the dried fruit mixture and stir well. Add the eggs, mixing until the ingredients are thoroughly incorporated.

4 Add the pineapples and cherries to the cake mixture and stir to combine. Transfer to a greased and lined 2-lb loaf pan and level the surface.

5 Bake in a preheated oven at 350°F for about 1 hour. Test the cake with a thin skewer; if it comes out clean, the cake is cooked. If not, return to the oven for a few more minutes. Cool and serve.

VARIATION

If you wish, add 1 teaspoon ground apple spice to the cake mixture, sifting it in with the flour. Bake the cake in a 7-inch round cake pan if you don't have a loaf pan of the right size. Remember to grease and line it first.

Rhubarb & Orange Crumble

A mixture of rhubarb and apples flavored with orange zest, brown sugar, and spices and topped with a crunchy crumble topping.

NUTRITIONAL INFORMATION

Calories 516	Sugars 45g
Protein 6g	Fat 22g
Carbohydrate . . .77g	Saturates 4g

15 MINS   45 MINS

SERVES 6

I N G R E D I E N T S

1 lb 2 oz rhubarb

1 lb 2 oz apples

grated zest and juice of 1 orange

½–1 tsp ground cinnamon

½ cup light soft brown sugar

C R U M B L E

2 cups all-purpose flour

½ cup butter or margarine

½ cup light soft

   brown sugar

⅓–½ cup toasted

   chopped hazelnuts

2 tbsp brown sugar (optional)

1 Cut the rhubarb into 1-inch lengths and place in a large saucepan.

2 Peel, core, and slice the apples and add to the rhubarb, together with the grated orange zest and juice. Bring to a boil, lower the heat, and simmer for 2–3 minutes, until the fruit begins to soften.

3 Add the cinnamon and sugar to taste and transfer the mixture to an ovenproof dish, so it is not more than two-thirds full.

4 Sift the flour into a bowl and cut in the butter or margarine until the mixture resembles fine breadcrumbs (this can be done by hand or in a food processor). Stir in the sugar, followed by the nuts.

5 Spoon the crumble mixture evenly over the fruit in the dish and level the top. Sprinkle with brown crystal sugar, if liked.

6 Cook in a preheated oven at 400°F for 30–40 minutes, until the topping is browned. Serve hot or cold.

VARIATION

Other flavorings, such as a generous ¼ cup chopped crystallized ginger, can be added either to the fruit or the crumb mixture. Any fruit, or mixtures of fruit can be topped with crumble.

Potato Muffins

These light-textured muffins rise like little soufflés in the oven and are best eaten warm. The dried fruits can be varied according to taste.

NUTRITIONAL INFORMATION

Calories	98	Sugars	........11g
Protein	.........3g	Fat	..........2g
Carbohydrate	...18g	Saturates	.....0.5g

20 MINS

35 MINS

MAKES 12

INGREDIENTS

6 oz russet potatoes, diced

¾ cup self-rising flour

2 tbsp soft light brown sugar

1 tsp baking powder

¾ cup raisins

4 eggs, separated

1 Lightly grease and flour 12 muffin pans.

2 Cook the diced potatoes in a saucepan of boiling water for 10 minutes, or until tender. Drain well and mash until completely smooth.

3 Transfer the mashed potatoes to a mixing bowl and add the flour, sugar, baking powder, raisins, and egg yolks. Stir well to mix thoroughly.

4 In a clean bowl, whisk the egg whites until standing in peaks. Using a metal spoon, gently fold them into the potato mixture until fully incorporated.

5 Divide the mixture between the prepared pans.

6 Cook in a preheated oven at 400°F for 10 minutes. Reduce the oven temperature to 325°F and cook the muffins for another 7-10 minutes, or until risen.

7 Remove the muffins from the pans and serve warm.

COOK'S TIP

Instead of spreading the muffins with plain butter, serve them with cinnamon butter made by blending ½ cup butter with a large pinch of ground cinnamon.

Butterscotch Melts

This delicious dessert will go down a treat with children of all ages. Bananas and marshmallows taste fantastic with butterscotch sauce.

NUTRITIONAL INFORMATION

Calories 385   Sugar 67g
Protein . . . . .2g   Fat 13g
Carbohydrate . . .70g   Saturates 8g

 5 MINS   5 MINS

SERVES 4

I N G R E D I E N T S

4 bananas

4 tbsp lemon juice

8 oz marshmallows

S A U C E

½ cup butter

⅔ cup light brown sugar

⅓ cup light corn syrup

4 tbsp hot water

1 Slice the bananas into large chunks and dip them into the lemon juice to prevent them from going brown.

2 Thread the marshmallows and pieces of banana alternately on to kabob sticks or bamboo skewers, placing 2 marshmallows and 1 piece of banana onto each one.

COOK'S TIP

The warm butterscotch sauce tastes wonderful with vanilla ice cream. Make double the quantity of sauce if you plan to serve ice cream at a barbecue. Ideally, prepare the kabobs just before they are cooked to prevent the bananas from turning brown.

3 To make the sauce, melt the butter, sugar, and syrup together in a small saucepan. Add the hot water, stirring until blended and smooth. Do not boil or else the mixture will become toffee-like. Keep the sauce warm at the edge of the grill, stirring from time to time.

4 Sear the kabobs over the grill coals for 30–40 seconds, turning constantly, so that the marshmallows are just beginning to brown and melt.

5 Serve the kabobs with a little of the butterscotch sauce spooned over them. (Use half of the sauce to serve 4; the rest can be used later.)

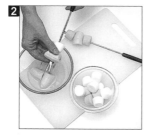

Traditional Tiramisu

A favorite Italian dessert flavored with coffee and Amaretto. You could substitute the Amaretto with brandy or Marsala.

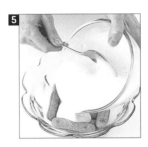

NUTRITIONAL INFORMATION

Calories 569   Sugars 28g
Protein ....12g   Fat 43g
Carbohydrate ...34g   Saturates 22g

 2¼ HOURS   5 MINS

SERVES 6

INGREDIENTS

20–24 lady-fingers,
  about 5½ oz

2 tbsp cold black coffee

2 tbsp coffee extract

2 tbsp Amaretto

4 egg yolks

6 tbsp superfine sugar

few drops of vanilla extract

grated rind of ½ lemon

1½ cups Mascarpone cheese

2 tsp lemon juice

1 cup heavy cream

1 tbsp milk

½ cup slivered almonds,
  lightly toasted

2 tbsp cocoa powder

1 tbsp confectioners' sugar

1 Arrange almost half of the lady-fingers in the base of a glass bowl or serving dish.

2 Combine the black coffee, coffee extract, and Amaretto together and sprinkle just over half of the mixture over the lady-fingers.

3 Put the egg yolks into a heatproof bowl with the sugar, vanilla extract, and lemon rind. Stand over a saucepan of gently simmering water and whisk until very thick and creamy and the whisk leaves a very heavy trail when lifted from the bowl.

4 Put the Mascarpone in a bowl with the lemon juice and beat until smooth.

5 Combine the egg and Mascarpone cheese mixtures and when evenly blended pour half over the lady-fingers and spread out evenly.

6 Add another layer of fingers, sprinkle with the remaining coffee, and then cover with the rest of the cheese mixture. Chill for at least 2 hours and preferably longer, or overnight.

7 To serve, whip the cream and milk together until fairly stiff and spread or pipe over the dessert. Sprinkle with the slivered almonds and then sift an even layer of cocoa powder so the top is completely covered. Finally sift a light layer of confectioners' sugar over the cocoa.

Pink Syllabubs

The pretty pink color of this dessert is achieved by adding blackcurrant liqueur to the wine and cream before whipping.

NUTRITIONAL INFORMATION

Calories 536	Sugars 17g
Protein 2g	Fat 48g
Carbohydrate ...17g	Saturates 30g

 45 MINS   0 MINS

SERVES 2

INGREDIENTS

5 tbsp white wine

2–3 tsp blackcurrant liqueur

finely grated zest of ½ lemon or orange

1 tbsp sugar

1 cup heavy cream

4 lady-fingers (optional)

TO DECORATE

fresh fruit, such as strawberries, raspberries, or redcurrants, or pecan or walnut halves

mint sprigs

1 Mix together the white wine, blackcurrant liqueur, grated lemon or orange zest, and sugar in a bowl and set aside for at least 30 minutes.

COOK'S TIP

These syllabubs will keep in the refrigerator for 48 hours, so it is worth making more than you need, and keeping the extra for another day.

2 Add the cream to the wine mixture and whip until the mixture has thickened enough to stand in soft peaks.

3 If you are using the lady-fingers, break them up roughly and divide them between 2 glasses.

4 Put the mixture into a pastry bag fitted with a large star or plain tip and pipe it over the lady-fingers. Alternatively, simply pour the syllabub over the lady-fingers. Chill until ready to serve.

5 Before serving, decorate each syllabub with slices or small pieces of fresh soft fruit or nuts, and sprigs of mint.

Berry Cheesecake

Use a mixture of berries, such as blueberries, blackberries, raspberries, and strawberries, for a really fruity cheesecake.

NUTRITIONAL INFORMATION

Calories 478   Sugars 28g
Protein ....10g   Fat 32g
Carbohydrate ...40g   Saturates 15g

  2¼ HOURS   5 MINS

SERVES 8

INGREDIENTS

BASE

6 tbsp margarine

6 oz oatmeal cookies

¾ cup shredded coconut

TOPPING

1½ tsp vegetarian gelatin

9 tbsp cold water

½ cup evaporated milk

1 egg

6 tbsp light brown sugar

2 cups soft
   cream cheese

1¾ cups mixed berries

2 tbsp honey

1 Put the margarine in a saucepan and heat until melted. Put the cookies in a food processor and process until thoroughly crushed or crush finely with a rolling pin. Stir the crumbs into the margarine, together with the coconut.

2 Press the mixture evenly into a base-lined 8-inch springform pan and set aside to chill in the refrigerator while you are preparing the filling.

3 To make the topping, sprinkle the gelatin over the water and stir to dissolve. Bring to a boil and boil for 2 minutes. Let cool slightly.

4 Put the milk, egg, sugar, and soft cream cheese in a bowl and beat until smooth. Stir in ¼ cup of the berries. Add the gelatin in a stream, stirring constantly.

5 Spoon the mixture onto the cookie base and return to the refrigerator to chill for 2 hours, or until set.

6 Remove the cheesecake from the pan and transfer to a serving plate. Arrange the remaining berries on top of the cheesecake and drizzle the honey over the top. Serve.

Mango Ice Cream

This delicious ice cream with its refreshing tang of mango and lime makes the perfect ending to a hot and spicy meal.

NUTRITIONAL INFORMATION

Calories 275   Sugars 25g
Protein . . . . .2g   Fat 19g
Carbohydrate . . .26g   Saturates 11g

 5¾ HOURS   5 MINS

SERVES 6

INGREDIENTS

⅔ cup light cream

2 egg yolks

½ tsp cornstarch

1 tsp water

14 oz cans mango slices
   in syrup, drained

1 tbsp lime or lemon juice

⅔ cup heavy cream

mint sprigs, to decorate

1 Heat the light cream in a saucepan until hot (but do not allow it to boil). Place the egg yolks in a bowl with the cornstarch and water and mix together until smooth. Pour the hot cream onto the egg yolk mixture, stirring all the time.

2 Return the mixture to the pan and place over a very low heat, whisking or stirring all the time until the mixture thickens and coats the back of a wooden spoon. (Do not try and hurry this process or the mixture will overcook.) Pour into a bowl.

3 Process the mango slices in a blender or food processor until smooth. Mix with the custard and stir in the lime juice. Whip the heavy cream until softly peaking and fold into the mango mixture until thoroughly combined.

4 Transfer the mixture to a loaf pan or shallow freezerproof container. Cover and freeze for 2–3 hours, or until half-frozen and still mushy in the center. Transfer the mixture to a bowl and mash well with a fork until smooth. Return to the container, cover and freeze until firm.

5 Transfer the container of ice cream to the main compartment of the refrigerator for about 30 minutes before serving to allow it to soften slightly. Scoop or spoon the ice cream into serving dishes and decorate with mint sprigs.

COOK'S TIP

Use the drained mango syrup for adding to fruit salads or for mixing into drinks.

Spiced Fruit Garland

There is nothing like the delicious smell of yeast cooking for creating a warm atmosphere. It must be something to do with the anticipation.

NUTRITIONAL INFORMATION

Calories	327	Sugars 28g
Protein	.........6g	Fat 11g
Carbohydrate	...55g	Saturates 5g

1½ HOURS   30 MINS

SERVES 12

INGREDIENTS

14 oz bread flour

½ tsp salt

¼ cup butter

¼ cup sugar

1 package active dry yeast

¾ cup warm milk

1 egg, beaten

FILLING

1 cup mixed dried fruit

¼ cup candied cherries, chopped

½ cup ground almonds

4 tbsp light brown sugar

1 tsp ground cinnamon

½ tsp ground nutmeg

2 tbsp butter, melted

TO DECORATE

½ cup icing sugar

candied cherries

chopped nuts

1 Sift the flour and salt in a large bowl. Cut in the butter and stir in the sugar and yeast. Make a well in the center and add the milk and egg. Draw in the flour gradually, mixing well to make a smooth dough.

2 Knead the dough on a lightly floured work counter for 8–10 minutes. Place in a lightly oiled bowl, cover, and set aside in a warm place to rise until doubled in size.

3 Knead lightly for 1 minute, and then roll out into a 16 x 9-inch rectangle. Mix together all the filling ingredients and spread over the rectangle, leaving a ¾-inch border around the edge. From the long edge, roll the rectangle into a cylinder, pressing the edge to seal it. Form the roll into a circle, sealing the ends together.

4 Lift the ring on to a greased cookie sheet and cut it into 12 slices, without cutting right through. Twist each slice so that a cut surface lies uppermost. Leave in a warm place for 30–40 minutes to rise.

5 Bake in a preheated oven at 400°F for 25–30 minutes. Cool on a cooling rack. Mix the icing sugar with a little water to make a thin frosting and drizzle over. Arrange the cherries on top and sprinkle with the chopped nuts.

Ground Almonds in Milk

Traditionally served at breakfast in India, this almond-based dish is said to sharpen the mind! However, it can be served as a delicious dessert.

NUTRITIONAL INFORMATION

Calories . . . . .314 Sugars 18g
Protein . . . . .8g Fat 21g
Carbohydrate . . .23g Saturates 3g

 5 MINS   10 MINS

SERVES 4

I N G R E D I E N T S

2 tbsp vegetable or pure ghee

¼ cup all-purpose flour

½ cup ground almonds

1¼ cups milk

¼ cup sugar

mint leaves, to decorate

1 Place the ghee in a small, heavy-bottomed saucepan. Melt the ghee over a gentle heat, stirring constantly so that it doesn't burn.

2 Reduce the heat and add the flour, stirring vigorously all the time to remove any lumps.

COOK'S TIP

Ghee comes in two forms and can be bought from Asian food markets. It is worth noting that pure ghee, made from melted butter, is not suitable for vegans, although there is a vegetable ghee available from Indian grocers and some health-food stores.

3 Add the almonds to the ghee and flour mixture, stirring continuously.

4 Gradually add the milk and sugar to the mixture in the pan and bring to a boil. Continue cooking for 3–5 minutes, or until the liquid is smooth and reaches the consistency of a creamy soup.

5 Transfer to a serving dish, decorate, and serve hot.

Boston Chocolate Pie

This lighter version of the popular chocolate cream pie is made with yogurt and crème fraîche.

🍰 25 MINS   🕐 35 MINS

SERVES 6

INGREDIENTS

8 oz shortcrust pie dough (see page 468)

CHOCOLATE CARAQUE

8 oz dark chocolate

FILLING

3 eggs

½ cup sugar

½ cup flour, plus extra for dusting

1 tbsp icing sugar

pinch of salt

1 tsp vanilla extract

1⅔ cups milk

⅔ cup plain yogurt

5½ oz dark chocolate, broken
   into pieces

2 tbsp kirsch

TOPPING

⅔ cup crème fraîche or whipping cream

1 Roll out the shortcrust pie dough and use to line a 9-inch loose-based flan pan. Prick the base with a fork, line with baking parchment, and fill with dried baking beans. Bake blind for 20 minutes. Remove the beans and parchment and return to the oven for 5 minutes. Remove from the oven and place on a cooling rack.

2 To make the chocolate caraque, put pieces of chocolate on a plate over a pan of simmering water until melted. Spread on a cool surface with a metal spatula. When cool, scrape it into curls with a sharp knife.

3 To make the filling, beat the eggs and sugar until fluffy. Sift in the flour, icing sugar, and salt. Stir in the vanilla extract.

4 Bring the milk and yogurt to a boil in a small pan and strain onto the egg mixture. Pour into a double boiler or set over a pan of simmering water. Stir until it coats the back of a spoon.

5 Gently heat the chocolate and kirsch in a small pan until melted. Stir into the custard. Remove from the heat and stand the double boiler or bowl in cold water. Leave it to cool .

6 Pour the chocolate mixture into the pastry shell. Spread the crème fraîche over the chocolate, and arrange the caraque rolls on top.

Apricot Slices

These vegan slices are ideal for children's lunches. They are full of flavor and made with healthy ingredients.

NUTRITIONAL INFORMATION

Calories 198	Sugars 13g
Protein 4g	Fat 9g
Carbohydrate ...25g	Saturates 2g

50 MINS   1 HOUR

MAKES 12

INGREDIENTS

PASTRY DOUGH

1¾ cups whole wheat flour

½ cup finely ground mixed nuts

⅓ cup margarine,
   cut into small pieces

4 tbsp water

soy milk, to glaze

FILLING

1 cup dried apricots

grated zest of 1 orange

1⅓ cups apple juice

1 tsp ground cinnamon

⅓ cup raisins

1 Lightly grease a 9-inch square cake pan. To make the pastry, place the flour and nuts in a mixing bowl and cut in the margarine with your fingers until the mixture resembles breadcrumbs. Stir in the water and bring together to form a dough. Wrap and set aside to chill in the refrigerator for 30 minutes.

2 To make the filling, place the apricots, orange zest, and apple juice in a pan and bring to a boil. Simmer for 30 minutes, until the apricots are mushy. Cool slightly, then process in a food processor or blender to a purée. Alternatively, press the mixture through a fine strainer. Stir in the cinnamon and raisins.

3 Divide the dough in half, roll out one half and use to line the base of the pan. Spread the apricot purée over the top and brush the edges of the pastry with water. Roll out the rest of the dough to fit over the top of the apricot purée. Press down and seal the edges.

4 Prick the top of the pastry with a fork and brush with soy milk. Bake in a preheated oven at 400°F for 20–25 minutes until the pastry is golden. Leave to cool slightly before cutting into 12 bars. Serve either warm or cold.

COOK'S TIP

These slices will keep in an airtight container for 3-4 days.

Fresh Fruit Compôte

Elderflower cordial is used in the syrup for this refreshing fruit compôte, giving it a delightfully summery flavor.

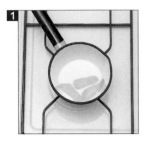  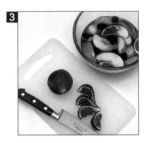

NUTRITIONAL INFORMATION

Calories 255   Sugars 61g
Protein . . . . .4g   Fat 1g
Carbohydrate . . .61g   Saturates 0.2g

 20 MINS   15 MINS

SERVES 4

INGREDIENTS

1 lemon

¼ cup sugar

4 tbsp elderflower syrup or fruit cordial

1¼ cups water

4 apples

1 cup blackberries

2 fresh figs

TOPPING

⅔ cup thick plain yogurt

2 tbsp honey

1 Thinly pare the zest from the lemon using a swivel vegetable peeler. Squeeze the juice. Put the lemon zest and juice into a saucepan, together with the sugar, elderflower syrup, and water. Set over a low heat and simmer, uncovered, for 10 minutes.

2 Peel, core and slice the apples. Add the apples to the saucepan. Simmer gently for about 4–5 minutes, until just tender. Remove the pan from the heat and set aside to cool.

3 When cold, transfer the apples and syrup to a serving bowl and add the blackberries. Slice and add the figs. Stir gently to mix. Cover and chill in the refrigerator until ready to serve.

4 Spoon the yogurt into a small serving bowl and drizzle the honey over the top. Cover and chill before serving.

COOK'S TIP

Greek-style yogurt may be made from cow's or ewe's milk. The former is often strained to make it more concentrated and has a high fat content, which perfectly counterbalances the sharpness and acidity of fruit.

Coconut Candy

Quick and easy to make, this sweet is very similar to coconut ice. Pink food coloring may be added toward the end if desired.

NUTRITIONAL INFORMATION

Calories 338	Sugars 5g
Protein 4g	Fat 34g
Carbohydrate 5g	Saturates 26g

1¼ HOURS   15 MINS

SERVES 6

INGREDIENTS

6 tbsp butter

3 cups shredded coconut

¾ cup evaporated milk

a few drops of pink food coloring (optional)

1 Place the butter in a heavy-bottomed saucepan and melt over a low heat, stirring constantly so that the butter doesn't burn on the base of the pan.

2 Add the shredded coconut to the melted butter, stirring to mix.

3 Stir in the evaporated milk and the pink food coloring (if using) and mix continuously for 7–10 minutes.

VARIATION

If you prefer, you could divide the coconut mixture in step 2, and add the pink food coloring to only one half of the mixture. This way, you will have an attractive combination of pink and white coconut candies.

4 Remove the saucepan from the heat, set aside, and leave the coconut mixture to cool slightly.

5 When cool enough to handle, shape the coconut mixture into long blocks and cut into equal-sized rectangles. Leave to set for about 1 hour, then serve.

Sweet Carrot Halva

This nutritious dessert is flavored with spices, nuts, and raisins. The nutritional information does not include serving with cream.

NUTRITIONAL INFORMATION

Calories 284	Sugars 33g
Protein 7g	Fat 14g
Carbohydrate ...34g	Saturates 3g

🍽 10 MINS ⏱ 55 MINS

SERVES 6

INGREDIENTS

1 lb 10 oz carrots, grated

3 cups milk

1 cinnamon stick or piece of
cassia bark (optional)

4 tbsp vegetable ghee or oil

¼ cup sugar

¼ cup unsalted
pistachios, chopped

¼–½ cup blanched almonds, slivered or
chopped

⅓ cup seedless raisins

8 cardamom pods, split and seeds removed
and crushed

thick cream, to serve

1 Put the grated carrots, milk, and cinnamon or cassia, if using, into a large, heavy-bottomed saucepan and bring to a boil. Reduce the heat to very low and simmer, uncovered, for about 35–40 minutes, or until the mixture is thick (with no milk remaining). Stir the mixture frequently during cooking to prevent it from sticking.

2 Remove and discard the cinnamon or cassia. Heat the ghee or oil in a non-stick frying pan, add the carrot mixture and stir-fry over a medium heat for about 5 minutes, or until the carrots take on a glossy sheen.

3 Add the sugar, pistachios, almonds, raisins, and crushed cardamom seeds, mix thoroughly and continue frying for 3–4 minutes more, stirring frequently. Serve warm or cold with thick cream.

COOK'S TIP

The quickest and easiest way to grate this quantity of carrots is by using a food processor fitted with the appropriate blade. This mixture may be prepared ahead of time and reheated in the microwave when required.

Fall Fruit Bread Pudding

This is like a summer pudding, but it uses fruits which appear later in the year. This dessert requires chilling overnight so prepare in advance.

NUTRITIONAL INFORMATION

Calories 177	Sugars 29g
Protein 3g	Fat 1g
Carbohydrate ...42g	Saturates 0.1g

10 MINS   15 MINS

SERVES 8

INGREDIENTS

4 cups mixed blackberries, chopped
   apples, chopped pears

¾ cup soft light brown sugar

1 tsp cinnamon

8 oz white bread, thinly sliced,
   crusts removed (about 12 slices)

1 Place the fruit in a large saucepan with the soft light brown sugar, cinnamon, and 7 tablespoons of water, stir, and bring to a boil. Reduce the heat and simmer for 5–10 minutes so that the fruits soften but still hold their shape.

2 Meanwhile, line the base and sides of a 3¾ cup pudding bowl with the bread slices, ensuring that there are no gaps between the pieces of bread.

3 Spoon the fruit into the center of the bread-lined bowl and cover the fruit with the remaining bread.

4 Place a saucer on top of the bread and weigh it down. Chill the pudding in the refrigerator overnight.

5 Turn the pudding out on to a serving plate and serve immediately.

COOK'S TIP

This pudding would be delicious served with vanilla ice cream to counteract the tartness of the blackberries. Stand the pudding on a plate when chilling to catch any juices that run down the sides of the bowl.

Semolina Dessert

This dish is eaten with pooris and potato curry for breakfast in northern India, but you can serve it with fresh cream for a delicious dessert.

NUTRITIONAL INFORMATION

Calories 676	Sugars 66g	
Protein 10g	Fat 31g	
Carbohydrate ...96g	Saturates 19g	

 5 MINS   10 MINS

SERVES 4

I N G R E D I E N T S

6 tbsp pure ghee

3 whole cloves

3 whole cardamoms

8 tbsp coarse semolina

½ tsp saffron

½ cup golden raisins

10 tbsp sugar

1¼ cups water

1¼ cups milk

cream, to serve

TO DECORATE

½ cup shredded
  coconut, toasted

¼ cup chopped almonds

¼ cup pistachios,
  soaked and chopped (optional)

1 Place the ghee in a saucepan and melt over a medium heat.

2 Add the cloves and the whole cardamoms to the melted butter and reduce the heat, stirring to mix.

3 Add the semolina to the mixture in the pan and stir-fry until it turns a little darker.

4 Add the saffron, golden raisins, and the sugar to the semolina mixture, stirring to mix well.

5 Pour in the water and milk and stir-fry the mixture continuously until the semolina has softened. Add a little more water if required.

6 Remove the pan from the heat and transfer the semolina to a warmed serving dish.

7 Decorate the semolina dessert with the toasted coconut, slivered almonds, and pistachios. Serve with a little cream drizzled over the top.

Baked Cheesecake

This cheesecake has a rich creamy texture, but contains no dairy because it is made with tofu.

NUTRITIONAL INFORMATION

Calories ....282 Sugars 17g
Protein ....9g Fat 15g
Carbohydrate ...29g Saturates 4g

2¼ HOURS   45 MINS

SERVES 6

I N G R E D I E N T S

4½ oz graham crackers, crushed

4 tbsp margarine, melted

⅓ cup chopped pitted dates

4 tbsp lemon juice

zest of 1 lemon

3 tbsp water

12 oz firm tofu

⅔ cup apple juice

1 banana, mashed

1 tsp vanilla extract

1 mango, peeled and chopped

1 Lightly grease an 7 inch round loose-based cake pan.

2 Mix together the graham cracker crumbs and melted margarine in a bowl. Press the mixture into the base of the prepared pan.

3 Put the chopped dates, lemon juice, lemon zest, and water into a saucepan and bring to a boil. Simmer for 5 minutes until the dates are soft, then mash them roughly with a fork.

4 Place the mixture in a blender or food processor with the tofu, apple juice, mashed banana, and vanilla extract and process until the mixture is a thick, smooth purée.

5 Pour the tofu purée into the prepared graham cracker crumb base.

6 Bake in a preheated oven at 350°F for 30–40 minutes, until lightly golden. Leave to cool in the pan, then chill thoroughly before serving.

7 Place the chopped mango in a blender and process until smooth. Serve it as a sauce with the cheesecake.

VARIATION

Silken tofu may be substituted for the firm tofu to give a softer texture; it will take 40–50 minutes to set.

Satsuma & Pecan Pavlova

Make this spectacular dessert for the perfect way to round off a special occasion. You can make the meringue base ahead of time.

NUTRITIONAL INFORMATION

Calories ....339 Sugars 36g
Protein ....3g Fat 21g
Carbohydrate ...37g Saturates 10g

2½ HOURS   3 HOURS

SERVES 8

INGREDIENTS

4 egg whites

1 cup light brown sugar

½ pint heavy cream

½ cup pecans

4 small oranges, peeled

1 passion fruit or pomegranate

1 Line 2 cookie sheets with non-stick baking parchment paper. Draw a 9 inch circle on one of them.

2 Whip the egg whites in a large grease-free bowl until stiff. Add the sugar gradually, continuing to beat until the mixture is very glossy.

3 Pipe or spoon a layer of meringue mixture onto the circle marked on the parchment; then pipe large rosettes or place spoonfuls on top of the meringue's outer edge. Pipe any remaining meringue mixture in tiny rosettes on the second cookie sheet.

4 Bake in a preheated oven at 275°F for 2–3 hours, making sure that the oven is well-ventilated by using a folded dish cloth to keep the door slightly open. Remove from the oven and leave to cool completely. When cold, peel off the baking

parchment carefully.

5 Whip the heavy cream in a large chilled bowl until thick. Spoon about one-third into a pastry bag, fitted with a star tip. Reserve a few pecans and 1 satsuma for decoration. Chop the remaining nuts and fruit, and fold into the remaining cream.

6 Pile on top of the meringue base and decorate with the tiny meringue rosettes, piped cream, segments of satsuma, and pecans. Scoop the seeds from the passion fruit or pomegranate with a teaspoon and sprinkle them on top.

Almond & Pistachio Dessert

Rich and mouthwatering, this dessert can be prepared well before the meal. It is best served cold.

NUTRITIONAL INFORMATION

Calories	565	Sugars	........37g
Protein	.........8g	Fat	..........43g
Carbohydrate	...38g	Saturates	......16g

🍮 1¼ HOURS   🕐 15 MINS

SERVES 6

INGREDIENTS

6 tbsp unsalted butter

1¾ cups ground almonds

1 cup sugar

⅔ cup light cream

8 almonds, chopped

10 pistachios, chopped

1 Place the butter in a medium-size saucepan, preferably non-stick. Melt the butter, stirring well.

2 Add the ground almonds, cream, and sugar to the melted butter in the pan, stirring to combine. Reduce the heat and stir constantly for 10–12 minutes, scraping the base of the pan.

3 Increase the heat until the mixture turns a little darker in color.

COOK'S TIP

This almond dessert can be made ahead of time and stored in an airtight container in the refrigerator for several days. You could use a variety of shaped cookie cutters, to cut the dessert into different shapes, rather than diamonds, if you prefer.

4 Transfer the almond mixture to a shallow serving dish and smooth the top with the back of a spoon.

5 Decorate the top of the dessert with the chopped almonds and pistachios.

6 Leave the dessert to set for about 1 hour, then cut into diamond shapes and serve cold.

Cherry Pancakes

This dish can be made with either fresh pitted cherries or, if time is short, with canned cherries for extra speed.

NUTRITIONAL INFORMATION

Calories	345	Sugars	.......25g
Protein	.........8g	Fat	...........11g
Carbohydrate	...56g	Saturates	.......2g

 10 MINS   15 MINS

SERVES 4

INGREDIENTS

FILLING

14 oz can pitted cherries

½ tsp almond extract

½ tsp apple spice

2 tbsp cornstarch

PANCAKES

¾ cup all-purpose flour

pinch of salt

2 tbsp chopped mint

1 egg

1¼ cups milk

vegetable oil, for frying

confectioners' sugar and toasted slivered
   almonds, to decorate

1 Put the cherries and 1¼ cups of the can juice in a pan with the almond extract and apple spice. Stir in the cornstarch and bring to a boil, stirring until thickened and clear. Set aside.

2 To make the pancakes, sift the flour into a bowl with the salt. Add the chopped mint and make a well in the center. Gradually beat in the egg and milk to make a smooth batter.

3 Heat 1 tablespoon of oil in an 7 inch skillet; pour off the oil when hot. Add just enough batter to coat the bottom of the skillet and cook for 1–2 minutes, or until the underside is cooked. Flip the pancake over and cook for 1 minute. Remove from the pan and keep warm. Heat 1 tablespoon of the oil in the pan again and repeat to use up all the batter.

4 Spoon a quarter of the cherry filling on to a quarter of each pancake and fold the pancake into a cone shape. Dust with confectioners' sugar and sprinkle the slivered almonds over the top. Serve immediately.

Index